CURT SACHS

The Commonwealth of ART

STYLE IN THE FINE ARTS MUSIC AND THE DANCE

W · W · NORTON & COMPANY · INC · *New York*

First Edition

Book Design by John Woodlock

PRINTED IN THE UNITED STATES OF AMERICA
FOR THE PUBLISHERS BY THE VAIL-BALLOU PRESS

Acknowledgments

THE AUTHOR gratefully acknowledges the loan of photographs from

Princeton University
The Institute of Fine Arts, New York University
The Museum of Fine Art, Rhode Island
Mr. Herbert Bittner, New York
Dr. Walter W. S. Cook, New York
Dr. Walter Friedlaender, New York
Dr. Alice F. Mühsam, New York
Miss Gisela M. A. Richter, New York
Dr. Judith E. Sachs, Princeton
Dr. Leonie F. Sachs, New York
Dr. Heinrich Schwarz, Providence

Contents

CONTENTS

Part Two The Nature of Style

CONTENTS

Plates

Between Pages 224 and 225

PLATES

Just as carefully as the pedant secludes his special learning from all other branches of knowledge, the philosopher strives to enlarge its domain and to re-establish their union. I say: to re-establish. Only abstract reasoning has built the partitions between the arts. The philosophical mind unites where the pedant parts. He is convinced that in the provinces of both the intellect and the senses all things are linked together, and in his desire for synthesis he cannot content himself with fragments.

FRIEDRICH SCHILLER (1789)

Introduction

THE COMMONWEALTH OF ART, the life and the concurrence of all individual arts under a common law and fate, is not a vain, utopian wish, to be realized only in a distant future. It has been a reality, an inevitable fact from the very outset of civilization. From whatever different sensations the arts may derive, from touch or vision or hearing—on to whatever the artists may project their visions, on statues or murals or melodies—they are one in spirit and meaning. They are as different and as one as the parts of the body with which a man expresses his glee and grief, his hope and despair: the bright or saddened eyes, the speaking gesture of eloquent hands, the cheerful or listless sound of the voice. They all, though controlled by different physiological systems, obey one motor impulse under one will or reflex. The arts, like gesture and speech, are expressions of man; they confirm and corroborate, in their own individual ways, what their sister arts reflect: man's emotive reaction to stimuli from without and within.

The artists themselves have not hesitated to profess the unity of art. Fifteen hundred years back, in the brilliant Gupta period of India (4th–6th century), painters expressly derived their art from dancing, and the dancers theirs from music. Vitruvius, the Roman, urged architects to make themselves familiar with melody and rhythm. Johann Reichardt, *Kapellmeister* to the court of Berlin around 1800, discussed the crescendo and decrescendo of the Mannheim orchestra as giving "a darker or a lighter shade to the whole coloring" and, in almost the same words, Dr. Charles Burney, musical sight-seer from England, characterized in 1773 the Mannheim achievement "as new colors—the colors in music having their shades as colors like red or blue have them in painting." And more than a hundred years later, Vincent van Gogh felt so strongly the sameness of painting and music that he eventually persuaded an old organist to teach him the elements of piano playing so he might better support his parallels.

Reichardt's and Burney's metaphors are not exceptions. Language often has freely borrowed appropriate words from the vocabulary of some other art whenever the terminology of one of the arts is defective; this very shifting to and fro acknowledges the close relationship between the basic qualities of either art. Melody is often said to describe a 'line' or a 'curve,' which might be 'smooth' or 'jagged'; orchestration gives 'color,' and the orchestrator has a more or less well-assorted 'palette.' Painters, on the other hand, have or have not 'tone'; a painting with much light is 'high' in 'key' or 'pitch,' and one with little light is 'low.' To such metaphors, which liken and unify the worlds of music and painting, language has added a number of semimetaphors which, making one forget that they have been transferred from art to art, bear witness to the existence of a common stock of qualities from which all arts are built, as: form and structure, symmetry, rhythm, color, clearness, movement, and numberless others.

Thus, inadvertently we often speak of what is dormant deep in our consciousness: that the basic forces at the bottom of art do not change whether we build, carve, paint, or compose.

This book, however, has no room for superficial comparisons or for the doubtful synesthesias in which some people associate colors, vowels, notes, tonalities, and even odors. Its purpose is to show that, and how, all arts unite in one consistent evolution to mirror man's diversity in space and time and the fate of his soul.

It also should be made clear from the very beginning that such an essay is little concerned with single personalities. Immeasurably strong as the importance and influence of individuals may be, the master, even the lonely genius, is never quite free from the bounds of his time and his nation; and while the things he has to say are greater, wider, deeper than those of lesser men, he says them in a language shaped by the anonymous, impalpable forces of ages and peoples. Indeed, the Himalayas can exist without Mount Everest, and the Sierra Nevadas without Mount Whitney, but Everest and Whitney could not be without their mountain ranges.

It has been essentially the fatal "tyranny of words" that precludes a full awareness of the unity of art history or even favors the isolation of the arts. As Mephistopheles sarcastically says to Faust:

> *Im ganzen haltet euch an Worte,*
> *So geht ihr durch die sichere Pforte*
> *Zum Tempel der Gewissheit ein.*

Which might in English be:

> Altogether stick to words,
> Then you will slip through the gate
> Of the temple of certainty.

One of the most momentous of these tyrannic words has been *style.*

The Greek word *stylos* literally means the writer's graver that scratched the letters in the wax tablets which served instead of paper in ancient Greece. Hence it figuratively denotes his personal mode of expression as Emerson's 'pen' or Rembrandt's 'burin' or Whistler's 'brush' denote the distinctive manners of the three men. In modern times, the conception of style has been expanded and used not only in literature but also in architecture, and was at last conferred upon all art, including the stage, the dance, and music.

Style, then, stands for the distinctive qualities of a certain group of art works, no matter what common traits have made it a group. It might describe the creations of one individual master and his followers—Palestrina's style or even Beethoven's last style; that of a whole generation or two—Louis Quatorze style; of a nation—

Flemish style; of like-minded artists—Romanticism; or even of some special pattern and technique—symphonic style.

Yet, the general public, under the fatal spell of a word, is still connecting the notion 'style' by preference with terms that once denoted successive phases of building only: Classic, Romanesque, Gothic, Renaissance, Baroque; they think of ancient columns, round and pointed arches, and gilded ornaments. They have been reluctant to share in the gradual expansion of these notions beyond the range of architecture, though they no longer hesitate to call the Chartres statues Gothic sculpture; the murals in Italian *palazzi*, Renaissance painting; the cabinets made in the seventeenth century, Baroque furniture.

The wider scope of these and other terms has been momentous; it implies the spiritualization of a once purely formal concept of style. If statues can be called Gothic, then Gothic is not just a pile of ogives, pinnacles, and flying buttresses; if Boucher's erotic canvases are Rococo, Rococo must be more than pierced shellwork and profuse decoration in curved lines. Style, it follows, cannot be defined in a few handy terms of architecture. It actually is the configuration of spiritual qualities that a certain man or age or country has created as the effigy of a certain will and emotion; and the easy characteristics that the handbooks teach are nothing but their outer marks.

Once we have shifted the focus from outer form and technique to the spiritual sources of style, we can no longer confine the field of view to architecture, sculpture, painting, and the minor arts. Will not the longing, mood, and character of living men in a particular age or place express themselves in music and the dance at least as well as in a carved chest of drawers or an illuminated Bible? Indeed, will not such expression be more spontaneous and powerful in these two arts, where matter and time do not interfere between the first impulse and the ultimate shape?

The question sounds almost rhetorical, and the expected answer seems to be a trite truism. And yet, when the author, from 1918 on, professed the unity of art history, he met with more resistance than encouragement. He was told by specialists (one did it "as a man and a Christian") to keep away from such dangerous, futile speculations and stick to music. Which is indeed much simpler.

One of the reasons so many people are not willing or able to see this unity is that, by nature or training, they are exclusively 'visual' or exclusively 'auditive' (not to mention those in whom no sense is properly developed). Because of this lack of balance, they are unfit to compare and to take their bearings by weighing similitude and dissimilitude—which after all is the basic form of all scientific reasoning—and they grasp the differences between the worlds of the eye and the ear more readily than their conformities. These aesthetic isolationists present us time and again with the old materialistic argument that music has developed according to immanent laws of its own and should be spared "false analogies" with other arts. So far, nobody has ever cared to show what these mysterious laws are like. Nor have their attorneys realized that, in establishing a self-sufficient, autonomous music history in which some symphony stems from some other symphony in virgin birth, they lead the catastrophic way to severing music from man and music history from the evolution of the human mind. This should not happen.

Rightfully, Erich Kahler says in *Man the Measure* (1943): "The autonomy of special departments of human activity is a disastrous phenomenon of modern times, and to extend the dividing lines backward into former ages is a falsifying interpretation of history. These fields developed as functions of man; their history is the history of their changing significance for man" (p. 25). And further on: Learning "will only be able to halt the growing process of specialization into fields that are increasingly losing connection with one another, if it accepts the artistic, philosophical principle of inner coherence and the trend toward a common order" (p. 517).

To be sure, comparison baiters will have the undoubted advantage of eluding the pitfalls of oversystematization and pedantry that lurk behind methodical reasoning. But they inevitably lapse into a complete negation of organic, meaningful growth—that is, into anarchy, indeed, into nihilism.

Damage almost greater than that done by the antiparallelists was caused when Friedrich Nietzsche, without denying a parallel development of the arts, spoiled the lawfulness of this parallelism by a wanton disregard of logic and historical facts: he seriously implied that music has always hobbled two hundred years behind the visual arts.

Many a naïve mind took this casual remark for gospel truth, and more than one delighted in elaborating on it. Indeed, not so long ago a German architect, Karl Weidle, author of a little book on *Bauformen in der Musik* (Kassel, 1925), tried to convince his public that Palestrina was an exponent of Romanesque architecture, Heinrich Schütz—after five hundred years!—of early Gothic, and Bach of central and late Gothic, and that Liszt was a Rococo master.

Whoever believes in pronunciamentos of such profundity must conclude that Bartók, Schönberg, and Stravinsky have at long last given an adequate musical expression to Louis Quatorze's courtly splendor and to Zinzendorf's sentimental pietism, while the actual chief composer to the *roi soleil*, François Couperin, ought to have lived in the times of Luther and Francis I; that Palestrina, so obviously misplaced in the time of the counterreformation by a stubborn law of nature, should better have provided the musical illustration for Boccaccio's *Decamerone;* and that, by right, Strauss should have performed *Salome*, *Electra*, and *Die Frau ohne Schatten* at the court of the first king of Prussia and of Queen Sophie Charlotte in Charlottenburg, not in William II's Royal Opera.

The reader should not smile. This is not exacting more of him than do the two misconceptions that gave birth to Nietzsche's hobbling theory: namely, that the Renaissance could conquer music only in 1600 instead of in 1400, and that Johann Sebastian Bach wrote Gothic music.

The Renaissance in 1600? Indeed, toward that year did not a

literary circle in Florence support the aesthetics of the latest music with copious quotations from Plato, most Grecian of all Greeks, and did not its members believe the newly created forms of the recitative and the opera to be a faithful renascence of ancient melody and drama?

The fact is correct but the interpretation naïve. Western scholarship has in all times been based on Greek and Latin studies, in the Middle Ages and in recent centuries as well as in the Renaissance. And if quotations from Plato and Aristotle were conclusive, all post-Greek Europe would have lived in a continuous renascence. Actually, the musical Renaissance began exactly at the same time in which the Renaissance in the fine arts started, however one wants to date this beginning. The following cross sections will give the proof. It set in when the spirit of balance, strictness, limpidity outweighed the intense, eccentric freedom of Gothic music; when modern harmony replaced medieval counterpoint; when the judgment of the ear became supreme; when texts, in a truly humanistic spirit, were respected as never before; when composers followed the Greeks in imposing poetical meters on their melodies.

Imaginative listeners endowed Bach, in his turn, with the misleading epithet of a Gothic straggler. Overwhelmed by his grandeur, archaic language, and piled-up polyphony, such listeners found themselves reminded of the grandeur, archaic language, and piled-up architecture of the great cathedrals in whose shadows they happened to live. They did not even know that the German Baroque as a whole—and not by any means just its music—was in spirit very close to the last style of the Gothic, so close that in the lifetime of Bach a few churches were actually built in the Gothic style, which proves just the opposite of the point to be proved.

In a similar way, some writers have likened Mozart to Raphael probably because, since both the artists died in their middle thirties, they embody the pathetic idea of youthful, unfinished mastership, and such scholars see Beethoven and Michelangelo as "struggling titans." Such comparisons are feasible no doubt. But they rest on mere impressions which of necessity are dim, incomplete, arbitrary, and open to the contradictions of adversaries who insist, not on common traits, but upon the differences that the comparer had failed to take into account. And for all these reasons, they are more entertaining than elucidating. Goethe was right when, in his Theory of Color, he commented on Johann Leonhard Hoffmann's *Versuch einer Geschichte der malerischen Harmonie* (1786) that such a train of thought "can amuse us only in as far as we play with certain vague similarities and, dropping one, seizing another, and so on, skilfully teeter hither and thither."

Vague resemblance or dim reminder will not do. Nothing but strictly methodical analysis can show that each generation has shaped its cathedrals, statues, paintings, and symphonies in the image of its will and dream exactly as emotion will shape at once the features, speech, and gestures of a man, to indicate one mood, one act.

In this analysis, we must not forget that, between the arts of space and time, there is the art that lives at once in space and time:

> Hence with her sister arts, shall dancing claim
> An equal right to universal fame.
>
> Soame Jenyns, *The Art of Dancing*, 1730

Even fashions, however erratic they seem, must not be omitted where the topic is taste and expression. Not before can we create the ideal history of art.

So comprehensive a history is not only more complete but also more unequivocal than the histories of individual arts. Just as we find in a man's gesture the confirmation of his words and vice versa, so the various arts confirm and elucidate each other's trends and those of their ages and nations. The history of the fine arts has the advantage of an older standing and the plain perceptibility of its objects. But the history of music (and to a certain degree the history of the dance) contributes its sharper contours: while there have always been reliefs, statues, and murals, which do not as such belong to any definite stylistic group, music has developed in clean-cut types—motets, fugues, sonatas—which, more precisely staked off in their lifetime, nationality, and social conditions than any form of sculpture or painting, leave no doubt of their stylistic relationships.

The three parts of this book are planned to sketch the scope and outline of such a comprehensive history. Part I, An Outline of Comparative Art History, gives not yet a true history but, as the initial step, a chronological sequence of cross sections, which co-ordinate the fine arts, music, and the dance of an age, with side glances at fashions and poetry. Part II, on The Nature of Style, tries to create an adequate terminology and to gain insight into the fundamentals that such co-ordination has in the ever-changing mind of man. Only then, Part III, on The Fate of Style, can lay bare a few of the hidden laws that rule the gigantic pageant of art history. It shows that neither the current trivial conception of eternal 'progress' to an ever greater mastership holds true nor—as readers of Part I might mistakenly suspect—the pessimistic idea of an eternal marking time on the same spot, in the sense of the resigned adage of the French: *Plus ça change, plus c'est la même chose*—the more things change, the more they are the same.

The Fate of Style, on the contrary, shows that the reversals from generation to generation are only parts of similar, larger reversals and that these latter, in their turn, are embodied in reversals, similar again, but of gigantic size. This eternal recurrence of general trends appears to be the inevitable law. But within the law, the style of art, man's truest mirror, has unlimited freedom and never repeats itself; just as man, within his human bounds, is never the same. "*Die Natur schafft ewig neue Gestalten; was da ist, war noch nie*"— Incessantly, nature creates unprecedented configurations; whatever lives, did not exist before. So Goethe said and to the pessimistic words of the French we oppose their optimistic inversion: *Plus c'est la même chose, plus cela change*—the more things are the same, the more they change.

There is no marking time or standing still. Nor is there a restless progress that aims at final, utopian perfectness and leaves to furnace and pickax all the once beautiful, now superseded, works of the past. But there is something better than progress: a ceaseless, ever-new adaptation of art to the changing needs of man. And in such adaptation, art slowly uncovers one by one the inexhaustible potentialities of human senses and souls, to which we bow in wonder and awe.

Writing such a book means incurring serious dangers. For it rests on the interpretation of facts, and no author can ever hope to elude the reproach of having misinterpreted the facts for the sake of his theory. Alas, the history of art, like all humanities, discusses the freedom and fancy of man and not the rigid laws of nature, from which the scientist derives irrefutable proofs. But then, in the physical world, too, only details, and nothing but details, can be proved. The ultimate conception of the universe and its forces has changed from age to age and remains no less debatable than any conception of the nature and fate of style in the commonwealth of art.

This is a solace, if a negative one, in the face of the fallacies of interpretation. The author has found another, positive encouragement in Walter Pater's memorable words, that "theories which bring into connection with each other modes of thought and feeling, periods of taste, forms of art and poetry, which the narrowness of men's minds constantly tends to oppose to each other, have a great stimulus for the intellect, and are almost always worth understanding."

PART ONE

An Outline of Comparative Art History

Introduction

> By lengthening the historic perspective, one gains power to throw off the partialities and relativities of one's immediate society; likewise, by facing the totality of human experience, one becomes aware of elements that the fashion or habit of one's own particular epoch may arbitrarily have neglected: archaic elements, primal elements, irrational elements, neglected mutation and concealed survivals, often overlooked by the wise in their too narrow wisdom.
>
> LEWIS MUMFORD, *The Condition of Man*, 1944.

THE IDEAL HISTORY of art should embrace all arts. It cannot reveal the essential issues unless it shows and compares the simultaneous reactions in every field of artistic activity. The ideal history of art should not be a collection of monographs, in which the individual arts or even the individual branches of one art are separately treated. Nor should it deal with the various nations one by one, unless they travel on byways rather than on the highways of Western civilization. All monograph collections disintegrate history and distort its perspective.

Nor is it advisable to organize the material in all too vast expanses of time. Centuries as means of chronology falsify the facts because they seldom coincide with spiritual revolutions; and conventional stylistic epochs, such as Romanesque, Gothic, Renaissance, Baroque, wrong the often so much more vital developments in shorter periods and take for granted the very slogans that every new approach to history ought to rechallenge.

OUTLINE OF COMPARATIVE ART HISTORY

The following short outline is based on the lifetimes of individual generations, that is, on spans in which a will and a trend have space enough to make their way, after which they generally yield to the different aims of another age. In accepting a plan based on generations, I have refrained from mechanically partitioning each century into three ages—as 1500, 1533, 1567. Rather I have selected years marked as focal by the significant coincidence of decisive events in the field of art. The introductory chapter on Prehistory and the Orient is of necessity vaguer in its chronology; the history of Eastern art provides but few reliable dates, the art of the primitives and of the Stone Age none at all.

The essay is based on architecture, sculpture, and painting, on music, and the dance. But wherever I felt that a casual glance at philosophy or drama, at poetry, or even at the costumes and coiffures of an epoch might round off the picture, I did not hesitate to call them to the witness stand.

Completeness of facts or names is not intended nor any exhaustive characterization of the styles and masters discussed. The outline confines itself to the traits indispensable from the particular viewpoint of this book. And wherever I anticipated that the reader might suspect me of being partial in stressing and interpreting these traits, I have taken care to quote the words of men to whom my train of thought was foreign.

CHAPTER ONE

Prehistory and the Orient

1. PREHISTORY AND THE PRIMITIVES

THE LATER PALEOLITHIC AGE, dawn of civilization, has left some documents of an astonishing art: small statuettes of women with exaggerated female details; bones engraved with figures, reindeers, and wild horses; and decorative objects of many kinds. Colorful murals in dozens of caverns in France and Spain represent the animals that the ancient hunters knew and chased, some in rest and some in an astounding movement, racing along, turning their heads to look back, or collapsing with an arrow in the flank—so incredibly done in daring realism and perfect craftsmanship that they were long thought to be modern falsifications.

In the later *Magdalenian*, last phase of the Paleolithic Age and culmination of nomadic life, style changed entirely. Murals in the caverns of eastern Spain give preference to man over animals. The proportions of the human body are willfully neglected and the torsos, immoderately stretched, often become mere strokes of the brush and almost ornaments. Their movement is powerful, intense, and concentrated. While the artist's concern glides away from the realistic conception of single objects, it focuses on rhythmic composition and in growing stylization leads to outright geometric designs.

It so happens that both styles also depict dances. In the abstract eastern Spanish group, a rock painting at Cogul in the province of Lérida shows nine dressed women dancing around a naked boy—a typical round dance, which in similar forms has survived in all countries of primitive civilization, in the branles of the Renaissance, and among our own children (Plate I).

In the naturalistic French group, on the contrary, we find mask dancers, attired with the natural heads and pelts of animals and moving in characteristic gaits. The most beautiful of these is a picturesque stag dancer in the cavern of the Trois Frères in Ariège in southern France.

This outlines a distinct dualism in the styles of at least two arts as far back as the Paleolithic Age, maybe ten thousands of years before our time: on the one hand, a vigorous extravert, sensory realism or even naturalism, descriptive and imitative; on the other hand, an introvert irrealism, imaginative, abstract, and stylized.

Careful research into the development of primitive art has, despite contradictory arguments, shown that the realistic, 'sensory' period can be divided into sections of growing realism, while the irrealistic, 'imaginative' period became increasingly abstract. The ultimate question, whether or not the former period represents the earliest stage of human art, has been answered in the affirmative by Herbert Kühn and a few other specialists in prehistoric art. I must confess that I am not convinced. Such a start would contradict the 'ontological' facts: it is not the way in which our children begin their artistic endeavors. The situation of music and the dance in the life of those primitives of today who have not developed much since the Paleolithic Age gives a different answer.

The prehistoric dualism that underlies painting and the dance reappears indeed in the music of living primitives and has been studied in detail in the author's book, *The Rise of Music in the Ancient World* (1943). Section One deals with two distinct styles, which I called logogenic or word-born and pathogenic or passion-born. The logogenic style is seldom more than a convenient vehicle for words, be they prose or poetry; it is strict in form, stylized, unemotional and often sung to dances of the round Cogul type. Its simplest and probably earliest melodies have a range of no more than two neighboring notes and slowly creep on in the endless repetition of a tiny motive (Example 1). Evolution in logogenic

Example 1. Botocudos *after Strelnikov*

music is additive: in the course of time, more and still more tones crystallize around the original nucleus of two, now above it, now below. But even before such development set in, primitives on the lowest level of civilization had from the endless repetition of tiny motives progressed to the well-wrought symmetry of answering phrases; to the distinction of a focal point similar to the one that we call the final or tonic; to the sequential repetition of motives on different pitch levels; to regular part singing; indeed, to a strict canonic imitation of the melody in a second voice (Example 2).

Example 2. Moni, Malacca *after Kolinski*

Logogenic music—like the murals of eastern Spain—has led the way to styles that rely on structure rather than on expressiveness and naturalism.

The opposite, pathogenic style does not try to carry poetry. It derives from violent outbursts of passion or ecstasy, from savage shouts and convulsive panting. Its earliest melodies are cataracts all through the range of pitches and intensities from high to low, from strong to weak, but these are eventually dammed up: the voice, still attacking at the peak of height and strength, no longer plunges in random jumps, but learns to mark and stress the essential musical intervals—octaves, fifths, fourths, and thirds—on its way down in a steady process of organization (Example 3). With all such development toward melodic strictness, the pathogenic style and all

Example 3. Zuñi Indians *after Stumpf*

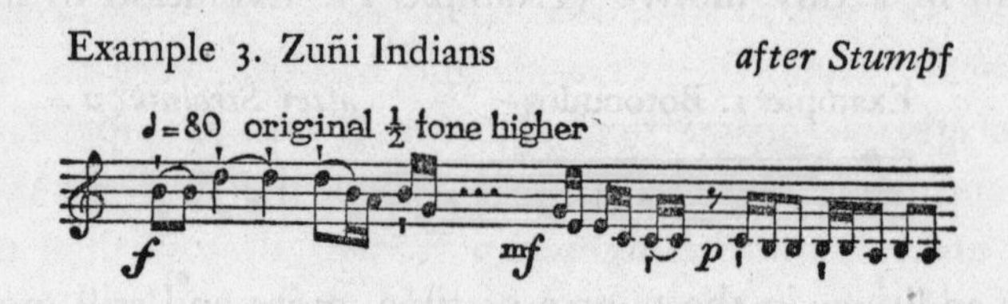

its descendants keep an improvisatory, spontaneous character and openly show the singer's emotions without submitting to frigid abstraction.

This dualism is partly a matter of race and geography. The logogenic style has its finest examples in the pygmoid districts of south and southwest Asia and, in this hemisphere, in Patagonia; and the pathogenic, in and off Australia and among our North American Indians. But a similar contrast often occurs between the sexes, even within the same tribe. In northwest Siberia, the men would sing in free, rhapsodic effusion without melodic or rhythmical ties while the women arrange their songs in simple, short, symmetrical phrases. A hundred similar examples could easily be added: all over the world, the character of man, impetuous and violent, forms unrestrained melodies; but woman, patient and careful, leans to tidiness and symmetry.

The two opposite styles also differ in rendering: the logogenic type, as a rule, is even and soft in performance; the pathogenic type, shaped by bodily strain and exhaustion, contrasts *fortissimi* and *sforzati* with almost inaudible *pianissimi*.

Which of the two styles preceded the other? One fact appears to favor the logogenic style, if we 'ontologically' presume that the child repeats the development of the species: it remarkably parallels the recorded babble songs of Western children three or four years old. The geographic and the sexual findings, on the other hand, appear to make the two styles simultaneous. But in neither way can the realistic, sensory style be claimed to antedate the irrealistic, imaginative style—not in music or in the visible arts.

2. THE ORIENT

EGYPTIAN ART was so static that even Plato, the purist, commended its stationary style. Its pyramids and obelisks were the most abstract imaginable geometrical patterns. It was as impersonal as art can be and never betrayed emotion: even the Wailing Women in Thebes are not more convincing in their despair than the hired professionals who served as the models. If Egypt did not strive for beauty in the Greek sense, it strove at least for permanence and absolute values. Art historians even have seen a binding canon of perfect human proportions in works of the Fourth Dynasty, two thousand five hundred years before Polykleitos.

Egyptian art was not irrealistic. Its painters were keen observers of nature. Their birds are paragons of exact rendition, and the Dog in Beni Hasan, so tense with his tail and ears up, is unforgettable. Man is depicted in all his occupations as a hunter, warrior, dancer, servant, or workman, in the fields and on the Nile, in the bakery, the kitchen, and the slaughterhouse; nothing is too petty. True, the many domestic scenes on the walls of Egyptian tombs are chiefly due to the belief that depicting the wealth and amusements of the dead secured an equally comfortable existence in the life to come. But then, the specification of such tasks is only possible in a realistic country.

Egyptian art was realistic; at the same time, it was nothing less than illusionistic. Painters never attempted actual perspective or three dimensions. Indeed, they thoroughly submitted to the law of frontality: all parts of the body were shown in their broadest views to avoid the detested accident of foreshortening—the head in profile, the eyes in front, the legs in profile, the torso approximately in front or one-half of it in front and one-half in profile—and women were given only the one breast that in the three-quarter view of the torso would affect the outline. Nor did the painters indicate shadows since these were accidental results of light, not permanent qualities of man.

Composition followed similar principles; always, the mental image mattered more than the optical impression. Persons and objects were drawn to different scales, with the chief figure often towering over the lesser ones. A proper arrangement in depth of the scenes represented, impossible without perspective, was circumvented either by displaying all figures side by side in one plane notwithstanding their actual position in space or by stacking such strips. Thus, multitudes usually appeared as a multiple repetition of the same figure. Empty spots were carefully avoided, and even hieroglyphic script was used to fill them.

Color, in tempera, was glaring and unbroken. The painters did not use it actually to contradict reality but in a conventional distribution—white for linen clothes, blue for water, green for all plants, black for hair, yellow with red dots for sand and desert.

This classic style of Egypt lasted to the end of the Old Kingdom, about 2200 B.C., and had its golden age in the Fifth Dynasty around 2700 B.C. There was not too much of a change in the Middle Kingdom (2200–1580 B.C.) although a certain pitiless naturalism, as in the wrinkled nude of an old woman in Cairo, has no parallel in earlier times.

One must turn to the New Kingdom, and particularly to the Eighteenth Dynasty (1580–1350 B.C.) to find a slightly freer spirit, liveliness and elegance, gesture and intimacy, a bolder conception of space and the human body, and an increased interest in things feminine. Nothing is more delightful from these viewpoints than the painting of the daughters of King Amenophis IV in the Ashmolean Museum at Oxford.

But the conservative spirit of Egypt did not permit a deeper change, and the art of the Eighteenth Dynasty was not much more than a brilliant episode in an otherwise uniform quiescence of three thousand years. The Nineteenth Dynasty (1350–1205 B.C.) already reverted to archaic, indeed, to cubic forms.

Our knowledge of Egyptian music and dancing is almost entirely restricted to the meager information from pictures of performing singers, players, and dancers and from a great number of actual instruments, kept intact by the arid sands. Facts from instruments are reliable but insufficient. Interpretation of dance pictures is dangerous, especially if, as in Egypt, the drawing style follows convention rather than optical impression. But it is safe enough to oppose the round and gliding movements of the Eighteenth Dynasty to the angular steps and attitudes of the Old Kingdom.

In music, too, a fateful change of style in the Eighteenth Dynasty, paralleling the principal change in the arts and the dance, can hardly be overlooked in the face of pictorial evidences and actual instruments. Performance passed partly into the hands of women. Among them were many slave girls imported from the newly conquered southwest of Asia with novel instruments—lyres, lutes, oboes, and the stimulating dance paraphernalia, timbrels and clappers. While this unmistakably hints at a turn to sensuality, the lute from Mesopotamia with its long neck, narrow-set frets, and one melody string must have brought to Egypt (as it did to Greece) the more refined tonal system based on the division of a string, to live alongside the older cycle of fifths and fourths.

We do not know at what time the subsequent reaction in the fine arts encroached on music. Anyway, a musical reaction must have been in full swing when the Greeks became familiar with Egypt. Herodotos related in the fifth century B.C. that the Egyptians excluded all foreign music. Shortly after him Plato reported with hearty approval how wicked music was being kept away from youngsters who, under the censorship of the priesthood, were allowed to learn only those melodies that bridled and purified the passions.

Ancient western Asiatic art, at home chiefly between the Tigris and the Euphrates in the successive kingdoms of Sumer, Babylonia, and Assyria, was for thousands of years more inert than any other art. Striving for permanence and reserve, it represented impersonal rulers in blocklike statues without the slightest gesture or even as much movement as one foot placed ahead of the other. This rigid art had neither the relative freedom of Egyptian art nor its charm and delight in life. On the contrary, it excluded whatever could appeal to human feeling: representation of women or younger people and, with them, of grace and emotion. Ornament was strict and symmetric, indeed heraldic, with preference given to those composite monsters, half-lion, half-eagle or bull-headed men, that after thousands of years the Romanesque art of Europe still preserved together with Babylonian vaults and portal-flanking sculptures.

Very late—after the collapse of the Babylonian empire and not before the maturity of Assyrian art about the middle of the seventh century B.C.—western Asiatic art achieved a certain degree of naturalism, dynamism, and picturesqueness. In their epic reliefs with landscapes and architectural backgrounds, sculptors made only modest attempts at perspective but they attained a mastery in representing lions, horses, and dogs, in which no later art has ever surpassed them.

The dance and the music of the nations between the Tigris and the Euphrates have unfortunately faded away without leaving more than insufficient traces.

Although we know a good deal about instruments and some generalities about temple singing, we have no musical relics nor even a clear idea of the scales that the Mesopotamians used. True, we are allowed to conclude from the attraction that certain music centers between the Tigris and the Euphrates had at the end of pre-Christian times—Al-Hira for instance—that music must have reached a respectable standard. We see from the form of religious hymn texts that the Assyrians, at least, must have performed in answering, antiphonic half-choruses as the Hebrews did; from the long-necked, fretted lutes and certain cosmological conceptions which linked the seasons to musical intervals, that the Babylonians devised their system, or at least one of their systems, according to the harmonic division of the string; from the headings of their psalms, that they had melodic patterns like those of the Jews, the Arabs, and the Hindus; from the description of Nebuchadnezzar's late-Babylonian orchestra in the book of Daniel, that, again as in the Arabian world, the individual instruments used to improvise in a first movement, while only in a second movement all instruments played together.

But all this is not enough to draw a parallel with the arts of the country.

The art of China has in all its amazing diversity one aim: to press on life and nature the seal of essence, dignity, unearthly aloofness, eternity. In its boldest realism, it is still unreal, fantastic, and dreamy; and the seeming simplicity of its subjects often conceals a profound religious symbolism. "The Chinese does not deal with a material, mechanical world. The world is still for him the passing expression of eternal spiritual Being. . . . He depicts not what he sees, but what he feels" (Fairbanks).

Against this common background, art history becomes set off in periods of different trends. The little that has been preserved from the Chou Dynasty (1111 or 1122–249 or 255 B.C.) is austere, solemn, and somewhat cubic. The subsequent Ch'in Dynasty (255–206 B.C.) shows unmistakable signs of grandiloquence. It indulged in giant bells and statues of bronze; Emperor Shih Huang-ti is said to have built two hundred and seventy palaces, the most famous of which, A-fang, needed seven hundred thousand workmen; it took eight days to traverse his capital; and his tomb has been estimated at a volume of fifty million cubic feet. The Han Dynasty (206 B.C.–A.D. 220) strove for more realism, elasticity, and elegance but its art was basically classic, clear, and almost heraldically strict, if not austere. In the centuries after the Han, painting came to the fore. A famous example, on silk, is the Admonitions of the Instructress of the Court Ladies from the fourth century, in which both space and depth are perfectly well indicated. The altar in the Boston Museum of Fine Art, of A.D. 593, and other sculptures around A.D. 600 began to separate body and cloth, to stress the third dimension, and to drop the conventional dreamy serenity of faces. Then, under the T'ang, from 618 to A.D. 907, art was particularly open to foreign influences. Sculpture again strove for gigantism and ostentation. The three hundred sixty foot rock Buddha of Chia ting fu (A.D. 730) probably established a record. Painting achieved striking portraits and an almost independent landscape and thus prepared for the human and sensuous styles of the Sung Dynasty, from 960 to A.D. 1279, which marks the beginning of modern times in China.

A complete outline of Chinese art history is not necessary, since Chinese dancing and music, particularly poor in chronology and without datable evidence, are hard to co-ordinate with the evolution of fine art. Still, their basic attitude is the same.

This shows at once in the 'genus' that dominates Far Eastern music: being pentatonic, the scale has only five, not seven, steps to the octave, three of which are whole tones and two minor thirds (like the sequence of black keys on our pianos). There is no semitone (Example 4) and consequently no leading note (like our B

Example 4. Chinese Song *after van Aalst*

before C) to secure, indeed, to enforce a purposeful march of melody: the Chinese pentatonic genus is thoroughly static. The same is true of the *salendro* genus in Java and Bali, in which this scale has been tempered to a uniform series of five (more or less) equal six-fifths of tones in the octave, and also of the Siamese genus with its irregular six-sevenths of tones. It is not true, on the contrary, of the (probably older) pentatonic genus of Japan with its two major thirds and two semitones beneath (in descending order: third—semitone—third—semitone) nor of its offshoot, the *pelog* genus in Java and Bali.

Besides, the music of ancient China, at least religious music, was founded on the essential importance and self-sufficiency of the individual, motionless tone: melodic movement was viewed as a set of such tones rather than as a configuration in itself. Each note according to its pitch and each instrument according to its material was involved in a complicated network of symbols and represented some cosmic force that connects with the seasons and months of the year, with the animals, elements, planets, colors, and cardinal points.

This at once symbolic and static character appears no less in the completely stylized dances of the Far East, the most colorful of which were the masked *Bugaku* ballets that Japan got from China and Korea at the end of the seventh century. The Chinese hymn to Confucius (Example 5)—to show one example only—was accom-

Example 5. Hymn to Confucius

panied in the temple by a dancing *corps de ballet.* However, "by the word dancing is not meant anything like the foolish jumping or endless turning to be met with in our ball-rooms; the dancers are grave performers who by their attitudes and evolutions convey to the eye the feelings of veneration and respect which are expressed by the words" (J. A. van Aalst, *Chinese Music*, Shanghai 1884, p. 31). Actually, just as music had stationary notes somehow connected to form the melody, the dance consisted in eleven positions, upright, stooping, kneeling, prostrate, forward, to the right, to the left, and so on, the passages from one to another being purely accessory.

Music, especially in the theater, seems here and there to veer to the realistic or even naturalistic side. But it always keeps an element of irreality; the singers would impersonate their ferocious heroes with unnatural falsetto voices and fantastic turns without ever attempting actual imitation.

Ferocity, though, has not been normal to Chinese music. "The noble-minded man's music," says Confucius, "is mild and delicate, keeps a uniform mood, enlivens, and moves. Such a man does not harbor pain or mourn in his heart; violent and daring movements are foreign to him." Music should be serene: *yüo*, music, and *lo*, serenity, had the same graphic symbol. No staccato, no accelerando, no strong crescendo had a place in such music, nor anything that might arouse unrest, passion, lust. A vulgar-minded man's performance, on the contrary, "is loud and fast, and again fading and dim, a picture of violent death-agony. His heart is not harmonically balanced; mildness and graceful movements are foreign to him." And vulgar was the noisy music of the tyrants of Hia and Yin, who "deemed the loud sounds of big drums, bells, stones, pipes, and flutes beautiful and thought that mass effects were worth while. They aimed at new and strange timbres, at never heard-of tones, at plays never seen before. They tried to outdo one another and overstepped the limits" (Lü Pu-we).

This antagonism is at once a piece of music history as well. For Confucius represents the classic ideals of the Chou period while Lü Pu-we, who lived in the third century B.C., witnessed the grandiloquent trends of the Ch'in Dynasty.

A similar coincidence of style in music and the fine arts appears during the T'ang Dynasty (618–907)—first of all in two qualities: large size and receptivity to foreign influences. Size is reflected in the climax of orchestral development; graphic ground plans of court orchestras record, among other instruments, no less than two hundred mouth organs, one hundred twenty-eight lutes, and a hundred twenty harps; and for outdoor processions, the imperial court entertained a huge band of 1,346 men. Receptivity to foreign influences shows in the cosmopolitan character of indoor music: the number of orchestras was increased to nine; these were imported from India, Japan, Burma, Cambodia, Turkey, and other Asiatic countries.

In a narrower sense we know three stylistic facts. The first concerns the music for mouth organs. The Japanese court orchestra, modeled after Chinese patterns in the time of the T'ang, still clings to an ancient Chinese technique of playing full chords of three, five, or six notes on the pipes of this small instrument; in China herself, these complicated harmonies have been given up for simple parallels in fourths and fifths. The second fact is the elaborate polyphony in which the Japanese court orchestra plays the ancient music, of which it claims to have an unadulterated tradition from the times in which the T'ang ruled China. The third fact is the adaptation of elaborate Indian patterns of poetical, and hence musical, meters. And it should be added that at that time, so very reminiscent of the Eighteenth Dynasty in Egypt, women played an outstanding role in Chinese music also: the emperor entertained a women's orchestra at court and founded a large female academy of music, The Garden of Everlasting Spring.

India's music has mainly kept to the emotional side. All its melodies conform to one of the dozens of *rāgas* or melodic patterns, in a way comparable to the three compulsory orders of Grecian architecture. They differ in the scales they use and in the moods they express. As early as approximately 400 B.C., in the great national epos *Rāmāyaṇa*, a *rāga* is expected to arouse one of the nine temperaments and sentiments—love, tenderness, humor, heroism, terror, anger, disgust, surprise, tranquillity. Indeed, the very word *rāga* means passion and color.

In contradiction to Chinese conceptions, the individual note has little meaning in itself; it gets its weight and character from added graces or *gámakas* and is subordinated to melodic movement. Even cosmic symbols and forces, connected with music no less in India than in China, refer to *rāgas* rather than to single notes. Structure is regular and rhythmically ruled by one of the *tālas* or metrical patterns, which organize the melodies as inexorably as the rhythmical *modi* did around 1200 in the polyphonic music of the Western church. However, such a strait-laced piece is preceded by an improvisation entirely free in rhythm and structure, the *ālāpa;* and, significantly, this unbridled, luxuriant prelude is often longer than the *rāga* proper.

It is almost impossible to outline any history of Indian music, since native sources show no interest in development and chronology and frequently even they cannot be dated. The main evidence of ancient music, Bharata, has in recent literature been given a time latitude of no less than a thousand years, from about 500 B.C. to about A.D. 500. The evolution of music in India seems to have been weak anyway; the musical system that Bharata describes is in principle similar to the system of modern Indian music.

It is therefore practically useless to present here a history of the other arts in India; co-ordination is feasible only in the common character of all Indian art, not in the parallelism of their developments.

The drama, queen of Indian arts, is definitely emotional—*rāsa,* the emotional reaction of the audience, is its dominating conception. And from the ancient Indian theater have come the earliest evidences of sympathy and applause, of clapping, smiling, laughter, acclamation, bristling hair, and jumping up.

Fine art in India presents a similar basic feature: it is emotional and even passionate, though never personal. It often strives for strictness and intricate rhythm but hates the frigid emptiness of unbroken lines and surfaces, decorating them profusely. Sculptures and paintings are often crowded and excessively agitated: on the temple in Aihole (sixth century A.D.), the limbs of Vishnu and his followers seem to serpentine like snakes. The approach is often realistic without much idealization; still, the artist does not study models or nature and rather relies on his memory images.

Some Indian architecture looks almost as tectonic as an Italian edifice of the Renaissance or Baroque but the architect hardly ever is satisfied with harmonic balance and simple contours. Often, as in the temple at Sanchi (first century B.C.), the outline is so jagged that the building almost seems to fly apart. The Lakshmana Temple at Sirpur (seventh century A.D.) is, from a Western viewpoint, overdone and destructive in its decoration. In the Kandarya Mahadeva Temple in Khajuraho (*c.* A.D. 1000) and other structures, all parts, the angles, the columns, the domes, are so redundantly multiplied that the whole gives the impression of a forest of stone. In Bayon (ninth century A.D.), a gigantic head unexpectedly and quite inorganically emerges from the front of a tower. Or, as in the overwhelming stupa of Borobudur in central Java (*c.* A.D. 800), sculpture obliterates architecture so much that we fancy we see a huge, though organized, mound rather than a building as we understand it. But then, the stupa or shrine is actually a rounded and, in principle, massive pile of earth devoted to terrene divinities.

Of historic developments within this world of dynamic art, the most striking is the turn it took in the seventh century A.D. The preceding Gupta Dynasty had been comparatively classic with trends toward balanced beauty, harmony, and limpid composition. But the period after the Guptas has on good grounds been called the Indian Baroque. Indeed, while Brahmanism developed into the colorful rituals of Hinduism, the arts and even architecture indulged more than ever in picturesque unrest, inebriate passion, and irrational profusion. But the characteristic monuments of the time, like the temples in Māmallapuram, could in their almost unbelievably piled-up redundancy of glittering details more rightfully be called flamboyant.

The nearest musical relatives of such stupefying, luxuriant growth are probably not the finely chastened chamber *rāgas* which dominate in modern India but rather the *gamelans*, the glistering orchestras of Java and Bali, with the confusing polyphony of dozens of hammers on resonant bronze. Javanese orchestral music seems at first hearing to be in continuous movement; the restlessly tinkling dissolution of the melody in the higher gong chimes, metallophones, and xylophones suggests motion. But it is a purely decorative motion—the movement goes on and on without leading anywhere. Rhythm and structure, very static, are of the regular square kind, the phrases and periods being cut in multiples of two; and the periods and sections are marked by disjunctive gong beats which serve as commas and stops. There is no passion; Javanese music breathes impassive serenity.

Bali's orchestras, however, similar but more archaic than those of Java, show a degree of dramatic tension, indeed of passionate violence, that gives the lie to the apparent serenity of Java. A glance at the loud and lively colors of Balinese batiks and the moderate and softer hues of Javanese batiks confirms that the present style of Indonesian art is of recent date.

The Indian dance is not social but spectacular and professional, like almost all the dances in the East beyond the tribal stage. Performed to be looked at and inextricably connected with temples and courts, it is on the highest technical level. It renders well-known scenes from Hindu mythology and from the national epics but its narration is long, long past the stage of realism. All the deeds and thoughts that it tells are frozen into conventional gestures of the hands, the head, the eyes, the brows, the neck—gestures of the highest beauty but not altogether comprehensible unless one knows the vocabulary. The Indian dance has become abstract and imaginative. And since all abstract art is two dimensional, its motion is sideward, and the parts of the body present themselves in frontal view on a plane.

The Islamic Orient from Morocco and Spain to Persia and India has generally lived on the dynamic side. Its art is irrealistic and mostly decorative rather than functional. This is true of architecture, with façades that rarely betray the organization of the interior, and with profuse decoration that often cuts across pilasters, panels, frames. And it also is true of the smaller province of book painting, in which, far from Western spatial conception, men, houses, trees, and animals are ornamentally displayed in carpet fashion. Ornament itself, in its gracefully twined 'arabesques' and geometrical patterns, vibrates with a life entirely its own. "Wherever the eye rests, it finds one design merging in another, a device fatiguing to the intellect but stimulating to the emotions" (Fairbanks). Slender, needlelike minarets, spiral towers, bulging domes, lobated ogives, stalactites in fantastic shapes, and forests of columns add to a restiveness that seems strange in a world of impassive stability.

The picture would not be complete without mentioning their curious delight in overwhelming sizes, as the colossal rock reliefs of Sassaniden times about the middle of the first millennium (and therefore pre-Islamic), or the palace of Balkuwara near Samarra, built A.D. 854–59 on a ground area of more than twenty-one million square feet.

All this art is strictly typical, never individual.

Islamic music, emotional and high-strung, is just as unindividual; it shows the same unconcernedness with tectonics and a similar interest in free effusion and ornamentation. Every melody is bound to follow one of the *maqamat* or patterns which, established once, forever determine its key, mode, curve, tempo, mood, and even certain melodic formulas. In a similar way, every melody is bound to follow one of the admitted rhythmical patterns. In ensembles, each instrument produces its own soloistic improvisation in florid *passaggi* without submitting to rhythm or form before the whole group joins in a strict and rhythmic movement. Coloratura and expression, unluckily parted in Western music, still live together in the East. The audience, rapt and often ecstatic, reacts with the same transport to well-done coloraturas, endlessly flowing and gracefully curved, as to the inimitable accents of love and mourning that Moslem musicians give their melodies.

Jewish music in Biblical times is clearly divided into two periods: the second millennium B.C., with the essentially vocal, Bedouin music of nomadic cattle drivers, and the first millennium B.C., with the more sophisticated and often instrumental music of sedentary townsmen, with a painstakingly organized temple music and an annexed preparatory music school, and with the motley influences of a royal court and its international host of singing, playing, dancing slaves.

There are no actual relics from either period. But tradition has been so strong that, from the forms of ancient poetry and modern musical practice, we can conclude the existence of two distinct styles. One is the style of women who, while singing, danced and beat their timbrels. It can be traced back to the times of Genesis and Judges, to Moses' sister Miriam as the leader of the women's chorus and to Jephtha's daughter welcoming her father. It is sufficiently well illustrated, both by the forms of poetry preserved in the earlier parts of the Bible and by remains found today in the secluded congregations in the Yemenite part of Arabia and the Isle of Djerba off Tunisia. Its melody is regular, symmetrical, repetitive, and clear in structure, since the lines are separated by drum or cymbal beats and alternate between soloists and choruses.

Alternation, in the two forms of response and antiphony, was also fundamental to the second style, as far as we know it from the later cantillation and the later lyrical forms of the Bible. But their meters and structures are free, dynamic, and expressionistic (Example 6). And when we read that instrumental music hypnotized

Example 6. Yemenite Jews *after Idelsohn*

the prophets so "that the spirit of the Lord came mightily upon them," we can assume such music to have been nearer to the second than to the first style. Whether or not the strict and the freer style represent in the main two subsequent phases is not quite certain.

Israel had unfortunately no genuine fine art to compare with its music. The earliest works that we hear of in connection with Solomon's temple were made by Phoenician artists and doubtless in the Phoenician style. While the Hebrews, like the Arabs, were willing to express themselves in verses and melodies, they hated to reduce to outer form what to them was boundless spirit. Hence the commandment: *Thou shalt not make unto thee a graven image, nor any manner of likeness.* And hence the words of Paul in II Corinthians 4:18: "We look not at the things which are seen, but at the things which are not seen: for the things which are seen are temporal, but the things which are not seen are eternal."

The words of Paul, spoken on the soil of Greece, were in a broader sense the Semitic answer to the Greek Aristotle, who once said that "evil was a form of the infinite, and good, of the finite." It is to this worship of the finite, of visible, tangible form that Hellas owed the bloom of her art, to which we shall presently turn.

CHAPTER TWO

European Antiquity

1. CRETE AND MYCENAE

CRETAN AND MYCENAEAN ART, the styles of the pre-Grecian inhabitants of Hellas, had overstepped their zenith long before the Greek invaders conquered the island and the Peloponnesos. After an abstract, geometrical period in the third millennium B.C., the arts of these lands, shortly before 1500 B.C.—in coincidence with the Eighteenth Dynasty of Egypt—revealed an unprecedented delight in life, nature, and movement. Motion—free, audacious, elegant—appeared in curling fish and the whirling corkscrew tresses of fashionable ladies; murals showed breathtaking circus and hunting scenes, landscapes, delicate flowers and admirably well-observed animals. Decoration, drawn from organic nature, ran and rolled without rest. And the very legend of the labyrinth on Crete—a reflection of the gigantic palace at Knossos—proves that picturesque complication was preferred to limpid simplicity.

At last (we do not know the exact time) the Cretans veered back from their gay naturalism to cold, geometric abstraction. The continental Mycenaean style, universally known by the strict, heraldic gate at Tiryns with the two lions face to face, had long preceded it in this process of denaturalization.

We know but little of music and dancing in Crete, and nothing of music and dancing in Mycenae. This is the more unfortunate, as not only Homer but also later Greek authors exalted the matchless perfection of Cretan dancers and their importance for their own art of dancing. On paintings and sculptures of the second millennium B.C., the Cretans dance around the lyre player; couples perform at religious rituals; large choruses of women dance in public, and professional female dancers appear in long and bellying dresses. Many group dances must have been accompanied by choral singing—another accomplishment that the Greeks admired and appropriated.

In the seventh century B.C., a famous Cretan musician, Thaletas, accepted an invitation to Sparta in order to fight the plague with the magic, curative power of Cretan paeans, which then passed into the hands of the Greeks as hymns in honor of Apollo, the god of healing. Thaletas is also credited with having introduced the Cretan sword dance *pyrrhiché* with its lively meter of two shorts, or eighth notes (♪ ♪). But the typical meter of Crete seems to have been the *kretikós*, a foot of long-short-long or five time units (♩ ♪ ♩) which in its spirited unevenness reflects the freedom of later Cretan art and its aversion to all too simple, static patterns.

Before leaving Cretan civilization, a glance at the remarkable costume of the dynamic, naturalistic Minoan Age will show—as in all times of a similar trend—that fashions strive for amplitude except for a narrow waist. Carl Köhler, who as the author of *A History of Costume* (Philadelphia, 1937) is better equipped to give a professional description than the author of this book, speaks of "skirts put together in an almost fantastic manner that betrays a highly developed knowledge of the technique of dressmaking. These skirts are constructed in tiers, separated by strips of rich ornamentation. There are even examples of what are called *volants*, or flounces —i.e., narrow strips of patterned material, the upper projecting over the lower, and, if we are to judge from the perpendicular lines, disposed in fine accordion pleats. Over these falls a rounded kind of apron. The waist is slender, and surrounded by a rolled girdle." How different is this costume from the dresses of classical Greece!

2. GREECE

AFTER THE DORIC MIGRATIONS (*c.* 1200 B.C.). the archaic arts of Greece were no less abstract and geometric than the last Mycenaean art had been. Even human figures on vases and in metal work were reduced to lines and triangles and arranged in simple, often superimposed, rows. Vase painting changed only at the end of the eighth century B.C. Color was introduced and the former serial arrangement of co-ordinated figures yielded to an almost unified composition; straight lines were replaced by curves; the figures of men and beasts gained volume and steadfastness; strict frontality succumbed to designs in several planes, to overlapping objects, to interlocking groups; and instead of domestic animals, Oriental models—as later in Romanesque art—suggested ferocious, fantastic monsters. While Asiatic and insular Greeks thus stuck to decoration, the mainland dropped all filling ornaments and developed realistic narration.

Modern authorities attribute the definite form of Homer's poems to these generations. For Homer, against all later classic ideals, sings of an immoderate world. He brings outbursts of passion, tirades, and eruptions of laughter; he dwells with relish on Philoktetos' stinking sore and the desecration of Hektor's corpse; he believes in size—the size of his own two epics and the size of the wooden horse which accommodates an important part of the army; and his analysis of the shield of Achilles shows that artists depicted scenes from the life of the gods and of men—just as his own two epics narrate them in detail.

During the seventh century, bold emancipation from static forms and ideas took place in music as well. Of the celebrated Terpander's work we have no clear idea, to be sure. But another great man, Archilochos, was by later writers credited with the use of lively iambic meters and complicated, changing rhythms, with the introduction of speechlike parts between melodic sections, and with the *kroûsis hypò tèn ōdén*, which, whatever the term specifically meant—playing under the melody is the literal translation—was a richer form of instrumental accompaniment than had been customary before.

The dynamic style lasted at least a hundred years. At the end of the seventh century, Attica seems to have reacted against the latest exuberance in subjects and style. However, Corinth, the important center of vase pottery, either went on with the older trends or else created a new descriptive style, which not only resumed the narration of mythological scenes but also depicted the workman's life in mines, by the oven, and at the potter's wheel.

Because of the uncertainty of most of the dates, it is hardly possible to follow the train of style generation by generation: art works of the sixth century are dynamic rather than static. But then that century witnessed Herakleitos' philosophy of universal change and flow. And it saw the creation of the tragedy (534 B.C.), which was essentially antiserene in its aim to stir up "pity and fear," however much it later periodically quieted down to less exciting expression.

Even painting and sculpture in their tempo *allegro molto* had a truly dramatic character. Everybody is in quick motion; a winged victory flies, and the goddesses on the frieze of the Siphnyan Treasury in Delphi (*c.* 524 B.C.) who are attending a meeting of the gods, act with the spirited eagerness of the stage. Though the sculptor most probably did not mean this scene to be comical (as it appears to us), art in the time of the tyrant Peisistratos and his sons (561–510 B.C.) had a good sense of humor, as a part of that sense of character and reality that showed in the delightful representation of old and young, dwarfs and Negroes, Egyptians and northern Barbarians. However, Peisistratian art marked a victory of the gentle, smiling genius of the Ionian tribes and even of the decorative, dainty costume of Ionian women. But the century also strove for the gigantic: the Naxians dedicated a colossal sphinx to Delphi; the temple of Apollo Selinos was given a length of no less than three hundred sixty-six feet; and Samos had a dyke thirteen hundred feet long and a hundred and thirty feet deep.

Dynamic, Dionysian styles had the lead in music, too. An unmistakable sign is the amount of consideration given Asiatic pipes at the cost of stringed instruments. Pipes, not lyres, accompanied the tragedy, and pipes as concert instruments were played at the public contests. Several detailed descriptions, written many centuries later, report how Sakadas, a piper and composer, was awarded a prize at the Pythian games of 586 B.C. for performing, on a single pair of pipes, Apollo's fight with the dragon in five movements—an introduction, the preparation for the duel, the challenge, the combat, and the victory with the last hiss of the beast and the trumpets of triumph. This remarkable piece of description shows that music shared with painting and sculpture the delight in narration. Dionysian, too, was the fact that the ecstatic Phrygian dithyramb, song of intoxicated followers of the god, was made an art form in the hands of Sakadas' contemporary, Arion of Methymna in Corinth, and later in the century, it was forced upon Athenian contests by Lasos of Hermione—again with the stirring pipes as the only accompaniment.

A less 'archaic' and less dynamic but essentially more realistic style sets in about 480 B.C. In contradiction to the stiff *koûros* type of naked men's statues in the sixth century, the famous Critian Boy from the Akropolis rests his weight on one foot only, and thus his perfect anatomy is slightly asymmetric. J. D. Beazley has nicely said: "The old kouros stood at the ready . . . his successor stands at ease." 470 B.C. is the approximate year of the Delphic Charioteer, described at the beginning of Part II of this book; and a little later came the admirable Zeus from out of the sea off Cape Artemision with his incomparable balance of strength and levity. All haste disappears; all forms are plain and pure; female statues sacrifice the pretty, plaited Ionic *chitōn* and go back to the graver, simpler Doric *peplos*. It is remarkable that the chief representatives of the style—the sculptures on the temple of Zeus in Olympia (*c.* 460 B.C.) and the lost, renowned wall paintings of Polygnotos—avoided showing violent action and preferably depicted the acts and moods preceding or following the climax: the preparation for the chariot race between Pelops and King Oinimaos, the morning after the taking of Troy, Odysseus after slaying the suitors.

There is no environment, though, either in time or in space. Scenes and individual figures are insulated.

The classic trends were not abandoned in the Golden Age of the second half of the fifth century. Repose and serenity were even deepened; but movement was varied and intensified, and the illusion of space became more important. Even the works of earlier sculptors of the time were full of life and daring in motion. Myron's Diskobolos, one of the best-known statues in the world, has been admired for the bold, almost baroque, contortion of the athlete who, poised on one foot, is about to rebound in hurling the disk. Myron is also said to have made the statue of a runner in the most breathtaking tension and movement "like Jean de Bologne's famous Mercury." His Sick Philoktetes was so true to nature that whoever saw him felt the pains himself. Even coins, which by their very character tend to the static rather than to the dynamic side, show delight in 'interesting' motion: bulls are turning their heads; the suffering Philoktetes, once more, is dragging his rotten legs along; or a silenos sits on the floor with legs far apart in audacious foreshortening.

The time of Athens' ruler Perikles, between 460 and 431 B.C., with the Parthenon (447–432), the sculptures of Polykleitos and Pheidias, and the paintings of Apollodoros and Zeuxis, set for thousands of years the paragon of classical style. It achieved, for once in mankind's history, the balance of all the counteracting forces that drag the artist forward and back: the real and the perfect, rest and motion, truth and beauty. It had indeed the "noble simplicity and quiet grandeur" that J. J. Winckelmann mistakenly attributed to all Greek art. The *Dorýphoros* of Polykleitos is a symbol of this balance. He could not be more real in his thorough anatomy and yet, in the classic sense of the word, he has a beauty that no single being has. He is all force and energy yet cool and relaxed. And the horse's head from the pediment of Pheidias' Parthenon, is truly *the* horse, not one of a million horses.

But in all its perfection, this style could not avoid the impassivity inevitably connected with balance and flight from the individual. Lewis Mumford is right in saying: "Life arrested meant art perfected. . . . Unfortunately, art perfected may also in time mean life denied."

Departure from the ideals of the Golden Age began as early as the Peloponnesian war (431–403 B.C.). The young generation, restive and individualistic, denounced the frigid standard of impassible serenity. Even Sokrates, though older, reprimanded the artists of his time with lack of expressiveness. "The sculptor should show the soul in visible form." The new goal was life, emotion, movement. Parrhasios led painting to psychic subjects and the expression of grief: the Battles of the Amazons and the Centaurs on the frieze of Apollo's temple at Bassae show a new type of dramatic agitation.

The drama itself had a parallel development: the "dignified grandeur" of Aischylos (525–456 B.C.) had yielded to the "reserved beauty" of Sophokles (496–406 B.C.) and the "violent passion" of Euripides (484–406 B.C.).

The musical situation is of necessity dimmer. Not more than eleven pieces and fragments of Greek music are left, and few of them can be accurately dated; nor do the bare notes of their melodies convey a sufficient impression of their true character. Greek music was primarily vocal; instruments had a subordinate position except in more dynamic generations. We conclude this from many facts—that Sakadas' single performance belongs in such an age; that Plato declaimed against instrumental music as a meaningless art; that the words *aulesis* and *kitharesis*, expressing the solo playing of pipes and lyres, occur much less often than the terms *aulodia* and *kitharodia* which, related to ode, denoted the accompaniment of a singer; and that instruments were kept in an amazingly primitive state down to the postclassical times about 430 B.C., when one Pronomos of Thebes devised keys which allowed the piper to modulate from one tonality to another. That generation was indeed 'modern.' A few literary sources of the time, sneering at the latest developments, leave no doubt that under the leadership of Phrynis of Mytilene, who lived during the Peloponnesian war, music broke away from severe simplicity and indulged in "patched-up melody."

The two generations between the end of the Peloponnesian war (403 B.C.) and Alexander the Great's accession to the crown (336 B.C.) vigorously increased the dynamic trends of the preceding age. Alexander's teacher, Aristotle, attempted—in Erich Kahler's words in *Man the Measure*—"to justify growth and decay and the varying conditions of earthly life by rendering dynamic the principle of the soul and spirit. To him the spiritual world was not, as Plato saw it, an immobile heaven where ideas hung like remote stars, and the moves and perceptions of earthly creatures were but dim, mirror images and shadows of eternal beings."

Growth and decay and the varying conditions of earthly life shifted to the focus of art. The ageless gods became young, and the watchful relaxation of Polykleitean statues turned to the playful, languid ease of Praxiteles' Hermes, on the one hand, and to the violent stress and torsion of Skopas' Raging Maenad. Naturalism reigned supreme. "Things," said Aristotle, "that in nature we cannot see without distaste, become pleasant when an artist represents them true to nature; as, for instance, ugly beasts or corpses." Preferring—in the words of Quintilian, the orator—"resemblance to beauty," the sculptor Demetrios pitilessly depicted the general Pellichos with his bald pate and paunch or old Lysimache, who had been priestess for sixty-four years; Skopas provided his statues with famous pathetic eyes; Silanion rendered Iokaste's deadly pallor by silver-inlaid cheeks; and the painter Aristeides caused a sensation by depicting pathological themes. At that, a sense of grandeur inspired the Artemision in Ephesos and the Mausoleon in Halikarnassos during the 350's. But the time was no less fond of elegance and appreciated the dainty proportions of the Corinthian order as much as it admired the graceful nudes of Praxitelian gods.

Music was no less revolutionary. Timotheos of Miletos, the best disciple of Phrynis and musical leader at about 400 B.C., who boasted that he did not sing "old stuff," was heavily scolded for his twisted style, lack of dignity, and display of virtuosity. Still, no lesser an advocate than Aristotle said: "Without Timotheos, we would miss many a beautiful melody, and without Phrynis, we would not have

Timotheos." The poet-composer Philoxenos introduced solo parts into the choral dithyramb and Timotheos added choral parts to solo forms.

These were the "leaders of musical illegality" who, in Plato's angry words, "frenzied and unduly possessed by a spirit of pleasure, mixed dirges with hymns, and paeans with dithyrambs." Timotheos also knew how to imitate all kinds of natural sounds and other noises in his music (though one of his contemporaries irreverently remarked he had heard more savage tempests in boiling waterpots). Other poet-composers were derided for bombast, both in music and verse; and though none of their melodies are left, at least we know Philoxenos' astounding word creation, *pyrbromoleukerebinthoakanthumiktritoadu*, which possibly proves that words were little more than vehicles of melody.

The age of Alexander the Great and of Hellenism persisted in shifting from classic ideals. Its extraordinary evolution is perhaps most evident in the growing elegance and lightness of architecture. Doric was replaced by Ionic or else, in elements and natural proportions, was mingled and mixed with Ionic, and the slender Corinthian was fully admitted as the third architectural order. A more important development led to a significant connection and interplay of the rooms inside to a façade, which expressed the inner organization of the building; to a definite orientation in space and therewith a purposeful relation to the surroundings instead of the earlier isolating all-round display; and to the conception of the individual building as an integral part in a unified whole, indeed, to town planning.

With an eye on such great and often gigantic tasks, the builders and sculptors strove for exceptional sizes and Wonders of the World: the lost statue of Zeus in Tarentum is reported to have been fifty-six feet high, and the bronze colossus of the sun god in Rhodes, a hundred feet; the Didymaion in Miletos had a length of three hundred fifty-three feet, and the Artemision in Sardes, of three hundred sixty-one feet; the lighthouse at Alexandria was nearly four hundred feet high; and the one relief of the Battle of the Giants on the altar in Pergamon measured four hundred and thirty feet.

Besides gigantic tasks, grandiosity, and splendor, much devotion was spent on small and intimate art. Delightful birds and kitchen still lifes were so delicately put together in mosaic that in one of them, of pigeons, three hundred seventy-five tiny tesserae have been counted per square inch—enough to fuse the single dots of color into one impression. At the same time, a busy industry of small terra-cotta figurines, in Tanagra particularly, amused its clientele with effigies, not only of charming girls but also of barbers, bakers, cobblers, and urchins.

At the same time, large-scale works in stone and paint did not lag behind. Tired of gods and heroes, they relished the malodorant reality of craftsmen, beggars, topers with rags and wrinkles in the spirit of Plautus' comedies and in strict parallel with the leveling doctrines and antiaristocratic habits of the Cynic philosophers. And while unheroic oddities became a recognized branch under the official title of *rhopography*, one Graphikos had to accept the personal pun-title *rhyparógraphos*, dirt painter.

But the artists were also deeply interested in specifically picturesque problems, in light and shadow, perspective, chiaroscuro, and, as with the powerful Battle of Alexander, in the masterful composition of masses in motion. Apelles was famous for his brilliant high lights, and Antiphilon has been cited for his painting of a boy blowing up a fire and getting its glare on the face. Even the sculptors, like Lysippos and his school, paid heed to the changing effects of light and combined them with a never heard-of momentariness in attitude and movement and with a new three dimensionality which allowed the onlooker to get a satisfactory view of the statue from all sides.

Masters of great art, Lysippos or Apelles, have left us gods, heroes, and mortals in beauty and grandeur (Plate II); they hardly ever lapsed into the lowlands of genre. But they did not refrain from appealing to the senses: the gods, once ageless, grew youthful and the goddesses, in classic times correctly dressed, exposed their charms unveiled. The athletes, on the other hand, often were no longer paragons of virile perfection but Herculean towers of brutish muscles. And even great art took to themes that stirred imagination. Orestes slaying his mother and stepfather, Cassandra's premonitions, the raving Thamyras, Demeter mourning for her daughter Persephone, Niobe with her dying children, Laokoön choking with his two sons in the constriction of serpents (Plate III) were subjects dear to the heart of later Grecian art.

In reports of Hellenistic dancing, the solemn *emmelic* patterns of the classic age were overshadowed by *kômos,* the dance of professionals performed with the generous exhibition of bodily charms but also with the display of repulsive deformities. Particular stress was laid on learning *phoraí* or gestures to express emotions and actions and *schémata* or gestures to characterize definite persons. Greek dancing had become emotional and descriptive and joined the novel art of portraying. True, Polybios, a writer of the first half of the second century B.C., relates that the Arcadians still performed public, nonprofessional group dances every year; but, from his description, this seems to have been an exception at so late a time.

However, the anticlassic trends of the Hellenistic age did not progress uninterruptedly. In the first half of the second century B.C., a replica of Pheidias' Athene for the King of Pergamon released a rage of ordering copies from older masterworks. Around the middle of the century, the creative artists themselves, led by the Peloponnesian sculptor Damophon of Messene, reverted to the styles of the Golden Age. Damophon's work testifies, to quote from Bernard Ashmole, to a new "sedulous study of the past. The forms in which this study manifests itself may be said to be two, which however merge into one another—the borrowing of older elements which are worked up into a more or less homogeneous but somewhat nerveless academic style, and the borrowing of older types which are modified and worked out in detail in the style of the day."

Two of the eleven musical relics from Greece, the two hymns in honor of Apollo engraved in stone in the Athenian Treasury at

Delphi, have on paleographic grounds been attributed by philologists to the middle of the second century B.C.—contemporary, then, with Damophon. And here, too, the style has unmistakable traits of reversion to earlier types, of "the borrowing of older elements." They are written in the so-called earlier enharmonion, a strange, archaic gender, in which the scale (like that of Japan) alternately jumps in major thirds and creeps in semitones. Since Euripides, three hundred years ago, had already composed in the so-called later enharmonion with the semitone cleft into two microtones—a short fragment from his *Orestes* is still extant—the Delphian hymns re-adopt a preclassical pattern abandoned hundreds of years ago. They are archaic also in their frequent modulation from the then usual modes organized in octaves (fourth *plus* fifth) into the corresponding obsolete modes organized in heptads (fourth *plus* fourth) (Example 7).

Example 7. Second Delphic Hymn

Small as our knowledge of Grecian music is, it gives unmistakable evidence of an evolution parallel to the essential destinies of the visual arts.

3. ROME

THE ROMAN WORLD, which in sculpture and painting more than in architecture greatly depended on Greece, reacted during the reign of the first emperor Augustus (30 B.C.–A.D. 14) against the exaggerations of later Hellenism and against the uncouth naturalism of its own 'Italic,' republican style. In an attempt to revive the quiet ideals of the Golden Age of Greece, the poets—Virgil, Horace, Ovid—

turned back to the standards of the Periklean century, to reserve and noble simplicity; and the artists did not stay behind. Cicero who, born in 106 B.C., belonged in an older generation, wonderingly asked why people were preferring ancient art to what he had been calling the much-improved modern style. There was no outstanding sculptor or painter, however; the great name of the age was Vitruvius, whose book *De architectura* has been the bible of all classicistic architects since.

However, in the following age, the Claudian emperors from Tiberius to Nero (A.D. 14–68) departed from the solemn coolness of the Augustean classicism and again tended to a moderate naturalism, based on Roman, un-Greek love for country life and nature. This dynamism climaxed in the 'Baroque' of the Flavian emperors (A.D. 69–96), and particularly of Emperor Domitian (A.D. 81–96). Gigantic buildings of a distinctly Roman character were then erected, the Colosseum and the almost seven hundred feet long Porticus Divorum on the Field of Mars. Sculptors overdid decoration, gave their picturesque reliefs architecture or landscapes as backgrounds, tried to present their scenes as casual sections from infinite space, and excelled in fascinating portraits of a pitiless naturalism. And murals of the so-called fourth Pompeian style were no less illusionistic than Italian murals of the seventeenth century. To make the picture complete, the ladies then wore enormously high coiffures in artful curls.

Reversion in the times of Trajan (A.D. 98–117) led to a new classicism. Under Hadrian (A.D. 117–138), overdecoration was avoided, composition became clearer and simpler, the backgrounds of reliefs again were left in the neutral emptiness of classical Greece, and the general tempo slowed down. It was consistent with such trends that the most stationary form of architecture, central building on a circular ground plan, reached its climax in the Hadrianic Pantheon, the Temple of All Gods.

Once more, a passionate, flickering Baroque succeeded under the Antonines between A.D. 138 and 192 until, in the early third century, another classicistic reaction set in. . . .

J. de Wit's recent book on later Roman portraits, *Spätrömische Bildnismalerei* (Berlin, 1938), justly characterizes the time from about A.D. 240 to 270 as impressionistic, and the following age as realistic. A subsequent period of expressionism reached from about 290 to the death of Constantin the Great (336) with increasing classicistic tendencies. Classicism in an Augustean sense was again in bloom under Valentinian I, about 370, and degenerated to mannerism under Theodosius I (379–395) and Honorius (395–423).

It was at about that time that the Romans began to illuminate their manuscripts which later, studied, copied, and imitated, begot the most important part of medieval painting.

Of the dance in Rome we know but little outside the facts that about 150 B.C. Scipio, the destroyer of Carthage, closed the dancing schools to which the Romans were sending their daughters and sons, and that Cicero, in the genuine rationalism of Rome, once remarked: "No sober person would dance." But professional dancing was highly developed under the influence of Etruria and Greece, and it might not be mere chance that the poet Lucian, though a Greek, recommended, in a special book on the dance, the greatness of pantomimic dancing in the empire at a time when the Baroque of the Antonines favored descriptive art.

There are no relics of Roman music, though several of the Greek remains doubtless belong in Roman times. What we know about Roman music comes mainly from poetic satires written against its nuisance and impropriety. Seneca, who lived in the age of the Claudii, complained that choruses and orchestras—never used in Greece proper—were growing to gigantic proportions, so that the theater often held more performers than it once had had spectators; and five hundred years later, Marcianus Cappella described lyres "as big as sedan chairs." Private teachers and conservatoires trained the daughters of the bourgeoisie to strum on the lyre—obviously, instrumental music played a role that Greece would hardly have tolerated and which seems to be confirmed by the fact that all the musical treatises from Rome present the scales in the ascending order characteristic of instrumental scales. Day and night, the slaves of the wealthy drove the neighbors mad with their singing and playing; and at table nobody could talk for music. At that, an intolerable host of virtuosos, capricious, insolent, intriguing, strutted the stage.

This is the picture Roman poets trace. But it must be incomplete. It is hard to believe that Roman music as a whole was in a state of disintegration for more than five hundred years. Such a prejudice is not compatible with the laws of evolution. And it is still less compatible with the fact that the cantillation of the church, generally treated under the heading Middle Ages, was actually a creation of Roman antiquity. To be sure, church music derived mainly from Jewish and Syrian sources. But as early as the fourth century, in the liturgy of St. Ambrose in Milan it had a character of its own, neither entirely Eastern nor entirely Western, which by way of elimination must be called Mediterranean and, still more narrowly, Italian (Example 8). Again, when two hundred years later St. Gregory undertook the redaction of the official musical liturgy, it differed not only from the Ambrosian version but also from the

Example 8. Jubilate Domino—Offertory—Ambrosian *after Gustave Reese*

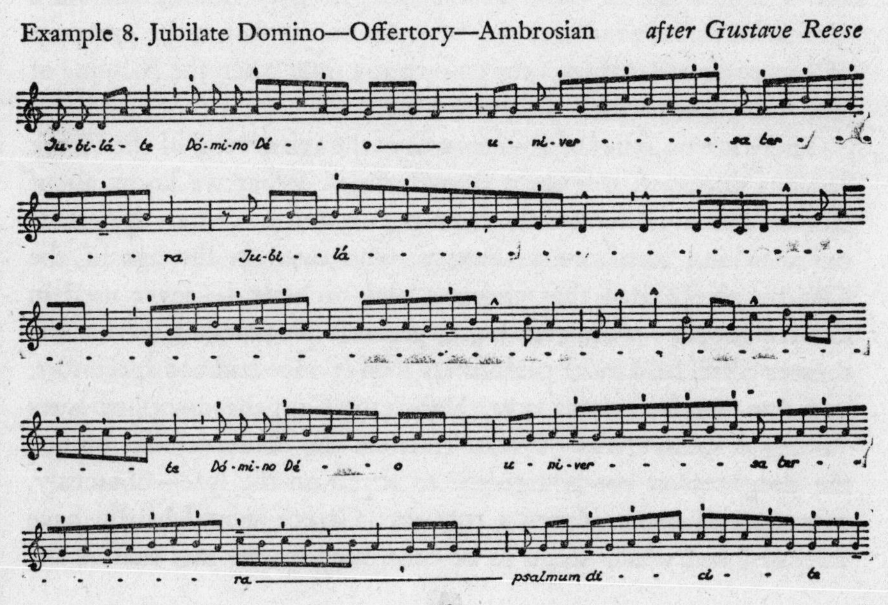

Byzantine, Syrian, Coptic, and Armenian chant; and so far was it from the ways of Western music that it had to be forced upon the Gauls and Germans who, as Roman singers complained "with their barbaric voices crushing the melodies in their throats," were unable to master the outlandish style.

It seems then that the musical mission of Rome was not so much the preservation or even the development of Grecian art and music, in which she would have failed in half a thousand years, but rather the anonymous evolution of an innate folk song, which in Italy is stronger, more general, and more beautiful than anywhere else in the world.

As the mature fruit of so precious a gift, Rome tendered to the Middle Ages the imperishable treasures of the Gregorian chant just as, along with her language, she handed over her architecture, mosaics, and illuminated books.

CHAPTER THREE

The Romanesque Middle Ages

A.D. *800*

THE TIME OF CHARLEMAGNE, which witnessed the passage from tribal to imperial art in the West and the center of Europe, the transition from wood to stone construction, and from ornamental to monumental expression, is the logical starting point for the medieval section of this book. It is the more logical, as the times before A.D. 800 provide no datable facts of music, let alone of the dance.

The style of Carolingian art is mainly due to influences from the Mediterranean world and its two civilizations—Rome in the West, and Byzantium in the East. Its outstanding architectural monument, the cathedral in Aix-la-Chapelle (under construction in 798), derived from a northern Italian church of the sixth century, San Vitale in Ravenna, and could not be more classic in the perfect balance of its regular octagonal form, tectonic neatness, and energetic disjunction of parts and subdivisions. Ivory carvings of the time, which mostly served as book covers, were symmetrical in structure and calm in pose (Plate IV); and the books themselves were under the supervision of the Imperial Office of Calligraphy illuminated in noble simplicity and moderation.

Charlemagne's efforts to introduce Italian architecture were in line with his fight for the (supranational) Roman chant in St. Gregory's edition against the (national) Gallican version of church music. This chant was occasionally given the richer, more festive polyphonic form of the *órganum*, in which a liturgical melody, solemnly proceeding in notes of equal, considerable length (like the hymn to Confucius in China), was accompanied throughout and note against note by a second voice moving on, as a rule, at the distance of a fifth or a fourth. Indeed, the principal voice could be doubled at the octave below, and the organal voice at the octave above, so that the melody advanced in four parallel lines (Example 9). No music could be more static or impassive.

Example 9. Simple Organum at the Fourth *after Gustave Reese*

850

UNDER CHARLEMAGNE'S SON, Louis the Pious, basilican churches were given transepts or cross naves, which must not be considered classical since Italy, homeland of the basilica, has always been averse to stressing such counteraccent. The one relic of secular architecture, a gate of the monastery in Lorsch, Hesse (*c.* 830), in its prim decorativeness, is no less against the spirit of classical art.

The ivories carved later in the ninth century, too, are unmistakably different from those in Charlemagne's time. All the figures are high-spirited, agitated, tempestuous; they rush and fling their arms beyond the framing vignettes while their garments float in a gale. The Adoring Magi on the cover of the gospel in Paris, Bibliothèque Nationale *fd. latin* 9393, almost dart to reach the Virgin and, in the Slaughter of the Innocents, one of the mothers, horror-stricken, shrieks and throws up her arms in helpless despair (Plate V).

Painting followed in the same direction, whether we reach for the almost illusionistic gospel of Aix-la-Chapelle, for the famous Utrecht Psalter of 867 in Leyden (despite its ancient models), or for the English *Liber Vitae* of the same time with its distorted postures, diagonal axes, and restive drapery. How precipitate is the movement in the two Bibles of the French kings Charles the Bald and Charles the Fat! How stormy is the opening illumination in the incomparable Golden Psalter at the monastery of St. Gall in Switzerland! King David on his throne is playing with his two musicians, while two dancers with fluttering streamers perform below. Everything is in violent motion: the very floor undulates as if the painter had meant to represent the agitated sea; all limbs turn out; all bodies twist; all garments flutter and fly; the king sits as if he were about to spring up, and his feet stand on a church model awkwardly placed aslant. Even the flanking columns which tradition has imposed are given energy and restlessness by golden spirals that all the way up to the capitals wind like the screw columns of Romanesque and Baroque times.

Describing the Bible of Charles the Fat makes it almost unnecessary to speak of the Gospels of Ada or of Lothar, or of the Bible of Moutier-Granval, which Alfred Leroy has called a *premier essai de naturalisme sans lendemain.* Indeed, "without a tomorrow." Did he expect a straight evolution?

The chant of the church cannot have been much less Baroque at that time. Otherwise, Archbishop Hrabanus Maurus of Mainz (776–856) would not have declaimed against the worldly, theatrical style of his singers.

900–981

IVORY CARVING, ONCE MORE, shows a reaction from the dramatic style of 870 to the strictest symmetry and reserve. The Liturgical Act in the Fitzwilliam Museum at Cambridge, England and the Celebration of the Mass in the Municipal Library at Frankfort on the Main are perhaps the strongest and most beautiful evidences of this return to classic ideals.

It is consistent with this attitude, as Chapter X (Addition and Unification) will show, that the outstanding edifice of the time, the older cathedral in Mainz, is, in the words of Paul Frankl's *Baukunst des Mittelalters,* "additive, composed of self-sufficient units."

Datable music or musical facts of the time are not available. True, two outstanding monks connected with music are known, Notker the Stammerer (d. 912) and Tuotilo (d. 915), both of St. Gall in Switzerland; but the textual and musical additions to the liturgical melodies, known as tropes and sequences—the invention of which is wrongly attributed to these two men—had in fact existed before their time.

Of the more dynamic middle of the century, it will suffice to mention the jerking, broken, violent dashes of the Aethelwold Benedictional in Chatsworth (A.D. 966).

It was in those dynamic times that the cathedral in Winchester, England, was given the earliest monster organ (between A.D. 935 and 951). From a Latin poem of that time, we learn that nobody ever saw its like. "A dozen bellows lie above and fourteen below, which, providing enormous masses of wind by alternate blasts, are worked by seventy vigorous men, who, sweating, labor their arms and egg their companions on to pump with all their might and make the spacious work with its four hundred pipes resound." Specialists of the organ might be interested to hear that the four hundred pipes were furnitures of ten ranks on forty sliders serving as the keys. One readily believes the poet when he admiringly tells his readers that "the audience stopped their ears with their hands" and that "the sound of the pipes was heard all over the town."

Toward the end of the century, style again reverted to calmer trends. The gospel lectionary for Archbishop Egbert of Trier, written and painted between 977 and 993 as the outstanding work of the illuminating school in the monastery of Reichenau on the Lake of Constance, fascinates us by its unexpected equilibrium. "It is indeed an introvert style, tending toward closed contours in the figure's silhouette," says C. R. Morey. The same is true of the illuminations in the gospel book of the German Emperor Otto III in the Staatsbibliothek at Munich, drawn in the quiet symmetry of the so-called Ottonian Renaissance.

The new monastery of Cluny was in 981 erected in a similar spirit: Paul Frankl praises its "limpid clearness" and "great and quiet train."

1050

1050 PUT AN END to the life of one of the greatest reformers in music, the Benedictine monk Guido d'Arezzo, to whose uncontested authority innumerable generations of European musicians have bowed. He introduced the four-line staff, to this day in use in Catholic chant, and reintroduced solmization, that is, the use of the tone-syllables *ut re mi fa sol la* notwithstanding the absolute pitch, *mi-fa* always denoting the semitone in the melody wherever it occurred—on *e-f*, on *b-c*, or on *f*-sharp-*g*. Thus, he facilitated the correct rendition and the memorizing of songs so that, in the words of a letter written to a monastic friend, "his choirboys were able to learn in a couple of days what before they had needed weeks to learn." Like most reforms, this, too, seems to indicate a loss of tradition and, hence, a new epoch.

In polyphonic music, both Guido's *Micrologus*, the musical Bible of the later Middle Ages, and the contemporaneous Winchester Tropers, more than a hundred and fifty *órgana* on one of the codices of Winchester in England, display an increasing interest in contrary motion (one voice ascending, while the other voice descends, or vice versa), especially in approaching the end. This means a definite estrangement from static ideals.

Of composers, the greatest known were two German masters: Heriman the Cripple, latinized as Hermannus Contractus, and Bruno of Egisheim, the later Pope Leo IX. Heriman's three beautiful antiphons and sequences in honor of the Virgin—*Alma redemptoris mater*, *Ave praeclara maris stella*, and *Salve regina misericordiae* (Example 10)—have lived to this day both in their original unaccompanied forms and disguised in polyphonic settings of later composers. Bruno of Egisheim's *Gloria in excelsis* in the seventh (Mixolydian) mode is no less a part of the present Catholic liturgy. And this holds true also of a fifth piece of the time, attributed to Wipo of Burgundy, chaplain to the German emperor Henry III, who died at the same time as the two other masters: the immortal Easter sequence *Victimae paschalis laudes* (Praise to the Easter victim), which has uneven verses, no rhymes, and the wide range of an octave and a fourth, unusual in church music. Not many pieces throughout the centuries are as ecstatic, powerful, and solemn as these five; not many have so passionate a tension.

Example 10. Salve Regina misericordiae *Hermannus Contractus*

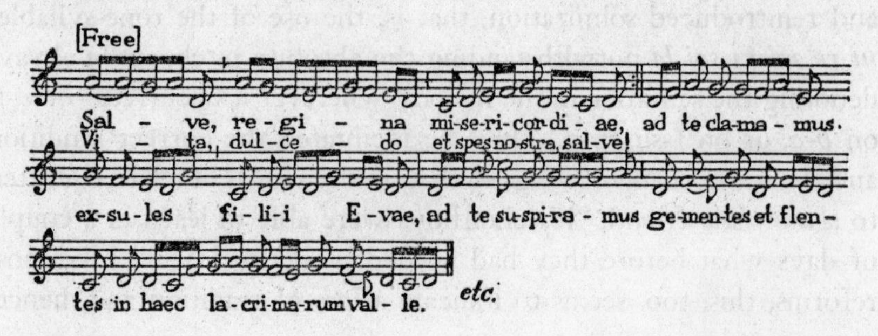

It was at that time, or shortly before, that Bishop Bernward (d. 1022) commissioned the bronze doors of Hildesheim Cathedral which—with their dramatic, picturesque scenes from the Bible and their twisted, excited relief figures—are one of the most remarkable relics of those agitated ages.

Painting, all through the first part of the century, with a climax around its middle, was fantastic, restless, violent. The Odbert Gospel in Boulogne (somewhere between 989 and 1008) and the gospels from Bamberg in the State Library at Munich, which must have been painted in the dozen years between 1002 and 1014, show the same excitement in the strong emotion, vivid gestures, and flowing garments of their figures. And still more exciting is the gospel in Amiens, Bibliothèque Publique no. 24, from the middle of the century, where the garments whirl like waterspouts around the bodies and the Evangelists, unreal and distorted, flare up in the crackling flame of an almost painful ecstasy.

Even as far away as Greece, in the Katholikon of Hosios Lukas in Stiris, the mosaic of Christ in Limbo shows the same spirit of dash and emotion.

It may be permissible to add here a unique work of art from the end of the eleventh century (a period that otherwise does not provide sufficient data for a section of its own)—the almost unbelievable Crucifix in the abbey church at Werden on the Ruhr, which with its exaggerated, suffering eyes is so strikingly expressionistic that nobody would be surprised to find it among the sculptures in a museum of modern art (Plate VI).

1120

THE YEAR 1120 approximately marks the culmination of Romanesque architecture with the rich chorus of the third abbey church of Cluny in Burgundy. And it also approximately marks the culmination of Romanesque sculpture in France. Inseparable from architecture and without interest in actual realism, this style adapted its objects to the panels or capitals to be filled in. And whether it represented the human body or plants or animals, it gave their motion a breathtaking tempo: legs run, arms jerk, robes flow, and ornaments creep in convulsive twist. On the tympan of Moissac in southern France (Plate VII), Christ, larger than life-size, is enthroned in the center while the many minor figures, small and crowded, are *secundum ordinem* aligned in horizontal tiers at each side and below. The tympan is almost static in its canonic majesty and symmetry and in the strictness of its hieratic grouping. But the souls and the evangelists and the elders revolt against confinement. Charged with excessive energy and restlessness, they claim an active part in the drama; they twist their bodies in eloquent gesticulation full of fervor and passion. How much this art is meant to be expressionistic can be read from the Latin motto of the Last Judgment on the tympan of Autun: *Terreat hic terror quos terreus alligat error*— Let this terror appall those bound in earthly sin.

It is in keeping with such trends that the cathedral of Modena sent for Master Wilhelm, a man from expressionistic Germany. His sculptures are coarse and ugly but full of life and drama and impressive in their tenseness.

These and other Romanesque figures are by no means realistic.

Their strong expressionism is due to inner vision rather than to keen observation—"the Romanesque sculptors, having eyes, saw not," says Salomon Reinach.

For the history of music and the history of the dance at this time unfortunately there are no dates available. It is true that the art of the troubadours had its first bloom, and that we know the life times of many of them: Marcabru of Gascony and Jaufré Rudel flourished about 1120. And it is true that their melodies look neat enough in the beautiful *chansoniers* in which they were collected. But, alas, the tidy squares and diamonds of their plain-chant notation do not reveal the time value assigned to the individual note, the spirit of the performance in general, or, for that matter, the instrumental accompaniment.

There has been much controversy as to whether and to what degree the time values depended on the poetic meters of the text—long–short, or short–long, or otherwise—the long syllables being supposed to have taken just twice the length of the short. With or without this hypothesis, the general idea seems to have been that the poetry of the troubadours had syllabic melodies with each note or at the most a ligature of two notes corresponding to one syllable, the whole tune following a strict and even beat. If this were true, then all the songs, in the two hundred fifty years of troubadour and trouvère music, would be on the side of simple, symmetrical, more or less unemotional structures. But there is no proof, and the whole idea may be merely one of those illicit backward projections of modern habits to which music history has so often fallen victim. Johannes de Garlandia, a theoretician of the first half of the thirteenth century, expressly said that certain melodies could be performed *aut sono ordinato*, that is, in strict form, or else *in florificatione soni*, that is, in free coloratura; and the English Anonymus confirms this statement. Both discuss church music, but such freedom, then, would apply so much the more to secular music. Actually, some troubadour melodies have survived on western Mediterranean islands in forms quite different from the sober notation the troubadours left. This island music is not at all syllabic or strict in

1120

beat but very free and expressive in the florid, melismatic style of southern Europe. The troubadours were southerners, after all, and the very fact that they always wrote their melodies in the noncommittal plain-chant notation, even after the introduction of mensural signs, hints at a basic vagueness of rhythm rather than the contrary. And as is true so often in older music, notation as a whole might have been skeletal. In this uncertainty, we had better refrain from assigning troubadour music to any definite style.

CHAPTER FOUR

The Gothic Middle Ages

1140

WHILE GERMANY AND ITALY adhered to the Romanesque style for a hundred years more, French sculptors and architects changed their idioms so thoroughly that from 1140 on, specifically from the building of the western portal of the cathedral at St. Denis near Paris (begun in 1137), most art historians believe that an entirely different style began—the Gothic. Sculptors were no longer interested in dragons, griffins, apes, or monsters with two bodies to one head or with two heads to a single body. No lesser man than St. Bernard, abbot of Clairvaux, had become aware of the *ridicula monstrositas* of late Romanesque church decoration and exposed it about 1130 in his famous *Apologie*. Restlessness disappears with the monsters and the once flowing garments quiet down: repose is the new ideal. Many porches are given typical column men: the statues of saints, instead of being decoratively pasted on the columns, now support the arches as parts of the structure, in the way the caryatids of ancient Greece had done.

And all over France, static ideals led the sculptor's chisel. The tympan in Conques, in the *midi*, which (in Porter's chronology) was carved "not much later than 1130 or 1135," is partitioned and hence less unified and flowing than the older ones. The scene of the keys of heaven being given to St. Peter in Nevers (central France), attributed to the middle of the century, has an almost classic sedateness. But these and the many other monuments of the new mentality are pale against the glory of the time—the Royal Portal of Chartres Cathedral (supposed to date from between 1145 and 1160, before the older church burned down)—pale, indeed, against the smiling majesty of its partitioned, symmetrical tympan and of the quiet, elongated column men in neatly draped garments which call to mind the fashions of ancient Greece (Plate VIII).

At this time, indeed, "whatever the material, the folds often have a crimped or gauffered appearance that recalls the early Ionic *chiton* of the Ancients," which "contrasts with the heavy 'Doric' draperies that preceded and followed it." This statement, found in Kelly and Schwabe's *Short History of Costume*, is a remarkable illustration of generational reversals, which play so dominant a role in the history of taste. Two distinctive feminine features of extreme fashion at this date were "first, the exaggerated prolongation of all parts, which was at times such an encumbrance that the draperies had to be shortened by tying them up in knots; secondly, the abrupt widening of the sleeves below the elbow into a kind of exorbitant streamers trailing sometimes as low as the ground." Thirdly, the upper parts of gowns were "skin-tight to below the hips." The ladies' hair made "an almost sensational appearance among the highest classes between *c.* 1120 and 1150, being parted in the middle and arranged in two long tails, either braided into plaits, twisted with ribbons, or enclosed in cases of silk bound with ribbon. These generally hung down in front and (length being a fashionable desideratum) were often eked out by means of false hair, tow, or other devices, reaching down to the knee or lower and ending in ornamental ferrules." No costume could be more vertical.

During this time in history, it is difficult to co-ordinate music with the other arts. The manuscripts have dates just as uncertain as those of the reliefs, to say the least, and the compositions that they include may or may not come from the time at which they were copied. The nearest musical monuments are the Codex of Beauvais and the Codex Calixtinus of Santiago de Compostela, both attributed to about 1140. But the notation of the polyphonic *órgana* and monodic *conductus* they contain fails to indicate time values and rhythm and hence does not convey a clear idea of living music.

The only composer's name that we know from this period was

Adam de St. Victor. About 1130, he became a monk in his abbey, died at a Biblical age in 1192, and therefore must have flourished about 1140. His field was the sequence, a strophic, nonliturgical poem to be sung on a nonliturgical melody during the service, and never was sequence simpler, stricter, and evener than Adam's.

All these traits coincide with a rebirth of classical learning, which has stamped the age as "the Renaissance of the twelfth century."

1170

FRENCH SCULPTURE RECHANGED its style after a very short time. There are the two almost violent ascensions in the cathedral of Cahors and the parish church at Collonges. But more violent are the Passion on the abbey church at St. Gilles, with the unruly drapery of its folds and the overdecoration of all structural parts, and the relief of Cain and Abel in the same church, where fantastic leafless trees are writhing in a gale. The high watermark seems to be the Death, Resurrection, and Triumph of the Virgin on the cathedral at Senlis (Ile de France), which in the powerful curves of its drapery and the dash of its movements suggests the epithet Baroque.

To this picture, England contributes a truly turbulent Last Judgment on enamel in the Victoria and Albert Museum. England also veers from the static Romanesque Anglo-Norman to a mature Gothic, the so-called Early English Style in architecture, with the cloisters of Fountain Abbey and the choir of Canterbury Cathedral (*c.* 1175–78) as its earliest monuments. And Spain contributes one of her best-known sculptures: the naturalistic, dramatic Puerta de Gloria of the cathedral in Santiago de Compostela, which Master Matteo carved from 1166 to 1188.

Fashion, the faithful, sensitive barometer, responds with a radical sinking of the waistline, which in all times seems to coincide with a dynamic trend in the arts.

At long last, the cautious search for musical contemporaries comes to an end. Around 1163, it seems, we are confronted with a world center of music, the school and choir connected with the cathedral of Notre Dame in Paris, and with its outstanding personality, Master Leoninus. An anonymous and probably English writer a hundred years later mentions him by name, in contrast to the impersonal attitude of the earlier Middle Ages in matters of art. He reverently calls him *optimum organista*, meaning, not an organ player but a composer of *órgana*. Leoninus wrote a whole *Magnus Liber* with a year's supply for all the mass and office services that needed such polyphony of soloists for the responsorial parts of the liturgy *pro servitio divino multiplicando*. Unfortunately this unique document is lost, but several copies have been preserved. In the *órganum* of Leoninus, sections of rigid counterpoint note-against-note in strictest rhythm with the Gregorian *vox principalis* below alternated with free counterpoints of long coloraturas, which in powerful tension and an almost rhapsodic freedom effusively flowed over the solemn, if not eerie, endlessly drawn-out pedal notes of the Gregorian *ténor* or 'held' melody (Example 11).

Example 11. Órganum *Leoninus*

[Free rythm]

etc.

1190

Perotinus of Paris, the earliest musician on whom his contemporaries conferred the title Magnus, the Great, remodeled Leoninus' *Liber Magnus* in the reserved taste of the turning century. He dammed the free effusion of the melodic voice parts in the *órganum* and forced them into clean-cut periods of answering phrases; he played with short motifs and sequences, interchanged the voice parts to create a limpid symmetry, and arranged the *cantus firmus* or *ténor* in regularly reiterated patterns (Example 12).

Example 12. Órganum *Perotinus*

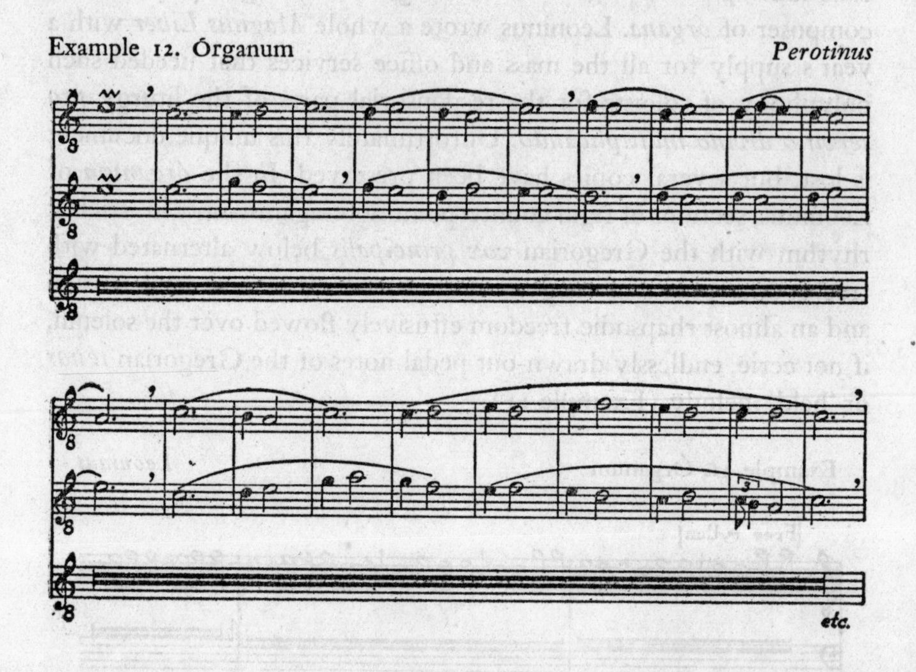

Out of the most clean-cut episodes in the *órganum*, Perotinus and his generation also developed a new, dominating form of polyphonic composition, the *motet* (which should not be mistaken for the later choral form of this name). A previously existing melody in lengthened notes was used as its *ténor*, and one or more additional voice parts, in shorter notes and strictest form, accompanied above. Each voice had a different text and later even a different language. Still, the texts were mostly somehow connected: one voice would sing *Virginale decus et presidium*, or *Gaude super omnia*, or *Anima mea liquefacta est*, a second, *Descendi in ortum meum*, while the *ténor* played the melody of *Alma Redemptoris mater*, August Savior's Mother, on some instrument. The result, truly Gothic in conception, is a unity in spirit rather than in sensuous perception (Example 13).

Example 13. Conduct *after Jacques Handschin*

So strict was Perotinus' generation that, going beyond the motet, it created in the polyphonic *conductus* a wholly unified form—*consonans*, says one writer. A melody with a metric Latin text was accompanied by one, two, or even three higher voices, vocal or instrumental, all of which followed the same beat and rhythm. Thus the parts, denied independence and individuality, grew together into a sequence of chords. An important, perhaps the most important step toward harmony had been taken.

French sculpture, in contrast to the preceding style of Senlis and St. Gilles, was classic, simple, sedate. Outstanding examples are St. Anne's portal of Notre Dame in Paris, dated "not much earlier than 1180"; the statues and reliefs on St. Trophime in Arles, "possibly 1185"; furthermore, St. Peter and St. Paul on the portal of St. Pierre de Maguelonne (1178); and the closely outlined statues from the shrine of Lazarus at Autun ("1170–89"), once in the cathedral, now in the museum of that town.

Italian sculpture had the same classic attitude and even provides some inscribed dates: Maestro Martino's wooden Virgin with Child in the Kaiser Friedrich Museum in Berlin (1199); or the symmetrical lunette of the principal doorway in San Michele degli Scalzi at Pisa (1204); or Maestro Marchinonne's solemn lunette in the parish church at Arezzo (1216).

In architecture, the year 1200 marks the first work on the Drapers' Hall in Ypres, so classic in its steady, uniform rows of windows under the dominant calmness of its overpowering gable roof.

Fashion accented this closeness by the new wimple, a tight-fitting linen cloth that framed the face of the lady.

In keeping with the strictness of the time, Pope Innocent III interdicted dramatic performances in churches in 1210 and the synod of Trier in 1227 renewed this ban at the climax of classicistic trends in the arts.

1230

THE EARLY THIRTEENTH CENTURY witnessed the beginnings of the chief group of Gothic cathedrals: Magdeburg in 1209, Reims in 1212, Amiens in 1218, Salisbury in 1220, Beauvais in 1225, Cologne in 1248. At the same time, France reached the climax of classic perfection in sculpture with the northern porch of Chartres, the porches of Amiens and Reims, the incomparable Virgin Portal of Notre Dame in Paris (Plate VIII), and the noble statue of the synagogue on the south façade of Strasbourg Cathedral.

In Germany, Naumburg Cathedral was at the same time given its famous 'classical' statues of the Prince and Princess, the *Schloß-kirche* at Wechselburg its Crucifixion, the cathedral of Freiberg in Saxony its Golden Portal, and the cathedral of Bamberg its St. Elizabeth (Plate VI).

Art historians have rightly compared this heyday of the Gothic style with the Golden Age of Greece: there are no archaic features left; all scenes are dignified and quiet without being stiff; symmetry has lost its hieratic rigidity; garments, in art and in life, are extremely simple and fall in a few, almost majestic, folds; and men and women have learned how to stand and to move, to smile and to mourn. In a similar sense of dignity, the council of Trier, in 1227, denounced the secular texts that had crept into hymns and plain song.

The outstanding, datable music relic is the *Dies irae*, Day of Wrath, which still forms the second section of the Requiem mass. But Thomas of Celano—if he is the composer—follows the age-old form of the sequence so closely that the time is not characterized.

The other relics are once more the songs of northern French

trouvères and German minnesingers and once more we do not know their rhythm nor their accompaniment. More important from the viewpoint of history are two developments in polyphonic music. One of them is the codification and, in a double sense, the classification of rhythm. Thus a whole piece from beginning to end, or one of the voice parts, was pressed into the strait jacket of one of the Greek poetic meters—trochees (2-1 units, ♩♪), iambs (1-2 units, ♪♩), dactyls (3-1-2 units, ♩. ♫♪), anapaests (1-2-3 units, ♪♩ ♩.), or otherwise—and therewith kept away from any free effusion of melody. The reader may form an idea of such modal compositions if he thinks of the dactyls at the beginning of the slow movement in Beethoven's Seventh or of the scherzo in his Ninth, or of the anapaests in Bach's Brandenburg Concerto for strings in G major.

In view of these *modi*, as the monks called the metric patterns, the author was pleased to read in Hans Karlinger's *Kunst der Gotik* (Berlin 1927, p. 78) that the contemporaneous Sixtus Portal of Reims Cathedral was to his taste "all too metrical in structure." This scholar, quite unaware of the implications of his statement, had found an extraordinarily strong sense of metric arrangement in the sculpture of that time, thus stressing that the musical codification of meter (probably unknown to him) was far from being exclusively a musical trait.

The rigid *modi* were fortunately valid only in polyphonic music, motets and conductus (Example 13, in the first, trochaic mode).

Secular monophonic melodies were, however, spared the *modus* regulation. We do not know their rhythmic organization, since their script ignored time values; but the very choice of so vague a notation seems to prove that rhythm played a rather subordinate role, indeed that the troubadours and other singers might not always have cared at all for regular time beats. Two or three generations later, Johannes de Grocheo in his fascinating treatise on music—to be discussed anon—significantly feels uncertain whether this kind of music should be described as immeasurable or as not so precisely measurable, since it was sung *totaliter ad libitum*, as you like it.

The stricter attitude of the times around 1230 was not satisfied with so vague a notation. To be sure, the plain-chant script, noncommittal and easy, was kept for all unaccompanied melodies (monophonies), both religious and secular, such as the chant of the church and the songs of the troubadours. But for polyphony, where the simultaneous progression of two or more voice parts had to be carefully related, the exact time values of the notes became so vital that a 'measuring' notation seemed indispensable. This *mensural* notation, the direct forerunner of our modern script, was achieved by assigning different shapes, and ascending or descending stems to the squares that symbolized the various time values, *longa, brevis, semibrevis* and, later, *minima* and *semiminima.*

With both developments, metric *modi* and mensural notation, the French polyphonists had radically turned their backs on the rhythmical vagueness of Leoninus' style. Both served strictness in structure and presentation.

1265

After the classical climax, Gothic art grew lighter, more elegant, louder, and livelier. In architecture, the turn is unmistakable in one of the most beautiful buildings of France, the Sainte Chapelle in the Court of Justice in Paris, which was finished in 1248 after six years of work. The edifice—in fact two chapels one above another—has scarcely solid walls; the stained windows occupy more space than had been usual before. All this interior, stone as well as glass, is lavishly colored; without color, the building would have little effect.

The English parallel of this postclassical Gothic is the so-called Decorated Style, which reaches from about 1270 to about 1370 and sets in with St. Ethelbert's Gateway, Norwich (1273–78), the choir and transept of Exeter Cathedral (1279–92), and the hall of the bishop's palace in Wells (1280–92).

Statues from the Sainte Chapelle, carved at a somewhat later date, but in the same century, are already Baroque in their prettiness and the would-be grandiosity of their bellying folds. At about the same time, the west front of the cathedral in Poitiers and the church of St. Seurin in Bordeaux (1267) are florid, overloaded, restive. But then, the turn had been visible as early as the west front of Amiens Cathedral (*c.* 1225–36).

In painting, the illuminations of the psalter of St. Louis (shortly before 1270) stand out with their dramatic verve, expressive contours, and eloquent gestures, and Witelo, a Polish friend of St. Thomas Aquinas, writes the earliest treatise on perspective. Fashions, in contradiction to the preceding mode, have "a certain amount of elaboration" (Mary G. Houston), particularly in the padded, netted hairdresses, and a "greater freedom of arrangement and gaiety of treatment." Significantly, the waistline descends.

Music, too, can be said to have grown lighter, more elegant, and livelier. The Franconian style in the second half of the century—named for Franco of Cologne, patriarch of mensural notation—abandoned the chordal conductus in favor of the freer motet and in the motet gave predominance, speed, and smoothness to the upper voice. The *ténor* or spine of the composition, once the melody proper, was reduced to a short and ever repeated *ostinato* motive, which could unhesitatingly be taken from anywhere, even from secular songs, from popular dance tunes, or from the traditional cries of Parisian street peddlers. At the peak of this style, under the leadership of Pierre de la Croix or Petrus de Cruce, upper-voice melody reached a highly expressive, free-flowing, and almost rhapsodic manner reminiscent of Leoninus a hundred years before (Example 14).

Italy, for centuries defenseless in the wake of Byzantine art, then at last emerged from its stupor and came to the fore with its earliest masterworks: the pulpits of the baptistery in Pisa (1260) and of the cathedral in Siena (1265). Their creator, Nicola Pisano, trying to reconcile archaic tradition and modern currents, avoided symmetry and other features of strictness (Plate IX). His reliefs are often crowded and always animated, dramatic, and even naturalistic: the Crucifixion in Siena, in its gamut from gloomy mourning to screaming despair, is one of the most moving works of all time. And it is probably more than mere coincidence that the naturalistic passion

Example 14. Motet *after Adler*

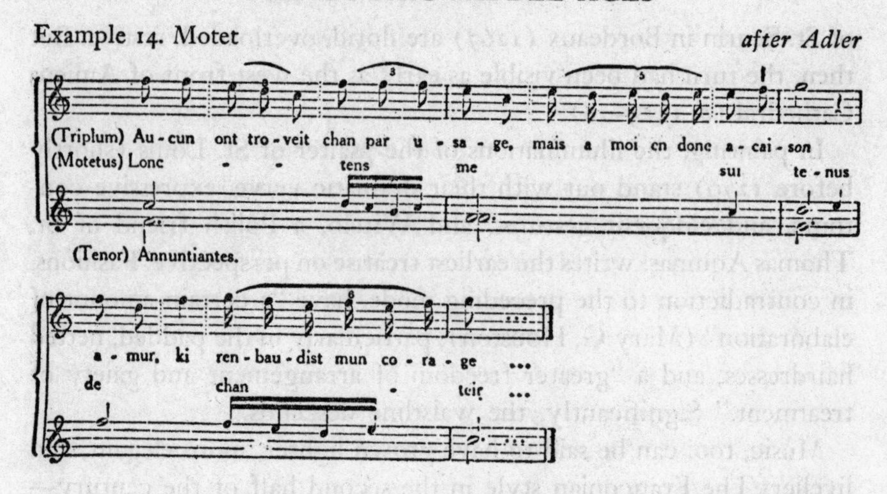

plays, representing the last days of Christ's life, were being introduced in these decades—in Padua 1244, in Rome 1264.

1300

AT THE BEGINNING of the fourteenth century, a victorious citizenry was taking over the cultural role of noblemen and priests; poetry began to admit the vernacular beside the conventional Latin, and things secular were slowly conquering a dominant place in spiritual life. Dante was writing the earliest of his greater works, *La Vita Nuova*, a book of prose and poetry thoroughly personal and Italian. Nor did his *Divina Commedia* refrain from the personal, the political, the Florentine.

To the greatest contemporary painter, Giotto, the saints, though solemn, were warmhearted human beings in Tuscan towns and settings who, with eloquent gestures, expressed their awe and bliss and passionate despair and, in their benevolence, did not hesitate to mingle with men of the street and beggars on crutches.

In a similar way, Duccio di Buoninsegna in Siena tried to rid his art of the static tradition in which he had been educated: the front of his *Maestà*, painted in 1311 for the cathedral, still clings to the solemn symmetry that the subject imposes; but on the back, the master depicts the life of Christ with an unparalleled dramatic power and freedom of conception.

An unusual genius led Italian sculpture into the fourteenth century: Giovanni Pisano, Nicola's son. His pulpits for Sant'Andrea in Pistoia (1298–1301) and for the cathedral of Pisa (1301–11) have an inner life and tension that no Italian master had ever achieved before him and that but few were to achieve in later times (Plate IX). In the years he was working in Tuscany, the west façade of the cathedral in Strasbourg was given its famous statues of the Foolish Virgins who, instead of being neatly aligned as a wall decoration in the customary way, perform a lively scene with stagy gestures, which the master might have seen in mystery plays.

The unsteady "Gothic sway" of the hips that gives these Virgins particular buoyancy—a common feature of many statues of the time (Plate VII)—has been called the expression of an excited mental state but also an affected mannerism (which it indeed became when it no longer had inner necessity). But maybe we should liken it to the contemporaneous trend in architecture toward sacrificing the capitals of columns to an urge for unobstructed verticalism and tossing the column ribs in one gigantic *élan* from floor to vault. A statue never would get such verve from steadfast verticalism but can easily get it from the graceful sway of the hips, which in its flexibility seems to relieve the pressure of gravity.

A similar trend appears in the tightening of modish gowns and tunics. Fashions turn radically away from the earlier reserve: the waistline sinks, the shoes grow in length, and the garments often become fantastically part-colored—the right half blue, the left half white or otherwise; coiffures are increasingly elaborate, and dignified gentlemen once again wear beards.

French music was still under the influence of Pierre de la Croix's intense and flowing melody. But it slowly moved to recognizing and using the third as a full-fledged consonance as the British had been doing for a long time. The clash of the two styles became manifest in an outstanding and fortunately datable musical document of the time. Interpolated in Gervais de Bus' satiric, anticlerical *Roman de*

Fauvel (1316) were far more than a hundred secular or secularized pieces—motets, rondeaux, ballads, and others. One easily distinguishes among them an older layer without, and a younger layer with, third consonances.

Another symptom of a turn away from the traditional standards of church music was the *Theoria* that Johannes de Grocheo, probably a Frenchman, wrote about 1300. While earlier authors, secluded and aloof, had busied themselves with quoting and interpreting once more the authorities in which the Middle Ages blindly confided—Nikomachos, Boethius, and Guido of Arezzo—with solving the thorny problems of intervals, of consonance and dissonance, and of an adequate notation, without ever deigning to look at secular music, Grocheo unexpectedly changes front. When he begins his treatise, "As certain young people asked me to give them a survey of music," we realize at once that he approached a public the scholarly musicologists had never considered. A few pages later, the unheard-of happens: music, he says, "differs according to different habits, different idioms, and different languages in different cities and regions." Let us then speak of the music "according to the usage of the Parisians, and how it is needed in the practice and intercourse (*convictum*) of the burghers."

There it is all at once: the rise of nationalism and regionalism, of the citizenry and the secular. The supernational knot, in which the Christian world had been tied by both church and nobility, was broken.

1324

THE COUNTERATTACK from the church came in 1324 with the intransigent bull against the "new school" in music issued by Pope John XXII. This new school, he contended, strove for artificial meters, invented new melodies in a new notation rather than singing the old ones, forced rapid tempos on sacred music, dissolved the melody by ornaments, rests, and polyphony, and grafted the holy words on secular tunes; in short, it disturbed devotion, intoxicated the ear, and perverted the listener.

The "new school" the Pope had in mind was very probably the free-flowing style of the preceding generation under Pierre de la Croix. The actual *ars nova* under the leadership of the versatile Philippe de Vitry—whom Petrarch addressed in 1350 as "the greatest, the only poet of the age" and Simon Tunstede in Oxford as "the flower of all the world of musicians"—shared with John XXII a spirit rather opposed to extravagance and aimed at strictness and balance. Reverting to an idea of the Perotinus generation, Vitry established his motets on the inexorable tectonics of isorhythm which will be discussed in greater detail in Chapter VIII (Symbols and Craft). Here it may be briefly described as the principle of forcing upon the melody a metrical pattern of some length—say, six, eight measures—and without any change repeating it as often as required to the end of the piece. In other words: the melodies of the various stanzas were different as to the sequence of higher and lower notes but similar as to the sequence of longer and shorter notes (as, with a very short meter, in the beginning of the slow movement in Beethoven's Seventh). On the other hand, de Vitry stressed the consonance of the third, an interval that the earlier theory had considered inadmissible and that even as progressive a writer as Johannes de Grocheo in Paris found too "hard on the ears" (*auribus dure*); and, quite in the spirit of 1230, he resumed a style dependent on chords.

It was in keeping with this turn toward harmony that the keyboard instruments which—contracting the independent voice parts of individual players to monochromic chords on one instrument, promoted, and depended upon, vertical hearing—were contrived at that time. We hear of a clavichord with nineteen strings in 1323 and shortly later of English, harpsichordlike *chekkers* or *exaquiers*.

While this was happening in music, Boccaccio wrote his classical epic *Teseide* (1341) in imitation of the ancients, and Giotto's personal style developed from the dramatic fugue of his Franciscan frescoes in Assisi to the solemn reserve of the murals in the Bardi and Peruzzi chapels in Santa Croce at Florence. In this new atmosphere of sedateness, Andrea Orçagna found his early style of sober, two-dimensional symmetry. And Lippo Memmi's or Ambrogio Lorenzetti's madonnas, "hieratic, Egyptian" as Bernard Berenson says, were no longer Sienese anachronisms but were in keeping with metropolitan trends.

There are at least some outer reasons for finding the same reactions in France since the Holy See was then in exile at Avignon in Provence; but the inner reasons must have been stronger. The tomb of Bishop Pierre de Roquefort (d. 1321) in Saint Nazaire at Carcassonne (near the Spanish frontier) is an excellent example of an almost archaic classicism. One should not minimize this testimonial by saying that the *midi* was anyway more classicistic than the North —the Rieux Chapel in Toulouse, which will be mentioned in the next section, was no less southern and yet entirely anticlassical.

A quite similar deviation from the dramatic ideals of the preceding generation appears in the sculpture of Germany, and in the quiet simplicity of fashions, too. The famous Lutrell Psalter (*c.* 1340) depicts its ladies in close-fitting, tight-sleeved gowns in one piece, which mold the bosom, waist, and hips.

1348

1348 was the fatal year in which the plague harassed the south of Europe. It gave Boccaccio the connecting link for his revolutionary set of one hundred short stories, written between 1350 and 1353, which, instead of evoking Mount Olympos or distant princely castles, lead the reader into the living rooms, bed chambers, and stables of lesser people. The hundred stories of this *Decamerone* or Ten Days are being alternately told by the members of a party of rich young gentlemen and ladies whom the plague has brought together in a manor near Florence to evade contagion. And every night, after having listened to ten tales, "the 'queen' ordered the instruments to come," and one or two voices united in singing.

The pieces that the elegant young ladies sang with their cavaliers were just as revolutionary as the *Decamerone* itself. Music of those days no longer gave preponderance to religious subjects but, on the contrary, fostered secular topics and forms, and in this field had created two almost unprecedented types, the *madrigal* and the *chace*.

Not the structure of the madrigal or, for that matter, of the ballad matters here; the number of lines and the place of the refrain are unimportant. Vital in their novelty are, in the first place, the renunciation of any cantus firmus and of counterpoint in medieval style for an almost chordal, harmonic accompaniment of the melody and, secondly, in connection with this change, the energetic turn to anecdotic texts as well as to anecdotic music. One of the boldest pioneers of the new style, Giovanni da Cascia of Florence, wrote a delightful little madrigal on a bathing girl (Example 15). "My visage concealed in the leaves, I stayed. . . ." Forgetting how artful the form is, you follow the longing watcher who cautiously draws nearer and nearer, and at last . . . "No," he says, "I am not going to tell you how I felt"; and he says it in the breathless patter that we know from the Italian opera stage. This is Boccaccio's spirit as far as the situation goes. Musically, the flexible adaptation of melody and rhythm to the sudden developments of an anecdote was entirely novel.

The same delight in life, descriptiveness, and one-way motion shows in the most curious form of the *trecento*, that of the *caccia* or, in French, the *chace*. Its structural principle, a favorite among fourteenth-century composers, was the canon, in which a second voice beginning later imitated the first voice note by note at the same pitch. But there is little resemblance to our childish little canons of eight or sixteen bars repeated ad infinitum; the second voice follows the first at a considerable distance, and repeats are avoided; from beginning to end, the melody develops in a one-way motion without ever falling back on the same formulas. Some texts, with their music, depict hunting as the name implies; others describe adventures

Example 15. Madrigal *Giovanni da Cascia*

of fishermen, some, fire and showers, and several even market life. In the latter, we hear the joyful cries of *Ho! Houp! Ayô!* flung to the dogs, and the din and bargaining and the voluble arguments of sellers and buyers.

Contemporary painters found a similar delight in depicting trivial detail and local color. A master like Altichiero of Verona (who flourished in the 1360's and 70's) reduced, as Bernard Berenson puts it, "the crucifixion to something not far removed from a market scene, and the spectator is in danger of forgetting the Figure on the Cross by having his attention drawn to a dog lapping water from a ditch, a handsome matron leading a wilful child, or an old woman wiping her nose."

As so often, delight in petty detail is paralleled by a sense of dramatic effects and even a pitiless naturalism. Dramatic is Simone Martini's Annunciation in the Uffizi (1333). The master could not avoid the conventional hieratic arrangement, the picture being evenly partitioned by Gothic ogives and columns. But he boldly took the two middle columns out to make room for an impressive scene: the Virgin, utterly thunderstruck by Gabriel's announcement, shrinks back from the archangel as far as the nearest partition allows, which by the contrast of its impassible verticality increases the violence of her panic (Plate X).

As to naturalism, nothing could be more impressive than the Crucified Christ by some painter of the Romagna ("Workshop of Baronzio," says the Metropolitan Museum, its present owner). The revolutionary creator of this blood-stained, livid torso with its protruding ribs has studied life and death themselves with greater devotion than the fixed patterns of his predecessors.

The best-known and most representative documents of the new naturalism, however, are the *Trionfi della morte* which, as a consequence of the plague of 1348, were painted here and there in Italy. The strongest of them is—alas, was up to the battles of 1944—Francesco Traini's mural in the Campo Santo at Pisa, so unforgettable in its pitiless grandiosity, which did not refrain from the ugly and the repulsive. Even as unnaturalistic a master as Andrea

Orcagna could not avoid creating a Triumph of Death in a naturalism quite foreign to his former abstract severity. And an inveterate Sienese like Pietro Lorenzetti, reneging the lyrical spirit of his town, carried the old themes—in B. Berenson's scolding words—"to the utmost pitch of frantic feeling. Form, movement, composition—even depth and significance—all have been sacrificed to the expression of the most obvious and easy motion. Such anarchy has seldom again overtaken an Italian master, even of the Bolognese. To find its like you must go to Spain and to certain Germans."

France was no less radical. Arthur Gardner, describing the sculptures in the Rieux Chapel at Toulouse (shortly before 1348), speaks of affectation, theatrical exaggerations, and "contorted attitudes with heads on one side, and hair and beards puffed out in most generous proportion, suggesting that they had been copied from actors masquerading in elaborate wigs."

Fashion, too, exaggerated again. The gentlemen padded their breasts and wore long streamers instead of flaps on their sleeves; the ladies widened their dresses and donned fantastic coiffures.

1372

TOWARD THE END of the century, the painter Melchior Broederlam, outstanding in the Netherlands, at long last gave up the spaceless ornamental backgrounds of the (northern) generations before him and laid his scenes in airy, perspective landscapes and architectures. A southern painter of the same generation, the Florentine Cennino Cennini, was then stressing imagination and its freedom at the cost of tradition and rules and recommending nature as "the most perfect guide" in drawing—in contrast to the ready-made canons and patterns used in the Middle Ages. Cennini actually wrote his *Tratto della pittura* years later; but he explicitly did it in the spirit of his master Angelo Gaddi, who had died in 1396. One of the very few dated documents of early French painting, King Charles the Fifth's illuminated *Bible historiale* of 1372, shows a "merciless naturalism" or, in the words of the French art historian André Michel: "*une ressemblance criarde, presque cruelle.*"

Sculpture went the same way; a statue like the one in Amiens from the 1370's that represents Bureau de la Rivière is striking as a naturalistic and even dramatic portrait.

In 1373, St. John the Baptist's Chapel in the cathedral of Amiens inaugurated the momentous last style of Gothic architecture, the 'flaming' Flamboyant, which then triumphed for more than a hundred years over solid weight and restful simplicity. Height grew at the cost of width. And the walls that were kept in this process of dematerialization dissolved in dizzying fireworks of delicate traceries in complex, curved, free-flowing, fantastic lines with swarms of niches, canopies, rockets, and pinnacles.

At exactly the same time, English architecture passed to what the British call Perpendicular Style which, not continental in its details, was nonetheless built on the same principles of atectonic, luxuriant ornamentation and avoidance of surfaces. It made its first appearance in Edward III's tomb in Westminster Abbey (1377), the nave and western transept of Canterbury Cathedral (1378–1411), and New College in Oxford (1380–90).

Fashionable dress became eccentric. Shoes were made immensely long and pointed; the new *houppelandes* or full and often part-colored coats, had fancifully scalloped or 'dagged' hems; and feminine hairdress, very elaborate, "reverted to the types worn earlier in the century," as Mary G. Houston states. The waist was very low.

Music presented closely related traits. It is true that the great composer, poet, and canon Guillaume de Machaut, its brilliant head at the time of the dawning flamboyant, preserved de Vitry's isorhythmic structure of the motet. But in spite of this archaic trait, once more all energy, tension and expression were condensed in the upper voice. Melody, free and almost rhapsodic, proceeded in everchanging beats and meters with rests, capricious syncopation, and frequent coloraturas; and the accompanying voice parts followed in contrasting rhythms and sometimes in the open work of rapid alternation with the melody in shortest rests and motives. It is hardly possible to separate this restless, glittering style from the laces of flamboyant tracery (Example 16).

Example 16. Motet *Guillaume de Machaut*

And one more trait, closely related to this splendor: Guillaume de Machaut himself, as the author of the epic poems *La Prise d'Alexandrie* and *Li Tems Pastour*, delighted in describing gigantic random orchestras at courtly feasts with no less than thirty-six different kinds of instruments and several players to the part.

Such delight in timbre and fullness gave the organ its earliest solo stops (beside the previously exclusive mixtures), a second manual, and pedals. Proudly, Machaut exalted it as "*de tous les instruments le roi*," the king among instruments.

Two passages in Machaut's letters addressed to friends should arrest our attention. One is the little adage:

Qui de sentement ne fait,
Son dit et son chant contrefait

which could be translated into

If you do not feel your song,
Words and melody are wrong.

This sounds almost romantic. The other passage stresses that he had never given away a piece without having heard it: the earliest evidence of an antimedieval attitude that makes the ear supreme controller.

The contemporary musicians of Italy, under the uncontested leadership of Francesco Landino, *poeta laureatus* and blind organist of the cathedral at Florence, were in a way abandoning the national style of the last two generations and openly accepting the influence of French flamboyant music. However, their chordal sonority and the long-drawn-out lines of their melody, now sweet, now grandiose, are unmistakably Italian (Example 17).

Example 17. Ballad *Francesco Landino*

1400

LANDINO'S ART, HOWEVER, was either too intellectual and far from the common taste of the public or else, which is more probable, the generational taste as a whole had changed at the end of the century. For one of Landino's madrigals, *Musica son,* I am Music, is a dreary lament of music itself:

> To see, for street-songs, fickle wits forsaking
> The sweet and perfect sounds that I am making.
> (translated by Gustave Reese)

Once more, the public preferred the simple, square-cut forms which in Italy have always counterbalanced freedom and sophistication. The Italian word Landino uses for street songs is *frottola.* A hundred years later, this same song form, ever alive, again counteracted the sway from France and Flanders.

But even in France, musicians after Machaut returned to chords, syllabic, unadorned diction, and regular beats. Baude Cordier's and Jean Tapissier's pieces in the so-called Apt Manuscript of about 1400 are good examples. But F. Andrieu's double ballad on Machaut's death, for two instruments and two voices on two texts (whence the term double), already had shown the same characteristics much earlier, in 1377 (Example 18).

Chords assume a significant role: at the end of Andrieu's lament, four weighty chords, insulated by rests and *fermatas* like as many monoliths, interrupt the regular pulse on the plaintive words *la mort Machaut* (and incidentally the upper voice descends in the same tetrachord with the augmented second in the middle of its four notes that plays so essential a role in Bach's Easter cantata *Christ lag in Todesbanden* on almost the same words: *Der Tod, der Tod,* Death, death).

Italian sculpture confirms the transition to classic ideals. The Metropolitan Museum keeps two outstanding examples of small-size sculpture—Baldassare degli Embriacchi's two sets of delicate bone carvings of about 1400. The two greatest sculptors of the time, Nanni di Banco and Jacopo della Quercia, created solemn, epic

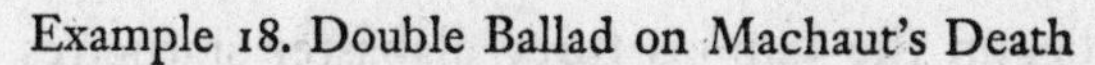

Example 18. Double Ballad on Machaut's Death *F. Andrieu*

statues full of quiet energy. Quercia's recumbent portrait statue on the tomb of Ilaria del Carretto in the cathedral of Lucca (1406) is the paragon of serene and noble simplicity. And classical in attitude also is the first (northern) bronze door of the baptistry in Florence, which Lorenzo Ghiberti created from 1401 to 1424.

But this is true of Italy only. French and Flemish artists carried naturalism to a climax of unusual strength. Cardinal Lagrange, who died in 1402, had himself portrayed on his tomb as a pitiful corpse, sunken, rotten, and desiccated; and his was not the only tomb in this macabre ideology.

The greatest master of the time, Klaas Sluter, was a naturalist, too, though a less penetrant one. He did not idealize the statues of Moses and Isaiah on his Well of Moses for the Chartreuse of Dijon, but lovingly depicted them after living models from the ghetto. At the same time, he had begun the famous forty alabaster statuettes for the tomb of Duke Philip the Bold in Dijon, which he left unfinished at his death in 1406. The figures, seemingly moving along a sinuous arcade around the sarcophagus in a funeral cortege, represent the mourners in all nuances of emotion, from the stolid apathy of the choirboys to the pathetic grief of the duke's next of kin, from solemn reserve to the bizarre attitudes and eloquent gestures of those unable to control their despair, and almost all in heavy, hooded mourning gowns, which betray the feelings of their wearers—"clothes that tell," Martin Conway called them.

CHAPTER FIVE

Renaissance and Baroque

1430

THE YEARS AROUND 1430 brought the Italian Renaissance, thus ending the Middle Ages and creating the ground in which our modern civilization has its roots. In this section, we will not attempt an exhaustive characterization of the crisis; far from anticipating the discussions of the Third Part of this book, we shall simply outline a few decisive facts that will later fall into pattern.

The unmistakable beginning is Filippo Brunelleschi's radical defection from the Gothic ideals and his creation of the Renaissance style in architecture with its well-known features: the semicircular arch instead of the ogive, the rehabilitation of the Roman column, a harmonious balance of vertical and horizontal forces and, hence, a clear, serene, and almost sober conception of space. In 1420 he was entrusted with solving the difficult problem of the dome of the cathedral in Florence, and in 1421, with designing the Foundlings' Hall in the same city (which has become so famous through Andrea della Robbia's swaddling children). In the following years, he built the Medici church of San Lorenzo.

While Brunelleschi's contribution was a half-classicistic restoration of native traditions after the Gothic interlude, the leading sculptors and painters complied with the new ideal from different sides. Donatello, *il terribile*, striving for realism against the predominant irrealism of the Middle Ages, created the striking portrait, characteristic of the Renaissance, with his statues of Job (1422) and Jeremiah (1426) and the almost illusionistic painted clay bust of Niccolò Uzzano in the Bargello (1432) (Plate XIII).

Masaccio, the greatest painter in Florence and probably in all Italy, laid his scenes in unified spaces, thus acting against the seriation of medieval art. Trained in the classicistic style of the early century, he turned to a passionately dramatic expression a few years before his premature death, which occurred in 1428 at the age of only twenty-seven. Two works, painted in 1426 and 1427, are particularly characteristic of this break at the eleventh hour. One is the Crucifixion in the National Museum at Naples, with St. John's desperate though quiet grief and the wild lament of Mary Magdalene who, prostrate at the foot of the cross, throws out her arms in almost hysterical violence. The other work is a set of murals in the Brancacci Chapel of Santa Maria del Carmine at Florence with the famous Expulsion from the Garden of Eden. Here, in pitiless naturalism, Adam, bent down and dejected, is depicted as he makes his exit with Eve who, repulsive in the miserable distortion of her face, is crying aloud (Plate XI).

Ghiberti's second (eastern) bronze door for the baptistry in Florence (1425–52) is both classicistic in a Roman sense and unified in the sense of Masaccio. Thoroughly picturesque, it combines the lowest relief for landscape and architectural backgrounds with half-relief for distant figures and high relief for the first plane, with a strong effect of light and shadow, convincing space, and a dramatic action that hardly lapses into staginess or agitation.

The opposite of both was Luca della Robbia, one of the most graceful and amiable representatives of quiet, classical trends. In whatever material he worked, in marble, bronze, or his favorite white and blue terra cotta, he was always strict and symmetrical in structure, simple and noble in drapery, and static—so static that his Resurrected Christ of 1443 does not fly to heaven, but quietly stands on a little mound behind the open sarcophagus. Two years later, he modeled his group of the Visitation for Pistoia in the spirit of truly Grecian reserve and purity.

It is only a seeming paradox that some men, unlike Luca, affected by the dynamism prevalent toward 1430 but too old to find their way to the Renaissance, developed a late Gothic style of an almost Baroque character. Nanni di Banco and Jacopo della Quercia, mentioned in the preceding section, had swerved from the ideals of their younger years. Nanni's manner had changed after his Saint Eloy (*c.* 1415). His famous Virgin in Glory on the northern portal of the Duomo in Florence (Plate XII) is all ecstatic motion, with floating gowns and wildly jerking folds. Quercia's conversion came at nearly the same time as Nanni's: the Virtues on the Fonte Gaya in Siena (1409–19), the tombs of the Trenta family (1416), and the altar of San Frediano (for which one finds the two dates 1413 and 1422), both in Lucca, not far from Florence, are almost Baroque in the twisted poses of men and women and the heavy garments with their tortuous folds. The architecture of the altar, Gothic in the Flamboyant style, overdecorated and lambent, may be a relapse into bygone times, but was a logical frame for the restless motion of his sculpture. Jacopino da Tradate's Pope Martin V in Milan Cathedral followed in the same direction as late as 1421.

After 1440, relapses into Gothic were no longer possible; the Renaissance had won. Even a master so anachronistically conservative and Gothic as Fra Angelico, who was but little concerned with tactile corporality or space and hesitated to give up the golden backgrounds of the Middle Ages, changed sides as much as was possible for him. But one of his madonnas in the Monastery of San Marco at Florence, painted before 1445, belongs in another world and suggests a measurable space. The golden background is replaced by an architectural wall with fine Renaissance pilasters that Brunelleschi or Michelozzo might have designed; the Child is a true child, no longer a diminutive man, and some attendants turn their heads to lead the onlooker's eye inward and out.

It was at this time that theory began to support the novel art. The learned masters were sitting down to find the laws of perspective. Indeed, Paolo Uccello, burning the midnight oil over studies of foreshortening and vanishing points, would answer his wife, who called him from the bedroom by "What a good thing perspective is!" Alberti, the true Renaissance universalist, also wrote the fundamental books *De pictura* and *De re aedificatoria* (1452). As a faithful disciple of the old Roman Vitruvius and an enthusiastic admirer of Augustean classicism, he exerted himself with a canon of 'good' architecture and the 'correct' measurements of columns, bases, and capitals. Were this endeavor insufficient to prove his radical classicism, one should read how, in his treatise, he flatly urges the painter to idealize his sitters and to attenuate their deformities.

Portraits themselves were at that time often medal-like, painted in the strictest profile and set off against a contrasting background, like Pisanello's Princess of Este in the Louvre (Plate XIV).

The North, Flanders and France, was not interested in classic revival or in theoretical research. But it shared with the South the thorough realism and a three-dimensional space, which the masters achieved through aerial rather than linear perspective.

In 1414, the death of the ducal maecenas put a sudden end to one of the most charming works of all times, Pol de Limbourg's exquisite illuminations for Duke Jean's hour book, *Les Très Riches Heures du Duc de Berry* in Chantilly. With unprecedented observation of nature and life and with an equally unprecedented delicacy of brush, the master describes the courtier's amusements and the workman's toil; lovingly, he displays to delighted eyes his flowers, trees, and animals and shows us airy, blue-green valleys with woods, meandering streams, and turreted castles (Plate XI).

Not many years after Pol de Limbourg had put his brushes down, Flanders was to receive the altar of St. Bavon in Ghent, the greatest work of older Netherlands art and the earliest known painting in oil. It is irrelevant for our purpose whether it was created by a single master Jan van Eyck or by Jan and his brother Hubert. We are more interested in its style, which is a strange magnification of an illuminator's style: in the photographic exactitude with which each hair and thread is rendered; the delight in accessory details; the well-kept, cozy interiors and the boundless vistas into distant sceneries; a scope which reaches from the nude humanness of Adam and Eve to the papal majesty of God the Father in Glory; a truthfulness in individual portraits, rarely reached and never surpassed; a quiet fervor and sincerity; and a total absence of eloquence, drama, or gesture.

The newly conquered landscape and widely opened space at last appears in southern Germany and Switzerland, too, and find their earliest climax in Konrad Witz's Geneva altar of 1444.

The two worlds, the North and the South, were connected about 1450 when the then outstanding Flemish painter, Roger van der Weyden, traveled to Italy on a portentous trip of give-and-take. He is said to have shown the art of oil painting to the Italians, who had known only the less glossy tempera painting until then and he brought home a decisive turn to the novel trends of the Renaissance. From then on, he renounced the profuse up and down of rustling, angular folds; he no longer neglected the third dimension or placed his actors all in a frontal row; and he restrained their lacrymose emotion and gesture. His Virgin with Saints in Frankfort on the Main was a true Italian *sacra conversazione* in symmetry and in quiet; and on the altar of the Three Magi in the Munich museum, he even allowed one of Mary's attendant maidens to look out from the picture in an unconcernedness entirely incompatible with the spiritual concentration of his pre-Italian works. One should not say all this was merely due to the accident of a stay abroad. For not just an accident urged him to travel but rather the fact that the northern style had no longer the unchallenged confidence of even its best representative while, on the other hand, the modern art of Italy had attained world importance and could not in the long run be ignored.

The general trend of calming down and classic purification in the second quarter of the century, which soothed even Donatello's violence, shows very clearly in the fate of fashion. From a determined reserve around 1400, it passed about 1425 to full and voluminous drapery and even to trains. The waistline fell; and hairdresses grew exaggeratedly large and fanciful. But in 1450 reserve was very strong again and, as Piero della Francesca's portraits of the Duke and the Duchess of Urbino show, remained very strong far into the 1460's. Indeed, the costumes were reactionary. Men wore the *capuchon* of the fourteenth century; gowns reverted to the tight-fitting *côte-hardi* type of the classical generation of the thirteenth century, and no longer were low waistlines, slashed skirts, or part-colored pieces fashionable. In Pisanello's portrait of a Princess Este in the Louvre (Plate XIV), an excellent example of feminine fashions, the waistline reaches the highest possible spot; the neck is free; and the hair, brushed back from the brow and up from the nape, is carefully tucked under a coif.

The evolution was no less unequivocal in music. In the dynamic days around 1425, Italian music under Matteo da Perugia and Bartolomeo da Bologna abandoned the strictness of the years after Landino and relapsed into the florid *bravura* of their grandfathers. But they were no longer in the van of the musical stage. Nor were the French or the Flemings in the lead. England had come to the fore, with Lionel Powers, John Bennet, and, one of the greatest masters of all times, John Dunstable. Parallel with the reawakened coloraturas of the Italians and very different from the preceding and following styles in the North, Dunstable's tense and ardent melody burst forth in boundless streams over the powerful chords of the lower two voices (Example 19).

Example 19. *John Dunstable*

Style changed after 1430. The place of honor among composers went to the Burgundians and, particularly, to Guillaume Dufay, their patriarch. His rise, toward the middle of the century, marks the dawning of another day; and Johannes Tinctoris, his not much younger apologist, was not so far wrong when he enthusiastically claimed that from Dufay "dated the first music worth hearing." This music was serene and blissful, not fervent and passionate as Dunstable's was. Divine things had lost their inexorability: God was good, the Virgin smiled, and Dufay smiled back. With such felicity, melody grew cantabile and 'beautiful.'

At that, Dufay had been one of the many Burgundian masters who, serving in Italian chapels, had succumbed to the charm, not of the sophisticated last generation of *trecento* madrigalists, but of Italy's semipopular, clean-cut *laude, giustiniane, strambotti,* and in general of Italian simplicity, balance, and clarity. Back home they were ready to lead the Gothic North away from Dunstable's rhapsodic style to stricter, soberer forms. Their rhythm obeyed a regular time-beating in three-four or six-eight, with an ever-growing importance of duple, not triple, time; and, in an almost obtrusive neatness, every tiny stretch of melody was given an emphatic cadence or ending of its own, so that the whole appears to be trimly parceled out. The upper voice was entrusted with the melody proper while the two lower voices, singing or playing, accompanied harmonically rather than contrapuntally and without disturbing the rhythm of the melodic part. Indeed, one of them, the *contratenor*, hopped up and down to fill harmonic gaps, without any longer pursuing a logical course of its own. Occasionally, as at the stupendous end of Dufay's motet *Alma Redemptoris Mater*, the three voices join in solemn, drawn-out triads, which recall Italian *laude* and anticipate a master more than a hundred years younger: Palestrina (Example 20). Dufay had indeed absorbed so much of Italy's taste that the cathedral of Florence could in 1436 be inaugurated with one of his motets.

Dancing, about the middle of the fifteenth century, does not allow of direct judgment, though we get a satisfactory picture from

Example 20. Alma Redemptoris Mater *Guillaume Dufay*

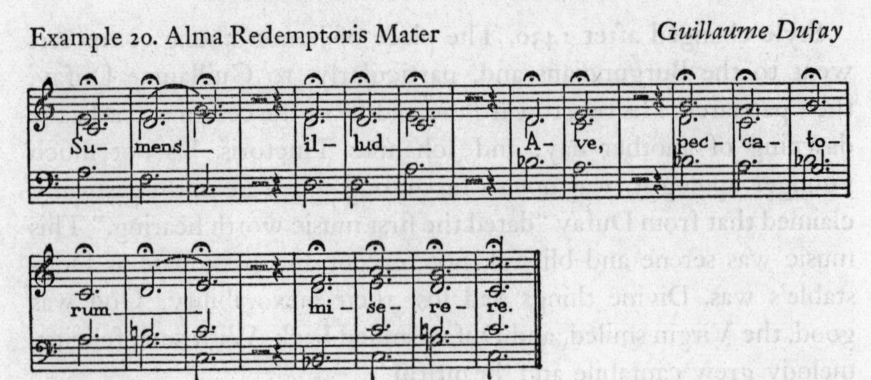

indirect sources. The first indication of a new era is the rise of a theoretical literature, climaxed in Guglielmo the Jew's undated *De praticha seu arte tripudii vulghare opusculum* and, 1455, in Antonio Cornazano's *Libro dell'arte del danzare*. Spontaneity has gone; past is the time when everybody danced from natural inclination and learned the steps from watching and participating. Movements have become restrained; the lively *piva* is no longer considered decent, and even the *saltarello* needs no leaps. The dance, once a child of impulse and passion, is now a ritual designed for the leading circles of the Burgundian and Italian courts. It is an art, the correct figures, positions, and steps of which must be memorized according to rule.

Of the world outside the arts, the searching eye is caught by humanistic poetry. Lorenzo Valla, in a treatise on the *Elegantiae* of Latin speech, exalted the glory of the Roman language. Julius Pomponius Laetus in Rome was the first to perform dramatic plays in Latin, for which he had to expiate his 'paganism' in a papal jail.

1460

In 1460, ANTONIO POLLAIUOLO in Florence painted his significant, large canvases with three of the tasks of Hercules. Few works have ever indulged in more savage action and crueler force. Its nudes are accomplished studies in anatomy: Pollaiuolo was indeed one of the earliest masters to dissect bodies and examine muscles, sinews, and bones. But facial beauty was not in his province; he disregarded it completely (Plate XV).

At the same time, Niccolò Alunno in Umbria painted another gruesome subject, the Martyrdom of Saint Bartholomew. Matteo di Giovanni joined him with a Slaughter of the Innocents in Sant'-Agostino at Siena. Both works are overcrowded, dramatic, ferociously naturalistic, and not much behind Spanish execution pieces of the time, such as Alfonso's bloody Slaughter of St. Medin (1473) in Barcelona or Sanchez's brutal Road to Calvary in Cambridge, England.

About 1480, Filippino Lippi, who has been given the title of a romantic, painted the Legend of Virginia (Louvre): pell-mell, *fortissimo* and *prestissimo*, the women race against and from each other and scream with mouths wide agape and gestures uncontrolled.

Not all the artists of that time proved their anticlassical mentality in horror painting. A few chose *genre* as their world of expression: the Ferrarese Bernardo Parentino descended to the lowest layers of society and even delighted in the fantastic and spooky. And visitors to the Metropolitan Museum will not easily forget the unusual Chess Players that Francesco di Giorgio created in an epoch that seldom admitted scenes from everyday life.

A greater man, Andrea Mantegna, up to the age of twenty-five had been an austere student of Greek and Roman paragons. About 1460, he was entering a new stage, in which on his former classicism he grafted Venetian delight in color, rich decoration (as on the altar at San Zeno in Verona), and the boldest perspective ever achieved. He would depict the body of Christ lying, enormous feet forward, in the most unwonted foreshortening or a ceiling, seemingly open, which showed the sky and, on the roof, some persons who leaned over the rail looking in—anticipating what centuries later Veronese and Tiepolo were to do with so much virtuosity.

The almost fanatic delight in perspective and spatial illusion of the age is perhaps best shown by the admirable little study from the palace in Gubbio (*c.* 1480) which the Metropolitan Museum keeps in its original form. The walls, inlaid in many-colored woods, suggest not only a bench running around the room but also, above it, shelves with books and instruments both musical and scientific.

Sandro Botticelli, the best-known master of the last third of the century, was neither a horror painter nor an outspoken virtuoso of perspective. He had the quiet dignity that few of his contemporaries were seeking, and yet he shared in their dramatic trends and love of floating movement. There is one picture, though, unique in its attitude and still characteristic of anticlassical times, the Derelict in the Pallavicini Collection at Rome. It shows a girl thrown out of a palace, with her few belongings hurled after her, sitting on a step in dull despair, while the thickness of the walls and the door so tightly shut accentuate her hopelessness. It does not matter whether or not the woman was supposed to represent Tamar or some other Biblical figure; whatever scene may have served as a pretext, the painter who had this unusual vision was keenly conscious of human tragedy beyond the idyls and the beauty that his priests and princes set between themselves and the world.

Before the century drew to a close, Leonardo had written the main part of his *Trattato della pittura*, in which he disowned the hard contours of earlier painting and laid the fundaments of *chiaroscuro* and *sfumato*.

Italian sculptors, like Mino da Fiesole and Desiderio da Settignano —"*il vago Desider si dolce e bello*"—had a peculiar technique, suggestive of the color terms *chiaroscuro* and *sfumato* and quite in keeping with the other trends of the age. In their flattened reliefs, *rilievi schiacciati*, all outlines were so delicately softened that no form was sharply set off against the background. And even in a wider sense, beyond the vague *sfumato*, most of Florentine and Italian sculpture was picturesque. What an amazing contrast between the noble simplicity of Luca della Robbia's pulpit in the generation before and Benedetto da Majano's pulpit of Santa Croce in Florence (*c.* 1475), so thoroughly ornamental and three-dimensionally picturesque! Or, for that matter, Vecchietta's relief of the Resurrection (1472) in the Morgan Gallery, New York, and Bertoldo di Giovanni's violent relief of the Horsemen's Battle. Andrea del Verrocchio's marble group of Christ and Thomas in one of the niches outside Or San Michele in Florence (1483) is almost Baroque in the loudness of its folds and oratorical gesture. And Baroque, indeed Berninesque, are the marble curtains on Donatello's tomb for Pope John XXIII in the baptistry at Florence or on Antonio Rossellini's tomb for the cardinal of Portugal (1466).

French sculpture was in a different way unclassical. The best example of its strong illusionism is Philips Pot's sepulchral monument in the Louvre (*c.* 1480), which represents the bier with the body, not resting on the floor, but carried by eight solemn, hooded pall bearers in natural size and color.

In architecture, the flamboyant of the French came to a last peak with the florid open work of the Palace of Justice in Rouen (1493–99). Of Germany, too, Wilhelm Pinder could say that the last part of the fifteenth century was more Gothic than the beginning had been. Spain was having its 'plateresque' counterpart, that is, the late Gothic overdecoration in the style of the silversmiths (*plateros*), which climaxed in the Palacio del Infantado in Guadalajara (1461) and in San Pablo in Valladolid (1463).

Inside Italy, the Vendramin Palace in Venice (1481) and Omodeo's façade of the Certosa near Pavia (1492) provide the ideal antipodes of the buildings cited in the cross section for 1430. Vendramin, almost devoid of walls—and not only because there was no necessity for fortresslike defense—is opened outward in windows and balconies where the Florentine palaces had been strictly closed. The Certosa, completely atectonic, is a dream—classicists would say a nightmare—of motley, profuse, almost Indian decoration, in which the eye has no rest and no guidance. Overdecorated, though in a different way, is even Sant'Andrea in Mantua, the last work by the classicist Leone Battista Alberti, which was begun in the year of his death, 1472.

Such delight in overdecoration shows impressively in Ghirlandaio's Birth of Mary in Santa Maria Novella, Florence (Plate XV). Profuse ornaments cover not only the architectural framework but also the pillars and pilasters, the ceiling, the friezes, the panels, and the very dresses of the calling and the attending women.

This general opening of form reappears in costume, which reaches a climax of foppish eccentricity. The shoulders are immensely broad and padded, and the sleeves, slashed at the elbows; the *chausses*, tight combinations of trousers and stockings, go straight up to the waist, and the shoes—*poulains*—become grotesquely long and end in needle points. Men's hair is allowed to grow freely and to overhang the forehead, and women's coiffures stick out. The fuzzy hair of the ladies on the Chess Players in the Metropolitan Museum and the well-known musician angels in Melozzo da Forlì's frescoes in the sacristy of St. Peter's in Rome are good examples. Or else, as in Botticelli's portrait of Simonetta Vespucci, the hair is an intricate nest of coils, plaits, and ribbons down to the bosom. Headgears take the forms of butterflies, horns, hearts, or steeples (*hennins*) and often reach a height of several feet.

Neither does Pulci's epic *Morgante* (1466–83), which "anticipated Rabelais," show classical trends in poetry. It was at that time that Matteo Maria Bojardo's poem *Orlando Innamorato* first mentioned the ribald dance *gagliarda*. This, however, was eclipsed by the wild, grotesque, and acrobatic twists of the *morisca* dancers that Erasmus Grasser carved in 1480 for the reception room of City Hall in Munich.

In the field of music, the Burgundian masters around Binchois and Dufay were yielding supremacy to the Netherlanders under the leadership of the Flemings Ockeghem and Isaac and the Dutchman Obrecht (Example 21). The Burgundian melody, neat and disjunct with strong harmonic trends, was put aside for a style, reminiscent of the later *órganum*, with a lengthy drawn-out cantus firmus and contrapuntal voice parts, which in boundless, flowing motion shaped fantastic, passionate lines. The number of voice parts was augmented from three in Burgundian times to four, and often many more. With this increase, the basso range, so anxiously shunned in the ages before, was now exploited to a maximum of depth and assumed a prominent role in the weaving of parts, as testified by Johannes Ockeghem's curious *Deo gratias* canon for no less than thirty-six voice parts.

Example 21. Mass *Jacob Obrecht*

The history of musical instruments, too, records two events in keeping with emotionalism and the conquest of the lower registers:

in 1491, the organ at Hagenau in Alsace was given the earliest tremulant, a device rapidly interrupting the sounds of all or several stops in order to cause a sentimental vibrato. And in 1493, Italy saw for the first time double-bass viols in the hands of Spanish players: *viole grandi quasi come me*, almost as tall as myself, reports Bernardo Prospero.

Exoticism, to be expected in an age of unrest and expansion in the arts, was not absent either: in 1477, William Caxton, the earliest English printer, published the *Dictes and Sayings of the Philosophers*, based on a collection of oriental fables and parables. And two years later, the republic of Venice sent her painter Gentile Bellini to the court of the sultan in Constantinople. But then, voyages of Bartolommeo Dias, Columbus, and Vasco da Gama are unthinkable without the impulse to join the world of the East.

1504

1504 IS THE YEAR of Raphael's earliest masterwork, *Lo Sposalizio*, The Wedding of the Virgin. The temple, in front of which the ceremony is held, occupies the very center of the rounded upper part of the painting and is seen in the strictest front view. Inlaid paths lead to it from all sides, thus emphasizing its central position; the middle path has its vanishing point in the small door that allows of looking across the temple at the sky beyond. This small door also determines, within the tall rectangle of the painting, where the height begins to exceed the width; and the two diagonals of the square thus marked would intersect in the wedding ring that Joseph is putting on Mary's finger. Needless to say, the high priest, the bridal couple, and the followers are also arranged in the strictest symmetry (Plate XVI).

The temple is a regular twelve-faced, domed rotunda, the very type of building that in its central structure has so often been a favorite of stationary, classical styles. The circle (and the polygon) is indeed "beautiful in its purity and simplicity, and wonderful in its continuity" (George Santayana, *The Sense of Beauty*, N.Y. 1896, p. 68). While Raphael drew its outlines, Bramante was building his little round *tempietto* in San Pietro in Montorio at Rome.

Raphael's School of Athens in the Stanze of the Vatican (1511) is riper, but no less classical than the *Sposalizio.* And with all due allowance for the mural style, we cannot help resenting the almost obtrusive interference of 'art' and 'perfection' with life and character. We are willing to give ourselves away to what the painter depicts, but the subject seems to recede from our eyes; indeed, it becomes a mere pretext for displaying symmetry, balance, and dignified aloofness. Not for one moment are we able to forget the stage director who, grouping and draping, rounds out a floating toga to fit in the semicircular curve of the mural; who lifts a man's arm to counterpoise it with his protruding leg; who shifts his groups until their outlines meet in the focal center where Plato and Aristotle pose, discussing. They are discussing, to be sure, but do not be mistaken: their golden words are carefully prepared, memorized, and rehearsed. In the end we leave Raphael's masterwork with the fervent wish for less perfection and beauty, and more life and character!

But then, the beginning of the sixteenth century was the age of rules and canons of proportions. In 1505, Jean Pélerin le Viateur published a *Perspective artificielle*, and the book that Luca Pacioli had printed in 1506, bore the characteristic title *Divina proportione.*

However, construction and calculation, standards and 'correct' measurements were certainly not the only aspects of that classical age. Leonardo da Vinci himself, who in his *Trattato della Pittura* established their theoretical foundation, warned against canons of any sort because of "the immense variety of nature." His own madonnas and the portrait of Mona Lisa seem to challenge ratios and standards. And yet they are classical, too: Mona Lisa, whose cryptic smile has so often been searched for hidden passion and secrets, is in her very inscrutability a paragon of composure and serenity.

The simplicity of her costume, too, is striking to anyone familiar with the extravagant fashion of the preceding generation. The hair is now smooth and parted; other ladies, and men also, wear their locks long, hanging down on the shoulders. "The whole trend of women's dress in the *fin de siècle* period of the fifteenth century displays a certain quiet, almost demure character when compared with the flamboyant costumes of the middle and late fifteenth century. . . . Before the end of the fifteenth century the influence of ancient Greek and Roman art had become a factor in determining the style of Italian costume" (Houston). The waist becomes higher, and upstanding collars yield to *décolleté* necks. The conical steeple was abandoned in favor of low, close-fitting caps. The *poulains* were replaced by round and square-toed shoes; and the *chausses* had to be divided into two separate parts.

Spain joined only reluctantly in the new classicism, but she could not evade it—witness the noble, reserved University of Alcalá, which was begun as early as 1508.

Even the Netherlanders underwent conversion. Gerard David, the greatest painter among them, had in 1498 presented the Skinning of the Bribed Judge with gruesome matter-of-factness. But his second period, commonly dated from 1499 on, ignored naturalism and brought serene unconcernedness, contemplation, stability, symmetry, and even beauty for the sake of beauty. In his last period (1512–23), he overdid the new 'classical' style and lapsed from his former chiaroscuro into bare, unbroken colors and from natural warmth into monumental, academic frigidity.

With David, Flemish national painting was interrupted until Peter Brueghel resumed it half a century later. In the meantime, Quinten Matsys, Jan Gossaert Mabuse, and Barent van Orley were caught in the snares of Italy. The tomb of Guillaume de Croy, Archbishop of Toledo (d. 1521), in the convent church at Enghien in the Flanders, is a pure example of Netherlandish Renaissance sculpture. Architecture followed a little later, with the House of the Salmon at Malines (1530–34) and the profuse Maison de l'Ancien Greffe Flamand in Bruges (1535–37).

England, France, and Germany also remained hesitant, except for the up-to-date attitude of their courts. In England, Cardinal Wolsey's palace at Hampton Court was begun in 1515 as the earliest intrusion of Italian ideals. It was followed by Pietro Torrigiano's

Italian tomb of Henry VII at Westminster. But on the whole, the native Gothic traditions survived.

In France, the stalls given the cathedral of Amiens between 1508 and 1519 were a flamboyant apotheosis of wood carving, unforgettable in their overwhelming beauty and the glittering unrest of their thousands of dazing details. Still, there too the Renaissance was coming: Leone Battista Alberti's treatise *De re aedificatoria* had already been translated into French in 1512, and four years later King Francis I had convoked Leonardo da Vinci.

The most astonishing work of a German contemporary master, Matthias Grünewald's altar from Isenheim (1512–16), now in Colmar, Alsace, is high-strung, expressionistic, and violent to the limit. Mary, at the foot of the cross, shrieks with all her might; the heavy lid of Christ's stone coffin flies off with a crash, the guards are hurled away, and Jesus darts up like a flame. Gales seem to agitate all drapery; and the tabernacle with the fiddling angels is so turbulently flamboyant that it hardly suggests solid material. Color overpowers drawing; in painting mystic skies and mountains, Grünewald achieves miracles unique in times before the nineteenth century. 'Beauty,' however, must not be expected; the angels are afflicted with pigs' eyes and turned-up noses, and not even Christ has noble, dignified features.

Albrecht Dürer, on the contrary, tried to join the Italian highway and, after a stay at Venice in 1508, proceeded to compositions as perfectly balanced as the Four Apostles in Munich, a German version of the typically Italian *sacra conversazione*, in which hardly more than St. Paul's angular folds recall the master's Gothic background (Plate XVII). Even the theoretical problems of the Italian Renaissance became his: he wrote a treatise on perspective, aimed at a canon of man's proportions, and in the same spirit of classicism claimed that perfection and beauty were found in the sum of all human beings.

Yet Dürer had too much of a Gothic spirit to become a classicist. High-strung, eruptive, mystic, he understood the Renaissance of Italy, but was neither able nor willing to lose his native heritage.

The man who better succeeded in absorbing the new ideals of the South was Hans Holbein the Younger of Augsburg. He was not quite twenty years old when he began to place his models against the pillars and arches of a decorative Italian Renaissance or the friezes of classic antiquity, and he was less than thirty years old when he composed his famous Virgin of the Burgomaster Meyer in Darmstadt (1526) as a typical *sacra conversazione*. But even without such all too obvious allusions, he had more need for the humanistic virtues of clearness, balanced form, restraint, and calmness than any other German of his time.

While Holbein was painting Italian architecture, his native city —probably all Germany—was given, around 1519, the earliest actual Renaissance building: the Fugger Chapel in St. Ann. In the same year, Peter Vischer created St. Sebald's tomb in Nuremberg as the first work of German sculpture in which the Gothic style was married to the Renaissance.

In 1504, the very year of Raphael's *Sposalizio*, the printer Petrucci at Venice published the first collection of musical *frottole*, that is, of northern Italian half-courtly, half-popular songs in strictest form, indeed in symmetrical structure, with a *ripresa* or refrain at the beginning and the end and between the stanzas, the whole being performed by a voice singing the melodic upper part and two or three instruments accompanying in plain chords note against note, without polyphonic complication (Example 22).

In 1508, a Milanese lutanist, Giovannambrosio Dalza, published, at Petrucci's in Venice, the fourth book of his *Intabulatura de Lauto*, which is the earliest preserved collection of printed dance music, especially of *padoane* or pavans. Compared with the motley, ever-changing *bassa danza* of the generation before, the newly accepted pavan was as static and simple as a dance can be. Just alternating between the two fundamental *passi* of the time: the single step (the second foot being drawn up to the first) and the double step (the second foot being drawn past the first, which then is drawn up to the second), it stood on the borderline between a solemn processional march and a dance proper, without pantomime or emotion but,

1504

Example 22. Frottola *Bartolomeo Tromboncino*

in Count Baldassare Castiglione's words, with *una certa dignità.*

In 1505, the Fleming Josquin des Prés, greatest composer of the time, published his second book of masses, including that known under the title *Ave maris stella*, which seems to have been written not long before. Flemish polyphony has after Ockeghem's generation again become reserved and limpid; indeed, it often yields—as in the *Incarnatus est* of Josquin's *Pangue lingua* mass—to a pure and simple chordal setting in the taste of the Italian *frottola.* The structure of these later works is quite regular and transparent and often rests on clearly separated phrases of three or four measures, which are frequently contrasted by the alternation of high and lower voices (Example 23), and the text is well laid out, as suits a

Example 23. Pangue lingua mass *Josquin des Prés*

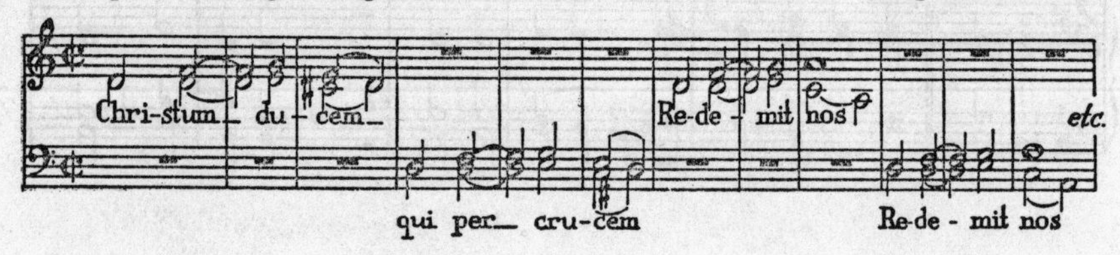

humanistic age. Indeed, one must agree with the words of Heinrich Besseler's *Musik des Mittelalters und der Renaissance:* "the pendulum, compared with Ockeghem, swung unmistakably and decidedly to the other side, to swing back only a generation later, with Nicolas Gombert."

Music paid its respect to the ideals of the Renaissance not only in the unwonted clarity and strictness of its style but also in an occasional bow to the little that the time knew of ancient music. In 1507, the Tirolese Petrus Tritonius, following a suggestion of Conrad Celtes, the humanist, published the odes of Horace in a simple chordal setting for four voices, which strictly obeyed the poetical meters of long and short syllables. Two greater men, Paul Hoffheimer and Ludwig Senfl, followed with *Harmoniae poeticae sive carmina nonnulla Horatii* (Poetical harmonies or some Horatian odes).

Celtes and other humanists had since 1497—the year of Leonardo's Last Supper—written Latin plays for the German Emperor Maximilian I with complete arrays of gods and muses, fauns and satyrs; and the earliest humanist of them all, Grünspeck, expressly sneered at the German language. Even in Italy, where the vernacular had been established in literature for two hundred years, Sannazaro, poet of *Arcadia*, had relapsed into Latin in the 1490's, and Pietro Bembo followed in a formal, frigid Ciceronianism. The *Arcadia* was a Virgilian idealization of pastoral life—"You have everything that you wish to imitate in that second nature, Virgil," said a contemporary, Julius Caesar Scaliger, in his *Poetices* lib. III cap. 4. In 1506, Count Castiglione responded with a pastoral drama, *Tirsi*. The greatest success however came in 1508 to Montalvo's romance *Amadis of Gaul*. But the period was classical-minded not only in the serene flight from reality and in the idealization of rural, careless existence or in the love and deeds of imaginary knights. It also created the first real tragedy in Trissino's *Sofonisba* (1515).

1530

CHRISTIAN EGENOLFF, printer in Frankfort on the Main, who three years before had published sophisticated songs on Horace's odes, offered in 1535 music in a quite different vein: street and horsemen's songs, *Gassenhawerlin* and *Reutterliedlein* which, though not exactly vulgar, showed a new delight in things unvarnished, vivid, and smart. In exactly the same year, the first collection of *Villote alla veneziana* answered with an equally popular style of dance songs. And six years later, Giovanni Domenico Nola presented the earliest *canzoni villanesche* or rustic songs: "a clownish matter," as Thomas Morley said, in dialect, parodistic and often uncouth, and set to a "clownish music" in irregular rhythms and in simple, often parallel, triads with the melody in the upper voice part.

It was the time when Pieter Brueghel painted robust and humorous scenes from the life of Flemish peasants (Plate XVIII).

Toward the middle of the century, the spoken drama deserted classical ideals and models. The tragedy, led by Cintio's *Orbecche* (1541), indulged in torture scenes, and the comedy descended to the rough milieu of peasants and shepherds, while Bandello's *Novelle* and Il Lasca's *Cene* told stories of unwonted atrocities with sexual emphasis. The new spirit is sufficiently characterized by the name of the body in which some poets were united: Accademia dei Rozzi, they called it—Academy of the Louts.

In France, Rabelais published a part of his juicy, comic monster novel *Gargantua et Pantagruel*, the poetic monument to the love of life, exaggeration, and immoderate loudness of its generation. And four years later, 1537, Bonaventure Despériers' *Cymbalum Mundi* was so audacious that the author incurred a prosecution for impiety.

Small wonder that the new French *chansons* had such an unusual popularity: one Parisian publisher, Pierre Attaingnant, printed two hundred fifteen of them in the year 1529 and again no less than thirty-five collections in the ten years 1539–49. Although this type of chanson is known as polyphonic, its polyphony is as a rule restricted to an imitative beginning; quick-witted and light-in-hand, it needed clean-cut, catchy melodies and spicy rhythms. Its words, sometimes sentimental and often, as Claude Goudimel put it, *lascives, salés, et impudiques*, required a speechlike conciseness for which there was no place in the music of other nations (Example 24).

Example 24. Chanson *Berchem*

While most chansons were short—a minute or little more in performance—Clément Janequin, leader of the generation of 1530, wrote, about that year, whole cycles of several similar chansons about eight, nine, or ten minutes long, to depict with humor and *esprit* one characteristic subject—*Les Cris de Paris* (The Cries of Paris), *La Bataille* (The Battle), *La Chasse au Cerf* (The Stag-Hunt), *Le Caquet des Femmes* (The Babbling Women), or *Le Chant des Oiseaux* (The Singing Birds)— in which four voice parts suggested all imitable sounds, far from the dry, unimaginative descriptions so common in naturalistic music.

The corresponding form in Italian music, first printed in 1533, was given the venerable title *madrigal,* but bore not much resemblance to its namesake in the fourteenth century. Its texts, in free, irregular verses, treated sentimental subjects with wit and delicacy and avoided too serious an attitude. The music drew on popular styles but followed the words more closely and shunned repeats and caesuras. This the new composers, Arcadelt, Verdelot, Willaert, attained by grafting the smoothly running polyphony of the Flemish motet upon the chordal style of Italy. No stylistic fusion could have better met the needs of that refined society of princes and patricians which had come to the fore after the decay of chivalry. Four, five, six singing partners, sitting down at a table, each with his part, and singing in perfect concert without the prevalance of one dominating voice—this was the ideal way of performing music in the best of taste for the singers' own delight (Example 25).

The madrigal, being a social, indeed an aristocratic form, had to display a certain finish that untrained eyes might easily mistake for classic reserve. But even in its beginnings under the Flemings Arcadelt and Verdelot, who clung to the square-cut strictness of the preceding generation, it reached a novel freedom. A few years later, in the hands of the Flemings Willaert and Rore, it lost all symmetry, all balance of sections, all petty partition. The close association of text and music—in itself a criterion of nonclassical styles—led to a kind of endless melody and allowed for all sorts of descriptive inter-

Example 25. Madrigal *Adriaen Willaert*

pretation incompatible with a classical attitude. On the other hand, the Venetian composers, led by Adriaen Willaert, Nicola Vicentino, and Cipriano de Rore, carried emotional expressiveness so far that they eventually destroyed tonality, invented chromatic melodies, and modulated, or rather shifted, from chord to chord to stress the poet's eternal *dolcezze*, *dolente's* and *haimè's*.

Religious music, too, broke through the walls of the rigid church tonalities and stressed emotional texts in bold modulations, which often were not indicated by sharps, naturals, flats, but were left to the penetrating insight of the singers. This *Secret Chromatic Art in the Netherlands Motet*, as Edward E. Lowinsky calls it in the title of his recent book (Columbia University Press, 1946), was partly identical with the so-called *musica reservata* of the time which as an esoteric art of those initiated was opposed to the obviousness of the *musica communis* and, by concealing stresses on certain words, had in the Netherlands the practical issue of hiding views that the church was not supposed to discover.

Meanwhile, the polyphony of the church again abandoned the classicalism of Josquin's style and under Nicolas Gombert's leadership reverted to the freedom of Ockeghem's diction.

In social dancing, the ceremonious pavan became obsolete after 1530 and was replaced by the lighter and livelier *passamezzo*. Italy, however, was rapidly losing her dominant position. As early as 1520, Duke Federigo Gonzaga had taken dancing lessons *alla francese*. The social power of the future, the French court, brought the sprightly, fanciful galliard to the fore and rehabilitated the branle, which Count Baldassare Castiglione's *Cortegiano* of 1514, the book of etiquette for Italian Renaissance society had permitted *in camera privatamente, ma in publico no così, fuorchè travestito*—only in private, but not in public, unless disguised. Branles were favorites of the French court under Henry II (1547–59)—branles from the French provinces and from distant countries, from Burgundy, Auvergne, and Champagne, from Scotland and Malte, where they had kept their exuberant vigor and life. And many of them were descriptive: the Washerwomen's Dance, the Pea Dance, the Dance of the Hermits, or the Clog Dance.

In this spirit of folklorism and exoticism the French court also accepted the tap dance *canaries* and two excessively strenuous dances from Provence, the *volta* and the *nizzarda*, in which the gentleman grasped his lady in a quite unorthodox way and flung her up so that, in Brantôme's words, he "always revealed something pleasing to the sight." And it was in the same spirit that the dance in Italy was somewhat stormy. Simeone Zuccolo da Cologna had cause to write a book on The Madness of Dancing, *La Pazzia del Ballo* in 1549, and to describe how the spectators egged the dancing girls on with shouts and cries. And in 1536, Antonius de Arena found himself reminded of a cockfight when he saw the galliard. Small wonder that the vocabulary of steps included forms, both vehement and angular—such as the several high leaps, *cadence*, *capriole*, and *saut*, or the thrusts of the foot, forward (*grue*), backward (*ruade*) sideward (*ru de vache*), and their combinations—which in no way agreed with the *aerosa dolcezza di movimenti* that the preceding generation had cherished.

Jean Goujon, twenty years old, was ready to lead French sculpture to agitation. Side by side with his wild relief of the Descent from the Cross, the Metropolitan Museum keeps an anonymous French Dormition of the Virgin, made about 1555–60 which, overcrowded and exaggeratedly lively, is frankly Baroque in the popular sense of the word. And speaking of 'Baroque' about the middle of the sixteenth century, the mind reverts to the noisy, excited groups of the Spaniard Juan Juni.

Even Italian sculptors swerved from the static ideals of the Renaissance proper. Michelangelo, who thirty years before had created the wonderfully restrained *Pietà* in St. Peter's and the 'close' Madonna in Bruges, was giving his statues in San Lorenzo at Florence (1524–32) the passionate tension that our eyes record as an audacious, powerful torsion of the body (Plate XIX). His architecture of the Biblioteca Laurenziana (1524–34), partly by his pupil Vasari, is no less Baroque. The steps of a tripled staircase bulge forward and again end in protruding rounds; volutes intensify the tempo of the rails; the columns appear in pairs; and out of an irresistible *horror vacui* every surface is filled to capacity. Such trends assume an almost intolerable form in the heavy, overdecorated, and restless tomb of Pope Julius II in San Pietro in Vincoli at Rome. Michelangelo was nevertheless so radically antinaturalistic that, as his biographer Vasari reports, he refused to make the likeness of anything, unless it was in an absolute sense perfect.

Michelangelo had many emulators and still more antipodes. Among painters, Daniele da Volterra might be called an emulator. Among antipodes, Benvenuto Cellini opposed overdecorated elegance to Michelangelo's overdecorated heaviness; against his austerity and hard-drawn, sculpturesque outline, Correggio held sensuality and the softness of *sfumato* and *chiaroscuro;* his Roman aloofness found its contrast in the Venetian Titian, who with dash and brilliancy presented life in all its gaiety and opulence (Plate XX). Recent art historians have summarily included not only Michelangelo's motley contemporaries but also the heterogeneous masters of the following generations into the seventeenth century, under the unfortunate title of mannerists, which in its vague generalization and at once derogatory connotation should not be accepted without reserve.

Like Titian's festive painting, Venetian architecture was inviting rather than haughty or cool. Saint Marc's Library (1536), Jacopo Sansovino's masterwork, has its façade dissolved in open arcades with lively clusters of pillars and columns in a vigorous relief that grants a picturesque play of sun and shadow. The following year, in Germany, the City Hall at Görlitz in Silesia was given an outer staircase which in its daring sweep was truly Baroque. Other Baroque elements appear in Italy from 1540 on: in Michele San Micheli's Palazzo Bevilacqua in Verona (1540), the fusion of the two upper stories by powerful through columns or, on Giulio Romano's church of San Benedetto al Polirone, the concave wedges or gussets along which the eye glides down from the central nave to the lower lateral naves.

Fashions, too, reflect the change. The 1520's, 30's, 40's are "the era of puffs and slashes"; the waist descends, men's codpieces attain boastful sizes, the shoes grow exceedingly broad, and beards reappear. The ladies begin about 1545 to fasten their hair high up on the heads and to display an extravagance in dresses, upright collars, coiffures, and jewelry, which oddly contrasts with the noble simplicity of the generation before.

1567

In the year 1567, the French poets Jean-Antoine de Baif and Pierre Ronsard, leader of the literary club La Pléiade, founded an Académie de Poésie et de Musique in Paris in order to force the spirit and the forms of Greco-Roman poetry on Frenchmen's verses. Étienne Jodelle, youngest member of the Pléiade, had as early as 1552 laid the cornerstone of French drama with his *Cléopatre captive,* a play so truly Greek that his friends of the Pléiade in rapture presented him with a wreathed he-goat, the *tragos* of the ancient tragedy (which present made him suspect of paganism).

In the field of music, the circles around Baif and Ronsard fostered *chansons mesurées à l'antique* that is, metrical compositions in the style of the Greeks with one time unit to every short syllable, and two units to every long syllable—just as Celtes had done around

1500. And Claude Goudimel who, as the chief creator of the Huguenot psalter from 1551 on, not only strove for sober simplicity but also was careful to do justice to the meter of its words.

In the same year 1567 in which the Académie de Poésie et de Musique was founded, Giovanni Pierluigi da Palestrina, the patriarch of the musical counterreformation, published his second book of masses, including the famous and, alas, so much romanticized *Missa Papae Marcelli* (Example 26). While his greatest contemporary, the Fleming Orlando di Lasso, was, as a versatile *homme du monde* and *grand seigneur*, living and traveling all over Europe and writing more than two thousand works, magnificats, masses, madrigals, motets, chansons, villanelle, and psalms in a truly Mozartian mastery of every style and mood, Palestrina never left his Roman homestead nor even the papal churches and was so intensely, uncompromisingly, and almost fanatically concentrated on church music that he printed apologies for having composed a few secular madrigals in earlier days. Reacting against the unbridled dynamism and the stress on polyphonic technique of the generation before, he resumed the Josquin style of 1500 with its predilection for symmetrical structure and quiet harmonies and gave it an austere serenity almost unique in postmedieval Christian art.

The counterreformation also stressed the static popular forms of religious music. Filippo Neri, founder of the Congregazione dell'Oratorio in Rome, fell back upon the age-old *lauda*, the simple devotional song of laymen's fraternities. And in the 1560's, he caused outstanding composers like Razzi, Animuccia, Soto, indeed Palestrina himself, to revive its sober, square-cut structure.

The dictatorial role of polyphony was no less challenged in the secular field: the simple music of one voice, writes Zarlino in his important *Istitutioni harmoniche* (1558), moves the heart much better than do the complications of counterpoint. The appearance of *canzonette* marks a further step; once a first collection of Neapolitan *canzoni* for three voices had been printed in 1570, the light-footed *canzonette* of the 1580's and, from 1591, the closely related *balletti*, incredibly successful all over the world, re-established the predom-

Example 26. Missae Papae Marcelli *Palestrina*

inance of Italian limpidity and 'naturalness,' which had gone underground when the Italo-Flemish madrigal appeared. In all these semi-popular art forms in dance character, the composers kept from affected words and subjects, from flowing rhythms and structures, and from polyphony which, as one or two generations later Father Marin Mersenne contemptuously said, "had been invented merely to cover defective melody and the ignorance of modern musicians." Once more, the beat was straight and strict; the forms were simple and symmetrical, the number of voice parts shrank, and melodies became natural, with *fa-la-la* refrains easily caught up. It is significant that early in that time of antipolyphonic trends, in 1558, Zarlino's *Istitutioni harmoniche* had established the logics of harmony, as based on the major and the minor triad and their inversions, and therewith had marked the end of the church modes.

This situation explains the antipolyphonic attitude of the Florentine Camerata, a group of noblemen, scholars, and artists who gathered in Count Bardi's house on the Arno to debate the aesthetic problems of the time in the spirit of Plato, the purist. The gist of their musical discussions, reported in Vincenzo Galilei's *Dialogo della musica antica e moderna* (1581), is: polyphony, responsible for the degeneration of music, must be abolished; descriptive music is ridiculous; a new monodic style ought to be created in faithful devotion to Plato's ideas and to Greek music (of which they only knew, and misunderstood, the theory). No doubt, Baroque music sprang from these roots, but in forms and a spirit that the erudite rebels of Florence could hardly foresee. The beginnings were a classical reaction.

Galilei's own test compositions are lost, but at least we know that they were vocal monodies with the accompaniment of viols. In this respect, he was by no means a pioneer. Recitatives of a somewhat wooden character occur in Alfonso della Viola's pastoral play *Sacrificio* (Ferrara, 1554) and also in the famous *Ballet de la Royne* that the court of France attended in the very year of Galilei's Dialogue. And, like so many features of that time, the recitative had been anticipated in the Raphael-Josquin generation. Count Castiglione's celebrated book *Il Cortigiano* exalts the delicate *cantare alla viola per recitar* of his days. Although later it was dynamic and dramatic, the recitative was in the beginning, just as much as Palestrina's art, directed against the autonomy of music which threatened to choke the words of the text.

Sculpture testified, in Brinckmann's words, to "a failure of Michelangelo's influence," which led to "a seeming relapse" instead of continuation toward the Baroque. Four outstanding spokesmen give an idea of leading trends in the fine arts. In 1563, Vignola, the architect of Il Gesù in Rome, presents his famous *Regola delle cinque ordini d'architettura,* Rule of the Five Orders of Architecture. In 1567, Vincenzo Danti's *Trattato delle perfette proportioni* brings the old classical idea of a perfect canon to the fore. Andrea Palladio, herald of Vitruvius' Roman order and builder of a Roman theater in Vicenza on which in 1585 Sophokles' *Oidipous* was performed, sets the fashion for more than two hundred years when his *Quattro libri dell'architettura* (1570) again and again insists on *regule* as the leading principle in art. In 1584, Lomazzo's *Trattato della pittura, scoltura, ed architettura* chimes in: without geometry and arithmetic nobody can hope to become a painter. Elsewhere, he adds that portraits should exalt the dignity and greatness of their models and suppress the subjects' natural imperfections.

The Florentine Angelo Bronzino, purest representative of idealizing portraiture, kept the classicistic tradition of Raphael alive, just as there were musicians in Gombert's time who had not forgotten Josquin. Bronzino's canvases never show emotion, action, emphatic gestures, or 'fussiness'; always quiet, always cool, they are the perfect paragons of reserved dignity. And they are firmly drawn, without effects of light or color, and still more so toward the end of his life (1572). The mannerism of Michelangelo's imitators hardly more than touched Bronzino's work. And yet, he was no reactionary nor even a belated leftover of times bygone, as is proved by the fact that his greatest admirer and protector, Grand Duke Cosimo I of Tuscany, was sixteen years his junior and in matters of art entirely up-to-date.

Paolo Veronese, with his worldly Venetian decorativeness, delight in brilliant color, and virtuosity in handling the boldest problems of mass composition, space, and perspective, was almost Bronzino's antipode (Plate XXI). And Nikolaus Pevsner is certainly right when he says, in his *Barockmalerei in den romanischen Ländern,* that while other painters shaped the soul of their time, "Veronese stands apart as a comforting, perfect evidence of the fact that no style reigns unchallenged." Yet even Veronese, so well able to play around with the intricacies of foreshortened obliqueness, quite often restrains himself to the strictest symmetry—not only in architectural canvases as huge as the Banquet in Levi's House (1573, Venice, Academy) but also in those smaller sizes like the Annunciation of 1581 in Venice or the Crucifixion at San Lazzaro dei Mendicanti in Venice, which also belongs in the 1580's.

The French scene, strongly under Italian influence, is similar. In the very year 1567, Philibert Delorme, creator of the Tuileries, published *Le Premier Tome de l'Architecture*, after the window painter Jehan Cousin had, in 1560, printed his *Liure de Perspective*, and the ceramist Bernard Palissy, in 1564, his *Recepte véritable*. It was the all-obliging *règle* that they were seeking. A few years later, 1570, the tomb of King Henry II in the Valois Chapel of St. Denis Cathedral indicated an energetic turn to strict classicism.

The English made their contribution to this movement in favor of form at the cost of content in a quite different and yet related way. In 1579, the poet John Lyly published the first part of his famous—or shall we say ill-famed—novel *Euphues*, which with its highly artificial preciosity was responsible for the 'euphuistic' style of the 1580's. Two years later, in 1581, Torquato Tasso finished polishing the noble, elegant verses of his epic *Gerusalemme liberata*.

These traits of strictness in form and restraint of expression would leave the picture incomplete and incorrect, unless we stress another, very different trend of the time, which was briefly touched upon in the couple of lines devoted to Palestrina. The Venetian Tintoretto, greatest of the painters who "shaped the soul of their time," developed, with some of his contemporaries, from personal, sensuous, palpable conceptions to a more and more impersonal visionary, and often almost ghostly style. In this evolution, Tintoretto drew very close to the flaming timeless and spaceless world of Greco's disembodied martyrs and saints and of the verses of Luis de León. But he also linked with the strangely rapt, immaterial style of the later Palestrina, who in his Song of Song motets of 1584 traced mystic, restless visions in flickering shadows and lights until he died in 1594, the year of Tintoretto's death. And it is far more than an accident that the spiritual connection between Italy and Spain, so manifest in the nearness of Tintoretto and Greco, became true of music also. The outstanding masters around and with Palestrina in Rome were two Spaniards, Cristobal Morales, born in 1512, also the year of Tintoretto's birth, and the great mystic Tomas Luis de Victoria.

The academicism and the mysticism of the period had in all their contrast a common front against the rule of the senses and unaffected joy in life and nature which only the later Baroque was called upon to restore.

1600

THE ANTIPOLYPHONIC ROAD that music took inevitably led to the opera. The first attempt in this direction was made in 1597, when Jacopo Peri composed music for Rinuccini's play *Dafne* and performed it in Jacopo Corsi's house at Florence for the learned Camerata mentioned in the preceding section. The work is lost, and we do not know its nature. What we know is the enthusiasm with which it was celebrated as the final recovery of Grecian tragedy. In 1600, Peri, and also Giulio Caccini, composed music for Rinuccini's play *Euridice*, and both these works are preserved. Seven years later, the decisive victory of the new form was won with the drama of man's fatality in grief and in mirth, in home and hell and heaven, in a myth of monumental simplicity and a musical language of timeless grandeur: Monteverdi's *Orfeo*. Breathtaking modulation and orchestral colors never heard before are preserved in this incomparable score; its melodies in sharp profiles and sweeping rhythms have withstood the changing tastes of centuries. Nothing is petty in this unique masterwork; the music flows in one powerful stream, now in spirited recitatives, now in terse and square-cut tunes.

The operas of 1600—or Emilio dei Cavalieri's scenic oratorio performed at Rome in the same year—have neither the passion nor the freedom and the boundlessness of Monteverdi's giant work. Their emotional expressiveness is limited; even the crucial moment, so deeply moving in Monteverdi's opera, when Orpheus learns that Euridice has died—*la tua diletta sposa è morta*—brings only a weak harmonic shift. The recitatives are not free and flexible; stiffly, they follow a uniform four-beat rhythm throughout and give way in all too frequent cadences.

In the music drama, for which *Orfeo* set the standard, music was faced with fully novel tasks. It had almost at one blow acquired the elasticity and striking power to follow the rapid changes of moods and actions. One year after *Orfeo*, the lengthy preface to Marco da Gagliano's opera *Dafne* demanded that music and action be strictly synchronized; every step and every gesture must obey the orchestra. The singer might pause after the first strophe and make three or four steps but always in time with the music. He should begin his step with the sustained penult and so on into the smallest details.

So minute a synchronization recurred only two hundred fifty years later in Wagner's Remarks on Staging the Flying Dutchman (1852) where the hero is meticulously told how to time his movements: "During the deep trumpet notes (B minor) quite at the close of the introductory scene he has disembarked, along a plank lowered by the crew, to a shelf of rock on the shore. The first note of the ritornello of the aria (the deep E sharp of the double basses) accompanies the Dutchman's first step ashore; his rolling gait, proper to sea folk on first treading dry land after a long voyage, is accompanied by a wavelike figure for the 'celli and altos: with the first quarternote of the third bar he makes his second step—always with folded arms and sunken head; his third and fourth steps coincide with the notes of the eighth and tenth bars . . ." Indeed, in its merging of poetry, music, action, and its painted wings, the early Italian opera was a *Gesamtkunstwerk* in Wagner's sense.

The musical backbone of these early operas was the recitative sung to the accompaniment of the chords set up on a thoroughbass or figured bass.

According to the nice definition by the Grand Chaplain Sébastien Brossard in James Grassineau's English translation of his *Musical*

Dictionary (London 1740, p. 195), the recitative "borders upon declaming, as if one declamed in singing, or sung in declaming." Vaguely imitating the natural inflection and meter of speech and avoiding purely melodic organization in rhythm and form, it rendered the sentence as a whole, stressed the main idea, and hastened the words of minor importance wherever epic and dramatic passages in their transitory character and rapid change of mood did not allow for the display of a steadily flowing melody.

The word *recitativo*, however, had a broader and essentially more melodic meaning around 1600 than it has today. It made possible the eloquence and unprecedented power that the divine word took on in the Spiritual Concerts of the German Heinrich Schütz but it also comprised the dramatic declamation of secular masters. For the recitative, proclaimed its loudest herald Giovanni Battista Doni, should be sung everywhere, on the stage, in church, at home, and in the oratory, since it allowed the words to be distinctly understood and although they were quite close to ordinary speech, yet to be emotional and expressive. After all, said the Frenchman, Father Marin Mersenne, in 1636, "a singer's performance should have the effect of a well-made speech." And more than three decades earlier, the composer Giulio Caccini who in the Florentine Camerata had been successfully trained to quote the Greeks, referred to Plato's words: "Music is in the first place speech and rhythm, and only lastly, tone." As a consequence of such an attitude Doni recommended good actors to serve as models to modern composers. Actors would teach them where the pitch should rise or fall, where the tempo must be slow and where more rapid, and how certain words should be stressed. Actors also would teach them how differently a prince speaks to his vassal or to some petitioner, and that a matron talks unlike a simple lad, a young girl, or a harlot.

This sounds engaging. And Doni would be a realist, if not a naturalist, were there not an irksome point. "Actors" would teach them how a prince or a matron speaks and not the prince or the matron themselves. This is the way not of naturalists but of those who, ignoring living models, take refuge in idealized paragons other artists have created. We know such expedience from the fine arts where academicists—Doni's French contemporary Poussin, for example—availed themselves of the ready-made poses on ancient reliefs instead of studying life and nature directly.

The thoroughbass to which the recitative was sung was performed by accompanying instruments. During the sixteenth century, in times that printed single voice parts but not scores, organists had prepared the thoroughbass as a short cut for the difficulties of co-operating with choruses, whether this meant supporting *a cappella* choruses while they were being rehearsed or actually playing some of the parts.

The special technique of the thoroughbass required two adaptations. (i) The frequent intersection of the lower voice parts was ignored; instead, a *basso continuo*, an uninterrupted bass line, followed the momentarily lowest notes, to whatever voice they might belong. (ii) The polyphonic weaving of a greater number of voice parts could not be rendered adequately on keyboards and therefore was replaced by chords that 'realized' the harmonic train of the composition. These chords, however, were not written but only symbolized in figures above or below the corresponding notes of the thoroughbass (3 for the third, 4 for the fourth, etc.) and their actual position, density, and connection were left to the player's discretion.

It is obvious that such practice broke up polyphony or, better, that such practice was possible only in a time in which polyphony was disintegrating and harmony, consolidating. Indeed, the organist's provisional score, supplementing the copyist's and printer's separate parts, was an eloquent witness to a growing vertical conception. By 1595 (Adriano Banchieri's *Concerti ecclesiastici*), conversion had gone so far that for the following one hundred sixty years no performance could be thought of without at least one keyboard instrument or lute to play the unwritten chords upon the thoroughbass, whether in opera, church, or chamber. Even most solo music was accompanied by a stringed bass and an improvising chordal instrument without any meaningful intermediate lines that could interfere with the all-important melody.

But lines there were; the texture of that music was certainly not as thin as printed editions would make one believe: we learn from Agostino Agazzari's treatise of 1607, *Del sonare sopra 'l basso con tutti li stromenti* (On Realizing the Figured Bass with All the Instruments) that each member of the orchestra was expected to improvise his own part on the thoroughbass.

The recitative upon the figured bass was then no longer the arid, antimelodic psalmody, the only concern of which had been not to threaten comprehension of the text. In the very year of *Orfeo*, to be sure, the preface to Monteverdi's *Scherzi musicali* (in a later edition subtitled *Arie, & Madrigali in stile recitatiuo*) pronounces that "speech be the master, not the servant of music." But this tenet no longer justified a recitative that secured the supremacy of the text only in virtue of its own melodic shortcomings. A new conception, the *stile rappresentativo* or style representing (emotion), had imbued the recitative with an unprecedented power of characterization and expressiveness.

Indeed, Father Marin Mersenne, who as a Frenchman belonged in a French and therefore an un-Baroque sphere of art, wondered at the convincing power of illusion which allowed modern Italian singers to make their listeners forget that they were merely playing roles and were not themselves the personages they were supposed to represent. Modern music, he says in his *Traité de l'Harmonie Universelle* (1636), "forces its way into the listener's soul to appropriate and lead it whither the composer wishes." Fifteen years before him, another Frenchman, René François, had in his *Essai des Merveilles de Nature* already described how an Italian lute player can easily do "what he will with men." A truly Baroque idea, indeed.

Since in impressing the listener's soul the way of least resistance pointed to the lachrymal glands, the 'lament' became a characteristic requisite of the new style. Nothing could better illustrate this tendency than the subjects of Vincenzo Galilei's sample compositions, spoken of in the preceding section—the monologue, from the thirty-third canto of Dante's Hell, of the unfortunate Count Ugolino, who starving saw his children starve; the responsorial Lamentations of Easter week; and the Lamentations of Jeremiah. Themes more lugubrious cannot easily be found.

Accordingly, the earliest operas were tragedies, though courtly rule imposed a happy ending. No comic opera was among them and they did not allow for humorous episodes. The greatest of their group, Monteverdi's second opera *Arianna* (Mantua, 1608), made history through an event less essential in itself than in its having been reported as unwonted (though not unprecedented). When the heroine, lamenting the desertion of her lover, burst out singing that deeply moving melody, *Lasciate mi morire*, Let me die, the aristocratic audience shed tears (Example 27). A similar result had been

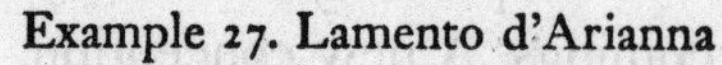

Example 27. Lamento d'Arianna *Monteverdi*

observed eight years before, at the performance of Cavalieri's *Rappresentazione di anima e di corpo*. This was a new effect and a new goal for music. In 1613, a certain Angelico Patto edited a collection called *Canaro pianto di Maria Vergine sopra la faccia di Christo estinto*, Lyrical Plaint of the Virgin Mary over the Face of the Dead

Christ; Biagio Marini composed *Le lagrime d'Erminia* in 1623 and *Lacrime di Davide* in 1655. As late as 1689, Purcell climaxed his opera *Dido and Aeneas* in a soul-stirring lament (Example 28). It is

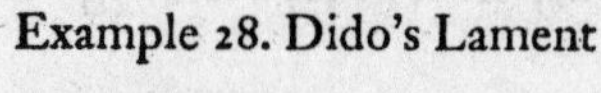
Example 28. Dido's Lament *Henry Purcell*

more than coincidence that a book which appeared in the same year as Monteverdi's *Arianna*, 1608, Constanzo Antegnati's *Arte organica*, makes the first mention of the lacrymose organ stop we know as *fiffaro* or *vox humana*.

It is also worth mention that Lodovico Viadana, switching back to the religious field, challenged polyphony in its innermost province: in 1607, the year of Monteverdi's *Orfeo*, he wrote a monodic mass *in stile rappresentativo*.

The imprint on Protestant music was stronger than that on Catholic music. Heinrich Schütz, the greatest German and Protestant master of the seventeenth century, published in 1629 the first part of his motets for solo voices and instruments, the *Symphoniae sacrae*. Familiar with the new Italian style as Giovanni Gabrieli's disciple, he knew the expressive power of the sung word and did not hesitate to introduce what he himself called the *stile oratorio* and to base his melody on the natural cadence of the declamatory word rather than on purely melodic inspiration without, however, striving for theatrical illusion.

The madrigal joined the new style in its own way. It became free in melody, rhythm, and structure, as its poetry was. It grew so definitely vocal that without words its melodic turns and harmonic shifts, indeed, its very rests would be meaningless. And far from being the moderately emotional expression of a group of singers, it became the individual, passionate, and highly dramatic outburst of self-centered composers—it became Baroque. To concentrate on the most original of the last madrigalists in the works of Don Carlo Gesualdo, prince of Venosa, polyphony had ceded the best of its former dominating place to a harmony in which simple triads rival bold inversions of altered seventh chords. These pieces moved in modulations of the weirdest kind with appoggiaturas, 'changing' notes, harshly dissonant entries, interrupted cadences, and chromatic progressions; they were always fascinating and often of irresistible beauty. Contemporary critics admired Gesualdo's madrigals as the creations of an incomparable genius, just as much as critics of the nineteenth century scoffed at them as the amateurish experiments of a "cavalier stumbling about in the maze of modulation." True, his modulation, logical from a coloristic viewpoint, was illogical when seen in retrospect from the angle of Rameau's harmonic system. True, he did not strictly confine his unwonted modulations to underscoring the ever-recurrent *io moro's* of his love songs. True, he overdid chromatics from sheer delight in eccentricity. These shortcomings should not be minimized. For they stamp Gesualdo not only as one of the boldest pioneers in music history but also as a genuine master of the Baroque, contemporary of the famous, if not notorious poets, Marini in Italy and Góngora in Spain.

Glancing at the picture of this highly dramatic, emotional, passionate style, we yet should not expect a naturalistic school of singers to thunder or shout. Lodovico Viadana wanted his epochal *Con-*

certi ecclesiastici of 1602 to be performed "with a soft voice, delicately and nicely." In Peri's *Euridice* of 1600, the singers were supposed to take *bellezza e forza* from improvised grace notes, and not only from those which could have been recorded in notation but more so from those which in their impalpable vagueness eluded the quill, as Peri himself wrote. And Monteverdi introduced the most genuine coloraturas under the pretext that *Orfeo* had to win over the dead of Hades.

This strange compromise between dynamism and Italian love of sensuous beauty seems in a similar way to have shaped the fate of painting in the same generation. It can be symbolized under the dualism Rome—Bologna. The Roman Caravaggio rejects all scenery and dips his figures into black shadows, the better to stress their force and tension with flashes of light. His movement is strong and audacious; how bold is the perspective conception of St. Paul in Santa Maria del Popolo in Rome, when the saint is thrown off his horse! To energy Caravaggio adds a sound naturalism. As a young man, he dares what nobody had dared before him, to paint just a basket full of fruit, and nothing else; and as a seasoned master, he risked occasional escapes from holy legend into the world of cheats and rogues and several times had his works rejected on delivery. Even in the holy legend, he could delight in a certain forwardness. In his Doubting Thomas (Uffizi), Christ does not just expose his scar to be reverently looked at but pulls the flesh apart and allows the apostle to rummage in the wound. Caravaggio's biographer Bellori tells indeed that "when some persons showed him the finest statues of Pheidias and Glykon and recommended them as models, he pointed at a crowd of men and said that nature had given him enough masters."

In Bologna, the works of the three Carracci, and above all, Lodovico Carracci's frescoes of the 1590's at San Michele in Bosco, represent about the limit of energetic movement, of loud and violent gesture, of crowded masses packed in a showy scenery. But the Carracci would not have referred to the masters given them by nature; they were eclecticists, not naturalists.

If Caravaggio may be looked at as a radical wing, and the Carracci as a center party, the other wing would be held by Guido Reni in Bologna, the pet painter of the millions. In his countless works, character is completely sacrificed to empty beauty which, being where it should not be, is a nuisance rather than a virtue. In the central figures, passion has yielded to the petty sentimentalism of skyward glances, and in the bystanders, to an almost indecent indifference.

Goethe was right when in 1786 he wrote in his Italian diary—I follow A. J. W. Morrison's translation of 1866, but take the liberty of correcting its mistakes—"No sooner are you attracted by the *gusto* of a Guido and his brush, by which nothing but the most excellent objects the eye sees are worthy to be painted, but you promptly withdraw your eyes from a subject so abominably stupid that the world has no term of contempt sufficient to express its meanness; and so it is throughout. You are always in the dissecting-room, by the gallows, in the carrion-pit—always some suffering, never an action of the hero—never an interest in the scene before you—always something for the fancy—some excitement accruing from without. Nothing but malefactors or fanatics, criminals or fools, alongside of whom the artist, in order to save his art, slips in a naked fellow or a pretty damsel as a spectator, in every case treating his spiritual heroes as layfigures on which to hang some beautiful mantle with its folds. In all there is nothing that suggests a human notion! Scarcely one subject in ten that ever ought to have been painted, and that one the painter has chosen to see from any but the right point of view."

With the dramatic and emotional trends of *rappresentativo* music, with Caravaggio's pitiless naturalism, with the Bolognese delight in "deeds of horror or convulsive sufferings, malefactors or fanatics," the door was wide open to the naturalistic, ecstatic, passionate, and cruel trends of Spanish art. Indeed, the eyes of Europe were for decades focused on Spanish painting and Spanish poetry, on El Greco, Cervantes, Lope de Vega, Alarcón y Mendoza. And the irresistible stamina of Spanish-American dances—*chacona*, *pasacalle*, *folía* and, above all, the *sarabanda* which "exhibited indecency in a thousand positions and gestures"—provides French and Italian dancing with the *dynamis* lost in the polish of courtly ballrooms.

German architecture at the beginning of the seventeenth century may be represented by two outstanding buildings: the *Friedrichsbau* of the castle in Heidelberg (1601–7) and the *Rathaus* in Paderborn, Westphalia (1612–16). The former, generally labeled German Renaissance and rightfully claimed as German, has features that liken it to the early Italian Baroque: rich motive and detail, interrupted pediments with rounded profiles and scrolls, statues between the windows, and a fascinating play of shadows. The *Rathaus* in Paderborn still clings to the old peasant type of German house, in which a huge, steep gable dominates, but two smaller, almost abutting replicas of the main building with its gable jut out from the front—so that no façade proper can be seen but a picturesque ensemble of projecting and receding blocks with charming contrasts of light and shadow.

1642

IN 1642, LORENZO BERNINI began the powerful sarcophagus for Pope Urban VIII in St. Peter's—one of the most characteristic Baroque works, full of exuberant energy, life, and profusion. Two years later, he devised the bulging, jagged tabernacle with Santa Teresa lying in the ecstasy of love under carved, gilded sunbeams which break through marble clouds (Plate XXIII).

The leading architect of the Baroque, Francesco Borromini, had just finished the church of San Carlo alle Quattro Fontane in Rome and was working on his most representative building, the Oratorio, in the same city.

In the North, Peter Paul Rubens had died two years before. His greatest Dutch contemporary and antipode was Frans Hals, who opposed genre to Rubens' *gran maniera*, and a predilection for the merry life of topers, fishwives, market women to his courtly leanings. And he painted with a brush so bold and vigorous that all the numberless genre masters of Holland after him seem tame and pale.

Also in 1642, L. von Siegen invented mezzotint engraving, which —a symbol of the trends of the time—dispensed with lines and only aimed at masses and gradations of light and shadow.

It was in 1642, again, that Rembrandt entered his third and last period and, with his monumental Night Watch in the Rijksmuseum, won one of the greatest victories of color and light over classical drawing, and of nature and freedom over academic pose and symmetry. His lesser contemporaries, men like Ostade, Teniers, Terborch, dedicated their busy brushes to painting life as it was and as the nation loved it at the tavern, in shops, and at home. Holland's writers, too, had their heyday in those years, and the books of manners that Vondel, Hooft, and Huygens printed were no more orthodox than Netherlands genre painting.

The genius of the South was the Spaniard Diego Velásquez, a colorist like Rubens, an impressionist like Hals, a light-and-shadow master like Rembrandt, yet wholly himself and almost a stronger naturalist than any of them.

In Italy, however, the high Baroque generation experienced a classical countercurrent from about 1620 on. Its leader, the aging Guido Reni, had lapsed into an unwonted simplicity of composition—witness his Contest of Atalante and Hippomenes in Naples, National Museum, where the action takes place on one frontal plane with bodies of an icy beauty arrested in rigid poses. To Borromini's architectonic excesses, this classical countercurrent opposed the almost pure Renaissance style of the Palazzo Rezzonico in Venice (1650). Along the same line, though with another, a moralistic approach, the style of the generation before was assailed by men of the church: by Cardinal Federigo Borromeo in a book on Sacred Painting (1634) and by the Jesuit Ottonelli, together with the painter Pietro da Cortona, in a Treatise of 1652.

Religious music climaxed with the splendor of the Italian, especially the Roman, polychoral style, in which from two to sixteen groups of singers and players with trumpets, kettle drums, and trombones, placed at different sides and altitudes of the church, united, contrasted, echoed, overlapped, or mingled in a confusing richness of what we, for lack of an adequate term, are tempted to misname vistas—auditory vistas.

When a French critic, Abbé Michel de Marolles, reprimanded Italian music of the time (1657) for its noisiness, frightful, monstrous leaps, and lack of sweetness, he was thinking less of this festive style than of the opera, which had in 1637 been given the first public theater in Venice and was rapidly becoming the outstanding representative of national music.

Also in 1642, thirty-five years after *Orfeo*, the aged Monteverdi wrote his last opera, *L'Incoronazione di Poppea.* More than ever, his music served the drama without asking much for itself. Choruses had disappeared, and instrumental interludes were reduced to a minimum. The form was wider open than at any time before and the recitative, admirably correct in its declamation and more flexible than in the earlier operas, easily slurred over all separating cadences.

Still, the same genius of form, which had reacted in the fine arts, was in the opera, too, rebeginning to counterbalance unbridled dynamism. In the Coronation of Poppea, lyric moments occasionally assumed the form of *da capo* arias, in which, after a contrasting second part, the first part is repeated to close the form. Moreover, the tragic love of Poppea and Ottone is duplicated and contrasted by the amourette of two attendants—an unfailing symptom of a more formal, static conception (cf. Chapter X, Disjunction and Conjunction). Lastly, the *Incoronazione* was the earliest opera with an historical subject; *la gran maniera*, the classical style in all arts, sneered at the irrational vagueness of myth and fable and preferred history as the proper object of sane reasonableness.

Form and classical attitude, imperishable in Italian art, had indeed reconquered most of the ground that the generation of 1600 had yielded. As early as 1626, the Roman composer Domenico Mazzocchi, prefacing his opera *La Catena d'Adone*, had spoken of the growing *tedio del recitativo*, and even Giovanni Battista Doni, the loudest herald of 'modern' music and of the recitative itself, warned that an opera exclusively recitativic was unbearable. Following this order of thought, Stefano Landi's *Sant'Alessio* led in 1634 to the 'classic' pattern of opera, with *da capo* arias, two *sinfonie* (which anticipated the standard overtures of the French and the Italian form), with the contrasting motive of a couple of *servitori*, and with a *castrato*, who sacrificed character to the sensuous charm of the voice, and nature to unconvincing affectation.

At the same time, the half-dramatic forms of oratorio and cantata, long before prepared in the musical life of Italy, became under Giacomo Carissimi's leadership important factors in the musical life of Italy. His melody, harmonically simple and rich in sequences, had already the classical beauty and noble grandeur of the coming turn of the century.

A new rhythm appeared: the slow measure of three halves, and particularly with a dot to the second half, either in the first or the second bar. This strangely hesitant rhythm is known as the rhythm of the saraband; but it also occurs in the passacaglia, the chacone, and many movements without specific dance names. The hesitant character of the three-two time is sometimes driven to extremities: much later, in the aria universally known under the nickname of Largo, from Handel's opera *Serse*, the initial notes of the first and second parts are drawn out so long that they actually form surplus measures.

The counterpart in costume was the long train which trailed behind the elegant ladies.

In the dance, treading and leaping movements are practically abolished; *saltarello*, *tourdion*, and galliard have disappeared from the dance hall; and folkloristic features have faded just as they have in contemporaneous literature. Practically all couple dances from the early seventeenth to the early eighteenth century had indeed the same fundamental step in three well-poised phases, *plier*, *lever*, *poser*, bend, lift, draw up, in keeping with the three-two rhythm and also with the solemn, hesitant motion betrayed by the art works, and by architecture in particular, with its preference for horizontal expanse.

In all this classicalism, contrasting with the unrest and exaggeration that popular conception gives to the Baroque, the French were much more radical than the Italians. Averse to the "noisiness, frightful, monstrous leaps, and lack of sweetness" that they disliked in

Italian music, they thought, in the words of Father Mersenne, that "melodies, composed with art and fitting their texts, can move the audience to pity and rue; but that their principal end was to delight the cultivated listener, and not, to rouse his passions." Thus, French music did what Perrin, the poet, claimed to have done: "banish the darker passions and stick to subjects unexpected, amorous, and spirited." As a true French rationalist, Mersenne distrusted imagination, sensuous perception, and any judgment based on it, and again and again stressed that music was a part of mathematics. In this attitude, he had the full support of the leading French philosophers of his time, of his friend Descartes and also of Blaise Pascal, who called imagination "a proud power hostile to reason" and, worse, "a mistress of error and falsity."

It is a comfort to pass from such frigid aesthetics to the work of a master like Champion de Chambonnières, the patriarch of French *clavecinistes*, who in all his noble reserve was a thoroughbred musician, inventive and spirited (Example 29).

Example 29. Rondeau *Champion de Chambonnières*

In the fine arts, France was no less un-Baroque—in the popular sense of the word 'Baroque.' In an influential book, *De pictura veterum* (1637), the Frenchman Franciscus Junius impressed upon the artist's mind the sacred duty of following antiquity to the letter. To the French, as to most Italians, the paragon of purist classicism was Raphael, and they knew no better title of honor for their painter Eustache Le Sueur than to call him the French Raphael. They sent a whole generation of painters to study in Italy: Poussin, Le Brun, Blanchard, and many others. And in the very year 1642, the greatest of them, Nicolas Poussin—who then, a few years before turning to his last heroic style, was painting in a sober, dry, and rational manner—met in Rome with the future chief of French official art, Le Brun, to seal the continuity of French classicism right in the face of Bernini and Borromini.

Their contemporary Claude Lorrain, so infinitely closer to modern eyes, was cast in a different mold. In his visionary landscapes, he dared to show the sun and sunlit spaces and even the mist enveloping water and air. He certainly was not a rationalist, almost rather a romantic. But he, too, held his visions in the iron clamp of classical discipline.

It was at this time that tragedy in France accepted the Aristotelian three unities of action, time, and place, and that it no longer tolerated crowds of murderers on the stage or heroes of less than princely rank. Corneille's *Cid*, played in 1636 in front of a multiple scenery, now went into a single room with four doors, to be used for any of Racine's tragedies as well.

Since all radical classicism inevitably leads to academism, the foundation of academies was a logical step. The Académie Française of language and literature was founded in 1635; the Académie Royale de Peinture et de Sculpture, in 1648; the Académie de la Danse, in 1662; the Académie des Inscriptions et Belles-Lettres, in 1663; the French Academy at Rome, in 1665; the Académie des Sciences, in 1666; the Académie d'Architecture, in 1671. They drew up elaborate charts of precepts for 'pure' art and prescribed the very subjects to be treated. Charles Le Brun, in one of his academic lectures, presented special rules for the 'correct' delineation of all human passions and sentiments in art, and demanded that painting be "founded upon a demonstrable science": geometry. Drawing became the leading principle, and color was relegated to the hindmost place, because, in André Félibien's words (1666), "it cannot be regulated scientifically." In a true Cartesian spirit, the epic of that time had, as a refrain, the verse: *Et sur mes passions ma raison souveraine.*

Even unacademic painting had somehow a classic attitude. In 1641, Louis Le Nain had done *La Charrette,* and in 1642, Antoine Le Nain finished his famous Family Reunion, both in the Louvre. In complete disagreement with the principles of the Academy, the three brothers Le Nain, and particularly Louis, the greatest among them, described peasant life and gave it color, light, and *plein air.* But there is not a trace of Baroque commotion or eloquent gesture; the peasants hardly move or speak, and some, such as the mother in Louis' Peasant Family, attain majesty.

The same was true of an England in which Palladio's ideals reigned supreme. Her greatest master, Inigo Jones, professed, in his own words, an architecture "solid, proportional according to the rules, masculine, and unaffected."

1675

In 1675 were laid the cornerstones of two outstanding buildings: the Dôme des Invalides in Paris, by Jules Hardouin-Mansard, and St. Paul's in London, by Sir Christopher Wren. Both were Baroque—not in the popular meaning of distortion or exaggeration but in the more serious meaning that the word has in modern art history, of a period prominent in central accents, richness of details, and thorough integration of all individual parts in one consistent whole (cf. also chapters VII, Ethos and Pathos, and XIV, The Cycle of the Later Ages).

This broader concept does not exclude classicism (which is the very opposite of distortion and exaggeration) but, on the contrary, includes it as one of the basic creeds of the time. Mansard's memorial church for the veterans is one of the noblest documents of strict classicism in its simplicity and quiet grandeur. And Wren, too, "was a supreme classicist, devoted to his Roman Orders and his geometry. Speaking of the different sorts of beauty, he said, 'But always the true test is natural or geometrical beauty.' He conceived of no nature apart from geometry; and outside the provisions of classicism he allowed no liberty. 'An architect ought to be jealous of novelties in which fancy blinds the judgment; but the glory of that which is good of itself is eternal.'" (Quoted from Frank P. Chambers, *The History of Taste*, N.Y., 1932, pp. 129 *ff.*)

French painting, however, was modifying its classicistic creed. An influential critic of the time, Roger de Piles, began to compare the great masters in all styles and in a truly academic spirit gave them credit points, which almost throw American colleges into the shade. Out of the optimum of twenty points, Michelangelo, for example, obtained eight for composition and eight for expression, seventeen for drawing, and only four for color. Rembrandt, on the contrary, was allotted fifteen for composition, twelve for expression, only six for drawing, but seventeen for color.

A generation ago, the academy had proclaimed: "drawing makes the merit of painting, not color," and Raphael had been its hero. Now, de Piles, from 1676 on, dared to call the colors of Raphael none too strong and his *clair-obscure* deficient; Caravaggio and even the three Carracci had done better. "Coloring is not only an essential part of painting, but is indeed its *differentia*, and is the very part that makes the painter a painter" (translated by Chambers). Progressive members of the academy were as the Rubenists opposing the old-fashioned Poussinists, and they got help from another side. Chambers rightfully stresses that Leibnitz's monadic philosophy also encouraged the new tendency toward a moderate naturalism: all individual objects were different, it taught, and only in the very divergence of their charcteristic traits were they truly real.

Even Dutch painting became ambiguous. Jan Vermeer van Delft, perhaps the most fascinating master of the time, was a colorist as few had been, and he also delighted in the little accidents of appearance, such as a face reflected in an open window or seen through the iridescent glass in the act of drinking. But he was almost uninterested in space or depth: his scenes are mostly closed in behind the figures by a wall parallel to the canvas, and the figures themselves appear in plain profile oftener than on the paintings of other masters. At that, they make no violent gesture and generally sit at some peaceful, if not immobile occupation, tatting, strumming the harpsichord, reading, or writing a letter. And the very colors, so attractive in the exquisite harmony of white, gray, blue, and lemon-yellow, are strangely cool.

Music, too, was basically on the static side with only a certain connivance at dynamic trends. The showy full-fledged orchestra at last succeeded even in England, where the idea of consort, a chamber music ensemble with one man to each part, had been strongest; in bitter words, the author of *Musicks Monument* (1676), Thomas Mace, already pillories the 'modern' orchestras with twenty violins and ten basses. The new form of the age, the concerto for solo instruments and orchestra, which Giovanni Maria Buononcini created in 1677 and Corelli and Handel led to a peak, was very regular in its structure: symmetrically, two rapid movements enclosed a slow one and, inside, *ritornelli* or refrains of the orchestra alternated almost rondolike with freer *divertissements* of the soloists. In a similar way Froberger's, Rosenmüller's, Locke's suites of four dance movements followed the symmetrical ABBA form: the two slower movements, allemande and saraband, stood at the beginning and the end, and the two faster ones, courante and gigue, in the middle.

Also in 1675, the greatest master of musical tragedy in France, the Italo-Frenchman Jean-Baptiste Lully, performed his opera *Thésée* in the Royal Palace. As a close collaborator of Molière, he was deeply interested in drama, diction, and eloquence, and willing to subordinate music to poetry. Faithful to speech, he followed the texts so scrupulously that the beat of his recitatives continually changed. They run smoothly into arias, which in general are short and do not differ much from recitatives. The all too faithful obedience to the caesuras and rhymes of the libretto results in a certain monotonous disjunction, and melody proper is avoided rather than desired. With all this, there is a strange coolness in his works, and even in the often colorful orchestration; emotion is not absent but moderate. The master imposed an iron discipline on his personnel, both on the stage and in the orchestra. He was very careful in his directions as far as he deemed them necessary but did not allow his performers to take arbitrary tempos or to indulge in ornaments and cadenzas of their own invention.

The ballet demanded much space on the stage of Lully and other Frenchmen. The dance had indeed reached a peak, nay, *the* peak, as Pierre Rameau, the *maître à danser*, claimed. However, the perfection that he had in mind was not expressiveness, vitality, or imagination but, on the contrary, technique, clarity, and balance. To secure these accomplishments, the masters devised and canonized basic, still-practiced 'positions,' five each, of the legs, the arms, the trunk, and the head, which allowed for all possible combinations of movements forward, sideward, and back without loss of poise. Movement was thus considered to be a transitory connection of stationary points, and nothing could better illustrate the static character of French art. The five positions expressly imply that the feet be never more than one foot apart—"close movement reigns supreme."

The masters of the so-called Neapolitan opera, led by Francesco Provenzale (whose earliest opera dates from 1653) and made world famous by Alessandro Scarlatti, were simple in their means but had the stilted attitude of *la gran maniera*. They stressed melody and overemphasized the *da capo* aria. They not only acted against polyphony, but also neglected proper rendition of the text, strangled the recitative, and frequently, failing to write it down, left it, as an unimportant accessory, to the improvisation of uninterested singers. In short, they sacrificed drama to the delight in sensuous melody and to an ever-more obtrusive stardom.

Lastly, it should be mentioned that in 1675, the German theologist, Jacob Philipp Spener, published his book *Pia Desideria* and therewith set up Protestant *pietism*, a strong movement to restore the piety of the heart and active Christendom against a cold and arid orthodoxy. His sentimental pietism heralded the torrid Baroque which was dawning over Germany.

1690

GERMANY'S BAROQUE CLIMAXED in the works of two extraordinary masters, the Austrian Fischer von Erlach and the Prussian Andreas Schlüter.

Fischer von Erlach, whose artistic personality recalls that of Francesco Borromini, started his career (though after the design of an Italian master) with the Holy Trinity Monument on the Graben in Vienna (1687). Perhaps more than any other work, it dissolves architecture into sculpture, and sculpture into shapeless clouds. Even in his buildings, and above all in the University Church and in St. John's Hospital at Salzburg (1696–1707), architecture flows almost insensibly into decorative sculpture and evaporates in carved clouds; façades bulge out or else curve in; and domes, avoiding commonplace rotundity, assume the elliptic shapes that Bernini had been the first to devise.

Much more moderate, like all North German art, are Andreas Schlüter's *Zeughaus,* arsenal, in Berlin and, in the same city, his excellent equestrian statue of the Great Elector Frederick William on a bridge near the Royal Palace (1703).

France, under the aging Louis XIV, was experiencing the heyday of Jules Hardouin-Mansard's grandiose classicistic Baroque, with the main parts of the palace of Versailles and, in 1699, the unmatched unification of the Place Vendôme at the end of the Rue de la Paix. More than the noble, reserved style of architecture, Hyacinthe Rigaud's portrait of the monarch gives an idea of the frosty, theatrical pompousness of the time (Plate XXIV). Spain, always prone to overdo dynamic styles, was enjoying the orgiastic excesses of the sculptor and architect José Churriguera, his sons, and numerous followers.

Italy, too, had a renewed 'wild' Baroque, witness to which is

Tremignan's façade of San Moisè in Venice of about 1680—"an orgy of decoration." It shows even more in stage decoration where imagination, unhampered by practical considerations, had the field clear for jotting down its dreams. Such dreaming found its realization in the overwhelming canvas palaces designed by the brothers Ferdinando and Francesco Galli da Bibiena. These buildings—the pride of the best theaters in Italy, Germany, France—were daring structures in the style of the time, presented in oblique view, with broken staircases and vistas into adjacent rooms; their incalculable depth and involution added an element of fear to the awe of richness and grandeur (Plate XXV).

While this happened in the fine arts, German poetry was degenerating into a truly Baroque pomposity and lasciviousness. Led by the literary society of the Pegnitzschäfer, Shepherds on Nurenberg's river Pegnitz—what a name!—the poets wandered into a sweetish dallying. It means quite a jump from the verses of these provincial *Spiesser* poetasters to the oriental trends in the drama of John Dryden or of Thomas Southerne and to the first translations into French and English of the *Arabian Nights*, in 1704. The latter testifies to the exotic leanings that we rightly expect from so dynamic an age and actually find in a quite different field: the *chinoiseries* or imitations of Chinese designs and lacquers on porcelain, furniture, even harpsichords.

In fashion, the waistline became low. The history of the dance contributes the remarkable fact that in Vienna the German emperor Leopold I (1658–1705), favoring the more dynamic native dances, flatly forbade the static, formal dances of France to be performed at court.

Passing to music, the eye is arrested by the strange yet beautiful form that makers in South Germany gave to their viols. The outline is fantastically undulated and lobated, the uneven front reflects the light in a delicate play of gloss and shadow on its varnish, and the irregular sound holes lick up like flames. New instruments of an exotic character were sought: in Hamburg, cymbals and triangles were introduced to stay and, in 1710, August of Saxony established a Polish band with four pairs of cymbals.

Perhaps the most Baroque of German composers was the Austrian Heinrich Biber. He wrote a monster mass nine hundred measures long, the *Missa Sancti Henrici* (1701). He again represented Christ's Passion and other holy stories in cycles of miniatures for the violin, which despite the inadequate medium evoke the memory of Fischer von Erlach's cathedrals, with their solemn façades in the sunlight and the dusk of their mystic recesses. Nor do these pieces omit rich and often meaningless ornaments. A violin and a harpsichord—that sounds commonplace enough. But the way Biber uses the violin is Baroque in its contempt for rule and tradition and the natural or conventional limitation of a given material. The strings seldom keep their usual pitches *g d′ a′ e″;* they are lowered, or sharpened by a semitone, a second, a third or even a fifth, and the resulting *scordatura,* mistuning, would read, say (Example 30). Chords otherwise

Example 30. Scordaturas *Heinrich Biber*

impracticable become easy, and all the mistuned strings, now dim, now strident, create unwonted timbres.

Biber's sonatas on episodes from the life of Christ, beginning with the Annunciation, are accompanied by small woodcuts serving as titles and are almost descriptive. But they render emotion rather than happenings. Other Germans did not hesitate to describe events and actions. Johann Kuhnau, predecessor of Bach at St. Thomas's in Leipzig, published in 1700 a Musical Representation of some Biblical Stories in six sonatas to play on the clavier (with a long apologetic preface which shows that he did not feel quite comfortable in his program music). And about the same time, a violinist Johann Fischer wrote, of all things, a Musical Composition on the World-famous Saltworks at Lüneburg. . . . Even young Bach, once and never again, paid his tribute with a *Capriccio sulla lontananza del fratello diletto*, On the Absence of his Beloved Brother.

It was in this naturalistic decade that the Germans changed the static ABBA structure of their suites into the more dynamic, open arrangement ABAB by giving the fast and nimble gigue the last place after the saraband. So deficient did the older form seem that a publisher in Amsterdam, Pierre Mortier, took care to reprint the *Suittes de Clavessin* of the long deceased composer Froberger set "in better order."

The picture would be incomplete without the truly Baroque opera in Hamburg, the first public opera in Germany. After decent beginnings in 1678, even the participation of Handel, Keiser, and Telemann did not prevent it from lapsing into the popular, and from the popular into the vulgar. Where once Biblical subjects like Adam, David, Esther had been given, the audience, used to the atrocities of Lohenstein's tragedies, rejoiced at stories from the local underworld with scaffolds, beheading, and genuine blood from pigs' bladders.

Italy and England went other ways. Arcangelo Corelli and Henry Purcell (Example 28), both exponents of an Italian style, were thoroughly aristocratic and seldom intimate even in their chamber music. They had the noble dignity and the well-poised stride of the *gran maniera* without its coolness—Purcell with the stress on vocal music and Corelli, exclusively devoted to music for strings, sonatas and, for the first time, *concerti grossi*, in which a *concertino* of two violins and a 'cello strove against the (sometimes a hundred and fifty) pieces of the *grosso*.

Although characterization of melody is the most delicate task in writing on music, a brief description of Purcell's or Corelli's musical language may be attempted. In the slow movements—where it seems to be at its best—orientation is purely harmonic; the melody, frequently just a broken triad, is a beautifully drawn connecting line along a set of simple chords which, from below are supported by evenly striding, dignified basses. Rarely following a straight path, it proceeds rather in sequences that repeat the same idea or motive on a higher pitch (which is reminiscent of the redundant clusters of bases, pilasters, or capitals in Baroque architecture but also of its ornamental volutes that repeat the same curve at an ever-increasing distance from the center). The motive is often so devised that in its repetition it suggests a springy, jerking lift rather than a continuous ascent. This simile is not rhetorical: few types of melodies are more suggestive of bodily motion and gesture—of the same expressive, broad, and noble gesture that we know from paintings of the time, dignified, eloquent, and on the fringe of theatricalism. The span is wide, both vertically and horizontally, and cadences, unavoidable in organized musical form, are veiled by a hasty interception of the ball before it reaches the ground. Still, the general attitude is simplicity; the melody keeps strictly to diatonic patterns without any of the chromatic spices so generously dispensed at the beginning of the seventeenth century; modulation sticks to the nearest tonalities and color is mostly monochromic, never motley.

1725

Both evolution and revolution put an end to the Baroque in the times of the French *Régence*, which bridged the reigns of Louis XIV and Louis XV—1715–23.

The evolutionary forces of the period are known as the Rococo. This name belongs in a narrower sense to a certain form of decoration in architecture and furniture, in a wider sense to the fine arts embracing this kind of ornament, and in the widest sense to all the arts that after the death of Louis XIV extricated themselves from the theatricality and the frigid academism of the later Baroque without however withdrawing from the courtly, aristocratic sphere in which this style had bloomed.

The Rococo originated in France in the 1720's as a typical end development, replacing power and heaviness by a light-footed, fanciful elegance, using Italian ornaments, best known under the French names *rocailles* and *coquilles*, rocks and shells, from which the style derived its name, but also scrolls and branches of leaves, the monkey motives of *singeries* and the Far Eastern motives of *chinoiseries* in atectonic, fantastic, unsymmetrical clusters. And all this freedom and profusion displayed a taste, a hovering lightness, a joy of living hardly ever precedented and never repeated.

The courtly buildings of the time of Louis XV, particularly in France, Saxony, and Bavaria, were dominated by decoration. Matthias Daniel Pöppelmann's *Zwinger*, museum court, in Dresden (1711–22) is almost unique in its fantastic overdecoration. All these buildings hardly contributed to the evolution of architecture proper, except in their lightness and elegance. The typical painters of the Rococo were the Frenchman François Boucher, who had the full-fledged amoral eroticism of the period and its playful decorativeness, though little human warmth or interest, and the Venetian Giovanni Battista Tiepolo who, more than others, had its hovering, light-footed volatility.

Music, often ahead when style turns from static heaviness to dynamism had reacted some twenty years before the fine arts. On the stage, André Campra, Philippe Destouches, and, later, Jean-Philippe Rameau presented pastoral operas of a radically unheroic attitude. And in the chamber, François Couperin Le Grand, the king's musician, seconded with equally unheroic pieces for harpsichord and for strings. While Lully had written ballets and operas for the great ceremonial performances, Couperin created his delightful four-part *Concerts Royaux* in 1714 and 1715 for informal Sunday afternoons in the palace of Versailles. In these pieces, solemn grandiosity yielded to playful elegance; melodic austerity to a decidedly melodic style with profuse ornamentation; full harmony to limpid broken chords. Fine and facile, the musical Rococo or *style galant* avoided both passion and heaviness.

Revolution in style and conception, on the contrary, found a weighty herald in the Neapolitan philosopher Giovanni Battista Vico who, in his greatest work, *Principi di una scienza nuova* (1725), dared separate art from law and reason and reinstate imagination as its essential quality.

The revolutionary forces that put an end to the Baroque have no handy name like the Rococo, which covers the evolutionary forces. But they can easily be described: they oppose human warmth to academic frigidity, sober simplicity to stilted pompousness, real life to a sham world, ethical standards to amorality, democracy to aristocracy.

Among painters, the Fleming Antoine Watteau was the earliest to burst into the world of Louis XIV. He fought the frostiness of the masters in charge with the poetic visions of his dreams; human and warmhearted, he ignored their rationalism, aloofness, and hard-drawn lines and dared to show man's soul and nature's charm. Uninterested in heroic acts or passions, he shunned cothurni and strutting Alexandrines. He painted tender couples embarking for Cythera, the blissful isle of love, or quietly sitting in parks unspoiled by Lenôtre's garden shears; or actors, in whom he saw the suffering soul through make-up and professional smiles.

Warmheartedness duly shows in music. In 1728, Bach's contemporary and compatriot Johann David Heinichen, a Saxon, claimed in a book on the thoroughbass (*Der Generalbass in der Composition*) that "the end of music was to move the emotions [*Affekte*]."

In that generation, the history of musical instruments lists a series of remarkable events. In 1711, a distinguished Italian author, Scipione Maffei, wrote in the *Giornale dei Letterati d'Italia:* "It is known to everyone who delights in music, that one of the principal means by which the skilful in that art derive the secret of especially delighting those who listen is the *piano* and *forte* in the theme and its response, or in the gradual diminution of tone little by little, and then returning suddenly to the full power of the instrument; which artifice is frequently used and with marvellous effect, in the great concerts of Rome . . ." (translated by E. F. Rimbault).

This paragraph served to introduce Bartolommeo Cristófori's revolutionary invention of our modern piano, the *gravicembalo col forte e piano*, in which, as Maffei explains, "the production of greater or less sound depends on the degree of power with which the player presses on the keys."

In the same year, 1711, in which Maffei introduced Cristófori's invention (made in 1709 at the latest), an English monk in Rome, Father Wood, devised a different type of piano; the Frenchman Marius followed in 1716, and the German Schroeter in 1717.

On February 8, 1712, the short-lived English magazine *Spectator* announced that "Mr. Abraham Jordan, senior and junior, have . . . erected a very large organ in St. Magnus' Church, at the foot of London Bridge, consisting of four sets of keys, one of which is adapted to the art of emitting sounds by swelling the notes, which never was in any organ before." The contrivance was a box for the pipes of one manual with a sliding shutter which could be gradually opened or closed at will.

It cannot have been mere coincidence that the organ was given its first intensity-changing device at exactly the time in which all countries were attempting to rid the harpsichord of its inflexibility. Still less was it mere coincidence that all the countries were interested in such devices at a time when the age "allowed man's soul to speak again."

The musical pioneer of the era was Domenico Scarlatti of Naples. While Bach and Handel shaped their ideas with the structural discipline of architects, he jotted his down with the capricious freedom of an engraver. Bach and Handel were 'tectonic,' and Scarlatti, 'atectonic,' without any concern for the even progress of a given number of voice parts. And while Bach and Handel, as a rule, wrote music in an almost abstract sense, without much caring for the medium of performance, Scarlatti, founder of the pianistic style, composed for harpsichord out of the spirit, sound, and technique of his instrument. The many hundreds of his short sonatas in one movement often alternate between a loose polyphony and broken chords, with rapid passages in octaves, sixths, or thirds, audacious jumps, and crossed hands. They are never dry or dull, seldom melancholy, often exultant, and always bold, witty, and brilliant (Example 31).

Giovanni Battista Pergolesi, celebrated composer of the *Stabat Mater*, and several minor masters stood at Scarlatti's side when the new spirit began to take shape. They hated pathetic gesture, cothurni, and pseudo majesty. Their goal was *cantabilità* and emotion, grace and intimacy, but also dash and delight in sudden changes of mood, which betrayed the ascendancy of the comic opera (*La serva pa-*

Example 31. Sonata *Domenico Scarlatti*

drona!) and soon resulted in the two contrasting themes of the sonata form, the masculine subject first and the feminine second.

The second campaign of the time was led by realism against the sham world of the late Baroque and the Rococo.

Jean-Baptiste-Siméon Chardin, not Boucher, was Watteau's actual complement. Like the older master, he spurned majestic forms and the pseudo heroism of theatrical gestures; and he, too, bathed his scenes in a warm and limpid *clair-obscure*. But far from being a dreamer who built a world of his own, he loved the simple realities of nature and everyday life. Devotedly, he would paint delightful still lives in silvery tones and cozy *intérieurs* of small people: he was a bourgeois in the best sense of the word and a herald of the honest, working *tiers état* (Plate XXVII).

Artistic and intellectual life was indeed gliding away from the court to salons and coffee houses; paintings were displayed in public exhibitions; and the weekly *Mercure de France* opened the era of journalistic art criticism. Again, Anne Philidor—a man—founded in 1725 the famous Concert Spirituel as the earliest public concert institution of France. In the same year 1725, Allan Ramsay's pastoral comedy *The Gentle Shepherd* foreshadowed the popular ballad opera of England, which only two or three years later reached its early peak in the unbelievably successful *Beggar's Opera,* with the catchy tunes that J. C. Pepusch had compiled to fit John Day's lampoons against the official Italian opera, the court, and the government.

Art was becoming democratic.

A significant fact from the history of the dance remains to be recorded: in the earliest attempt to do away with the unnatural, conventional garbs of the ballet, Mademoiselle Sallé, celebrated ballerina of the Parisian opera, who scorned mere technique, saults, *entrechats, pirouettes,* advocated and in 1733 introduced authenticity of costume as to country and period on a starring tour to the Covent Garden Theater in London. On March 15, 1733, the London correspondent of the weekly *Mercure de France* reported that in one of her own ballets, *Pygmalion,* she "had ventured to appear without *panier* or skirt or anything but her own hair on her head. She wore nothing in addition to her bodice and petticoat save a simple robe of muslin draped and adjusted after the model of a Greek statue."

While the *Beggar's Opera* celebrated its first triumphs, William Hogarth, the English painter and engraver, was busy finishing the six canvases of *A Harlot's Progress,* the earliest English work to point at the vices and follies of the time and to oppose the inexorability of actual life to the pseudo life of those that he called the nature-menders. When Reynolds, one of these menders, was thirty years old, in 1753, Hogarth published a book, *Analysis of Beauty,* in which he lashed out against nature-mending in the memorable words: "Were I to paint the character of Charon, I would thus distinguish his make from that of a common man's; and in spite of the word low, venture to give him a broad pair of shoulders, and spindle shanks, whether I had the authority of an ancient statue, or basso-relievo, for it or not."

Classicism was indeed not dead, even outside conservative England. True, the reversal of the 1720's had the same target everywhere: the Baroque and its theatrical grandiloquence. But while in

France this wide-scoped, motley style had found expression in a cool and rigid classicalism and therefore had met reaction from anti-classical forces, the hot and boundless Baroque of Italy and Germany, contrariwise, cooled off to soberness, simplicity, and moderation in a process for which antiquity, the versatile cure-all in crises of style, again had suitable models ready.

In Italian architecture, Carlo Fontana's Palazzo Bolognetti in Rome (1700) had anticipated the reversal, which a generation later became perfect in Ferdinando Fuga's characteristic additions to the Palazzo Corsini in Rome (1729–32). The theory of this reversal was written by Carlo Lodoli (1690–1761), who, in Venturi's words, "was the first to consider the beauty of an edifice as the representation of its function."

Germany joined in the 1720's. Nothing could be more significant than Fischer von Erlach's two monuments in Vienna: the incredibly turbulent Trinity Monument on the Graben (1687–93), discussed in the preceding cross section, and the moderate Fountain on the Hohe Markt (shortly before 1723); or, for that matter, the contrast between the orgy of his University Church at Salzburg (1696–1707) and the Roman classicism of the Karlskirche in Vienna or the sober simplicity of the Imperial Stables, on which he worked until his death in 1723. In a similar way, another great Viennese, Georg Raphael Donner, led sculpture from the convulsive, flamboyant South German Baroque to tectonic, indeed, to classicistic forms.

German poetry chimed in: from 1730 on, Johann Christoph Gottsched, professor in Leipzig, tried to force the rules of French dramaturgy on German tragedy.

England had at that time the supranational ideas characteristic of classical periods: John Toland's pamphlet *Pantheisticon* was in 1710 printed in 'Cosmopolis' and Alexander Pope addressed his *Universal Prayer* to the

> Father of all! In every Age
> In every Clime ador'd
> By Saint, by Savage, and by Sage
> Jehovah, Jove, or Lord.

One cannot well leave a cross section of 1725 without having reverently bowed to Handel and Bach, the greatest masters of the time, and having tried to assign them places of honor. Paradoxical as it sounds, these places are not easily found. Bach and Handel, both born, like Domenico Scarlatti, in 1685, two years after Rameau, were titanic epilogues to the passing Baroque rather than heralds of the time to come. Handel, who in 1725 wrote *Rodelinda* and *Apollo's Feast*, had the full dramatic spirit of the Baroque; and Baroque were the heroic style of his historic operas and Biblical oratorios, the splendor of his anthems, the power and breath of his choral fugues, and the pompous stride of his themes.

Bach was no less Baroque. Witnesses are the gigantic size of the B minor Mass and the Passion according to St. Matthew; the Venetian double chorus at the beginning of the latter work; the central position that he gave to the fugue, as the strictest, most unified, and most progressive form; the density of his scores and the riches of their harmony; the golden glitter of his Gloria trumpets; and also the acrobatic play with inadequate means in the neck-breaking polyphony for solo strings.

Yet there are things in his music that belong in the present and future rather than in the past. Take the profuse Rococo ornamentation of his chorale-preludes. But then turn to the Brandenburg Concerto in D major of 1721: nothing could be more human, more heartfelt, more intimate, and therefore wholly un-Baroque. Take the many compositions in which the second theme of the coming sonata appears, as in the Italian Concerto or the C major Concerto for Two Harpsichords. Take all his transcriptions from Italian contemporaries and on the whole his eagerness to study the modern styles of France and Italy.

But the magic force of genius defeats analysis: though Baroque, Rococo, and what not, he is not just the sum of all these but their integration in a higher unit, in which they almost lose themselves.

CHAPTER SIX

The Latest Past

1760

"NATURE! NATURE! And our compositions must be beautiful; let us renounce art, when it is not simple; it convinces only when it is concealed; it triumphs only when it is unrecognized and is taken for nature . . . We must not merely practice steps; we ought to study the passions."

The French ballet master Jean-Georges Noverre wrote these words in 1760 in his *Lettres sur la Danse et sur les Ballets*, one of the most revolutionary essays in the history of the arts. Nature, character, soul, truth, and passion are his key words; mere technique is worthless. The dancers must if necessary give up their prescribed movements in exchange for a soul; they must forget their feet and legs to concentrate on facial expression and gestures. Away with the old masks which had banned the play of feature from the dancer's domain; away with the long and cumbersome court dresses which covered up the free play of the body; away with the classical symmetry of figures—they injure truth and kill illusion.

Social dancing could not but follow similar trends. Thirty, forty years before the manuals had totally ignored whatever dance existed besides the classic, restrained minuet; now, the modern manuals, such as De la Cuisse's *Répertoire des Bals*, a *Théorie-Pratique des Contredanses* (1762), would in their turn ignore the vanishing minuet. The old court dance was actually given its last manual a few years later, in 1767, while a new dance, the waltz, was taken over from German mountaineers and rapidly spread all over the world. "Every dance must have character and soul, express passion, imitate nature!" proclaimed its heralds.

Nature, against the stilted aloofness of the Italian *opera seria,* was the war cry of Gluck, when, in 1762, he entered a new phase in his development with a music drama which had more than just the subject and the title in common with Monteverdi's *Orfeo.* Gluck's reform, coincident with similar innovations in Jomelli's and Traetta's works, once more made the drama paramount. Unity of action, deep emotion, and moral ideas were required, while the scores had no place for musical vagaries, coloraturas, or even polyphony. The dominant role of the recitative was re-established; the sketchy *secco,* hastily sung to the dry accompaniment of the harpsichord, yielded to a more elaborate form with accompaniment of the orchestra, while the *da capo* aria, antidramatic and self-sufficient, lost its monopoly. The chorus, almost forgotten, came back with Handelian vigor as the "ideal spectator." The orchestra stressed dramatic accents and emotional atmosphere with an individualization and artful combination of instruments that has granted Gluck's scores a place of honor in all the manuals of orchestration up to modern days.

Gluck even complied with the contemporary demand for exotic subjects. He wrote two charming comic operas with the scene laid in the Islamic Orient, *Le Cadi dupé* (The Cheated Judge) in 1761, and *La Rencontre imprévue ou les Pélerins de la Mecque* (The Unforeseen Meeting or the Mecca Pilgrims) in 1764, and gave exotic episodes to his *Iphigénie en Tauride* (1779). Noverre, too, experienced the appeal of exoticism, though his acknowledgment sounds somewhat didactic: he thought that a "ballet well done was an animated picture of the passions, customs, usages, ceremonies, and costumes of all peoples of the world." It was the time when James Macpherson had a tremendous success with his *Fragments of Ancient Poetry Collected in the Highlands* (1760), *Fingal* (1761), and *Temora* (1763), allegedly translated from the Irish bard Ossian; when Johann Gottfried Herder was compiling the folk songs of all peoples, primitive and civilized; and Paul Whitehead, in a prologue to Arthur Murphy's *Orphan of China* (1759), sang:

Enough of Greece and Rome: Th'exhausted store
Of either nation now can charm no more . . .

Mademoiselle Clairon of the Comédie Française dared in 1755 as the first actor on a French stage to appear in Chinese costume in *L'Orphelin de la Chine*, and in a Near-Eastern costume in *Roxana*.

And again in the Comédie Française, Voltaire shouted at Clairon's colleague, Mademoiselle Dumesnil: "You take that too tamely . . . it lacks force and fire." "How?" demanded Dumesnil; "one would have to have *le diable au corps* to strike the tone you want me to take." "Right," answered Voltaire, "*le diable au corps* is the thing. Without it—no good poets and no good actors" (Thomas Wood Stevens, *The Theatre from Athens to Broadway*).

"*C'est la nature vivante, animée, passionnée, que la sculpture doit exprimer sur le marbre, le bronze, la pierre.*" This was the creed of one of France's greatest sculptors and most implacable foes of Rococo and classicism: Falconet. About 1760, he created the delightful timepiece with the three Graces in the Camondo Collection of the Louvre, and seven years before, he had given a beautiful all-round group of Leda to the porcelain manufacturer at Sèvres. Shortly afterward, he made the most vehement sculpture of the time, the monument to Peter the Great in Leningrad (1766–78). Masters of the Baroque had before him set their riders on wildly prancing horses but Falconet even sneered at the idea of an elegantly carved socle and placed the hind legs of the steed on a rough, unhewn monolith of more than three millions of pounds. It was almost a symbol that he had jotted down the first idea of his work on Diderot's table, who, to give him the tenderest pet name called him the Jean-Jacques (Rousseau) of sculpture.

Nature, soul, imagination, character, warmth reappear in the writings of Diderot, d'Alembert, Grimm, and the other Encyclopedists or authors of the gigantic *Encyclopédie* which as the greatest spiritual monument of the age was published between 1751 and 1766. While they enthusiastically espoused the cause of Gluck and Falconet, they aimed their wits at academies, classicalism, and rationalism. The Vitruvian system of measures, paramount in France and

Italy, "seems to have been invented only for monotony and for the suffocation of genius." And elsewhere: "The exact imitation of nature might make an art that is poor and mean, but never false."

"Nature! Back to nature!" exclaimed Rousseau, the most famous of the Encyclopedists, who in 1761 published his epochal novel *Julie ou la Nouvelle Héloise*. Extravagant, passionate, melancholy, patron saint of democracy and romanticism, he fought against reason for the judgment of the senses. As a musician, he severely criticized the decorative playfulness of the contemporaneous French *ballet-opéra*, and particularly of Rameau's compositions. And, deeply impressed by Pergolesi's charming comic opera *La Serva Padrona* and its unexampled success in France, he even tried his hand at writing a light musical comedy of his own: *Le Devin du Village*, The Village Seer, in which, as once in Adam de la Halle's *Robin et Marion* five hundred years before, plain rural life and unassuming tunes replaced stilted action and bombastic arias (Example 32).

Example 32. Le Devin du Village *Jean-Jacques Rousseau*

From 1760 on, or, more exactly, from 1759 on, Rousseau's amateurish seed bore blooms in a powerful school of operas in the lighter vein under the leadership of Monsigny. Germany responded with the simple actions in the vernacular and the catchy, popular melodies of the Singspiel, which came to live with Johann Adam Hiller's *Der Teufel ist los* (The Devil to pay), 1766, and *Lottchen am Hofe*

(Charlotte at Court), 1767, and lead in a straight line to the *Freischütz* (1821).

The unnaturalness of the *opera seria* was attacked from still another, opposite angle. Reasoning that music had an expressive power beyond the spoken drama, but that in the catastrophies of their lives, people after all do not sing, the generation created the *melodrama*, in which all words were recited, not sung, while the orchestra expressed what the actor left unsaid. Again, Jean-Jacques Rousseau inaugurated the new form in his *Pygmalion* (1762) and was soon joined by the German Georg Benda. The melodrama, so dear to Beethoven in the following age, has never since disappeared. Arnold Schönberg's *Pierrot Lunaire* (1912) is its latest realization.

The very landscape cried for nature. Fashionable parks were changing from the classical French to the anticlassic English garden. The Royal park in Versailles had been typically French, in André Lenôtre's strictly symmetric array of aisles left and right from the dominating central aisle which, rhythmicized by fountains and water basins, opens into the country far beyond. And French are the trees so stiffly cut to geometric forms and hedges as even "as were the verses by Boileau" (Theodor Fontane). But awe (read: boredom) yields to comfort and delight when you enter the English garden behind Marie Antoinette's Petit Trianon, with its informal natural beauty, where the trees grow freely from the lawn and the footpath meanders in leisure through boskets and arbors.

Nevertheless, classicistic resistance was greater in England than anywhere else. English architecture clung to the classicistic trends of the Georgian style, and American architecture followed suit. An outstanding example, the Craigie, or Longfellow, House in Cambridge, Massachusetts, was built about 1760, and at the same time George Washington erected Mount Vernon with its curious Palladian window.

Even in matters of painting the English followed a classicistic line, at least officially. Sir Joshua Reynolds, the leading master and first president of the Royal Academy since 1768, recommended "obedience to the rules of art . . . grand subject matter . . . the purest and most correct outline." Color, to him, was "unworthy of regard . . . The whole beauty and grandeur of the art consists, in my opinion, in being able to get above all singular forms, local customs, particularities, and details of every kind." This sounds almost like Plato's creed. But Reynolds was no zealot and recognized true art even when it was presented in anticlassical forms.

Four years younger, Thomas Gainsborough cared little for antique statues or grand subject matter. His actual interest was not devoted to society portraits—in which, however, he achieved perfection—but to the charms of English landscape: "Madam Nature, not Man, was then his only study," wrote his contemporary, Philip Thicknesse. This was new enough to rouse antagonism. Disdainfully, some critical saucebox wrote: "He fills his canvas with unthatched cottages, and their bare-legged inhabitants. This is vulgar nature—pray avoid it."

All this struggle for nature implied inevitable secondary currents, of which the strongest were simplicity, bourgeois spirit, emotionalism, belittlement of craft and, hence, the important role of the amateur.

"Let us renounce art when it is not simple," Noverre had said. Most music of the time, not only that of the Singspiel, is simple in spirit and technique, and he who, with old Bach's grandeur in mind, turns to the generation of his sons must resent their sober, meager melody-and-bass style. It was in keeping with the ideal of simplicity that composers expressly addressed the world of children: one of them, Johann Adam Hiller, presented *Lieder für Kinder* (Songs for Children) in 1769, *Geistliche Lieder für Kinder* in 1774, and a *Kinderfreund* (Children's Friend) in 1782.

German architecture behaved similarly. In 1770, the elector of Bavaria decreed that all ecclesiastic building should be kept pure and regular, that "all superfluous stucco-work and other meaningless and ridiculous ornaments" should be cut away, and that "a noble simplicity" should be the goal.

Such simplicity could not fail to celebrate the simple life of everyday instead of "grand subject matter." In Germany, Gotthold

Ephraim Lessing had, in *Miss Sara Sampson* (1755), written the first tragedy of common life. And two years later, Diderot had with *Le Fils naturel*, The Natural Son, established the French *drama bourgeois*. Denmark followed in 1772 with Wessel's *Love without Stockings*. The painters, preceded by Chardin, chimed in. In Germany, Anton Graff made hundreds of informal portraits and Daniel Chodowiecki depicted people in comfortable circumstances who play their cards by flickering candlelight. Jean-Baptiste Greuze, in France, painted actual peasant life and with his Village Bride aroused in 1761 what Goncourt called "a riot of enthusiasm."

Such bourgeois realism, however, was very far from the outwardly similar ways of the Dutch a century earlier, because it lived on a delight in emotion that the Netherlands had hardly ever known. Sometimes such emotion rose to actual passion in works which, in Diderot's words, being "terrible or sensuous, at the same moment that they charm the ear, carry love or terror to the depths of your heart, dissolve your senses and purge your very soul."

Oftener, emotion dwelt in the shallow waters of a lacrymose sentimentality. Greuze, with his charming girls in difficulties, leaned to this side more than to passion. But his age, which had in downright earnest accepted La Chausée's *comédie larmoyante*, found in Greuze's melodramatic paintings only *la sensibilité* that it was striving for. And it was in the spirit of the age that, when Emperor Joseph II of Austria once visited Greuze's studio and asked from where he took his themes, the painter answered: "Sire, they are in my heart."

Diderot himself, admirer of passion, was equally open to the delight in melancholy longing close to sentimentality that the romantics were to resume. He loved wild scenery and the sweetish sadness of solitude and once explained: "A palace must be in ruins to be an object of interest." Both picturesque and melancholy, ruins were indeed so much à la mode that certain painters could specialize in rendering crumbled walls and broken columns. One of them, the Frenchman Hubert Robert, called himself *Robert des Ruines* and was by his compatriots given the unprecedented title of *ruiniste*.

The "sweet melancholy of solitude" was in keeping with a curious, little noticed byway of music. Oliver Goldsmith's celebrated novel *The Vicar of Wakefield* (1761) remarks that English ladies of the time "would talk of nothing but high life . . . pictures, taste, Shakespeare, and the musical glasses." The last was a set of tuned drinking glasses (still to be seen in this country) which Benjamin Franklin, about the same year, was converting into a well-constructed instrument, the glass harmonica. Rubbed with moistened fingers, it yielded an indescribably pure, vague, and immaterial sound which "seemed to emerge from infinite space and to fade away into endlessness" and thus "anticipated one of the romantic ideals" (the author's *History of Musical Instruments*).

Thirteen years before Goldsmith, James Thomson had in his romantic poem *The Castle of Indolence* praised another immaterial instrument, the wind-blown aeolian harp:

> Ah me! what Hand can touch the Strings so fine?
> Who up the lofty Diapason roll
> Such sweet, such sad, such solemn Airs divine,
> Then let them down again into the Soul?

It is consistent with this taste for sentimental, intimate instruments that Germany, the most sentimental and at that time truly lacrymose nation, neglected the rigid harpsichord in favor of the older tiny clavichord. And the latter, weak, affectionate and overdelicate, allowed the player's fingers to give the individual notes *vibrato* and stress and therewith an emotional life, indeed, a soul denied to other keyboard instruments.

Even England, then the foremost land of harpsichord, felt the impact of sentiment. But it was in vain that in 1760 the Anglo-Swiss manufacturer Burkat Shudi in London forced a Venetian swell box (in the form of horizontal blinds above the strings to be opened or shut at will) upon the harpsichord. Superseding this instrument as well as the clavichord, the modern piano, designed to render keyboard music with all the shades of changing intensity, after sixty years of penury, came to the fore for good. In 1768, it first appeared as a solo instrument in a public concert in London, played by Bach's youngest son Johann Christian, and quickly overthrew both the feeble clavichord and the rigid harpsichord.

Nowhere did the emotional needs of the time more firmly materialize than in the music of Bach's sons Carl Philipp Emanuel and Johann Christian and in the so-called Mannheim style. Carl Philipp Emanuel, the elder son, once an outstanding representative of the *style galant*, at last anticipated Beethoven's personal language, and Johann Christian, the youngest son, preceded Mozart in his heartfelt *cantabilità*. In Mannheim on the Rhine, the duke of the Palatinate, Carl Theodor, entertained a court orchestra of world renown, which from the 1740's on, when Johann Stamitz and Franz Xaver Richter held the baton, became epochal in discipline, in a passionate, truly symphonic style, and in the development of emotional crescendos and decrescendos over longer passages. Characteristically enough, it also gave its name to a (then already existing) ornament, the appoggiatura: the Germans called it the Mannheim Sigh.

It was almost inevitable that the triple ideal of nature, simplicity, and feeling should lead to a typically romantic belief in inspiration and a certain contempt of professional craft and academic rules. Diderot claimed that not the imitation of insipid models but "the artist's inspiration is the breath of the Divine." And elsewhere he added: "There is something in that that none of your rules can achieve."

In Germany, Gotthold Ephraim Lessing chimed in. Attacking the musical critic Marpurg in Berlin, he rhymed:

Nun tadle mich, daß ich die Regeln schmäh',
Und mehr auf das Gefühl, als ihr Geschwätze seh',

which might in English verses be:

Do nag at me for hating all their rules,
I heed the feeling heart more than the prate of fools.

At about the same time, in 1767, Lessing was writing his *Hamburgische Dramaturgie* to free the German drama from the fetters of French classicism.

Rousseau in France and Doles, Bach's disciple and one of his successors at St. Thomas's, sneered at the fugue and other contrapuntal forms, and Handel is reported to have contemptuously said that his cook knew more counterpoint than Gluck.

It was only natural then that such a time allotted a big share to amateurs. Rousseau composed his Village Seer not despite his being a dilettante but with a particular stress on this fact and refusing to correct his little shortcomings lest such polish might interfere with his personal stamp. Germany's music greatly depended on laymen. Sperontes or, more soberly, Johann Sigismund Scholze, who in 1736 published the earliest collection of German songs under the title *Singende Muse an der Pleisse*, Singing Muse on the Pleisse (Leipzig's river), was a lawyer; Johann Friedrich Graefe, who edited the following collection, *Sammlung verschiedener und auserlesener Oden*, (1737–43), was no musician either; and Christian Gottfried Krause, the leading spirit of the Berlin school of the Lied, again was a lawyer. One should not forget in this context that most German orchestras and choruses of the eighteenth century were *Liebhaberorchester* and *Akademien* of amateurs.

No doubt, a good many of the art works created as alloys of simplicity, bourgeoisdom, and sentimentalism were of necessity superficial and feeble. Strong opposition was aroused in the *Sturm und Drang*, Storm and Stress, in which the younger generation of German poets fought for independence, passion, and vigor against tradition and academic standards, against the frigid formalism of older French and French-inspired poetry and the insipid optimism that ignored the miseries of life and social wrongs. Shakespeare and Rousseau were their gods; Schiller and Goethe, authors of the *Robbers* and of *Werther*, their leaders. So anticlassical were they, that Goethe laid the scenes of *Götz* and *Faust* in the Middle Ages, and, in face of the Münster of Strasbourg he was, as a student, moved to a wild (and hitherto unwonted) enthusiasm for Gothic art. Seen from the viewpoint of parallel developments, it is remarkable that in that very year 1770, Horace Walpole, ancestor of the Gothic Revival, erected an imitation abbey in Strawberry Hill, London.

In painting, this movement anticipated, as it did in poetry, the romantic realm of blood-curdling horror. Johann Heinrich Füssli's Nightmare of 1781 (the year of Schiller's *Robbers*) is one of the most powerful documents of the high tension of those days.

The composer who more forcefully than any other musician embodied the trends of the time was Joseph Haydn. Unlike Mozart, he delighted in nature and country life, and in his fifth symphony of 1761, long before the *Seasons*, he dared replace the courtly minuet by a genuine Austrian *Ländler* with stamping accents on the downbeats. Even before the German poets entered the Storm and Stress period, he began to cut his flowing melodies by sudden, ominous halts or brusque interjections, to veer abruptly from major to minor, and to modulate boldly to far tonalities. And when in the 1770's that literary movement came to its climax, Haydn, whom trashy writing on music has falsified into a good-natured daddy, gave music its full share in rendering man's passion and tragedy. His greatest achievement, though, was the growing unification of the sonata form, with the organic development of often tiny particles of his melodic themes (Example 33).

Example 33. Trio in E flat major *Joseph Haydn*

From here, the doorway opened wide into the modern music of all nations and, most directly, into the world of that genius—who almost naïvely solved the problem of the time in reconciling heart with reason, Italian *cantabilità* with French *esprit* and German *Weltschmerz,* classical and anticlassical trends; to whom it was given to be boundlessly free and never shapeless, to be serene in sorrow and in joy and never frigid, to be dramatic, never stagy—Mozart.

Mozart, unlike Haydn, was not interested in nature. But on him, too, the Storm and Stress of the 1770's left its mark and particularly on the (earlier) G minor symphony (Köchel V. no. 183), composed at the age of seventeen, which in its whipping *sforzati* and counteraccents is the drama of a tender heart under the impact of inexorable fate.

Mozart's gift for reconciling opposites, however, represented in a way the common destiny of art in the age of Louis XVI, and particularly in Germany. But what to the genius meant reconciliation and synthesis at a higher level became insipid eclecticism in the hands of minor prophets. Johann Joachim Quantz, teacher of Frederick the Great, said point-blank in chapter XVIII §87 of his celebrated Essay on Flute Playing, *Versuch einer Anweisung die Flöte traversiere zu spielen* (1752): "If one knows how to pick the best qualities out of the musical styles of various nations, one obtains a mixed style, which without being arrogant one could call the German style."

Eclecticism was no less recommended in painting. In 1762, the year of Gluck's reform, the painter Raphael Mengs published his curious Ideas on Beauty, *Gedanken zur Schönheit,* which urged artists to combine Raphael's design with Titian's color and Correggio's chiaroscuro, without realizing that these elements excluded each other—that Raphael's color had to be Raphael's, not Titian's, and that Titian's drawing had to be Titian's, not Raphael's.

In all this lack of character and decision, the arts not only jumped from Italian to French and German styles, not only from Raphael to Titian and Correggio, but also from Gothic to classic ideals. And so we watch the most unexpected result: that with its enthusiasm for

Gothic cathedrals, Storm and Stress, and Dutch-inspired realism the age knew how to reconcile an almost violent love of classic antiquity. The connecting link was the common ideal of simplicity and 'nature' as opposed to the ecstasy and noisy eloquence of the Baroque and Rococo with their carefree, amoral, overdecorated gracefulness, grown meaningless in a world of enlightenment and democratic ideals on the threshold of the great revolution. Besides, antiquity recommended itself by its very definite ideas on the moral role of art, so dear to an age in which art, in Diderot's words, should render "virtue adorable, and vice repugnant."

In 1762, when Gluck was performing his *Orpheus*, two Englishmen, James Stuart and Nicholas Revett, printed their epochal *Antiquities of Athens;* and in 1764, Johann Joachim Winckelmann published his famous *Geschichte der Kunst des Altertums*, History of the Arts of Antiquity, the earliest art book called a history. In the same year, Paris saw the beginnings of the Madeleine in the style of ancient temples and was soon to see the Panthéon and the triumphal arches on the Carrousel and Etoile squares. And in 1766, Lessing wrote his famous dissertation on the antique Laokoön group.

The heralds of antiquity praised the noble simplicity and quiet greatness of the Greeks. But the statues Winckelmann had seen in Italy were Roman statues or copies; the Laokoön group Lessing analyzed was a Hellenistic sculpture of about 50 B.C.; and the models of Parisian architecture stood in Rome, not in Athens. It was not the genius of Pheidias that the classicism of 1760 evoked. A year before, Sir William Chambers, the builder of Somerset House in London, had in his influential *Treatise on the Decorative Part of Civil Architecture* (1759) expressly said: "Since the Grecian structures are neither the most considerable, most varied, nor most perfect, it follows that our knowledge ought not to be collected from them, but from some purer, more abundant source; which, in whatever relates to the ornamental part of the art, can be no other than the Roman antiquities yet remaining in Italy, France, or elsewhere."

If this eager statement proves that the classicism of the age was not too close to Periklean ideals, we find an unmistakable hint at dynamic trends in the fashions of the 1760's. Men's toupees grew higher, and the ladies broadened their skirts until, some six feet wide, they were forced to sidle through the doors; they pulled their hair high up on vertical stays until they had to stoop below the lintel, and donned no less enormous hats.

Only the following age was classicistic in earnest.

1793

As early as 1780, Goethe, withdrawing from Storm and Stress, had in *Tasso* created a drama truly classic in spirit and form, and six years later he wrote from Venice that he had rid himself "for all times, thanks God," of "grouchy Gothic saints, packed above one another on little corbels" and of "tobacco pipe columns, pointed turrets, and flower jags."

The revolutionary generation displayed no passion, unrest, chaos. Nor did the political emancipation of the *Tiers État* beget a bourgeois style. Quite to the contrary, it turned away from genre and decorativeness and strove for severity, classic grandeur, and great, historical subjects. Jacques-Louis David, leading master and official dictator of painting in the Revolution and "grave-digger of the *Dixhuitième*," utterly despised Fragonard's impressionism and decorative elegance as well as Greuze's petty sentimentalism. He would not condescend to glorify the sugary distress of sweetish dairy girls or the giggling lust of pink *baigneuses*. His subjects were Leonidas, Andromache's Grief, the Oath of the Horatii. And he presented them in the severest form, in sober, hard-drawn lines and cool, contrasting colors. 'Natural' they certainly were not—"what matters truth if the poses are noble," he said. But once again, it was not the serene Periklean spirit that David's classicism evoked but the pitiless genius of Rome, in its blend of austerity and showiness, of grandeur and pose.

David's strongest fellow classicists were two Italians, Vittorio Alfieri, the dramatist, and Antonio Canova, the sculptor, last of the great Italian masters. Canova's earliest works still have the dynamic temperament of the 1770's and 80's in forms almost Baroque; but at about 1787, when he was thirty years old, he quieted down to so pure a classicism that some of his works can hardly be told from Greek or Roman statues. His two tombs for popes show the difference: the earlier one depicts Clemens XIV in the act of blessing, his body shaken by a true Michelangelesque passion, the garment floating, the arm thrust forward in magic violence; the later one represents his predecessor Clemens XIII serenely kneeling down in static profile.

The names of two northern masters may be called as further witnesses to classical sculpture: the German Johann Heinrich Dannecker and the frigid Dane Bertel Thorwaldsen, who used to say he had been born on the day he arrived in Rome, and whose Blessing Christ is still the obligatory requisite of Protestant ministers' parlors.

German painting in a quite different way was affected by classicism. Asmus Jacob Carstens drew austere cartoons of ancient and religious subjects. His direct or indirect pupils, Peter Cornelius, Johann Friedrich Overbeck, Philipp Veit, and others, wandered to Rome in a somewhat romantic escapism and founded a brotherhood in 1812 with its seat in an abandoned monastery. These 'Nazarenes,' precursors of the English pre-Raphaelites, were purist, out-of-the-world idealists who, scorning naturalism and Storm and Stress, and also official academicism, reverted to the 'naïve' and 'honest' ways of Italian painting before Raphael. In a palish style, they attempted Biblical subjects in hard-drawn lines with raw and unrelated colors.

Architecture still kept to the Roman Revival inaugurated by the 1760's. It reached its peak in the Empire Style under Napoleon's court architects Fontaine and Percier, who blended solemn grandeur with severity and elegance, and in the less decorative and more organic creations of England. Outstanding monuments of the Revival, besides the Madeleine and the Arc de Triomphe mentioned in the preceding section, were Thomas Jefferson's designs for the Virginia State Capitol in Richmond (1785) after the Maison Carrée at Nîmes, at which he once had gazed "like a lover at his mistress," and the Brandenburger Tor in Berlin, which Langhans built from 1788 to 1791.

It is almost trivial to mention the classicistic trend in feminine fashion that became victorious about 1793: the rejection of everything unnatural, of powder and stays, of the wig and the bustle, the adoption of affectedly simple, close-fitting Roman dresses, and the raising of the waistline to the highest point ever reached; and, for that matter, the fancy for rectangular shawls like the *chlamys* of the ancients, helmets *à l'Athène* or *à la Minerve*, vanity bags decorated to represent Greek vases, and guitars in the form of Greek and Roman lyres.

Music swerved from classic ideals for but a few years, and mostly in the field of opera. It there complied with the horror of the early 90's and gave birth to a noisy, naturalistic style. One of the most gruesome was Jean-François Le Sueur's *La Caverne*, the almost unbelievable success of which may be understood from turning the pages of its truly dramatic score, where motivic development in Haydn's sense is spiced with voices that sing at extreme height, with lavish syncopation, and with the ceaseless excitement of tremolos and agitated passages in the strings.

But after the short lifetime of the horror operas, Le Sueur changed his style with disconcerting swiftness. He professed his belief in Gluck and became no less classicistic than David. He emulated antiquity not only in its spirit but even in its technique; prefacing his opera *Télémaque* (1796), he wrote this astonishing sentence: "Pursuing a strict musical unity in this opera as much as possible, I have at the same time tried to apply the various qualities of the modes, nomes, rhythms, and melodic patterns (*mélopées*) of ancient music to the passions, dramatic situations, and pantomimic movements." The overture is, as he says, written "in the hypodorian mode, the spondaic nomos, and a mesoid melody" (which did not hinder the composer from disowning the mode by the naturalization of the very first F sharp). Indeed, the score of his *Adam* (1809) warns the performers on nearly every page to play with the "pathetic sentiment that the ancient Harmony had" (whatever he fancied this to be).

Luigi Cherubini, born in the same year as Le Sueur, 1760, never lent himself to writing horror operas. Even his *Médée* (1797), so savage in its atmosphere of murder and infanticide, kept within the moderation and economy of a truly classical style, in which a single, carefully saved high A flat at the end of the overture affects the hearer like the ultimate scream of demoniacal possession.

Mozart—who spanned the entire scope of music, in church, concert, chamber, and theater, and, in the drama, all the range from tragedy to comic operettas—had died two years before 1793. Still, *The Magic Flute*, finished shortly before his death, gives evidence of the growing ethical attitude of art. Designed by its libretto poetaster to be an entertaining, motley Singspiel, it became in Mozart's hands a serious opera, in which the vulgar and the petty traits were driven back to give even stronger relief to the victory of moral power over the evil forces of weakness. And it is significant that the master of *cantabilità* and motivic development found in this late and often flippant work the way to Bach: to his fugues in the overture, and to his austere chorale variations in the grandiose cantus firmus ("When in the hour of utmost need") of the two guards.

Beethoven was not yet to take this way. Like Michelangelo, he accepted classical balance and ultimate serenity, but only as the issue of a violent struggle. The *Eroica* (1804), earliest giant among his works, is dynamic, if this none too fortunate word has any meaning. The symphony dispenses with the customary slow introduction; two whipping lashes of the full orchestra and the battle is on—not the military battle with guns and bugles that Beethoven's biographer Marx had in mind but battle in the abstract, essentially against the forces of weakness in ourselves. The writing could not be bolder; at the peak of the development, there is even a clash of two keys sounded together. And yet, the Heroic Symphony, like all Beethoven's works, has an almost classical strictness and an entirely unromantic self-discipline. Beethoven always conquers in his struggle against himself.

1819

ALPHONSE DE LAMARTINE who, in Sainte-Beuve's verse, knew nothing but his own soul—"*Lamartine ignorant qui ne sait que son âme*"—wrote in 1819 his ecstatic *Méditations poétiques*, the earliest document of self-centered Romanticism in French literature. And in the same year, Sir Walter Scott reached the height of his fame with *Ivanhoe*. In Germany, E. T. A. Hoffmann was publishing his *Serapion Brothers*, and Arthur Schopenhauer, *The World as Will and Idea*.

Romanticism in French painting, too, began in 1819, when Théodore Géricault exhibited his masterwork, *Le Radeau de la Méduse*, the raft with the survivors of the ship Medusa. Its naturalism was unprecedented: the artist had bought and studied corpses, and after interviewing some of the rescued and the carpenter who had made the raft, he had almost obtrusively depicted death and horror to the last detail. He also painted dashing horses, battles, bodies of executed men and, not long before his premature death in 1824, he ventured upon some no less challenging subjects, madness and paralysis.

Eugène Delacroix took up the banner Géricault had had to drop. When he exhibited Dante and Virgil in Hell (1822), the critics shook their heads; when he displayed the *Massacre de Scio* two years later, they called him savage, delirious, drunken, barbaric. But while he was hot and immoderate in the ecstasy of creation, he had at the same time the patience of the cool observer and man of research. He avoided Italy, as the homestead of classic influences, but went to Morocco and indulged in the light and life of the south. "Observe first that which strikes the eye and the mind; observe the character of things." Rubens was his god; Rembrandt, whom Winckelmann had called "an ape of nature," he placed above Raphael, and color —from which he excluded gray, as the impressionists did later— above mere drawing. Once, he even ventured to utter that "painting has not always need of subjects." In consequence, Delacroix has been claimed as their patriarch by both the impressionists and our modern apostles of objectless art.

His antagonist, Louis David's cool and static pupil Ingres, could not with all his matchless mastery check the march of anticlassical art (Plate XXVIII). While he was drawing hard, uncompromising lines, while in his scorn of color he was painting gray in gray *grisailles,* two English landscapists, Turner and Constable, had discovered how air and light dissolve contours and surfaces.

Joseph Turner, starting as an unconventional painter of heroic, dramatic landscapes of England and the Continent, ended as the creator of impressionistic, airy land- and seascapes, in which all objects drown in the vagueness of light-flooded blue and yellow mists.

John Constable was simpler and perhaps more serene but he explored similar grounds, and history can hardly separate them. He is said to have been the first painter to plant his easel right in the face of a countryside instead of recollecting it in the studio. The two currents, the French and the English, met in the momentous year 1824, when Constable sent his canvases to the Salon in Paris, and Delacroix, deeply shaken, went home to repaint the background of his *Massacre de Scio.*

Caspar David Friedrich's high-strung, gloomy work, however different from the French and the English landscape in its mentality, shows that Germany, too, was being carried along by the same wave.

Architecture, on the contrary, unable to conform to romantic ideas, still lived in the Classic Revival. The year 1819 saw Benjamin Henry Latrobe erect the Bank of the United States in Philadelphia, and Thomas Jefferson, the campus of the University of Virginia in Charlottesville, both in classic forms; in London, the Bank of England (1823) was being planned; and in Berlin, Karl Friedrich Schinkel had in 1819 just finished the guardhouse (*Hauptwache*) Unter den Linden, was designing the Royal *Schauspielhaus* on the Gendarmenmarkt, and paid a further tribute to Roman art with the delightful Pompeian murals that he gave some of his interiors.

Sculpture had a similar difficulty in leaving classic paths. In the 1830's, however, Germany's greatest sculptor, Gottfried Schadow, evolved to a style of motion and significant gesture. And in France, the leading master, François Rude, created his incomparably dashing, violent relief on the Arc de Triomphe (1836), which his compatriots have rightly called the Marseillaise in Stone.

The costume of the time developed away from closeness, nature, and simplicity. Gentlemen adopted the top hat and often the loose and flowing *cravate à la Byron;* ladies lowered the waist, wore fuller skirts with starched or padded petticoats, reintroduced the bodice stays which the Revolution had abandoned, and puffed their sleeves to exaggeration. They gathered the curls of their parted coiffure in rolls high up on top and sides, and donned enormous, broad-rimmed hats with feathers, ribbons, and flowers. Even muffs became colossal.

The musical picture is at first sight rather confusing. In 1819, Gasparo Spontini, newly appointed director general of music to the king of Prussia, took a fatal step down from Gluck's dramatic ideals with his opera *Olympia*. Daniel-François Auber performed *Le Testament,* and François-Adrien Boieldieu was preparing for *La Dame blanche*, both in lighter vein. Gioacchino Rossini, the Swan of Pesaro, wrote no less than three operas in that one year and was about to intoxicate the audiences of all Europe with the sweetmeats of his glittering coloraturas.

But east of the Rhine, Beethoven was creating the *Hammerklavier-Sonate*, the Ninth Symphony; Franz Schubert wrote the 'Trout' quintet and the powerful lied *Prometheus;* and Karl Maria von Weber was working on the *Freischütz,* with its romantic world of woods and hunters' horns, of enchanted bullets and haunted ravines.

Olympia, *Le Testament*, and Rossini's three operas are forgotten, and *La Dame blanche* leads the peaceful existence of a venerable dowager. The future belonged, not to Spontini's pompousness, not to Rossini's delicacies, not to the gentleness of the French composers, but to the greatness, fervor, and warmth of the German masters.

Beethoven has been warmly claimed by both the classicists and the romantics, and he has even been called a transition between the two styles. This last diagnosis is nonsensical, like all alleged transitions in an evolution the very essence of which is continuous flow and transition. And his classification as either a classicist or a romanticist depends upon what definitions the classifier chooses to give the two trends. Even then, it would still be true of Beethoven, as was said in Cross Section 1730 of Bach: that "the magic force of the genius defeats analysis." Altogether, Beethoven is neither a classicist nor a romanticist, nor a transition between the two, nor their sum, "but their integration in a higher unit, in which they almost lose themselves."

He portrayed the storms in his soul and was so self-willed that a critic of as early a work as the *Eroica* (1804) disapprovingly commended some conventional E flat major symphony by an obscure composer as a model of better discipline. And yet, no one was more opposed to the lenient, feminine egocentricity of romantic music. He never allowed his melody to lapse into effeminate chromaticism nor did he break its power in sentimental, weak appoggiaturas. Many of his themes are truly granitic, fateful, inexorable. Authors have spoken of his heroic style. Heroic he was, ever fighting and often triumphant, but never theatrical.

In the last ten years of his life, from 1817 to 1827, he created fewer works than before—it took him longer to give them final, irrevocable shape—and no two of them were alike: each one, unique and solitary, was an individual document of his relentless struggle. Their size became larger and larger; the number of movements within a work increased, and the ranges of voice parts grew excessive. Unity was his ideal; the whole C sharp minor quartet is worked out of the theme of the opening adagio. Accordingly, cadenzas and caesuras were concealed, and the hemless weaving of fugal forms, neglected in Beethoven's earlier works, was called to play a prominent role in his last period. He challenged the exclusiveness of major and minor tonalities, introduced archaic modal scales, such as the Lydian, and created on the whole an atmosphere less material, more spiritual, almost mystic.

Beethoven's symphonies demanded larger orchestras than had

been used before. Music as a whole, indeed, was steadily developing toward éclat and quantity. The technical shortcomings that had kept brass wind instruments, kettledrums, and harps from regular membership in the orchestra were being done away with. Gerhard Cramer in Munich had in 1812 invented a device to act simultaneously upon all the tuning screws of the kettledrum so that it might quickly join the orchestra in all its moves from key to key. Blühmel and Stölzel in Berlin were constructing and improving the additional crooks and connecting valves that give complete chromatic ranges to trumpets, cornets, and horns. And in 1820, Sébastien Érard in Paris, developing the so-called double action, supplied the modern harp with an equally completed range. Érard's name itself and with it the name of Broadwood in London stand for the evolution of the piano away from the tamer ideals of the clavichord and the harpsichord to superlative power. Here too Érard's invention of double action—in another form—in 1823 inaugurated the modern era of the piano.

1854

In 1854, RICHARD WAGNER finished the composition of *Das Rheingold*, first night of the *Ring des Nibelungen*, and began the score of *Die Walküre*. With a gigantic orchestra, he accompanied, nay led, a gigantic drama which, having grown backward out of Siegfried's tragedy, claimed no less than four nights of performance. And gigantic was the subject: the saga of the North had been remelted to shape the myth of the gods, from the proud erection of Valhalla, symbol of their might, to the end of the world, when the flames from Siegfried's pyre destroy the castle with its heroes and its gods.

While Wagner proceeded from Wotan's sunlit palace to Hunding's lowly hut, Johannes Brahms was beginning his First Symphony —the Tenth, as Hans von Bülow later jubilantly called it. Brahms tried indeed to ignore the 'music of the future' and to continue where Beethoven had laid down his pen. Like his idol, and like Mendelssohn, he submitted to an iron self-discipline and an inexorable strictness of form, to protect his music from romantic degeneration through subjective lawlessness. But what had been convincing in Beethoven and natural in Mendelssohn was often forced in Brahms. That his retrospective leanings created a classicistic countercurrent but not a reversal, in the art of the age, was due much less to a lack of creative spirit or power than to the fact that—as Chapter XIV (Cross Section 1225) will show—the time, dynamic and naturalistic to excess, lacked what the Greeks would have called *kairós*, the fateful moment, for any reaction.

While Brahms was timidly beginning his First Symphony in C minor, Liszt presented a *Faust Symphony*. The mere titles betray their antagonism: Brahms wrote absolute music, to be soberly cited by opus number and key; Liszt insisted on extramusical connotations, indeed, on a literary program (which however was spiritual rather than factual). Liszt, too, was thinking of Beethoven; like that master, he climaxed his symphony in a chorus and a tenor solo to sing the mystic ending of Goethe's work. But he felt free to subordinate symphonic form to the needs of his poetic subject. The general programmatic character, however, is perhaps less important than one musical detail: the great unison that opens the symphony (and reappears later in the second act of Wagner's *Walküre* when Sieglinde awakens). This meandering, searching exposition, a forceful chromatic sequence of four decomposed, 'augmented' triads (Example 34) in which there is no major or minor, and not even a

Example 34. Faust Symphony *Franz Liszt*

key seems to be the earliest symptom of harmonic disintegration, atonalism, and even impressionism.

While Wagner was attacking the conservative Brahms party in aesthetical pamphlets, the classicists found their herald in the Viennese Eduard Hanslick, who, again in 1854, published his famous, often re-edited book *Vom musikalisch Schönen,* On the Beautiful in Music.

Of the remaining great masters, one, a favorite of operatic audiences, and a second, hardly ever in the focus of public attention, were past their prime: Meyerbeer published his *Etoile du Nord* in 1854, and Berlioz was writing his oversized *Te Deum* in connection with the Crimean War. In the same year, a greater composer, Robert Schumann, left the world of work and sanity.

A few years later, the 'Mighty Five' of Russia, Balakireff, Cui, Borodin, Mussorgsky, Rimsky-Korsakoff entered the musical life of the west as pioneers of the folk-inspired national groups, Slavic, Scandinavian, Hungarian, which had a necessary and important place in the music of a naturalistic-romantic age.

Intensity of sound was ever increasing. Wagner's *Ring* orchestra included no less than thirty-three wind instruments, of which seventeen were brasses; the wind pressure of the organ, in earlier times between four and seven and a half centimeters, was up to twenty-two centimeters (to rise to fifty-five in 1867); and under the leadership of Steinway, who had founded his New York firm in 1853, the cross-stringed piano was striving for the utmost power.

French painting had two power centers, which after all were less distant from one another than is generally assumed. The older was the school of Barbizon, a group of eight masters, including Théodore Rousseau, Corot, Millet, and Troyon who retreated to a little village near Fontainebleau, devoted their brushes to landscapes and peasant life—without sentimentalism, without passion or drama, but also without idealization. "It is," thought Millet, "only an immense pride, or an equally immense folly, which makes people think they can rectify the supposed faults and bad taste of nature. What authority have they for this presumption?" Within such simple, honest realism, the masters of Barbizon were as different as possible, embracing all the scope of painting from the epic greatness of Rousseau's trees, Millet's workers, and Troyon's patient cattle, to the retrospective lyricism of Corot's delicate, misty, silvery woods.

In 1854, Gustave Courbet, who was born the very year 1819 in which Géricault's *Radeau de la Méduse* inaugurated Romantic painting, created his powerful rustic *Rencontre*—Good Morning, Monsieur Courbet!—had it promptly turned down by the Académie and the Salon, and showed it with forty-three other works in an independent exhibition, which he called the *Pavillon du Réalisme.* "The basis of realism," he said. "is the negation of the ideal and all that the ideal means . . . If you want me to paint a goddess, show me one." Small wonder that he was reproached with depicting the outer appearance of things and neglecting their spirit.

To span the whole enormous scope of painting in France at that time, we must furthermore mention its three extremes—Daumier, Puvis, and Manet.

Honoré Daumier, very different from Courbet, was a fine, independent painter—how 'modern' are his windmills!—but more, a great and pitiless cartoonist who with an easy, infallible pencil exposed the human tragicomedy behind good manners and impressive officialdom.

Puvis de Chavannes, painter of the *Panthéon* and the *Sorbonne*, was in his quiet and almost two-dimensional primitivism one of those masters who, to paraphrase the words of Camille Mauclair, make the heart but little throb yet stimulate the mind and pacify the soul. Puvis' final recognition as the greatest muralist of his time dates from 1861. In this year another monumental master, Anselm Feuerbach, entered the age of maturity as Germany's outstanding antinaturalist.

From another angle, classicism and romanticism were challenged by the impressionists under the leadership of Edouard Manet. Turning his back on the dynamic trends of the century, he was quite unemotional and unrhetorical. Nor did he care for the plastic qualities of three-dimensional or geometrically constructed space; he neglected backgrounds and often arrayed his figures frontally in simple planes—Courbet once reproached him with painting playing cards. All objects were dematerialized, and color became supreme—color in the ever-changing play of air and light, as it impressed the painter's sensitive eye.

After Manet, impressionism lost itself in technical problems and experiments—the unavoidable consequence of this attitude. More and more, its original realism vanished under the impact of the eternal question of how to represent things. Finally, the how became so strong an obsession that the what no longer had interest, and the American Whistler was right when he called his canvases *Nocturne in Black and Gold*, or *Symphony in White*, or *Arrangement in Gray and Black*.

In 1854, James McNeill Whistler drew illicit sketches on the margins of the austere coast survey plates that his superiors expected him to delineate, and the next year, the young man, as a failure, shipped to Paris to become an artist. Also in 1854 the treaty between the United States, Great Britain, and Japan opened the way for Japanese art to enter and to fascinate the West. Without Japanese woodcuts, Whistler, the impressionist, would not have been what he was.

No greater contrast is imaginable than that between Whistler and Dante Gabriel Rossetti, the leader of the newly founded Pre-Raphaelite Brotherhood, who took up the strife for unconventional truth, morality, and the religion of the Nazarenes without the naïveté of the Romano-German group. (It should be remembered that religion was reconquering a part of the domain lost to science and materialism and that, in 1854, the Pope could announce the dogma of the immaculate conception.) Where Whistler was a genuine painter, interested in the impression of his eye rather than in the material subjects of his pictures, Rossetti sacrificed the pictorial problems to his religious, legendary, mystical subject, to *The Girlhood of Mary Virgin* or *The Beloved*, or *Dante's Dream*. If we add to his name that of the pre-Raphaelite John Everett Millais, paragon of humble photographic fidelity, we have a rough cross section of painting in London that reflects the tremendous scope of all the arts about the middle of the nineteenth century.

In sculpture, the works of Jean-Baptiste Carpeaux may show how the masters availed themselves of the picturesque play of light and shadow to compete with both the romantic and the impressionistic trends of the time.

Under the impact of such trends, the Classic Revival in architecture yielded to a Gothic Revival, which allowed the romanticists to revert to the national past and provided picturesqueness for the impressionists. After Horace Walpole's anticipated revival of 1770, Benjamin Henry Latrobe had made a timid experiment in this direction in Segeley near Philadelphia as early as 1800. In Germany, Karl Friedrich Schinkel had followed with the sketch for a 'national,' and therefore Gothic, church on the Leipziger Platz (1816) and the Friedrichwerdersche Kirche near the Royal Palace (1821–23), both in Berlin.

Not before the 1830's did the growing enthusiasm for the anticlassic style of the cathedrals become an actual movement. Heralded in 1831 by Victor Hugo's novel *Notre Dame de Paris*, it won victory with Sir Charles Barby's Houses of Parliament in London (1840) and was in the following year given its bible with Augustus W. N. Pugin's *Principles of Christian Architecture*. In 1854, the title year of this section, John Raphael Brandon's Gothic Apostolic Church in Gordon Square, London, was built. An American example is Richard Upjohn's Trinity Church on Broadway opposite Wall Street in New York (1846); and an Austrian one, the *Votivkirche* in Vienna (1856).

Fashions, too, were as far as possible from classic ideals: the ladies wore full skirts ten yards round and spiders' waists and, in order to get rid of the numberless wadded, starched and stiffened petticoats necessary to support and stuff the outer skirt, reintroduced the age-old hoop-skirt farthingale under the new name *crinoline*.

Must we add that in such a time the dance was unrestrained? As early as 1845, Perrot and Robert wrote in a book *La Polka Enseignée sans Maître* (The Polka taught without a Teacher): "To dance the polka men and women must have hearts that beat high and strong. Tell me how you do the polka, and I will tell you how you love." And in 1856, one Baron Hübner said of the balls in Paris that "our mothers of families danced like women possessed." The new dance of the age was the galop.

1892

THE YEAR THAT BROUGHT us Gerhard Hauptmann's social, indeed, revolutionary drama *Die Weber* (The Weavers) and, at the opposite pole, Maurice Maeterlinck's fragile tragedy *Pelléas et Mélisande*, was one of the most fateful years in music. Anton Bruckner wrote the Eighth, the last of his finished symphonies, and MacDowell his first suite for orchestra; Claude Debussy who later transformed the Pelléas play into an opera, composed his earliest work of world renown, the colorful symphonic *Prélude à l'après-midi d'un Faune* in the face of his conservative adversaries Saint-Saëns and Fauré; and Ruggiero Leoncavallo conquered the lyrical stage with his veristic opera *I Pagliacci*. The year before, Gustav Mahler had presented his First Symphony, and Richard Strauss, his symphonic poem *Macbeth;* the year after, Verdi performed his last opera, *Falstaff*, Tchaikovsky his Pathetic Symphony, and Dvořák his Symphony From the New World.

This is a truly confusing list, a kaleidoscope of pitiless naturalism, of mystery, dream, and idyl, of materialism, symbolism, and pious idealism, of belated romanticism and neoimpressionism. The end of naturalistic and also of romantic trends is at hand, and the beginnings of expressionism stand out against the motley background of the past.

In a way, most of these contradictory trends had shaped the man who was greatest in the field of sculpture, Auguste Rodin. With all his grandeur, he had not lost the picturesqueness resulting from the contrast of light and shadow or his belief in realism: "What a teacher the street is!" he exclaimed. But he never rested satisfied with mere reality and boldly pushed forward to expressionism: "Rodin's marbles express the surging tumult of a soul at grips with life," says Malvina Hoffman in *Sculpture Inside and Out*. But already looming was the impassive, unromantic art of Aristide Maillol.

Impressionistic painting had come to an end with Paul Cézanne. There is no movement in his works, no emotion, no space, no atmosphere. They are detached and cool, if not cold, and his figures often have, in the words of his eulogist Novotny, "an almost puppet-like rigidity, while the countenances show an emptiness of expression bordering almost on the mask."

While Cézanne was bringing impressionism to an end Vincent van Gogh had opened the path of expressionism: he would say that in one of his landscapes he had wished to express peace of mind, and in another, sorrow and loneliness. He had taken his life two years before 1892, without having completed the desperate journey from the gloomy darkness of human life to the burning glare and sereneness of a southern sun in his paintings.

Ferdinand Hodler, the Swiss, fought romanticism from exactly the opposite end. Symmetrical, frontal, interested in surface rather than in space, in line more than in color, he created a new austere monumental art, in which frontality and symmetry never interfered with an incomparably vigorous movement; in which the surface did not kill the third dimension; and in which the colors added to the almost unparalleled power and life of the lines.

Feminine fashions still clung to 'back-full' skirts, spiders' waists, bustles, and leg-of-mutton sleeves. But the tide was turning. "After 1892 the back-fullness grew much less pronounced. The skirt was no longer draped, but cut in gores which swept out behind" (Agnes Brooks Young, *Recurring Cycles of Fashions*).

As the sun set on the day of Romanticism, minds were singularly attracted by the East and the West as sources of rejuvenation. The year 1892 found the painter Paul Gauguin in Tahiti, trying his brush at Polynesian colors and forms. About twenty years before, Louis-Albert Bourgault-Ducoudray had transcribed *Trente Mélodies populaires de Grèce et d'Orient* (Thirty Popular Melodies from Greece and the Orient) "hoping to extend the horizon among the musicians of Europe." But though it reached a second edition, it was a failure as far as the horizon was concerned. His vision came true when Claude Debussy, deeply impressed by the charms and possibilities of oriental music, devised his famous whole-tone scale—inspired by the *salendro* genus of five equal steps per octave, which he had heard from a Javanese *gamelan* in Paris—to help him on his way out of modern harmony with its 'leading' semitone, without which there is no 'functional' connection of the two principal chords, the tonic and the dominant.

At exactly the same time, American ragtime with its awkward syncopations and shifted accents made its first appearance in Europe and recommended itself as a liberation from the yoke of uniform beats that harmonic music had had to accept. And with American ragtime, Europe experienced the beginnings of a steady influx of American social dances: the Brazilian *maxixe*, in 1890; the one-step or turkey trot, around 1900; the cakewalk, in 1903.

It was more than mere coincidence that the lore of primitive and oriental music, so-called comparative musicology, was established in this country in 1890, when Dr. Walter Fewkes, using Edison's phonograph for the first time in the interest of musical science, recorded the songs of the Passamaquoddy and the Zuñi Indians.

1921–1946

OUR TIME IS 'STRICT' and antiromantic. We have departed from the dark and heavily curtained interiors of late Victorian days, so hopelessly jammed with bric-à-brac and upholstery in vague and meaningless colors, to strive for air and light, for limpid display and unbroken colors. Architecture spurns the inane imitation of bygone styles, of sham Greek temples, counterfeit Gothic cathedrals, or would-be Renaissance palaces; it shuns all false pretension and shrinks from meaningless glued-on decoration. Under the leadership of pioneers like Le Corbusier and Walter Gropius, it has turned to *Sachlichkeit*, to practicality or matter-of-factness, which demands the derivation of outer form from inner necessity and usefulness in keeping with Louis Henry Sullivan's law: "Form follows function." In its simplicity and functionalism, it often achieves a high degree of perfection and beauty: the airy elegance of George Washington Bridge and the overawing verticalism of Rockefeller Center in New York are examples familiar to most of us. And what we all know is the unpretentious, convincing beauty of streamlined engines, cars, and ships.

Sculptors, painters, stage designers have fled from space, perspective, illusion, realism, indeed from sensuous perception. They are no longer interested in the experience of their eyes. Instead, an earlier group, around 1920, outdid and ended naturalism in the utmost intensification of the human, the personal, the 'soul,' which we call expressionism, including those who followed man into the unfathomable depths of the subconscious of dream, and of nightmare. Another group—in fact a set of groups—under the names of cubism and constructivism has raised the flag of pure and abstract form, in which the object is meaningless in itself and can or should be altogether ignored. When finally the surrealists in their manifestoes claim to look for things as they ideally 'are' behind their outer appearance, they have, as the Second Part will show, a Platonic program, although it is open to doubt whether Plato would have endorsed the work of Dali.

Music is definitely antiromantic, 'neo-classicistic,' indeed, antiemotional. With Arnold Schönberg, who calls himself a constructor, not a composer, music has reached a climax of purely functional, structural trends, and his once so elemental antipode Igor Stravinsky has since *Le Sacre du Printemps* (1912) been developing more and more toward austere simplicity, to diatonic themes, indeed, to classicism.

In another province of music, the works of 'ancient' masters are being revived together with all kinds of ancient instruments, and particularly with the so-called Praetorius, Bach, or Baroque organs, which are designed to keep the clean-cut music of pre-Romantic times from being drowned in the messiness of nineteenth century organs. But all this is more than sterile, retrospective historism or a snobbish fad. It is a symptom that we ourselves have changed and are aware, consciously or subconsciously, that certain prior times have succeeded where our own age is still striving and struggling. What superficially looks like archaism is actually a step into the future.

Passacaglias, fugues, *concerti grossi*, toccatas of bygone times invaded our concert programs as curios from the historian's antique shop. But the very year 1921, in which the first Praetorius organ was built, witnessed the publication of Ferruccio Busoni's 'neoclassicistic' *Toccata, Preludio, Fantasia, Ciaccona* and of K. R. Heyman's book on *The Relation of Ultramodern to Archaic Music*. Not much later, Paul Hindemith turned from expressionism to a new structuralism, which in many respects evokes the memory of the 'horizontal' counterpoint of the Middle Ages.

Jazz, too, has, like most musical styles of our time, dissolved the function of harmony. It is, in a way similar to Hindemith's and medieval counterpoint, horizontal. It needs ears willing and able to hear the simultaneous but independent course of superimposed voice parts (═), not, vertically, the chords resulting from their con- or dissonances (|||). Jazz, however, has not the constructiveness of present 'art' music. In its shallow, crooning sentimentality, it appeals to the emotions of adolescents, and its improvisational character is about the contrary of balance and strictness. Actually, the commercial jazz and swing of today no longer represent what they used to be around 1920. Nor does 'official' music any longer pay its respects to jazz since Constant Lambert's *Rio Grande* for voices and orchestra (1928). In other words, jazz was a normal feature in the heyday of expressionism but is at odds with the stricter trends of today.

It is certainly in keeping with such trends that the *New York Times* of October 9, 1945, advertised under Fashions, as a "Formality for the Evening Scene," a sheer white jersey, "intricately draped and shirred in a gown that shows a Grecian derivation." And on December 26, 1945, the same paper depicts a coiffure under the title "For Classic Formality" with the caption: "The hair is brushed up from the brow, rising to a graceful Psyche knot at the center back of the head. A Grecian band encircles the knot."

Compare these advertisements to the fact that the waistline had reached its lowest point in 1922 and 1923 in the heyday of expressionism, and you have one more proof of the closest synchronism in the evolution of all aesthetic trends.

PART TWO

The Nature of Style

CHAPTER SEVEN

The Basic Dualism

1. ETHOS AND PATHOS

THE PRECEDING OUTLINE of a comparative history of art shows that in the to-and-fro of shaping trends two ideals have alternately acted as magnetic poles. The fact itself has not been entirely unknown, although it has scarcely been acknowledged outside the history of fine art. Neither were the adjectives unknown that the author provisionally and very reluctantly used to designate the two ideals: *classic* and *static* on the one hand and, as their counterparts, *baroque*, *romantic*, and *dynamic*. He used them reluctantly because they take undue advantage of the privilege of many technical terms: they are so disconcertingly ambiguous that redefinition seems unavoidable whenever their services are needed.

The word 'classic' is particularly dangerous since it has three different meanings, all too readily confused: (i) the first rank or class, in contradiction to either second-rate or—especially in the language of music—to popular art; (ii) certain, conventionally so-called groups of masters, as the Greeks in the fine arts or the three generations of Haydn, Mozart, and Beethoven in music; and (iii) any style, notwithstanding in what art, country, or time, that expresses a need for moderation, harmony, and serenity, as opposed to the Baroque or Romantic. This third, modern conception of 'classic' contradicts the second meaning of the word, since neither the Greeks nor the Romans were serene, harmonious, or moderate throughout the fifteen hundred years of their culture and art. To make things worse, most architects and sculptors during and after the Renaissance claimed to be admiring followers of classic antiquity (second meaning), and even Bernini, the most Baroque of sculptors in the Baroque, used to call himself an ardent classicist; which he was if we think not of (third meaning) the classicism of the Periklean age but of the immoderate, unbalanced, passionate, indeed Baroque, ideals of Hellenistic Greece or Antoninian Rome.

The word 'baroque,' and for that matter the word 'romantic,' are however just as misleading and dangerous as the term 'classic.' There is again contradiction between the popular and the historical meaning: Baroque, in Webster's *Dictionary*, for example, denotes (1) "irregular in form," (4) "grotesque, in bad taste" which, mirroring the common use of the word, is derogatory. Only (2) defines it as "of, pertaining to, or designating the style of art and architecture prevailing from about 1550 to late in the 18th century," to which the book unfortunately adds that this style was "characterized by the use of curved and contorted forms" which, to say the least, is an oversimplification in the face of powerful trends in the opposite direction during the more than two hundred years of the style. This, then, is another case of confusion: a popular, prejudiced, derogatory catchword versus a gigantic, many-sided phase of history in which regular form, purity, and good taste were more in demand than their contraries.

Romantic, on the other hand, is an attitude compatible with all kinds of styles; it is hardly a style itself. As Irving Babbitt rightfully says: "It requires courage in any one who aspires to be looked on as a careful thinker to use the word at all."

The terms *baroque* and *romantic*, which do not even do justice to the various and changing aspects of Baroque and Romanticism themselves, do certainly wrong the seemingly similar trends of other ages to which they are being applied. No doubt, baroque and romantic qualities reappear in many periods of art history, and a careful use of the two characterizing words is helpful and must not be opposed. But it should never be forgotten that all epochs, far from being mere anticipations or repetitions of the Baroque, Romantic or any other phase of style, are unique in their particular configurations. Rash connotations about developments of the seventeenth or nineteenth would easily expose them to disastrous misinterpretations. As a makeshift—but only as such—I have preferred the word 'unclassic.'

Recently, the antithesis in question has been called *static-dynamic*. The contrast is taken from physics, where 'static' means "pertaining to bodies or forces at rest or in equilibrium" and 'dynamic': "pertaining to bodies or forces in motion" (Webster). These are excellent terms. They avoid the inadmissible extension of the names of specific styles and unmistakably express the more universal character of the two basic trends. But they have their shortcomings, too. Taken at face value, they suggest a contrast so radical, so black–white, that they inevitably wrong the subtle nature of art. No style is actually motionless, that is, inert, neither the Periklean arts nor the music of Haydn, Mozart, or Beethoven, not to speak of the dance, which is motion *ex definitione*. As a classic, Beethoven himself would be assigned to the static side; but should he not be unanimously called dynamic, if ever there has been a dynamic master? And would not the same be true of Michelangelo?

Similar pairs of terms have been coined to express the same dualism from other angles: idealistic and naturalistic by Konrad Lange, geometric and imitative by Alois Riegl, *einfühlend* or 'empathetic' and abstract by Wilhelm Worringer, ideoplastic and physioplastic by Max Verworn, and, best of all, imaginative and sensory by Herbert Kühn. All the first terms denote estrangement from nature in stylization or geometrization and all the second terms, realism and dominant interest in the perception of our senses.

But all these terms refer essentially to sculpture and painting only and cannot without strain be used to describe the common traits of all the arts. Even so, we had better shun such rather specific terms, lest they force an all too easy, distorting formula upon the motley diversity of style all over the world and throughout the ages. It is unfortunate that any less specific terms imply a greater vagueness. But this is the minor evil.

The Greeks set up such a pair of wider, vaguer terms. I am not speaking, though, of Friedrich Nietzsche's often used, and oftener misused, antithesis Apollinian and Dionysian, or wisely moderate and passionately immoderate, which, meant for two contrasting attitudes in Greek mentality, can only sometimes be applied to the un-Greek styles of Western art in the Middle Ages and the period from the early fifteenth to the early twentieth century which we are going to call the Later Ages. I speak rather of the two antonyms in which the Greeks expressed the decisive imprint left on their lives and arts by the collectivism of the Periklean age and the growing individualism after the Peloponnesian war: *ethos* and *pathos*.

The word *ethos* indicated the serene calmness of the soul that the philosophers praised as *sophrosyne*, the wisdom of self-control, the privilege—in Lessing's and Irving Babbitt's words, "never in any matter to do too much or too little." An explanation is hardly necessary; a glance at the composure and coolness of Pheidian gods illustrates the unemotional reserve of serenity. The pose of statues was steadfast; their gestures were so restrained that the limbs seemed anxious to return to rest; and their lack of feeling borders on impassivity.

Ethos, however, implied more than stand-offish reserve and impassibility. It referred, in Plato's words "to the better part of the soul," which was "prone to trust to measure and calculation." It meant *kalokagathía*, the sameness of beauty and virtue, and implied belief in absolute, unalterable values, in perfection, norm, and permanence.

But no individual being or object can ever be perfect or permanent; both perfection and permanence exist as ideas, as archetypes only. Consequently, ethos ignored the characteristic features of actual persons and their passing moods, acts, and appearances. Instead, it abstracted the elements of beauty from the most beautiful specimens, melted them into one, and "trusting to measurement and calculation," it devised synthetic beauty in what it thought were the perfect proportions of the human body, thus doing what, in the words of Byron, "nature could but would not do."

The Greek word *pathos*, on the contrary, meant passion and suffering, and also all outer, accidental influences that might affect a thing or a person. The trend of style that took this name did actually veer from sereneness to emotion and passion, from hieratic impassibility to human suffering, from unaffectable idealism to naturalism with all its 'accidents.'

With the principle reversed, a general shift of ideals, aims and ends was inevitable. Permanence yielded to growth and change, typified perfection to personal character, and uninteresting beauty not seldom to fascinating ugliness. Norm and canon, the patterns of common traits, gave in to emphasis on individual differences; motion and action got the better of cool inertia; and picturesqueness supplanted sober statuesqueness. Life, nature, and truth were the slogans.

The notion of nature, however, calls for an adjustment, since the terminology of aesthetics has given prominence to a pair of unhappy categories, often opposed and still oftener confused: realism and naturalism.

They are neither synonyms nor antonyms. This book calls realism an artist's fidelity to the forms, proportions, and functions that nature has created. A realist gives his figures two arms, not four or six as a Hindu might do; he renders them in natural proportions and makes their muscles act in a physiologically correct, convincing way; and he places them in three-dimensional spaces. The logical antonym of realism would be irrealism.

What this book calls naturalism is a similar fidelity to nature; all naturalists are realists. Their particular attitude is to cherish nature in its innumerable characteristic forms of appearance, whether they are 'imperfect' or not. Indeed, in taking sides against the host of sweetish idealizers and, as Hogarth called them, nature-menders, they might accent the ugly and the imperfect—*la grossière nature* of the French academicians—and print, with Hindemith (Op. 25), as the headline of a movement: *Wild. Tonschönheit ist Nebensache* —fiercely. Beauty of tone is secondary. The correct antonym of naturalism would indeed be idealism.

In keeping with this terminology, ethos is idealistic, and pathos, naturalistic. Both may or may not be realisitic.

Irrealism appears in two main forms. One is the grotesque, dream-born art where, as the author once said of the Melanesian dance masks, "unfettered, free of all physical ties, the creative fantasy molds into new formation what nature has divided strictly into types and classes . . . And we have all of us set foot upon that kingdom where the masked dance had its real beginning: that dream world in which our horrors and our fears, quite apart from logic and reality, lump themselves into irrational apparitions."

The other main form of irrealism might also, and perhaps more appropriately, be called prerealism. Its followers are not interested in observing and copying nature, but rather, as children are, in giving shape to memory pictures. Weak and vague, these images are not organic wholes but disconnected details. A man is remembered as a complex of a head, a chest, and four limbs, all of which live in the artist's memory in their broadest, most characteristic aspects without foreshortening and without relation. Only in profile do you see the significant angles of the brow, the nose, and the lips with the chin, and the back of the head at the nape of the neck. The eye, on the contrary, with its long-drawn almond shape and the circular iris, appears in full front. Unconcerned with reality proper, the artist does not hesitate to compose a human body out of these disconnected mental images. The head is drawn in profile but the eye in front and the chest in full or three-quarter front, while the legs with the feet are given in profile, like the head. The same is true of group formations in painting and reliefs: they are never the products of snapshot observation but of a mental assemblage, whether or not the represented persons ever met at the same place or time. This is the law of Mesopotamian, Egyptian, and archaic Greek art. Indeed, not even the classic art of Hellas was entirely free of unorganic frontality.

Abstraction, as a type of style, is the willful neglect of reality in life and nature: it is irrealism. Uninterested in the exact, photographic representation of objects or scenes, the abstract artist has one of two very different goals. One is the elimination of snapshot accidents in the search of law, simplification, and archetypes. It is in a mild form manifest in the triangular patterns of composition that the Renaissance preferred and in the various canons of 'correct' and ideal proportions imposed on the human body, both in antiquity and the Later Ages. It is devitalizing in the radical geometrization of Egyptian and of modern art, in the sober prisms of pyramids and obelisks as well as in the paintings of cubists.

The other goal of abstraction is just the opposite: expression. There are two ways to reach this goal. One of them starts from life and nature but violates and stretches correct proportions in order to dematerialize the bodies. This is what the sculptors of the twelfth century did, and it is what Greco used to help his saints in conquering their earthly, mortal bounds.

The second way leads to vitalizing meaningless dashes in ornaments which convey energy, restlessness, infinitude—those ornaments that we find in the decoration of ancient Scandinavia, in the initials of Irish codices, and in the ravels of oriental arabesques.

Needless to say, the first goal of abstraction, thoroughly static, belongs to ethos, and the second goal, so fully dynamic, to pathos. Indeed, the two types of irrealism that we call abstraction are the extremes in either direction. In between, and facing both of them, is stretched the vast expanse of realistic art.

The word abstraction has been used in music to distinguish a fugue of Bach or a Mozart quartet in which nothing 'happens,' from some program symphony in which the composer describes or narrates an extramusical subject. The term is none too good. It implies neither the search for simplified archetypes nor the vitalization of lines meaningless in themselves (since this latter criterion would be true of the majority of melodies). In the interest of clearness, music, allegedly abstract, should rather be called 'nondescriptive.'

The basic difference behind all these partial antitheses is that ethos aims at the thing in itself, and pathos, at its changing aspects: the first wants the thing as it ideally *is*, and pathos, as it *appears* to the senses. Accordingly Sophokles is reported to have said that, while he himself drew men as they ought to be, Euripides drew them as they were. What he actually meant is better expressed in a similar pronouncement ascribed to Lysippos: that he carved men as they appeared, while Polykleitos had carved them as they were.

The two polar words *ethos* and *pathos*, though formulated in and for ancient Greece, express an eternal antithesis, which is general and flexible enough to lend itself to the different conditions of all nations, times and arts, and yet they are sufficiently specific and rigid to show the immutable factors in the evolution of style. Consequently, we keep them throughout the book, although, nay because, they are vague and often inadequate. For the less a term is specific, the better it suits those intangible complexities in art which elude determinate titles. The natural adjectives ethical and pathetic, on the contrary, have not been used. They would evoke undesirable connotations of a moral and an affective kind. And they would also be too handy: easy terms are easily misused.

Dualism is in any case prone to mislead into the fallacious thought that an art work necessarily belongs to one or the other side exclusively. The reader will see that this is hardly ever the case: *the two categories imply the courses steered toward one of two poles rather than the poles themselves.*

2. *ILLUSTRATIONS*

A FEW EXAMPLES will show how the antithesis *ethos—pathos* applies to the most heterogeneous manifestations of art.

The first is the Doric temple, main architectural expression of preclassic and classic Greece. Erected on a few steps, it is rectangular, wide rather than high, with one of its smaller sides turned toward the arriving worshipper. The front, or the front and the rear, or all four sides, are rows of powerful columns with their horizontal 'entablatures' of architraves and friezes, which again support the shallow gable roof. Above the architrave, the vertical movement of the columns resumes in vertically channeled tablets or triglyphs, which partition the frieze; and it is inverted, suggesting descent rather than ascent, in the tiny 'drops' below the triglyphs and even in the gables. Contrasting vivid colors and the alternation of shadow and light played an important role in keeping the individual parts from each other (Plate XXIX).

To the principles of balance and contrast, of simplicity and closeness in outline, the Doric architect added the principle of seriation: column–space, column–space—even and equidistant—follow without integration into higher units. And he added the principle of symmetry: from whichever side one looks at the temple, symmetry is perfect.

With symmetry and seriation, the Greeks of the fifth century B.C. were so much interested in 'being' and so strongly averse to casual 'appearing' that in one of the most amazing paradoxes they introduced deforming 'appearance' instead of correct 'essence' where the eye threatened to falsify the impression of 'being.' Greek temples are indeed not wholly devoid of irregularities deliberately arranged in a regular frame. To quote from H. van Buren Magonigle's book on *The Nature, Practice and History of Art* (New York, 1924): "In the Parthenon, for example, the columns are not spaced at equal distances; as they approach the angles of the temple they are set closer together; the corner columns which are seen against the sky and which the light therefore seems to consume somewhat by halation, are made thicker to correct this optical illusion; the outline of the columns is not straight but has an exquisite outward curve or *entasis;* and they diminish in diameter toward the top; the axis lines of all the columns not merely incline backward, but lean toward the center also to an extent that would cause them to meet at a height of about a mile; the walls incline backward; the *stylobate* or series of steps on which the columns rest is curved, springing upward toward the center; the line of the architrave, or lintel stones which rest upon the columns, follows another, similar curve. The only straight lines are those of the pediments or gable ends of the roofs, and in the Theseum, built a few years later, these, too are slightly curved."

What Mr. Magonigle wishes to prove is "the freedom of Greek design from any preoccupation with symmetry." What he actually proves is just the contrary: the Greeks were so anxious to create full symmetry that they eagerly acted against any optical misapprehension interfering with straightness or symmetry. They protected essence from appearance by making the appearance convey the essence.

Since the balance is perfect, since the equilibrium of vertical and horizontal forces, of supporting and supported parts bars any excess of power, since the even seriation is—or is made to appear—impeccable, the onlooker is not impressed with any one-way motion; his eye might follow the upward trend of the columns, but smoothly glides back along the soft ramp of the gable. Each part, at that, is strictly detached from neighboring parts by its shape and its color: the columns from their capitals, the architrave from the frieze, the cornice from the pediment. Nowhere is the visitor allowed to lose himself in vague distances; nowhere is his imagination stirred. Everything is open, direct, and sane; and the whole building, restful and unproblematic, breathes serenity.

The Gothic cathedral of the fourteenth century shoots high up over the lowly houses crouching at its foot. When you face it, turning around the corner of a narrow street, you stop short in rapture before the huge, confusing mass of ogives, turrets, towers that jerk your eyes up to the sky—"star-high and pointing still to something higher" (Plate XXX).

On entering, you lose yourself in a mystic tangle of naves, transepts, and chapels and in the twilight of heavy shadows scarcely lighted by the glittering fireworks of scarlet, yellow, bluish panes. In the main nave, you experience the same dizzying verticalism that the exterior has forced on you: unresisted and uninterrupted, bundles of slender pillars and ribs flow up to unreachable heights and intersect in the pointed vaults. But you cannot halt and yield to this pull; an invisible power pushes you from arch to arch toward the altar; in flesh or mind, you climb and advance.

From the parvis to the apse, the cathedral develops against symmetry. Even frontal symmetry, although accepted in principle, is willfully spoiled by architects who continue when the original designers have died, as show the one tower of Strasbourg, the differing towers of Chartres, the unequal portals of Notre Dame in Paris or Notre Dame in Mantes. The balance, too, is intentionally violated; the middle nave is from two to three times higher than wide, and flying buttresses must help to counteract the surplus of weight. There is no quiescence; everything seems to move. Strict caesuras are avoided. While in earlier Gothic churches the columns have still sharply marked capitals beyond which the ribs resume the upward surge, the later Gothic style suppresses all disjoining links and makes the columns with the ribs one piece from the ground to the vault; conjunction supersedes disjunction. To the plainness of the Greek temple, the Gothic cathedral opposes picturesqueness, and to its moderation, a tendency of growing to gigantic size.

The Charioteer in Delphi and the Gaul with His Wife are excellent paradigms of the basic antithesis in sculpture.

The Charioteer, made about 460 B.C., stands like a column, tall and slim, and channeled with the straight, vertical folds of his long robe. The outline is austere and close; even the hair fits tightly; and the feet firmly planted on the ground, are parallel. There is neither motion nor emotion (Plate XXXI).

The Gaul who has killed his wife and is stabbing himself to death was made about 200 B.C., approximately two hundred fifty years later, and has a Hellenistic character. Everything is pathetic, high-strung, restless, and open. The warrior, who with his left hand gently grounds the flaccid body of his wife and with the right hand thrusts the sword into his breast, presents himself in fourfold torsion. The legs are wide apart, the arms project, the muscles work, and a piece of cloth floats wildly to help in the *stretta* of the drama's closing scene (Plate XXXI).

The Last Supper was a favorite theme of the fifteenth and sixteenth centuries. Painted on the wall of some refectory it lifted the meal of the monks from bodily satisfaction to a spiritual community with God.

In the most famous Last Supper, Leonardo's fresco in Milan (1497), the dining room is strictly frontal and symmetrical; the supper table extends frontally all across the mural and by its four trestles and the knotted corners and ornamental stripes of its tablecloth emphasizes flawless symmetry. Christ, arms spread evenly out, sits right in the center before the middle window with his head in the vanishing point of the architectural lines. The twelve disciples to the right and the left are arranged in similar groups of three (Plate XXXII).

Decades later, Tintoretto tried his hand no less than seven times at the theme of the Last Supper. All his versions differ among themselves but unite in a common front against Leonardo's solemn, classic style. Where there had been strictest symmetry, balance, austere restriction to the necessary, and dignified tranquillity, Tintoretto used to place his table to the side and had it run obliquely into the depth of the room. Of food there is plenty, including fruit and dessert; Christ sits somewhere among the apostles or rages wildly with the stormy gestures of a wind god; unmannerly boon companions loll in their chairs, feed beggars and dogs, while cats impatiently try to get at the dishes and pans; and empty spots are filled with well-stuffed pantries, eager attendants, or bored and boring extras (Plate XXXII).

Music, far as it seems to be from the apparently visual dualism of 'being' and 'appearing,' of permanence and change, develops between exactly similar poles of tension. The rondo from Mozart's Sonata in C Major for piano, written 1788 (Koechel's *Verzeichnis* nr. 545) and a Toccata for Harpsichord or Organ by Johann Jacob Froberger (d. 1667) may serve as impressive examples.

Mozart's theme, graceful and unsophisticated, extends over four measures, ends in suspense on the dominant, but is at once answered with a full cadence on the tonic. This regular period of eight measures is repeated and then relieved by another theme also four measures long. But the first theme comes back and this time yields to a third theme; and thus the principal theme alternates eight times with some other melodic material. Schematically, it is ABACAD etc. (Example 35).

We need not look for new concepts or terms to describe the basic qualities of this music; most words can be taken from the description of the Doric temple without any change, however far the temple is from a rondo, Greece from Austria, and the ancient builder from Mozart. The alternation that leads to no definite ending is a typical form of 'seriation' and 'return' motion: the term symmetry has in the current language of music already passed from visual phenomena to the 'period' of two similar 'phrases,' the 'antecedent' and the 'consequent,' of which the first is semicadential and 'open,' and the second, full cadential and 'closed'; the marked caesuras at the end of each four measures make the piece essentially 'disjunct'; and the structure as a whole is clear and concise.

Johann Jacob Froberger's toccata, on the contrary, begins with

Example 35. Sonata *Mozart*

a powerful chord, sustained until one voice breaks loose and entices the other parts to free themselves and dissolve the heavy chordal harmony in a torrent which during sixteen long measures pursues its way, now soft and hesitant, now in violent cataracts. At last, the voices rally in a *fugato* on two themes, chase one another in chromatic modulation, get entangled in the oddest counterrhythms, and end in a thunderous cascade (Example 36).

There is development and one-way progression—quite free in structure, without alternation or symmetry, without caesuras, more diffuse than concise, and showy rather than reserved. Mozart's piece has no emotion except the minimum granted to playfulness. In Froberger's toccata, on the contrary, the hearer is from the first to the last note under the spell of an inspired improvisation in which the composer opens an escape, a very personal escape, to feeling and passion.

A last contrasting pair may be taken from descriptions in the author's *World History of the Dance* (New York, 1937).

The minuet, leading court dance between 1660 and 1760, "was performed in open couples; spectators and partners were saluted with ceremonial bows. With dainty little steps and glides, to the right and to the left, forward and backward, in quarter turns, approaching and retreating hand in hand, searching and evading, now side by side, now facing, now gliding past one another, the ancient dance play of courtship appears in a last and almost unrecognizable stylization and refinement" (p. 405).

Voltaire, a pioneer of dynamism, once ridiculed the minuet when he compared the metaphysic philosophers to dancers "who, most elegantly adorned, bow a few times, mince daintily across the room exhibiting all their charms, move without progressing a single step, and end up on the very spot whence they started" (p. 407).

The minuet was indeed more static, balanced, and unemotional than any other dance.

The strongest contrast will be found in the dances of primitive peoples. When the Wayeye in East Africa dance their frenetic full-moon dances, "all the parts of their bodies begin to shake, all their

Example 36. Toccata *J. J. Froberger*

muscles play, their shoulder blades roll as if they no longer were a part of their bodies. The drums resound louder and louder. The movements of the dancers become wilder and bolder. Their bodies are bathed in sweat from head to foot. Now they stand as though changed to statues. Only the weird jerking of the muscles over their whole body continues. Then when the excitement has risen to its highest point, they suddenly collapse as if struck by lightning and remain for a time on the ground as though unconscious . . ." (p. 18).

The few analyses on the preceding pages make evident that comparable styles exist everywhere—in the fine arts, music, and the dance; in antiquity, the Middle Ages, and modern times; in Greece, in France, in Italy. They also broaden our stock of stylistic qualities: to those that a quick comparison of the Hellenic styles has yielded—serenity, perfection, norm, permanence, beauty—they add the notions of symmetry, seriation, balance, return motion, disjunction, and several more, each with its antonym.

In this chance enumeration, the terms convey empty words rather than useful conceptions. But once they are properly arranged, they grant a firm foothold for further insight. They express (i) abstract notions which guide the artist, (ii) concrete qualities which the artist gives to his work under this guidance.

The abstract notions, all similar in scope, form

the perceptual antithesis: essence–appearance
the aesthetical antithesis: beauty–character
the correlative antithesis: impersonality–personality
the normative antithesis: limitation–boundlessness
the emotional antithesis: serenity–passion
the ethical antithesis: perfection–imperfection

all of which are comprised in the general antithesis: permanence–change.

It is hardly necessary or even advisable to discuss the one great contrast under each of these six headings. To avoid tedious repetition and overlapping, it will suffice to picture the general antithesis under the two aspects of the normative antithesis (Chapter VIII:

Limitation and Boundlessness) and the perceptual antithesis (Chapter IX: Essence and Appearance). The subsequent Chapter X will treat all structural features under the heading Close and Open Structures.

CHAPTER EIGHT

Limitation and Boundlessness

1. THEMES

ALL ETHOS STYLES have strict commandments—Thou shalt not . . .

Artists of the pathos side laugh at such restrictions. Art, they say, has not and cannot have eternal laws; it obeys the will of masters who, freed of the strait jacket of rigid tradition, create whatever and however their personalities impel them to create. The Roman poet Lucian, who lived in the 'baroque' times of the Antonine emperors, wrote: "The poet's fancy is the only law of poetry." Seventeen hundred years later, the German archromanticist Friedrich Schlegel proclaimed that the "caprice of the poet will suffer no law above itself" (translated by Irving Babbitt); and a few years after him, the Frenchman Victor Hugo emphasized that "There are neither good nor bad subjects, but only good and bad poets."

Thou shalt not . . . But people get weary of the eternal gods with the eternal smile in eternal beauty. How great is life, how boundless nature! Should we not plunge into its abundance instead of fleeing into the pale realm of normalized beauty? Should we not open our eyes to see how fascinating man is—not the immortal and therefor lifeless god but the mortal, living human, on the throne, in the workshop, in the street; not in the soulless serenity of Mount Olympos but in the bitter fight for life and death, and even in the petty doings of daily existence. Things so habitual that we have forgotten to notice them unveil their charms, but also things remote and rare—romanticism, says Walter Pater, is "strangeness added to beauty." Artists, then, would take to exoticism: the Greeks made their earliest portraits of the outlandish faces of barbarians; Rembrandt moved to Amsterdam's ghetto to have handy models out of the beaten track; Puccini laid the scenes of his operas in Italy, Germany, France, America, China, and Japan; and Charles Lewis Fox, depicting Indians of Maine, exclaimed: "The mission of art is too world-wide to confine itself to beauty alone."

Pathos artists are truly what Diderot was called by his own contemporaries: expansive, and what Irving Babbitt used to call eleutheromaniacs, freedom-ravers.

It has not always been a merely sensuous delight in character and variety that drives the artists away from serene and normalized beauty. Interest in the characterful ugliness of the queer and the ill-fated often creates understanding and sympathy, uses art as a powerful mirror to reflect the tragedy of man without make-up, and tries to stir and to help. Not writers alone have pilloried prejudices and wrongs; the Dickenses, Ibsens, and Zolas are not the only fighters on this side. As early as the fourteenth century, daring painters challenged authority by relegating popes and emperors with tiaras and crowns to the damned in their Last Judgments; in the seventeenth, Jacques Callot's fascinating etchings, *Les Misères de la Guerre*, protested against the barbarism of warfare; in the eighteenth, Hogarth exposed the vices of his time; around 1800, Goya gave a strong prosecuting touch to his engravings; and again one hundred years later, Käthe Kollwitz drew the poor man's doom with all the silent eloquence of her crayon.

Such preacher's fervor has been common to many pathos styles, although in different shades and intensities. It is what Father Mersenne meant when in his portly *Harmonie Universelle* of 1636 he emphasized that music should force its way into the listener's soul and lead him whither the composer wishes.

Thus it is no contradiction that Zola started the twenty volumes of *Les Rougon-Macquart*, the natural and social life of a French family under the Second Empire, while Wagner was working on the *Nibelungen*, or that *Parsifal* and Ibsen's *Ghosts* came out at the same time. No greater contrast could be imagined: the naturalistic writers, who soberly and almost scientifically kept the readers in the present world, and Wagner, who grandiloquently led his listeners away into the misty land of myth and saga. Yet both belong in the climate of pathos, of forcing their "way into the listener's soul."

One might hesitate for a moment: does not myth in its agelessness represent the element of permanence required in styles opposed to actual life? Was not myth the almost exclusive theme of the ethos age in Greece? True, Hellenic mythology, in its unworried serenity, if not beatitude, had indeed the proper atmosphere of ethos styles. But not so Nordic mythology. Far from perfection, sereneness, or permanence, its scenery is wild and cheerless and its events are stirring, strange, and even exotic despite all actual or alleged ties of consanguinity. Everything is immoderate, extreme: ice and fire have created a world inhabited by tiny dwarfs and by giants so huge that two of the gods, Loki and Thor, once passed the night in the thumb of one of their mittens. Muscular strength is unbelievable, and unbelievable is the capacity of stomachs: Thor, the thundergod, would eat an ox, eight oversize salmons besides the cakes prepared for all the women, and he would drink two barrels of mead. There is action all the time—galloping, fighting, hunting, storming. And far from being serene, Nordic mythology is deeply tragic and death-conscious. Odin, father of the gods, gives one of his eyes for winning insight into the future; and the future he sees is impending disaster: *ragnarök*, the Twilight of the Gods, the end.

2. *DESCRIPTIVENESS*

Objects absolutely beautiful, so Plato says, cannot represent or imitate. Representative or imitative art, he holds, does not contain its own essence and is, therefore, not autonomous.

In times of pathos, on the contrary, without limitation of, and interest in, absolute beauty, the individual arts put up with tasks beyond their capacities. Indeed, many of their masters have particularly delighted in exacting of their arts more than their fathers had risked. This does not mean the dubious achievements and tricks of technique—not the overdelicate traceries of the Flamboyant style which call for wood or wrought iron rather than for stone; not the inadequate performance of Beethoven's violin concerto on a mandolin (which actually occurred in the 1920's); not the cheap imitation of silk and velvet in marble on Italian tombstones; nor the bronze blood that in Cellini's Perseus statue protrudes from Medusa's neck like the stuffing of a doll; not even Bernini's attempt to force the shapelessness of immaterial clouds on rigid blocks of marble. I mean, in a more spiritual sense, the trend to overstepping the natural boundaries imposed on every art by its very nature and to prescribing for one art such themes as would more convincingly be treated by some other art.

We all know the misled authors who hopelessly exert themselves to describe in a torrent of words sceneries that a painter's brush perfectly conveys in a few dashes or those who, with the poet Leconte de Lisle, require that "the first concern of the man who writes in prose or verse should be to set in relief the picturesque side of outer objects." To which Gotthold Ephraim Lessing had already about a hundred years before objected that "any one who would paint directly with words some visible object is forced to enumerate one after the other the different parts of it, and a blurred and confused image must necessarily result from this piecemeal enumeration of details, from this attempt to render the coexistent by means of the successive" (the two quotations from Irving Babbitt, *The New Laokoon,* Boston–New York, 1910).

The opposite way, however, is much more usual: to borrow from literature and to thrust upon the fine arts, music, and the dance such topics that rather need the unequivocal precision and descriptive force of the word; or to violate statuesqueness by charging sculpture with stories of hasty transition, thus inverting Lessing's words and attempting to render the successive by means of the coexistent.

Perhaps the most astonishing example of the latter type is Lorenzo Bernini's early marble in Villa Borghese at Rome, probably of the 1620's, which describes how Daphne, fleeing from Apollo, is pitifully changed into a laurel tree when she can no longer escape. Apollo, for sculptural reasons too close to his victim, looks like an eager attendant rather than a lover; and the nymph, in whom metamorphosis has already set in, seems misshapen—half-woman half-tree—because a sculptor can show how a certain person looks at a certain moment but is unable to show transformation. The group is an audacious challenge to the natural laws and limits of sculpture; it renders unsuccessfully what a poet has narrated in an incomparably better way (Plate XXIII).

Ovid's poetic metamorphoses, of which Daphne's is one, have not eluded seizure even by musicians. In 1785, the Austrian composer Karl Ditters von Dittersdorf wrote twelve symphonies 'expressing,' as the title says, one metamorphosis each—Phaeton's crash, Actaeon and the Lycian peasants being changed, one into a stag, and the others, into frogs, Perseus rescuing Andromeda, the petrification of Phinaeus, and seven more. It was fortunate and certainly necessary that a novelist, Johann Timotheus Hermes, retranscribed the twelve from music into words. But then, had not Ovid's words been better?

Trespassing, alas, is well, all too well known in music. It has led to a handy term, program music, to heated arguments pro and contra, and consequently to many controversional books and papers. Most of them could have been left unread and unwritten. Their authors, under the naïve delusion that music began with Bach, have acted as attorneys either for the prosecution or for the defense of that incriminated branch of music without even knowing the documents.

Whether with or without council's permission, descriptive music has existed since the infancy of mankind. For it rests on one of the fundamentals of all art: on the eternal delight in making-believe without lying; in creating illusion without trying to dupe; and in finding analogy in divergence. Bushmen reproduce to the point of illusion the gaits of animals with a light rod that taps the single, weak-toned fiber string of the musical bow; and Siberians imitate cackling geese, barking dogs, and cantering horses on their jaws' harps; just as the horse's gallop has been counterfeited in Liszt's

Mazeppa and Wagner's *Walküre*. Church bells and chimes, from the heavy drones of the largest to the delicate tinkling of the smallest, have been depicted in the sixteenth century—by *a capella* singers in Senfl's Bells of Speyer, and by a harpsichord in Byrd's famous piece from the Fitzwilliam Virginal Book; human voices have imitated warbling birds and wauling cats, cackling women, drums and trumpets in chansons and madrigals—indeed, Béla Bartók has given us in his *Mikrokosmos* an ingenious, witty *Diary of a Fly*. So frequent is imitation that music history has produced some special monographs on Thunderstorms in Music, Water in Music, Horses in Music.

In larger forms, such episodes of sound imitation cannot avoid a somewhat scenic connection: the idea of galloping horses widens into the vision of a hunt with horns and dogs and all the hurry of the day or the imitation of bird calls develops into the picture of woods, in which the birds awaken one by one to greet the dawn.

In a way, Honegger's *Pacific 231* for orchestra (1923) and George Antheil's *Airplane Sonata* for piano (1931) are stragglers of this seminarrative style. True, Honegger denied having "aimed to imitate the noise of an engine." But the musical expression of "a visual impression and physical enjoyment," which opens with "the quiet breathing of the engine at rest . . . and finally reaches the lyrical pathetic state of a fast train, 300 tons of weight, thundering through the silence of the night at a mile a minute," can hardly be looked on as 'absolute' music.

There is no sharp borderline between these larger forms of description and actual narrations, in which composers try to relate in the language of music some story of their own or, oftener, of a poet's or a painter's invention. A story told by a poet, a mood created by a painter find their way to a musician's imagination more easily than stories untold and moods unshaped by a previous artistic concentration. Algerian Kabyls describe the combat against the lion on a single flute; similarly, the Greek Sakadas won the Pythian prize in 586 B.C. by a performance on a pair of pipes of Apollo's fight with the dragon; and in later Greece, the paean depicted through music all kinds of human activities and natural phenomena. An almost uninterrupted pedigree reaches from that day to Richard Strauss's *Alpensymphonie* (1915), with some truly naughty children around 1700. This adjective does not so much apply to Johann Kuhnau's six Biblical sonatas for clavichord or harpsichord (1700) where, for instance, the flight of the Philistines from David as a breathtaking fugue in presto is today as convincing as it might have been in its own time. Johann Fischer's idea, however, of describing how they work salt in the pits of Lüneburg in an overture, an entree, an aria, a minuet, and two ballets is, to say the least, bewildering. But then did not Marin Marais in 1717 write a piece for viol and harpsichord to give a *Tableau de l'Opération de la Taille*—the operation for stone in the bladder (Example 37)!

Example 37. L'Opération *Marin Marais*

Romantic narration, from Berlioz to Strauss, has partly turned away from the description of acts and facts to egocentric psychology: the Fantastic Symphony or *Lélio* or Harold in Italy are no less Berlioz himself than *Zarathustra, Don Quixote*, and *Ein Heldenleben* are the confessions and portraits of Strauss.

Altogether, there is no rigid separating line between absolute and program, between nondescriptive and descriptive music. They run into one another, as ethos runs into pathos, as white runs into black in a gamut of grays.

DESCRIPTIVENESS

Not all descriptive music is narrative or imitative in the sense expressed above. There has been a species that for readers with a liking for nice Greco-Latin terms might adequately be called synaesthetic concomitance: the reinforcement of an idea, mood, or act by using two mediums and addressing two senses instead of one, just as we reinforce the spoken, audible word by a visible gesture or smile. Consciously or subconsciously, composers avail themselves of appropriate musical gestures to strengthen conceptions expressed in the text.

The Gregorian chant would trill or coo when birds occur in the words—*Passer invenit sibi domum* (the sparrow hath found a house); and notions high and low have in all times affected the course of melody—rarely have such words as *ascendit* or *descendit* not been answered by some rising or falling group of notes. Bach once prescribed an actual *campanella*, a carillon connected with the keyboard of the organ, to toll in his cantata *Schlage doch gewünschte Stunde*. And in certain requiems—Verdi's, for instance—the allusion to the Doomsday trumpet in the *Dies irae* on the text words *tuba mirum spargens sonum* releases long drawn-out trumpet signals in the orchestra. Berlioz, finding the effect too poor, has instead devised four full-fledged brass bands high up in the corners of the church with cornets, trumpets, trombones, and ophicleides. But the result is empty noise not awe or terror. Composers of the non-illusionistic type, like Brahms, would never attempt so hopeless an undertaking.

Such synaesthetic concomitance, however, is only the inner field of description. In a spacious outer zone, all music—seemingly absolute and certainly neither imitative nor narrative—is actually inspired by, or at least suggestive of, some definite character, mood, or event. Of this kind are the little pieces—*Charakterstücke* in German—from Farnaby's *Toye* and Peereson's *Fall of the Leafe* in Elizabethan times to Robert Schumann's *Kinderstücke* and Debussy's *Cathédrale engloutie*. And we should include the numberless *tombeaux* composed, from about 1640 on, as éloges and mostly in the form of some dance, with their admirable straggler, Maurice Ravel's

Tombeau de Couperin (1914–17). Nor should we ignore the more or less well-done portraits beginning with *Doctor Bull's my selfe*, the humorous harpsichord piece in the Fitzwilliam Virginal Book (*c.* 1600) which so nicely closes in a doubtful question mark, and concluding with Edward Elgar's *Enigma Variations* (1899), with each variation addressed to one of his friends.

Actual borderline cases between descriptive and absolute music are not designed to describe or to transcribe but to express with musical means the mental atmosphere that some poetry or painting has created in the composer's imagination. It is in this spirit that Ossian's alleged verses gave their mood and color to Mendelssohn's Hebrides Overture; that Wilhelm Kaulbach's mural of the battle against the Huns inspired Liszt's symphonic poem *Die Hunnenschlacht*, and Böcklin's painting *Gefilde der Seligen*, Weingartner's symphonic poem of the same title; but also, the other way around, that the music of Brahms evoked the visions of Max Klinger's *Brahmsphantasie* etchings.

'Absolute' music, however, is by no means in itself indicative of ethos. Quite the contrary, ethos periods, fond of reason and definiteness, have generally given preference to vocal music and its unmistakable meaning, while purely instrumental music needs a good amount of pathos in its native soil to allow for its fancy and vagueness. The famous challenge "*sonate, que me veux-tu?*" (sonata, what do you want of me?) came from a country whose music has mostly been on the ethos side.

In such a vocal spirit, the Golden Age of Greece rested satisfied with musical instruments in a truly primitive stage and confined their role chiefly to mere accompaniment. Plato, fanatical prophet of ethos, had in the second Book of the Laws something to say against musicians who "divorce melody and rhythm from words, by their employment of *kithara* and *aulos* [lyre and pipe] without vocal accompaniment, though it is the hardest of tasks to discover what such wordless rhythm and tune signify." This is nothing less

Women's Dance around the Man. Paleolithic rock painting from Cogul, Spain

Paleolithic Mask Dancers

Cavern of Teyjat, Dordogne

Cavern of Trois Frères, Ariège

Homer. National Museum, Naples

PLATE II

Laokoön. Vatican Museum, Rome

PLATE III

Ivory book covers

Cambridge, Fitzwilliam

Frankfort am Main, Municipal Library

PLATE IV

Ivory in the Gospel, *fd. latin* 9393, Bibliothèque Nationale, Paris, middle 9th century (*after Adolf Goldschmidt*)

PLATE V

PLATE VI

Head of Christ. Bronze Crucifix, Werden, Abbey Church

Saint Elizabeth. Cathedral, Bamberg

Tympanum of portal. Abbey Church, Moissac (*University Prints, Newton, Massachusetts*)

PLATE VII

PLATE VIII

The Ancestors of Christ (?). Column men, west front, Cathedral, Chartres (*University Prints, Newton, Massachusetts*)

e Presentation of the Christ Child in the Temple, Pulpit of Nicola Pisano. Baptistry, Pisa
(*University Prints, Newton, Massachusetts*)

unciation and Nativity, Pulpit of Giovanni Pisano. S. Andrea, Pistoia (*University Prints Newton, Massachusetts*)

PLATE IX

Mourners from the Tomb of John the Fearless, Klaas Sluter. Museum, Dijon (*University Prints, Newton, Massachusetts*)

Annunciation, Simone Martini. Uffizi Gallery, Florence (*University Prints, Newt Massachusetts*)

PLATE X

Expulsion from Eden, Masaccio.
Brancacci Chapel, Florence

Miniature of the Hours of Milan, Palazzo Madama, Turin

PLATE XI

The Creation and Fall of Man, Ghiberti's doors. Baptistry, Florence

Madonna, Nanni di Banco. Cathedral, Florence

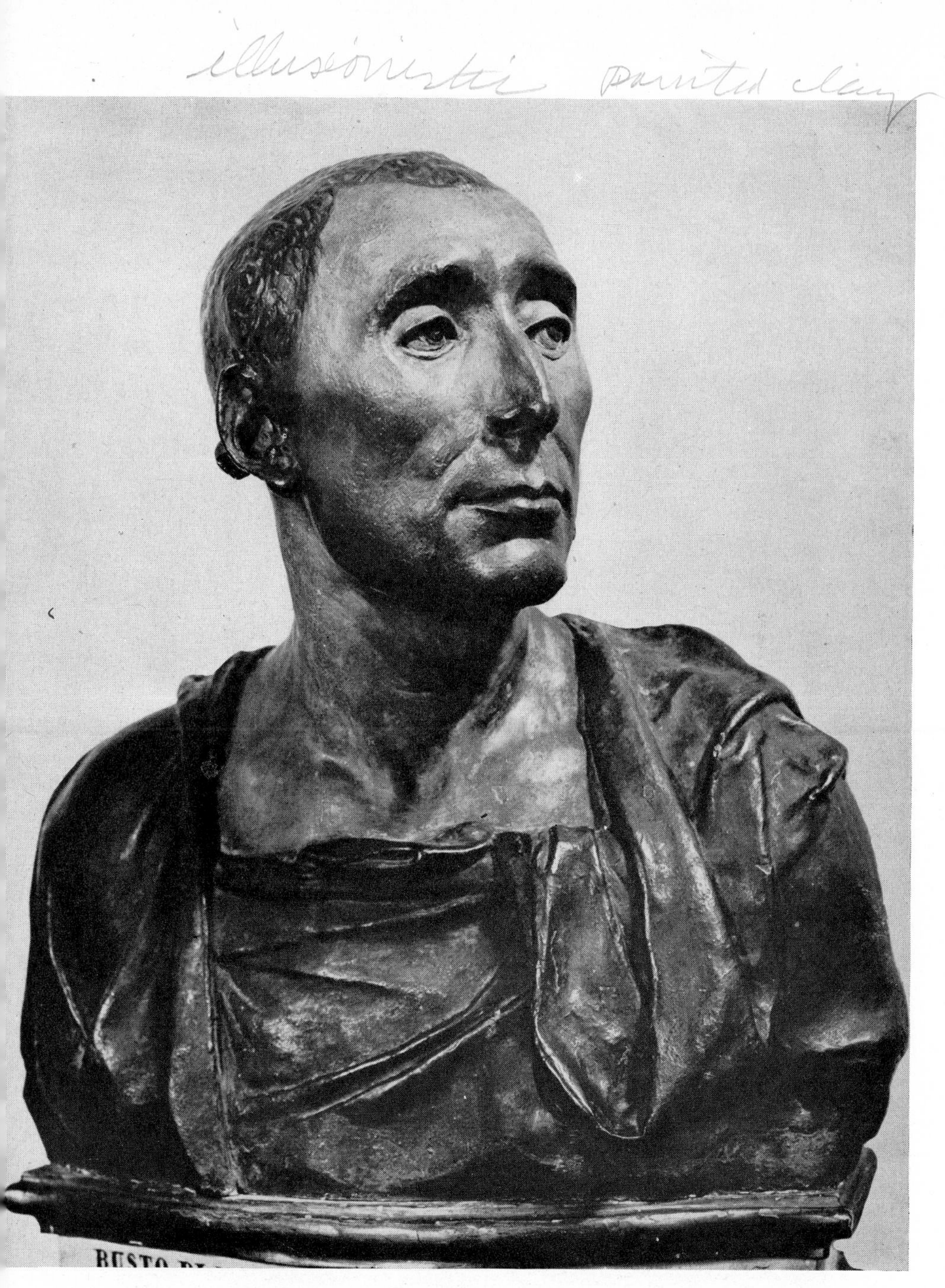

Niccolò Uzzano, Donatello. Bargello, Florence

Princess of Este, Pisanello. Louvre, Paris

PLATE XIV

Confinement, Ghirlandaio. Santa Maria Novella, Florence

Tasks of Hercules, Pollaiuolo. Uffizi Gallery, Florence

PLATE XV

Sposalizio, Raphael. Brera, Milan

PLATE XVI

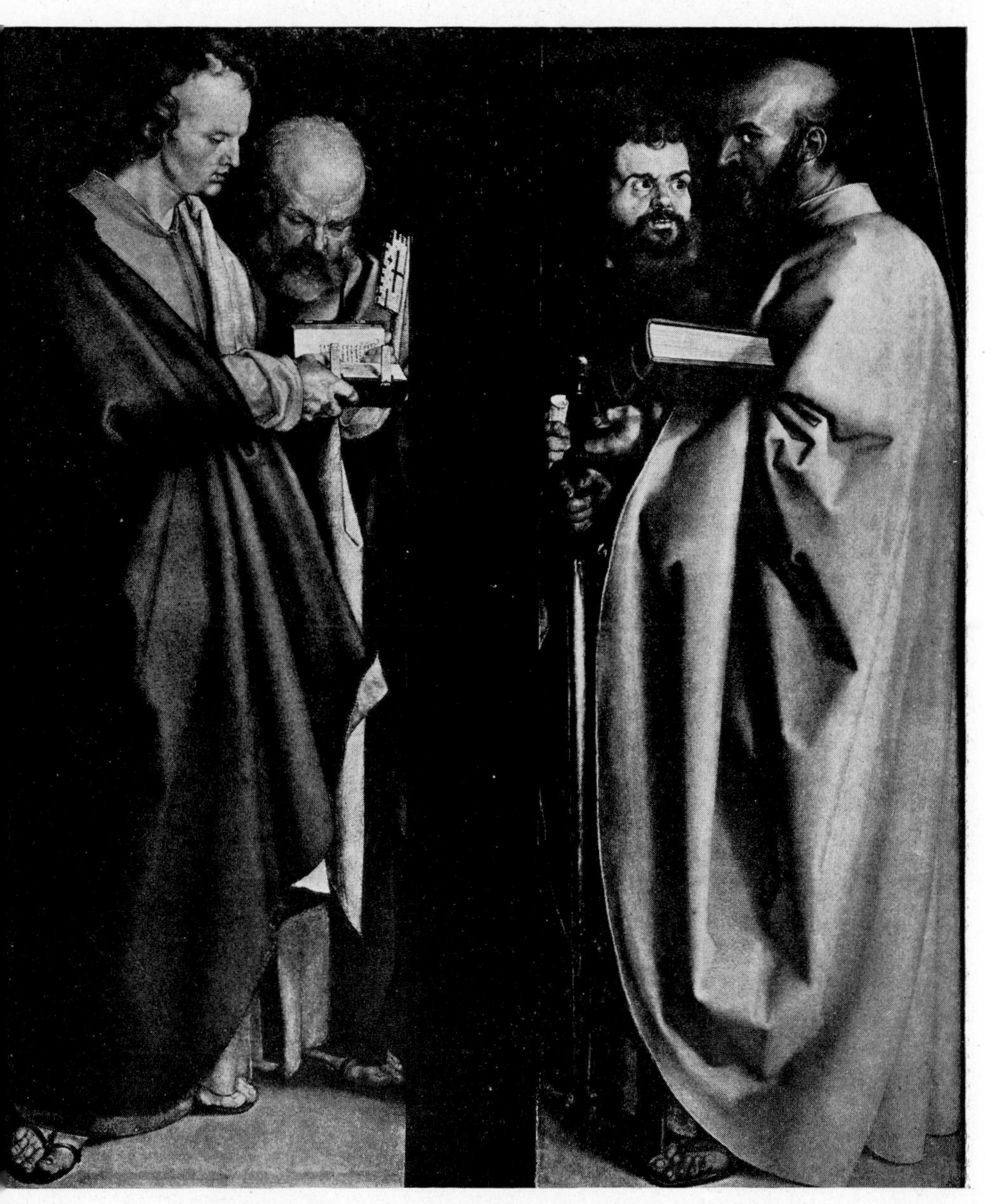

Apostles, Albrecht Dürer. Alte Pinakothek, Munich

PLATE XVII

PLATE XVIII

PLATE XIX

Tomb of the Medici, Michelangelo. San Lorenzo, Florence

Christ, Michelangelo. St. Peter's, Rome

Laura de' Dianti and Alfonso da Ferrara, Titian. Louvre, Paris

PLATE XX

Wedding at Cana, Veronese. Louvre, Paris

PLATE XXI

David, Lorenzo Bernini. Villa Borghese, Rome

PLATE XXII

PLATE XXIII

Daphne, Lorenzo Bernini. Villa Borghese, Rome

Saint Theresa, Lorenzo Bernini. Santa Maria della Vittoria, Rome

Louis XIV, Rigaud. Louvre, Paris

PLATE XXIV

Stage decoration, Bibiena

PLATE XXV

PLATE XXVI

Graces, Chardin. Louvre, Paris

PLATE XXVII

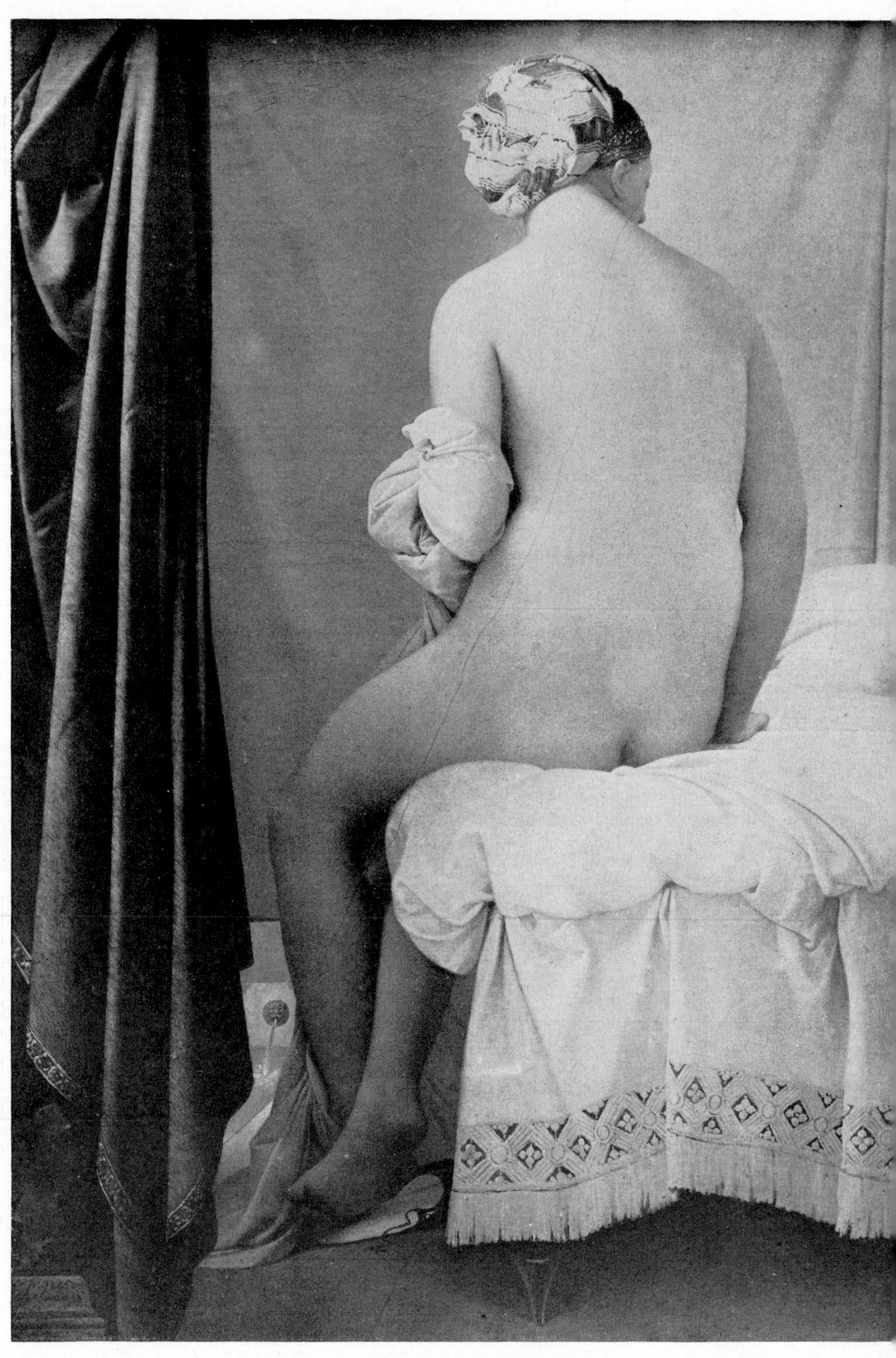

The Bath, Ingres. Louvre, Paris

PLATE XXVIII

The Parthenon, Athens

PLATE XXIX

The Cathedral of Rouen

PLATE XXX

PLATE XXXI

The Delphian Charioteer

The Gaul with His Wife

The Last Supper, Leonardo da Vinci. Santa Maria delle Grazie, Milan

The Last Supper, Tintoretto. S. Trovaso, Venice

than a wholesale damnation of instrumental music. Hellenism and Rome, on the contrary, seem to have allowed for a good deal of self-sufficient instrumental music and accordingly had instruments with technical improvements.

In the Middle Ages, there was but little mention of instrumental music in Romanesque times. In the Gothic centuries, however, all music for dancing, ballads, *rondeaux* and *stantipedes* passed into the hands of pipers and fiddlers; huge orchestras met in extempore 'jam' sessions; and at last, an independent literature for keyboard instruments and lutes sprang up. Again in the Later Ages, the Renaissance, as the period of vocal *laude*, *frottole*, madrigals, and chansons, was followed by the Baroque and its stress on instrumental forms, on consorts, sonatas, toccatas, suites, and concertos. But there, again, the earlier, rather ethos-minded generation had questioned instrumental music: in 1600, Emilio dei Cavalieri, the composer of *La Rappresentazione di anima e di corpo*, had deemed all music without words boring.

More than a hundred years later, in 1712, a London daily, *The Spectator*, insisted that music is "only valuable as it is agreeable to and heightens the Purpose of Poetry . . . ; to say it shorter, mere musical Sounds are in our Art no other than nonsense Verses are Poetry." Again one hundred years later, Beethoven's contemporary, Justus Thibaut, the famous professor of law in Heidelberg, as the center of an influential circle of purists, interceded in favor of *a cappella* music against the recent flowering of instrumental forms in the nineteenth century. This unprecedented bloom of instrumental music in the nineteenth century—of symphonies, symphonic poems, overtures, chamber and piano music—would have been quite impossible in a less pathos-minded time.

The dance has always granted a dominant role to description: the dancer shares his motor impulse and gesture with the nondancer, who far from art conveys ideas, moods, and facts to fellow men. There is no definite borderline separating anybody who wishes to express himself from the actor, and again separating the actor and the dancer. Many dances of primitive and half-civilized man are descriptive. He imitates the animals in their gaits and behavior, and acts out his planting, rowing, hunting, fighting, his courtship, love, and death. Without a program, a complicated performance might be unintelligible; husbands would confess they did not understand what their wives were dancing and vice versa.

India, the nation paramount in well-established gesture, has molded the elements of descriptive dancing in an incomparably sophisticated system. But sophistication is not compatible with ethos: the Hindu dance is far beyond the stage of expression in the sense of pathos.

The same is true of the dances in classic antiquity. Tradition, convention, systematic regulation took possession of descriptive dances created in periods of pathos—the Cretan *hyporchémata*, which in rhythm and gesture rendered the mythical action of the text, the sword dances, and the original, orgiastic Dionysian dances from which the drama was created. They methodically taught *phoraí*, the gestures conveying emotions or acts, and *schémata*, the gestures portraying some person. The Romans placed the pantomime in the center of the dance. Lucian, Greek poet in Roman days, could say: "the dancer's principal task is to draw continually upon an unfailing memory of ancient story, and this memory must be backed by taste and judgment. He must know the history of the world, from the time when it first emerged from Chaos down to the days of Cleopatra the Egyptian . . . Since it is his profession to imitate and to show forth his subject by means of gesticulation, he, like the orators, must acquire lucidity."

Group dances of the Middle Ages were full of description. Maddened dancers acted their own crafts in haunting the graveyards—ploughing, weaving, spinning. The *moresque*, out of which the modern ballet developed, once represented the combat of the crusaders against the Saracens. The *ballo*, one of the most distinguished social dances of the fifteenth century, often pictured characters or little scenes and had appropriate titles: *La Mercantia*, the woman who confers her favors on all, performed by a lady with three gentlemen, one beside her and two behind or *La Sobria,* the lady who bestows her favor on only one—a group of three, the lady between the two men. These pantomimes, however, had apparently lost the traces of action, of byplay and gesture, and were successions of figures, which did not actually depict the scene, but suggested it in a more abstract way to those who knew.

Even in the sixteenth century, most dances had pantomimic elements at the beginning of their careers. In the galliard, the man traversed the hall once or twice with his partner; but the lady retreated to the opposite end; there, the dancer courted her with increasing intensity until the music finished. In the courante, three young men invited three girls, led them one after another to the opposite side of the room and, retreating, left them standing there. Then they went back with amorous looks and gestures, dusted their shoes and arranged their shirts. The ladies, however, refused their hands and turned their backs, and the dancers had to retreat again without having achieved their purpose. At the end, all three came forward and, on bended knees and wringing their hands, begged for mercy. In a similar way, the early waltzes and polkas, if not pantomimic in a narrower sense, were at least significant, meaningful.

But all social dances, of whatever century, lost their pantomimic or significant traits after awhile and survived as mere step patterns.

Painting and sculpture need hardly as much space as music in a section on descriptive art. Acting through and upon the eyes, they are bound to visible form and thus must keep much closer to the descriptive than to the nondescriptive pole. But in principle, the dualism of descriptive and nondescriptive music is paralleled by the dualism of objective and nonobjective styles in the fine arts. One of its extremes is the latest objectless painting, which aims so much at purity of rhythm, structure, and color that all objects from life and nature are dismissed as unessential and even disturbing. And sculptors, still more referred to visible form than the painters, have not only deindividualized but actually dehumanized their statues in order to express movement in the purest form. In a last abstraction, nonobjective art becomes mere ornament (of the nonnaturalistic kind), that is, an arrangement of lines which, like the arabesque or the meander, convey some form of motion, force, and temperament without evoking the memory of living objects.

The other extreme is the kind of anecdotic illustration, in which nothing much matters besides the story it tells. This is the case in the spiral strips of relief that climb the memorial columns of Roman emperors to commemorate their campaigns and victories or in Bernini's Baroque metamorphosis of Daphne, described earlier in this section. Examples of anecdotic art in later ages, around 1760, are the sentimental paintings—The Village Bride, the Father's Curse, The Punished Son—by Jean-Baptiste Greuze who, in his contemporary Diderot's admiring words, was the first "to link events of which it would be easy to make a novel." Somewhere between the two extremes, Whistler emphasized his concern with problems of painting beyond or even above the object, by calling his portrait of some girl a *Harmony in Yellow and Gold*, or the portrait of a gentleman, *Arrangement in Flesh-Color and Black*.

But matters are not that simple. Different from music, most art, if not always anecdotic, has at least been illustrative. It conveys stories, scenes, and objects that people know and understand. A madonna, a portrait, potato diggers, a reading girl, and even a landscape or a still life are in the first place intended to convince the onlooker by the very rendition of their subjects. How much the artists might have thought of merely artistic values above and beyond this rendition is in retrospect hard to decide; and it is still harder to know how much of the artist's personal contribution was appreciated by the laymen. However this may have been, painting and sculpture, as extravert arts, have mainly kept to the objective and music, as an introvert art, to the nonobjective side.

Architecture has no place in this section. It *is;* it does not depict.

A discussion on overtaxing the means of art should not pass by the excessive demands that certain styles have made on the operatic stage and—the spectators.

Demands on the stage were highest in the Italian opera around 1700, which has accordingly been called the machine opera. Abbé Raguenet's interesting pamphlet, *Parallèle des Italiens et des François en ce qui regarde la musique et l'opéra* (1702) describes it in detail: "I think, the genius of man in stage-engineering cannot progress beyond what it is in Italy today. In 1697, I saw in the opera at Turin how Orpheus charmed the animals with his beautiful voice; and there were many kinds, like boars, lions, bears; nothing could have been better acted. A monkey did his antics; he climbed on the backs of other animals, scratched their heads, and did whatever monkeys do. On another day, I saw an elephant on the stage. He fell to pieces, and an army stood in his place: the soldiers had formed the elephant merely by their shields, and as perfectly as if he had been a real elephant. In 1698, I saw on the stage of Capranica in Rome a puppet woman surrounded by guards. She opened her arms, stripped, and became a palace with façade, wings, and additional buildings in delightful style; when the guards pounded their halberds, they were transformed into fountains, cascades, and trees to be its park. Nothing could be quicker, nothing more artful and miraculous than these metamorphoses."

Demands on the spectator's capacity and willingness to be deceived were made in the nineteenth century. A hasty look at Wagner's music dramas catches the burning palace in *Rienzi* and the pinkish couple that at the end of the *Flying Dutchman* is towed to heaven; the cardboard swan in *Lohengrin;* the *Rheingold* giants who supplant size by clumsiness, and the dwarfs who unsuccessfully stoop; and, worst of all, the end of the *Götterdämmerung*, where a steed, supposed to bound into the flaming pyre, happily trots from the stage while the paper tide of the Rhine swallows the silently crashing canvas palace and high up in the sky a rosy transparency tries to convince the spectator that fire is consuming Valhalla with its heroes and gods. Indeed, it is but a step from the sublime to the ridiculous. And we had better close our eyes to the unreal realities of the scene and let imagination play.

Wagner would have been within his rights had he objected to our comparison of his would-be illusionistic stage with the complicated *macchine* of the late seventeenth century. Wagner's stage indeed served the meaning and action of his dramas, not sensation or surprise. Yet both phases in the evolution of the opera agree in challenging the spectator's readiness to be deceived and in overtasking the illusionistic possibilities of the stage.

Such readiness on the part of the public and, in general, delight in overcoming inadequacy seem indeed to be characteristic traits of pathos. What else is the meaning of Heinrich Biber's *Passacaglia* for solo violin or of Bach's *Chaconne* and his other works for one unaccompanied instrument, which in deadly earnest exact of one soloist and his more-than-limited means the complicated polyphony of an entire group of players or at least a suggestion of such polyphony?

As Goethe said: "*Den lieb' ich, der Unmögliches begehrt,*" I love him who pursues a hopeless cause.

3. THE MIXING OF THE ARTS

ALL THESE FACTS have touched upon the antithesis: purity versus merger. Critics solicitous about purity in art, who object to the liberal acceptance of themes and to overtaxing the capacities of the individual arts, must likewise resent the unconcerned mixing of arts and art forms.

Thus Lucian, Greek writer of the second century A.D., vigorously objected to mixing the genres in poetry; and long before him, Plato, the purist, had scorned the new men of his time who dared to mingle dirges with hymns and paeans with dithyrambs. What would he have said had he lived to see John Dowland's *Lachrymae or Seven Teares, Figured in Seaven Passionate Pavans* (1605) or, similarly, the *tombeaux* of the seventeenth century, which were dirges, frequently written *en forme d'allemande*, that is, in the form of a dance (an idea that Maurice Ravel resumed in 1899 with his *Pavane pour une infante défunte*). What would he have thought had he seen the fusion of a French overture with the suite of dance movements to form the modern sonata or the mixture of the concerto and the symphony in the nineteenth century. Indeed, what would Plato have said of composers who, anxious to give their works a maximum of intensity, add the impressiveness of singing voices and the definiteness of words to the vaguer speech of instruments—of Beethoven, Félicien David, or Liszt, who ended symphonies in choral climaxes, or of Arnold Schönberg, whose second string quartet Op. 10 culminates in two soprano songs on words of Stefan George.

All vocal music, to be sure, is in itself a merger of two arts. But, strictly speaking, it is less a merger than a primeval sameness since poetry, normally and originally, cannot be separated from singing. Thus, ethos has not only tolerated but even favored vocal music; indeed, Plato, and many purists after him, on the contrary proscribed wordless instrumental music as vague and irrational. But in doing so, they have given to one of the two combined arts a dominant place, while the other has to be content with an auxiliary role.

The Greeks gave the first place to poetry; melody followed the poet's inflections and meters so closely that composers rarely indicated the time values of their notes. This kind of supremacy has not existed in Western civilization because European meter distinguishes its syllables by accent, not by length. Instead, Western ethos has favored neutral melodies with unpretentious accompaniments of simple chords lest the listener's attention might be distracted from the words. No wonder that, in the 'classic' period around and after 1800, Goethe preferred his friend Zelter's respectable settings of his poems to Schubert's meddlesome vagaries. Such neutral music—to which many of our folksongs, anthems, church tunes must belong—lends itself easily to heterogeneous poems and, within a poem, to each of its stanzas, different in character as they may be. It is bound to a certain pattern of verse and rhyme, not to any particular mood or action.

But ethos admitted melogenic just as well as logogenic music:

the composer, reading and rereading a poem, would find a melody springing up in his mind and allow it to follow its own way even if it wronged correct enunciation. The works of Brahms are full of such melogeneity: he would accent *Holder klíngt der Vogelsáng*, where the words require *Hólder klingt der Vógelsang.*

Pathos, on the contrary, has always striven for higher units in which no component was allowed to dominate. Hugo Wolf's *Lieder* (around 1890) are the outstanding examples that refute both Zelter and Brahms. His music is never overbearing and never mere accompaniment in the ordinary sense; while it faithfully follows every syllable of the poem, both in the voice and the piano, it intensifies the poet's verses and says what words alone are not given to convey.

Lust for intensity led to unexpected issues. About 1900, some German protagonists of pathos propagated that lieder should only be sung at the appropriate time of the day—cheerful morning songs before noon, and songs with twinkling stars and an amiable moon, at night. Indeed, they postulated that carefully chosen perfumes be sprayed in the audience to create the right emotional atmosphere. From this it was not far to the "first experimental perfume concert in America" given in 1902 at New York in the Carnegie Lyceum. But do not bear malice toward the *fin de siècle:* as early as the first half of the eighteenth century, the Frenchman Father Castel had planned a *clavecin des odeurs.*

Readers of Joris Karl Huysmans' novel *À Rebours* (1884) cannot help thinking of its hero Des Esseintes who, in the words of Irving Babbitt, "built into the wall of his dining room a cupboard containing a series of small kegs arranged side by side, and each having a little silver spigot at the bottom. He connects these spigots with one another so as to form a kind of keyboard on which he can play his mouth-organ . . . Des Esseintes drank a drop here and there, played inner symphonies for himself, succeeded in procuring for himself in his throat sensations analogous to those that music pours into the ear . . ."

After all, scent hearing was not too far from color hearing which, whether or not physiologically founded, has been a perfectly legitimate *synesthesia* or coupled sensation familiar to many people—Vincent van Gogh for example—and has led to the merger of a chorus plus orchestra, organ, and piano with many-colored, changing lights in Scriabin's symphonic poem *Prometheus* (1913), and to the experiments of Laszló and others in the same field. And here, too, Father Castel had anticipated the idea in his *clavecin des couleurs* of 1734.

Sculpture and painting have in pathos styles been merged in two forms: as the combination of carved figures with painted backgrounds, particularly in the *Stationen* or episodes of the Passion and in the *Krippen* or crèches, both characteristic of the South German Baroque; or else in the realistic coloring of Spanish wooden statues between the sixteenth and eighteenth centuries. In recent times, the Russian Alexander Archipenko resumed the combination of both arts on the irrealistic, unillusionistic side as 'sculptopaintings.'

Architecture has often in a similar way combined with sculpture and even with painting. Later Gothic churches are unthinkable without their stained-glass windows, and in many styles the walls were nearly meaningless without their murals. South German painters of the sixteenth century covered whole façades with paintings, the best known being by Hans Holbein the Younger and Georg Keller. It is significant that one of the most important architects of the second half of that century and the author of the leading book on *Architectura* (1593–94), was Wendel Dietterlein, a painter.

Not that ethos styles have excluded paintings, reliefs, or statues from their buildings; but they have always confined them to filling in empty surfaces, as in the pediments and friezes of the temple in Greece. In pathos styles, on the contrary, sculpture has frequently been an organic part of the edifice or has even fused with it. In the Erechtheion on the Akropolis, karyatids instead of columns support the tablature, and in the cloister of St. Bertrand-de-Comminges, from the twelfth century, the statues of the four evangelists fuse to form a column.

In the piled-up sculpture on certain Romanesque churches, Notre

Dame de la Grande in Poitiers for instance, and, very like them, on Indian temples and *stupas* such as the Borobudur in Java and the Angkor Vat in Cambodia, the orthodox-classical concepts of architecture have lost their meaning. Chartres Cathedral is said to contain no less than ten thousand figures, and the roof of the Duomo in Milan, two thousand. And how much the Gothic column men were considered parts of the building can easily be seen on churches in France where iconoclasts of the Revolution struck them out of their grooves. The Italian Renaissance kept architecture and sculpture strictly apart but the Baroque again delighted in fusing them. "In the finest work of the Baroque," says H. V. Lanchester in his book on Fischer von Erlach, "no dividing line can be found between architecture and sculpture, as the one flows insensibly into the other."

The peak and almost a caricature of mixing the arts in the Baroque period is Narciso Tomé's noted or notorious *Transparente* in the cathedral of Toledo (1721–32), a huge altar of jasper, marble, bronze, and painting in illusionistic perspective with the light stagily shining through the film-thin stone—which an enthusiastic Spaniard has called the eighth wonder of the world and a Frenchman, cooler and less polite, a *fricassé de marbre*.

If I add a paragraph on the merger of music and the dance, I risk being reproached with truism. However, I do not mean the self-evident accompaniment of the dance but rather dance and action that accompany music.

The essential fact is that primitives and, in general, men of pathos leanings are hardly willing or able to disconnect the various ways in which we express ourselves: gesticulation, the voice, and facial movements; any impulse of motion or emotion releases them as one inseparable complex. Disconnection is, as we daily experience, a result of natural or educational restraint and reserve, that is, of ethos. Our own civilization tends to suppress gesticulation in talk and public speeches and, in a similar way, it discourages performing musicians from facial expression and time stamping. Hence the unwillingness to allow a singer to convert his motor urge into dancing.

An impressive illustration of disconnection as a symptom of a civilization turning to ethos is the famous passage in II Samuel 6:16: "And as the ark of the Lord came into the city of David, Michal Saul's daughter looked through a window, and saw King David leaping and dancing before the Lord; and she despised him in her heart." David, once a shepherd, was a survival of nomadic days, but Michal, the daughter of the first of Israel's kings, already shared in the new mentality of a resident, settled society.

Between the two extremes, disconnection is not necessarily abrogated but it is at least artistically controlled. I think of the ancient Elamic court players who, on a well-known Assyrian relief of about 650 B.C. (in the British Museum), advance with the lifted knees of hop dancers. I think of women all over the Near and Middle East who, like the Biblical Jewesses, like Miriam or Jephtha's daughter, sing and dance and beat the drum in one. And I think of the Yemenite Jews, who never sing their antiphonies "without one or two couples of men dancing—slowly at first and thereafter in an ever increasing tempo up to a frantic prestissimo" (the author's *Rise of Music in the Ancient World*, N.Y., 1943, p. 95) or of Robert Lachmann's Kabyl flutist in Algeria, who in a crouching position acted the horse as it shied from the lion and who, in a later episode, managed to free one hand to illustrate how a girl ground barley and did her hair. And above all, I think of the carefully studied gestures and dance steps of Greek theatrical choruses from which choreography itself derives its name.

All these partial mergers have been outdone by the opera or musical drama. Poetry, action, singing and the orchestra, the dance, and the painted stage with its props unite to give a drama utmost intensity, without (in principle, not in fact) allowing any of these components to dominate. Wagner called it the *Gesamtkunstwerk*, the work embracing every art. But the idea itself was not entirely Wagner's nor was it a child of the romantic nineteenth century. It had guided the Italian masters who founded the opera of 1600 and had reappeared in the eighteenth century in the reforms of

Gluck and, without poetry, of Noverre, after ethos trends had alienated the opera from its original ideals of fusion.

An episode of 1865 illustrates the contrasting attitude. Wagner, rehearsing the first act of *Tristan,* shouted at the extras who were mooring the ship and winding up the hawsers that, if they did not strictly conform to the characteristic rhythm of the orchestra, his music was written in vain. Peter Bayersdorfer, a Munich art critic of the ethos side who had attended the rehearsal, went home and sardonically entered in his diary: "This we will not forget, Mister Wagner; you concede that your music does not mean a thing unless somebody pulls the ropes!" . . .

4. THE FUSION OF THE DIVINE AND THE SECULAR

PATHOS ART, prone to set aside all limitations, can hardly be expected to honor the often artificial boundaries that separate the religious and secular spheres. A charming French legend from about 1200, *Del Tumbleor Nostre Dame,* The Tumbler of Our Lady (re-edited in *Romanische Texte* 1, Berlin 1920), tells how an old juggler, who did not know how to sing or read or pray in Latin, renders his ecstatic homage to the image of the Virgin in his own way, performing dances of Champagne, Lorraine, and Brittany, whirling, jumping, somersaulting, and walking on his hands. And the pious friars peep into the church, wonder, smile, and understand.

Three or four hundred years later, two Spaniards, Juan Timoneda and a certain Salvá, dedicated their pavans to the Mother of God, though it must be said that the Holy See, less pathos minded than the artists of Spain, at least put the former on the Index.

Jan van Eyck, who worked in the first quarter of the fifteenth century, left a delightful painting: smiling and placid, the Virgin has descended from the altar and with the Child in her arms is walking in the deserted nave of the church. The day is drawing to a close; the heavenly queen is now only a mother. She is showing her child the stained-glass windows which shine in the last rays of the sun, and perhaps will let him touch the embroidered chasubles and the crucifixes with their gleaming gems. The cathedral itself seems transformed: from a gigantic, unapproachable temple it has become God's quiet home.

Petrus Cristus, little younger than van Eyck, depicted a Netherlands goldsmith's tidy shop with an engaged couple who try their wedding rings—a slim circular line around the master's head, and nothing but this line, makes known that he is Saint Eloy, patron saint of the goldsmiths, and that consequently the little painting has a religious subject.

But one visit to a larger museum leads to the realization of how often painters have given the Mother of God traits and forms that normally lead to courtship rather than to worship. In the 1440's, Jean Fouquet perpetuated the memory of Agnes Sorel, his sovereign's beautiful mistress, in a portrait (today in the Museum of Antwerp) that represents her as the Virgin with the Child on her lap, exposing the most provocative breast ever painted. This is the spirit in which Paul Heyse's and Hugo Wolf's *Italienisches Liederbuch* dreams: "Would that thy charms were painted . . . that all should now turn Christian and love thee. Of ev'ry heathen straight 't would converts make, they'd all be Christians true for thy love's sake." Three years after Wolf had composed this song, Rodin conceived a Christ and the Magdalen, in which the beautiful nude embraces and kisses her crucified Savior in a paroxysm of awe.

Things were worst in the seventeenth century. In a hymn *O Jesu meus amor*, published in 1688 in a Venetian collection with the title *Philomela angelica*, an Italian nun sings, indeed gasps, after her Savior as if he were her lover in the flesh: *Veni, veni, veni, veni, amo te, mea felicitas, mea lux . . . ô ô ô ô veni, meum cor*—Come, come, come, come, I love you, my sunshine, my light . . . oh, oh, oh, oh, come, my heart. So she ejaculates and the melody pictures concupiscence as no other melody has done. Short, breathless phrases, interrupted by rests, all gliding downward, jerk and rage and palpitate and re-start in growing excitement a seventh, octave, ninth above. Saint Theresa, as Bernini has sculptured her in Rome—a lady in silk, prostrate in ultimate carnal rapture and surrender while a knowingly smiling Cupid aims his dart—Saint Theresa would sing this hymn if her mouth, agape to receive Christ's kiss, could burst into melody (Example 38).

Example 38. O Jesu meus amor *Anonymous Nun*

Germany's contemporary religious movement, pietism, indulged in a similar salacity though with less power and taste. This kind of poetry is not easy to translate into English; but the attempt may be made with one of the least bombastic poems, Friedrich Spee's *Gespons Jesu*, that is, Spouse Jesus:

Das Flämmlein das ich meine	The flame I have in mind
Ist Jesu süßer Nahm,	Is Jesus' sweetest name,
Es zehret Mark und Beine,	It gnaws at pith and bone,
Frisst ein gar wundersam,	It oddly eats at one,
O Süssigkeit in Schmerzen!	Oh sweetness in the suffering!
O Schmerz in Süssigkeit!	Oh suffering in the sweetness!
Ach! Bleibe doch im Herzen,	Alas! Stay in my heart,
Bleib doch in Ewigkeit.	Stay for eternity.

To musicians, heaven was no less close to earth. The learned chapel master, sitting down to write a new mass, did not silence the familiar tunes that buzzed in his head: *Se la face ai pale* (If my face is pale) or *L'Homme l'homme l'homme armé* (The armed man) or *Le serviteur* (The servant). And unhesitatingly he used, as many had done before him, one of them as the cantus firmus or melodic spine of his work, without thinking that such connection of the religious and the secular could be a sacrilege. Only the ethos generation of the Council of Trent and of Palestrina in the 1560's put an end to the indifferent intrusion of worldly melodies.

Protestantism was equally unprejudiced. Luther and his followers took entire melodies from well-known love songs, and no congregation resented the fact that the chorale *Von Gott will ich nicht lassen* originally read *Einmal tat ich spazieren* (One Day I Took a Walk); that *Auf meinen lieben Gott* had come from Jacob Regnart's *Venus du und dein Kind* (Thou Venus and thy Child); that *O Haupt voll Blut und Wunden* had originally been Hans Leo Hassler's lied *Mein G'müt ist mir verwirret von einer Jungfrau zart* (My Mind is all Confused About a Tender Maid). Nor does it hurt American feelings that the hymn *Holy Spirit, Truth Divine* is a pious disguise of Louis Gottschalk's piano piece *The Last Hope.*

5. THE FUSION OF ART AND LIFE

THE CONTRASTING TENDENCIES toward purity, on the one hand, and fusion, on the other, lead to opposite needs—either to insulate the work of art from the life without or to shun such insulation. Rather, we should avoid the term 'work of art.' As long as we enjoy a work of art as such, we are conscious of its distance from life and nature; no fully illusionistic work belongs to art. Within art, there is still an enormous span from simple realism to quasi-illusion, from the delight in a convincing rendition of life and nature to the almost complete deception which leaves no space for aesthetic values. Realism may be almost at zero and just allow recognition of an object as such or it may be so strong that in curiosity, horror, or sympathy we can hardly detach ourselves from the subject. And it seems that moving from lesser to greater illusion we move from ethos to pathos.

Illusionistic is the 'diorama'—a picture, without the usual kind of frame, which you see through a window. When you change your position, the borders change with you—as in nature—and you easily imagine yourself attending the scene depicted.

This illusionism is climaxed in the 'panorama' of the later nineteenth century, where a battle is painted on a huge, endless canvas running round about the spectators' central platform and, under a cleverly devised light, gives the illusion of miles and miles of horizon, while a few full-clad dummies of killed soldiers and some real equipment adroitly arranged before the canvas mislead the eyes. Genoese palaces of the Baroque age are not basically different from panoramas, when their flights of court yards and stairs climb up the hills and end in painted vistas which make one believe that other court yards continue and at last open into a park.

The sculptural counterpart of diorama and panorama is provided by waxworks, which are not expected to give aesthetic pleasure, but rather to fascinate by their exceedingly small margin between reality and skill.

Not basically different were the later times of Greece when the lust for illusion, trespassing upon this margin, threw life and art together. Young men, we learn, demanded to be locked up in the temple at Knidos to pass the night with the statue of Aphrodite; and legend tells how Daidalos, the sculptor, had to chain his statues lest they run away, or how Pygmalion fell so desperately in love with the image of Galatea which he himself had carved that Aphrodite brought her to life and married them.

While writing this paragraph, I attended a performance of Shakespeare's *Othello*, and when at the end the actors came out and bowed to the applauding public—Othello, who had just committed suicide, hand in hand with Desdemona, whom he had just strangled, and Iago, reunited with Emilia, whom he had stabbed to death—I thought of *Parsifal*, where no applause or bowing singers was permitted. This too shows a bit of ethos and pathos: in *Othello* illusion, indeed, the work of art itself, are brusquely cut off, and the actor is restored to his own personality; in *Parsifal,* illusion is intended to persist, and both the singers and the public are only gradually dismissed from the world of appearances.

Having broached on theatrical reminiscences, I might add an episode from Max Reinhard's staging of Offenbach's *Orphée aux Enfers* at the beginning of this century. In the formal meeting of the gods, Venus, severely asked by the presiding Jupiter why she was giggling, answered: "Wassmann is tickling me!" The name of the actor, not that of his role, dis-insulated the play at one blow.

Gradual dismissal from the world of the stage was in the Baroque age counterbalanced by a gradual admission of the audience to the scene: engravings of theater interiors show that the stage continued the columns and friezes of the house which step by step assumed the character that the act required.

Musical conducting has known the same antithesis. Chorus leaders in ancient Greece and Rome used a thick sandal made of two hinging boards with cymbals inside, which under the stamping foot clapped together with a sharp metallic sound. Lully died in 1687 from an infection he had incurred when his long baton pounded his foot instead of the ground. In the sixteenth century, on the other hand, Stefano Vanneo, Bermudo, Sancta Maria, and others had condemned all audible beating; later, Jean-Jacques Rousseau complained that the Parisian opera did not abandon noisy time stamping. And in 1786, Goethe wrote angrily from Venice that he would have enjoyed the oratorio in the Mendicanti church, "had not the d . . . ed conductor beaten the time with a roll of music on the grill and clapped as impudently as if he were teaching schoolboys . . . I know, the French do it; but I would not have expected it from Italians."

Such practices were indeed abuses. But they could occur only where audiences were able and willing to insulate music from accidental noise. The late King Fuad I of Egypt told me how once, attending *Parsifal* in Bayreuth, he had furtively looked at his watch, and how at the click of its case a thousand devotees had indignantly turned toward him. This is the other extreme.

Insulation and encroachment as problems of composition will be discussed in their proper place in Chapter X (Addition and Unification).

6. SIZE AND DENSITY

No EXAGGERATION—*medèn ágan* and *nil nimis*—was the claim of Greeks and Romans in classical times. Ethos, with moderation as the dominant rule of conduct, has always steered a golden middle course; carefully dodging extremes, the size of its works of art is measured by the size of man himself. A classic period never would have created the gigantic statue of Helios in Rhodes, one of the Hellenistic Wonders of the World, or the Colosseum in Rome (A.D. 72–80) which, six hundred twenty feet long, accommodated some hundred and ten thousand spectators; or, for that matter, the three hundred and sixty foot tall rock Buddha of Chia ting fu (A.D. 730). It would not have covered a thirty by seventy-three foot wall in the Ducal Palace at Venice with the one monster mural of Tintoretto's Paradise; nor would it have raised the Empire State Building in New York to the height of 1,248 feet.

Size has been most conspicuous in the fashions. Tall steeple and sugar-loaf hats, over-long pointed shoes, broadening epaulettes, lengthening tails, and swelling crinolines are typical pathos features, which would not have been possible in Greek antiquity or in Florence around 1510.

In music, size has shown in the duration of individual pieces, in the numbers of performers, and in the dimensions of instruments or even of score books.

We do not know how long representative pieces were in the classical and the nonclassical times of Greece and Rome. And we are not too sure about the length of music pieces in the Middle Ages either. But we are perfectly safe in more recent music. Even the most unsophisticated concert goer and opera fan knows the impressive length of the unabridged Passion according to St. Matthew, the B minor Mass, the *Götterdämmerung*, or, for that matter, the whole four-night cycle of the *Ring*. The music historian would add that the performance of Monteverdi's *Orfeo* (1607) lasted eight hours, and that a *nūba*, an Arabo-Andalusian cantata, has similar dimensions.

Pleasure in mass and number can easily be traced to certain phases of antiquity: the Chinese T'ang Dynasty had several court orchestras, of which one outdoor band comprised no less than 1,346 men. In Rome, delight in size is about the only trait of music made known in the existing sources.

The courtly poets of the fourteenth century indulged in enumerating the many kinds of instruments that played at the festivities given in honor of their heroes. Guillaume de Machaut, composer and poet, recites thirty-six types of instruments played in the princely feasts described in his epos *La Prise d'Alexandrie*, and twenty-eight, in his poem *Li Tems Pastour*, with several men to each or at least to some (since he puts most of them in the plural and mentions, among others, more than ten pairs of horns—*cornes, plus de dis paires*). All players, "kempt and scrubbed," performed together in chance orchestral ensembles, and "such melody was never seen or heard before." The orchestras of angels that contemporary painters depict confirm that the poets were not fibbing.

Larger orchestras and choruses have in all centuries been characteristic of pathos generations. At a Roman banquet in 1564, the year of Michelangelo's death, the chorus had fifty voices and the orchestra, eighty pieces. Exactly one hundred years later, Sebastiano Locatelli found in Lyons between forty and fifty viols and between fifteen and twenty violins in the orchestra which, he said, made a noise as if they called to battle. And while England, untouched by Baroque tendencies, refused as late as the middle of the seventeenth century to duplicate parts, Corelli performed his *concerti grossi* in 1682 at Rome with no less than a hundred fifty instruments. It is hardly necessary to speak of the last act: the continuous growth of the orchestra from Beethoven and Berlioz to Mahler, Strauss, and Schönberg is generally known; and the nickname of the Symphony of the Thousand which a clever manager has given to Mahler's Eighth characterizes the idolatry of size in the prewar world.

The size of orchestras is a dangerous criterion, however, and should be handled with care. Money and other extramusical factors have often interfered with purely aesthetic trends. Just for this reason, Hector Berlioz's vision of an ideal orchestra is more effective than reality with all its limitations could actually make it. Topping the three hundred players and four hundred singers in Lesueur's *Messe du Sacre* for Napoleon's coronation (1804), he dreamed of four hundred sixty-five instruments, including one hundred twenty violins, forty-five 'celli, forty violas, thirty-seven double basses, thirty harps, and thirty pianos. Berlioz had indeed the pathos sense of size. When he saw St. Peter's in Rome, he was so much impressed by its overwhelming dimensions that he at once planned to match them in an *oratorio colossal*, The Last Day of the World. Luckily, he forgot about it but later realized at least one of the outstanding features he had planned to give it: in the *Tuba mirum* of his Requiem (1837), as already mentioned, he tried to give an adequate idea of the terrifying Doomsday trumpet by letting off no less than four complete brass bands in the four corners of the church besides the orchestra proper and a battery of sixteen kettledrums.

Berlioz's dream, however, could not have competed with the realities of Patrick Gilmore, the "supersalesman of music" in America, who between 1864 and 1892 conducted concerts with a band of a thousand pieces and a chorus of ten thousand, with fifty anvils, bells, and a battery of cannon outside firing on the beat, for which he had in 1869 built the Temple of Peace in Boston to seat an audience of fifty thousand . . .

How happy Gilmore would have been had he lived to see Convention Hall in Atlantic City and hear the organ with its seven manuals, more than twelve hundred stops, and 32,882 pipes!

The size of recent organs, too, and in general of instruments has indeed been a symptom of pathos. In the dynamic time of 1376 a Frenchman mentioned *grosses bombardes*, bass shawms, as *nouvelles;* in the no less dynamic year 1614, a certain town musician Hans Schreiber in Berlin constructed the earliest octave trombone, twice the size of the ordinary tenor trombone; and in 1618, the same man was working on a double bassoon; "if he succeeds," writes his contemporary Michael Praetorius in *Syntagma*, "it will be a marvellous instrument, the like of which nobody has seen heretofore." Praetorius' hope hardly came to pass; both instruments were unsuccessful in their time. But both were revived in pathos times, the double bassoon by Joseph Haydn and Beethoven, and the double trombone by Wagner for the *Ring*.

Speaking of Berlioz, we should not forget his enthusiasm for Jean-Baptiste Vuillaume's *octobasse*, a giant, clumsy double bass thirteen feet high, which had the strings stopped by seven pedals and played with a bow supported by blocks. And speaking of America, we cannot ignore the wide and sparkling bell of the sousaphone, which so impressively towers over the heads of the band and adds so little to its musical glamor.

If size means growing outward, density means growing inward. Density in music shows in the number of voice parts, in an opaque orchestration, and in a profuse harmony.

French and Flemish composers at the end of the fifteenth century occasionally increased the usual number of voice parts; Brumel wrote an *Et ecce terrae* for twelve voices, Josquin des Prés a *Qui habitat* for twenty-four, and Johannes Ockeghem a canon *Deos gratias* for thirty-six voice parts.

Two generations later, the English court organist Thomas Tallis composed a motet *Spem in alium*, and Striggio another, *Ecce beatam lucem*, both for no less than forty voices.

When—again two generations later, in 1628—Salzburg inaugurated its new cathedral, Benevoli had written a brilliant gala mass for eight choruses vocal and instrumental, the whole accompanied on two organs. There are fifty-three staves upon one another in a score almost three feet high and twenty-two inches wide.

Notwithstanding a few stragglers, the end of the polychoral style was reached in the first half of the eighteenth century with a *Kyrie* for forty-eight voices by Giuseppe Ottavio Pitoni (d. 1743). The composer must have looked with particular relish at the three foot seven size of his score.

Density also shows in harmony. The most instructive illustration of German density versus Italian rarity is Bach's translation of Vivaldi's concertos for violin and orchestra into concertos for harpsichord *solo,* where he stuffed out the original wherever it was too thin to his taste, and particularly by adding sevenths to the simple triads of Vivaldi's scores.

To see what dense and rare mean in orchestration, it suffices to compare the horn-crammed score of *Tristan* with Verdi's *Falstaff:* they are typical of the difference between the ideals of Germans and Italians. Density, to be sure, is where it belongs when Wagner holds the pen. There are quite different cases, though. Hans Leo Hassler's playful madrigal *Mein Lieb will mit mir kriegen* (My love would battle with me) in the grandiose double-chorus setting of Venetian gala motets, the harmless fairy-tale opera *Hänsel und Gretel,* with the full *Meistersinger* orchestra to paint the innocent sleep of two little children, or the even more heavily clad *Sinfonia Domestica* in which Richard Strauss describes his life at home with wife and child are among those slips in taste that occur in pathos times and lands more easily than in the province of ethos.

Just as the pathos musician shuns limpidity and vacuum, his fellow painters and sculptors have often overcrowded the scenes on reliefs and canvases without allowing their figures space enough to move or breathe. It suffices to compare the loose composition of the Olympia and Parthenon pediments with the closely packed reliefs on Roman sarcophagi.

And this is true of architecture, too: nothing could be more confusing than the piled-up domes and columns of St. Mark's in Venice or the Romanesque Church of St. Front in Périgueux. Where one column with one capital would suffice to carry its part of the wall, where one pilaster would be enough to separate two panels, the pathos architect often clusters three, five, seven of them, the more to impress what he wishes to express: overwhelming force and riches. Such clusters are characteristic of certain phases of the

Romanesque and the Gothic style and also of the Baroque. Masters of the seventeenth century like Borromini in Rome would even take a step further and arrange their clustered pilasters at different angles so that the eye, drawn inward and outward, is much more strongly affected than if the pilasters stood in parallel planes. This is increased density; but it is also duplication and redundancy.

7. *REDUNDANCY*

REDUNDANCY is nowhere more critical than in the dance.

There is no country in which people dance without some sort of musical accompaniment; there is no epoch in which dances are performed in silence. Dance cannot exist without music. Primitive dancers stamp the ground, strike their bodies, clap their hands, or beat the drum; and if not the dancers themselves, then the bystanders do. Take the castanets from a Spaniard and forbid him to snap his fingers: he will hardly be able to dance. The two arts are basically one, and the Greeks were right when they embraced both under one name, orchestics.

Such oneness, however, poses a fundamental problem. Is it meant to be redundancy, that is, reduplication, or rather a difference which produces unity on a higher level? There are a few strange facts in primitive dancing: with certain North American Indians and Eskimos, the rhythm of the dance is entirely different from the rhythm of the accompanying drum, as nine-eighths against eight-eighths. And one East African people dance more and more slowly as the tempo of the accompaniment increases. In the famous whirl dances of Egyptian dervishes there is no apparent relation between the whirl and the music: neither melody nor rhythm duplicate the movement of the dancers, nor do they anticipate or imitate corporal gesture. And yet the spectator feels that this, and no other, is the right music: it supplies an inspiring background, with which the dancing blends into a higher, spiritual unity.

This may also be the mystery of the Javanese and Balinese dances. Dreaming, the leader starts to play a soft and almost unreal melody, and presently the gongs and xylophones unite in a tinkling, clattering symphony from which we see the dance arise. But the dancers are entirely indifferent to the musical details and do not try to render them by steps or gestures. The orchestra provides the mood, the motor impulse, and a rhythmic inspiration; it never gives the dance itself. The music has but little meaning without its dance, or the dance without its music. Alone, each is incomplete.

Incompleteness of either partner is in fact the justification of partnership: sharers are not expected to duplicate their work but to contribute, with assigned parts, to a common success.

Again and again, some of our dancers put self-sufficient music pieces on their programs and while there is a regular concert on the stage, they hopelessly try to translate the music into body movements—a loud note by a vigorous stamp, a soft one by a soothing, gentle gesture. When the melody rises, the head and the arms are likewise lifted to worship nobody knows what idol; and when the next melodic step goes down, the dancer drops his arms, inclines his head and, abandoned by his god, tumbles down, a picture of dumb despair.

It is obvious that dancers and, for that matter, all 'kinetic,' motion-conscious persons, feel a motor urge in response to melodic contours and that, by virtue of their particular gift, they react with a bodily gesture. But it makes a decisive difference whether we spontaneously answer to a stimulus or deliberately create a work of art for others to look on. Quite certainly a melody is born out of a motor impulse similar to that which leads the dancer to a corporal gesture or attitude. But the gesture that a melody seems to convey is essentially different from the bodily gesture. It has none of the restrictions to which the dancer's body is submitted; it knows no bone or joint or ligament; it is invisible and impalpable; it is the abstraction, the last essence, the soul of a gesture. The dancer who tries to translate a musical gesture actually pulls back to the earth what has glided away into the realm of ideas. He takes possession of a freed soul and reimprisons it in a body; he embodies the spirit when he ought to spiritualize the body.

What, then, can be done? The answer is: when the dancer has no music made to order, he should choose music in which subjectivism, emotion, and duplicating gesture are repressed to a minimum—in other words, music of the ethos side.

Redundancy in a more intellectual sense has been frequent in the musical drama. Its typical form is the leitmotiv, leading motive, a short musical phrase given as a permanent escort to a person (Siegfried), some fateful object (the ring), an important notion (the curse), and is heard whenever these appear on the stage or in the thoughts of those present. Some are of the gesture type: the motive of the ring in Wagner's *Nibelungen*, which describes a circle of thirds and reverts to its starting note; or the motive of Wotan's, Siegmund's, and Siegfried's sword, which suggests the weapon drawn, brandished, and flashing in the sun. But most are of the character type: the Valhalla motive with the megalithic monumentality of its simple D flat major chords; the stubborn, defiant, and almost barking rhythm of the Hunding motive; or the tender motive of Brünnhilde's love with its ecstatic turn to the upper sixth.

The leitmotiv is redundant because it generally duplicates: all spectators see Siegfried enter the scene and yet the orchestra, as a reliable commentator, announces, "And now, Siegfried is coming." Somebody on the stage retells the story of the ring, of the gods, of the Välsungen, and again the commenting orchestra hurries to hammer in every person, every object mentioned in the tale.

In a broader sense, redundancy is not only concerned with leitmotivs proper, but also, and more so, with all musical illustrations of the text. One characteristic example that occurs to me can be read in the score of Strauss's *Salome:* when John the Baptist urges the princess to scatter ashes upon her head, you hear three slight and almost dusty triplets, starting very high and coming down—delicate fingers sprinkling three pinches of ash (Example 39). I personally like this passage, so full of *esprit* but it makes me smile, which is not quite in the spirit of St. John's sermon, though the composer him-

Example 39. Salome *Richard Strauss*

self might have smiled when he was writing it down. Giovanni Battista Doni's *Trattato della musica scenica* had, three hundred years before Strauss, stated that musical illustration of details was best at home in the world of humor.

8. SYMBOLS AND CRAFT

It is dangerous to call such illustrations symbols. The true musical symbol is redundant, too; it re-enforces some notion just as these motives do. But it is neither audible nor intended to be heard; it appears graphically, only in the notation of a piece, not in its sound, and can at best be seen and grasped by those who perform it. Motets and madrigals of the sixteenth century were particularly full of symbols. Where the poet spoke of light, day, white, or pale, composers often answered with notes unfilled and white; and, in the opposite case, they rendered darkness, night, and blindness by notes filled-in and black. The word *crux*, cross, was illustrated by two dovetailed melodic steps; and in Luca Marenzio's madrigal *O bella man* (O beautiful hand), the line *Di cinque perle oriental colore* has in the basso part five equal minims, round and white like a set of five white pearls. Other examples can be found in Alfred Einstein's paper on Ocular Music in the Madrigal in *Zeitschrift der Internationalen Musikgesellschaft* XIV (1912–13), pp. 8–21.

Still more remote from audibility is the derivation of melodies from words and letters. Schumann, Liszt, Rimsky-Korsakoff and other composers of the nineteenth century celebrated the sacred memory of their idol Bach in pieces for which the sequence of the (German) notes *b a c h*, that is, *b* flat, *a*, *c*, and *b* natural provided the theme. The idea was not entirely new. When, sometime around 1500, Johannes Ockeghem was writing his motet *Ut heremita solus*, he put his melody together out of the syllables of solmization that these three initial words provide: *ut* or *c* from the incipient word, *re-mi* or *d-e* from the second, and *sol* or *g* from the third, as Hans T. David recently explained in *A Birthday Offering to Carl Engel* (New York, 1943). Similarly and about the same time, Josquin des Prés found the title motive of his Hercules Mass by substituting solmization syllables for the vowels of the dedication: *Hercules Dux Ferrarie*, namely, *re* for *e*, *ut* for *u*, *re* for *e*, in the first word, *ut* for *u* in the second, and again *re*, *fa*, *mi*, *re* for *e*, *a*, *i*, *e* in the third. And Ockeghem and Josquin were by no means the only masters in their time to make what we would all too rashly dismiss as musical puns.

These substitutions were not puns, at least not around 1500. They must be understood out of an ethos mentality that took things similar for connatural, so that one of them could be thrown (*bolon*) together (*sym*) with the other as a symbol—not in the pale sense of a conventional emblem, but as an additional identity to reinforce and deepen the first.

Such symbolism, taken at its face value, is possible only in times in which *ratio* is more important than creative imagination.

This atmosphere of reason and immanence explains the overestimation, in certain epochs, of technique at the cost of imagination, perception, and inspiration. Frank P. Chambers has said of the medieval architect: "The mason's ideal was skill, not beauty; like Villars de Honnecourt, he may have been a showman, overkeen sometimes to execute a *tour-de-force*, an artist's trick for the trick's sake" (*A History of Taste*).

This is also true of the medieval composer. One of his tricks was the isorhythmic structure of a voice part, which our Cross Section 1324 characterized as a procedure in which "the melodies of the various stanzas were different as to the sequence of higher and lower notes but similar as to the sequence of longer and shorter notes."

A complication of this isorhythmic principle resulted from the overlapping of melody and metric pattern when the two were of different length. In case the metric pattern is shorter, the melody would come to an end only somewhere in the middle of the *repeated* metric pattern. As a consequence, its own repetition does not begin where the pattern begins, but somewhere within the pattern, and then proceed in this and all the following repetitions in an ever-changing meter. Here, the listener is confronted with a unifying device that his ear is not able to perceive.

The fourteenth century was particularly fond of such devices. It favored the *canon,* in which a second voice, setting in a few beats or measures later, imitates the first voice note for note; and even a more than sophisticated device, anticipated in the thirteenth century, the *crab canon,* in which—as in the spoken palindrome "Madam, I'm Adam"—the melody, whether read forwards or backwards, is exactly the same.

Why notation was often left so incomplete and incomprehensible that it required a special key and that such a key was concealed under an enigmatic form is another problem. Guillaume de Machaut would write a *rondeau,* text and music; the music consists of one staff, and the poetic text explains how to read from the few notes the whole piece in all three voices. "*Ma fin est mon commencement,*" my end is my beginning, it begins, that is: the top part is the inversion, note for note, of the tenor. It continues: "My third song three times reverts on itself and thus ends"—the third voice again is a crab canon. And so on. Another example: the tenor in Dunstable's *Veni sancte spiritus* obeys the precept *Et dicitur primo directe, 2° subverte lineam, 3° reverte remittendo tertiam partem et capies diapenthe, si vis habere tenorem*— First sing it as it is written, the second time invert all intervals, and, the third time, transpose it to the lower fifth and sing it backwards." A third master has his text begin: "*Je suis défait si vous ne me refaites*"— I am undone unless you redo me.

The modern reader, at a loss to see what all this has to do with art, should be reminded that most peoples have had a peculiar predilection for enigmas. The riddles of the Sphinx and of the Chinese princess Turandot are the most famous among them. Our own generation gets a vivid idea of what we could almost call the riddle rites from the first act of Wagner's *Siegfried,* in which Wotan the Wanderer and Mime the Smith pump one another with posers. In the later Middle Ages, the riddles were an important part of esoteric communication between fellow professionals, but also in the end a social amusement.

It could be conceded that playfulness was necessarily the ultimate outcome. But at the bottom of the musical 'artifices' and their cryptic disguise was the truly Gothic idea of developing a work of art out of one kernel, excluding anything foreign, unorganic, accidental, arbitrary, and to make the performers a party to the plan.

The knowledge of esoteric tricks created a true freemasonry of those initiated. Indeed, the modern fight for, and against, the mysterious transposing notation for *cors anglais*, clarinets, F-horns, B-trumpets shows that we have preserved remainders of such a secret-society mind: I myself remember my late master Hermann Kretzschmar saying in criticism of Felix Weingartner's unified notation that a score with all the voice parts printed in the same key did not look professional.

Craft and imagination balance one another. The Middle Ages emphasize craft and do not mention imagination. But in the sixteenth century, Giorgio Vasari, the biographer of Italian artists, believed in inspiration and genius. Benvenuto Cellini, in his precious modesty, called himself *un maraviglioso ingegno*, a marvelous genius. But one generation later, the blind painter Giovanni Paolo Lomazzo, a leading figure in the theory of art at the onset of the Baroque, was on the contrary more than cool toward what he called "the Fury of Apollo and the Muses." Now, Vasari wrote his *Vite* in 1550, Cellini lived from 1500 to 1571, and Lomazzo published his *Trattato* in 1584: the first two were typical pathos men, while Lomazzo was the exponent of an ethos-minded age.

Two hundred years later, Sir Joshua Reynolds cautioned the Royal Academy in London "against that false opinion but too prevalent among artists, of the imaginary powers of native genius, and sufficiency in great works." At the same time, Jean-Jacques Rousseau denounced all "fugues, imitations, *doubles desseins,* and other arbitrary and purely conventional beauties, which have scarcely any merit except to have overcome a difficulty, and were invented in the early days of art to make a show of knowledge." So he wrote in his *Lettre sur la Musique françoise* (1753). One year before, he had himself composed the first French comic opera although, or even because, he was an amateur. "Much as I approved of the changes that my friends saw fit to make," he wrote in his preface, "I do not, for several reasons, deem it wise to adopt them today. In the first place, inasmuch as this work carries my name, it should be entirely mine, even if it suffers thereby . . ." (which in a way foreshadows another Rousseau, the painter and customs official Henri, whose penetrant naïveté has been the delight of all snobs).

A few years ago, two outstanding composers, one American and one German, discussed in the author's presence what share technique and inspiration had in shaping a work of music. One of them granted 95 per cent to technique; the other offered 3 per cent more. Both avoided the shamefully romantic word inspiration and preferred to speak of an "unknown remainder." Neither of them knew that in such overestimation of mere craft he was a spokesman of ethos.

The great antithesis appears indeed in a strong belief in rules, technique, and craftsmanship on the one hand, and in imagination and inspiration on the other hand, even at the cost of professional skill and experience. Those who strive for nature and against mere art can hardly avoid assuming that the full mastery of technique backs meaningless artificiality, while nature, opposing routine and abstraction, is better taken care of in the hands of him *der nichts weiss von der Tabulatur,* rendered as "who knows not of the rules." This is not only a quotation from the *Meistersinger;* it is the basic conflict in Wagner's opera—of the masters who depend on rules and recipes and of Walter von Stolzing who learns his tunes from the birds.

As a consequence of such conflict, the ethos party has often reproached pathos masters with lack of technical skill. Handel told whoever wanted to listen that his cook knew more counterpoint than Gluck, and anti-Wagnerians used to say scornfully that Wagner would never write a decent symphony or quartet. (Would Brahms have written a good music drama?)

Seen from this antagonism of skill and inspiration, a strange fact becomes important: artists of the ethos side like to write on the technique of their art, while artists of the pathos side indulge in aesthetics, art philosophy, and criticism. Leone Battista Alberti, who lived from 1404 to 1472, wrote his two standard books *De re aedificatoria* and *De pictura* about the middle of the fifteenth century at the same time that Cornazano and Guglielmo Ebreo composed their treatises on the *bassa danza.* The leading technical volumes of the sixteenth century, Zarlino's *Istituzioni harmoniche* (1558), Vignola's *Regola delle cinque ordini d'architettura* (1567), Palladio's *Quattro libri dell'architettura* (1570), Lomazzo's *Trattato della pittura, scoltura, ed architettura* (1584), and Thoinot Arbeau's *Orchésographie,* were published in the interval between two pathos styles. The ethos period around 1720 saw Gottfried Taubert's *Rechtschaffner Tantzmeister* (1717) and Pierre Rameau's *Maître à danser* (1725), the most important works on the dance, and furthermore Jean-Philippe Rameau's *Traité d'harmonie,* the fundamentals of modern harmony, and Johann Joseph Fux's *Gradus ad Parnassum,* the bible of counterpoint. The leading masters in the middle of the nineteenth century, Berlioz, Schumann, Liszt, Wagner, published aesthetic and critical pamphlets—Berlioz even wrote his pseudo manual *Traité de l'instrumentation* as a poet rather than a technician. And again in our own age, Schönberg, Hindemith, Toch, Piston, and other composers have published books on harmony, counterpoint, melody, and form. Imagine a theory of counterpoint by Wagner, or an opus on aesthetics and *Weltanschauung* by Hindemith.

Overestimation of structure is possible only in times when reason matters more than creative imagination and the arts are meant to have an existence beyond the mere appeal to our senses, that is, to have essence beyond appearance.

CHAPTER NINE

Essence and Appearance

1. IMMANENCE AND ACCIDENT

ZEUS, SO PHEIDIAS would have argued, must not be caught in his passing moods or actions as the benevolent, fatherly or angry, thundering god nor even as the victim of incidental light and color. He should be Zeus simply, unrelated, abstract, and absolute; not in his outer, casual appearance, but in his very idea and essence, of which his appearance could just be a meaningless shadow—a shadow's shade, Plato would say.

Lysippos, sculptor in Alexander's time, might have answered: This is a truly noble conception but, in the end, philosophy rather than art. Destined to make ideas visible, palpable, audible, art appeals to the senses and must not, cannot, avoid appearance whether you like it or not. There is no Zeus "in himself," not even in poetry, and what you call idea is nothing but an empty shell. We, warmhearted artists of today, do not care for forms eternal, immutable, dead; we strive for change and life and action.

This dialogue was never held and yet has been at the bottom of all the struggles of pathos artists against the men preceding them and following them.

As a vital implication, ethos, in its struggle for perfection, immanence, and permanence, found its ultimate standards in the immutable laws and forms of mathematics. Egyptian pyramids were plain and regular stereometrical bodies. To the Greeks, all beauty, resting upon geometric proportions, had a mathematical character; Pamphilos was "the first painter who was thoroughly trained in every branch of learning, more particularly in arithmetic and geometry;

without which, so he held, art could not be perfect" (Lionello Venturi). In 1584, at the beginnings of Baroque, Giovanni Paolo Lomazzo maintained that without geometry and arithmetic nobody could hope to become a painter; and our Cross Section through the year 1642 shows how the French of the seventeenth century echoed this thought.

Computed canons of 'correct' proportions as the basis of beauty were the necessary consequence and, as a curious but logical issue, beauty became synthetic: Duris of Samos relates that Zeuxis, the painter, selected the most beautiful parts from several women and put them together, since no individual human body was perfect. Two thousand years later, Albrecht Dürer, as a proselyte of the Italian Renaissance, and again Vincenzo Danti, were to repeat what Zeuxis had felt and done.

It has been one of the direct consequences of believing in canons and perfection that art of ethos times has concentrated on human beings without age. Accordingly, our First and Second Chapters had to relate that the Babylonians refrained from representing younger people and that the Greeks gave features of adolescence to their gods in postclassic times only.

But the case of the Child is still more striking. Everybody has with consternation seen how medieval artists, when in representing Christ, St. John, or the Innocents they could not avoid the Child, used to show him as a thoroughly disagreeable creature of adult proportions though smaller in size—disagreeable, because it caricatures grownups the way children dressed up in adult clothing do. The typical ethos man would hardly feel this repugnance. To him, there is but one perfection and beauty—the body in its full development of which senility and more so infancy are morbid, illicit deviations, indeed, embarrassing accidents. It is the pathos man who recognizes children's claims to a beauty of their own, disdains the dead, immutable beauty of arrested growth and permanence and dares to open his eyes to the changing beauty of growing, unfolding bodies, which is a challenge to the frigid rigor of canons. Hence the unexpected predilection for children in Hellenistic art and the almost eruptive delight the early Renaissance took in man in the bud; hence Andrea della Robbia's swaddling infants, Verrocchio's chubby-faced *putti*, Desiderio's delicate maidens.

The animal, too, in ethos times does not often have the privilege of a rendition true to nature. With the dominant position given to the representation of man, animals were hardly admitted as more than symbols and were as such refused convincing reality. Even the lion in Villard de Honnecourt's sketchbook of about 1250 (cf. our Chapter XIV, The Cycle of the Middle Ages), which according to its caption was "drawn from life," shows the queer assimilation to human features that we so often find in the art of the Middle Ages. The artist's eye may be a photographic, impersonal lens—what he actually sees is not a photographic picture but his personal interpretation.

The renunciation of the Middle Ages—from this viewpoint—was in Leonardo's postulate: "The knowledge of the human form is no longer sufficient. The painter must be clever enough to represent all appearances of nature, even fogs, clouds, rains, dust, smoke, in their different densities, the transparence of water, and the stars in the sky" (quoted from Venturi).

Still, the relapse to earlier positions, so characteristic of the evolution of thought and style, did not fail to appear in time. In 1666, the classicistic architect André Félibien said in his *Entretiens sur les Vies et sur les Ouvrages des plus excellens Peintres* that—I quote from Lionello Venturi's translation—"since the figure of man is the most perfect work of God, he who paints man is the most excellent among painters; next comes he who paints living animals rather than dead things without movement; then he who paints landscapes, and finally flowers and fruits."

It needed the mild pathos in the mind of Félibien's fellow Frenchman Roger de Piles, a few years later, to restore landscape to its rights: "If painting is a species of creation, it bears the marks of it even more sensibly in pictures of landscapes than in others" (translated by Venturi).

But exactly a hundred years after Félibien, and in almost the same words, a German classicist, Gotthold Ephraim Lessing, firmly stated in his *Laokoon*, that "the highest bodily beauty exists only in man, and even in him only by virtue of the ideal. This ideal already finds less scope in the beasts, and in the world of plants and inanimate objects has no place at all. We can infer from this the rank of the flower and landscape painter . . ." (translated by Irving Babbitt).

2. *THE PLAIN AND THE PICTURESQUE*

Picturesque we call a broad-rimmed Rubens hat with plumes put on askew; a Ruysdael landscape with gnarled and twisted trees; Claude Debussy's symphonic poem *La Mer*, which forces an irresistible vision of storm-whipped seas upon the audience; some exceptionally vivid, impressive description in a poem; or a sculpture fascinating through the glittering play of light and shadow rather than through tactile form.

The term 'picturesque' has been defined as antiplastic by the art historian Oskar Wulff, and as antilinear by Heinrich Wölfflin. Either definition is evidently true of the visible arts of which alone these writers were thinking. And Wölfflin's definition also applies to music: a composition is picturesque when, being antilinear, it relies on the shades of harmony, intensity, tempo, and orchestration more than on the solid weaving of polyphonic voice parts or the regular, functional march of chords. Still, both definitions—as all too brief definitions—are probably not wide enough. Our examples cited above oppose not only the clarity of well-drawn lines and tactile forms; they also suggest appeal to imagination, fancy, motion, dash, and challenge sober matter-of-factness. Thus, the plain and the picturesque are only shades in the basic antithesis: permanence—change.

It is typically a case of change and accident as against permanence and immanence when, appealing to imagination and fancy, the painter introduces looking glasses into his picture to catch some indirect and therefore nonessential, casual vista in addition to the direct and normal view from the front. A good example is Titian's double portrait of Laura de'Dianti and Alfonso da Ferrara in the Louvre (Plate XX).

In similar strife for picturesque 'change,' architects of the Baroque age carved pilasters, sills, cornices, and pediments in stronger relief to make the shadows play and enliven the slumbering stones with moving, incorporeal shapes.

Passion for life, change, and movement has led to a dread of completion and finish; for things complete and finished have ceased growing, changing, living. Pliny the Elder, who perished in 79 B.C. and hence belonged in an age of strongest pathos, found it "quite curious and noteworthy . . . that people admire less the finished productions of an artist than his last works, left incomplete, as, for instance, the Venus of Apelles. In fact, people appreciate the interrupted sketch and the first idea of the artist" (translated by Jex-Blake). The Gothic age must more than other periods have experienced the specific charm of the unfinished: the masons' scaffolds never taken off and the eternal interruption of work on the giant cathedrals, almost unique in the history of architecture, cannot in the ordinary way be excused by wars, disorders, and lack of funds. To say the least, the later Middle Ages did not mind façades with only one of two towers, as in Strasbourg, or towers never capped with spires, as in Paris, Laon, or Reims.

A similar victory of the casual over the permanent, although with entirely different means, can be read from Carlo Crivelli's Madonna in the Bache Collection in New York, a typical painting from the pathos age of the late fifteenth century: the (painted) label with the master's signature is crinkled and has lost one of its four thumbtacks, and the stone balustrade in the foreground has a crack.

However, the crack and the missing thumbtack denote a turn in the pathos aversion to neatness and finish different from the dragging, unfinished cathedrals. It is the turn from the simple delight in life and growth to the delight in death and decay which, too, are aspects of life and growth, though from the opposite side. In this same spirit, Diderot said around 1750 that no palace could be attractive unless it was in ruins; Panini and Hubert Robert, the *ruiniste*, spent a lifetime each in painting broken shafts and crumbling walls; and the fashionable English gardens, 'picturesque' against the architectural park of the French, could hardly do without a set of artificial ruins. In Gothic ages, imagination was youthfully aimed at the future; in romantic times, at the past.

Again in a different approach, the architects of the Baroque interfered with completion when they boldly interrupted the pediments above the windows or portals and kept the two ends at the left and the right as broken stumps without connection: the onlooker's attention was roused, the eye staggered, and imagination had to step in and fill the gap.

The picturesque sculptor has similar ways. He counts on the lively play of lights, reflexes, and shadows and even would, as did the Romans, bore out the hair with drills to make it more 'picturesque' with its black perforations against the white of the marble (Plate II). He also delights in ruins though in his own way when, in an attitude so strangely far from our natural repugnance to living cripples, he experiences the particular charm of ancient marble torsos found without their arms or legs. Indeed, some recent sculptors—Aristide Maillol and Archipenko for example—avail themselves of marble blocks too small for their purpose and carve them to artificial torsos. It should not be forgotten, though, that any kind of bust (reintroduced about 1400 after Roman models) is no less a torso.

The changing treatment of ancient torsos and the differences of opinion on the problem of restoration would be a fascinating subject of history: in the ceaseless debate as to whether the mutilated remnants of antiquity should be kept as they were excavated or be given deceptive protheses, the mania for deceptive restoration has raged mostly in ethos times, to which the torso as something atectonic, imperfect, and ugly must be a shock.

The sculptor, again like the architect, is in pathos times inclined to achieve the charm of growth and change by replacing the 'no longer' of the torso by the 'not yet' of the intentionally unfinished work. The most outstanding example of recent times is Rodin's Thought (1886), a head not fully emerging from the shapelessness of the uncarved marble block.

The fittest form for picturesque trends is the relief. While to the statuesque sculptor it means a flattened projection of round forms on a plane, it becomes the opposite in the hands of picturesque sculptors, a painting in plastic forms which detach themselves from a plane. The statuesque sculptor, therefore, leaves the background, as an ideal reference plane, bald and untouched; the picturesque sculptor shapes it in lowest relief as a backdrop with landscapes or houses, in front of which the figures move and act in layers of ever-increasing roundness. The second of Ghiberti's celebrated bronze doors on the baptistery in Florence (Plate XII) is a fine example of picturesque relief (against the first door, say, or the pediments of the Parthenon); later, the principle came to a climax in the wild exaggeration on carved altars of the German Baroque: Hans Degler's in Augsburg 1607), Jörg Zürn's in Ueberlingen (1604–1607), Hans Gudewerdt's in Preetz (*c.* 1640).

It is hardly necessary to translate these traits into the idiom of painting proper. The picturesque painter, too, operates with light and shadow and chooses figures, poses, objects that stir our motor impulse and imagination. He would omit those lines which the spectator's eye is willing and able to supply itself, and, while he rarely leaves his work unfinished so that the virgin canvas shows, he shuns at least the all too perfect spick-and-span completion which classicists so often deem desirable. His works, as the art critic of the London *World* blamingly wrote against Whistler's etchings of Venice in 1880, "rather resemble vague first intentions, or memoranda for future use."

The picturesque, finally, implies a suggestion of movement by means of round instead of plane and straight formations. Architects of the Baroque age, eager to give a breath of life and motion to lifeless matter, took a fancy to sinuous fronts. After Peruzzi had broken tradition by giving his Palazzo Massimi alle Colonne in Rome a convex face (1535), they often delighted in concave, receding façades. The Palazzo Carignano in Turin (1680) even has the end sections plane, the neighboring sections concave, and the central section convex: receding and protruding, the building seems to move. The Baroque, averse to towers, crowned its roofs with domes and cupolas which smoothly lead the eyes up to the lantern. The Romans, pathos-minded, vaulted their ceilings and bridged their columns with arches, which the ethos-minded Greeks of classical times had never considered. The contrast between the two styles of prehistoric painting—stylized and naturalistic—was also the contrast between Greek vases before and after 700 B.C. And is not this general antithesis (round and straight) ultimately responsible for the swaying hips in fourteenth century sculpture as opposed to the rigid column men of the twelfth?

A curious confirmation seems to be found in the history of the human body and of its costume: the ideal of ethos-minded ages has always been the slender man and the slender, almost boyish woman; pathos times, the Roman, the Baroque, the late Victorian world, have preferred, or at least not resented, obesity and have with corsets, *culs*, and other odd devices supplied what nature would in honest stubbornness not grant.

How far the costume of a time is consistent with the trends of art and music, we have shown here and there in Part I. In for a penny, in for a pound: fashion must be granted a place in the Nature of Style. And since its fluctuations are chiefly determined by the antithesis: plain–picturesque, fashion's place is in the present chapter.

It is a delicate subject to discuss the share of fashions in the generational reversals of style. Costume, even more than the arts, depends on imponderables, which either delay response under the sway of tradition—as in man's wear today—or else precipitate changes under the impact of a mania for novelty which often enough is sponsored by commercial interests but might possibly represent a faster to-and-fro than we find in the reversals of art. This question must be left open. Still, a number of characteristic correlations can be traced.

As a rule, ethos generations demand reserve and simplicity, close contours, and often transverse divisions to avoid the prevalence of verticality. Women have their hair smooth and low, and men shave or else wear beards as close-lined frames rather than as jutting-out projections. The waistline goes up.

Pathos generations exaggerate in fashions as they do in art; they open contours and avoid transverse partitions. In the last third of the fifteenth century, the steeple hat of ladies à la mode reaches several feet in height, and the shoes of gentlemen, affectedly pointed and turned up, are often three times as long as the foot. Men's shoulders are broadened and padded, and their trousers and hose made in one piece; ladies' dresses are puffed, full, and trailing. Fuzzy hair sticks out, or else it is plaited in tresses and arranged in complicated nests of ribbons and coils. In many pathos styles, the men wear beards or perukes. The waistline falls.

Typically 'picturesque' in a narrower sense is the costume in Tournière's portrait of the dancing master Louis Pécour (Plate XXVI): the beret, boldly askew with the tuft of feathers up, the collar open with the carelessly dangling lace, the tassels of the golden embroidery, the wide-sleeved gown, and even the dance script book with the corners of its pages slovenly turned up.

3. LINE AND COLOR

Color in ethos times is subordinated to drawing, to firm, uncompromising lines. It is even looked at with a certain amount of suspicion as something nonessential, irrational, and sensuous. It may be accepted to balance and contrast the parts of a work of art but has no meaning in itself. Indeed, color may not even be required to conform with nature in the broadest sense of the word: some horses carved on Grecian pediments apparently were just as blue as those on Etruscan tomb murals of the time and as, in modern years, those of Franz Marc's painting, The Tower of the Blue Horses, in the Kronprinzenpalais, Berlin (c. 1910).

Whenever a generation turns to pathos, it rediscovers the illusionistic and emotional qualities of color—in Hellenistic times as well as in the fourteenth century, in the Baroque, and the middle of the nineteenth century. Plutarch, who lived around A.D. 100 in Roman 'baroque' times, promptly wrote that "coloring is superior to drawing, and produces a more living impression on the mind, because it is the source of a greater illusion" (in *Quomodo adolescens poetas audire debeat*, translated by Lionello Venturi, p. 61).

Raphael and Bronzino could at the worst have done without color; Velásquez or Canaletto could not, because to them it meant creative inspiration and dominant quality. In a nutshell, the antithesis may be formulated in Roger de Piles' already quoted words against the academic attitude of the French about the middle of the seventeenth century: "Coloring is not only an essential part of painting, but is indeed its *differentia*, and is the very part that makes the painter a painter."

Orchestration as a consciously used means to create emotional atmosphere dates, it seems, from the middle of the sixteenth century —from the same time in which emotional color developed in painting; and the two have since been synchronized. In a courtly *intermedio* of 1569—*L'Amico fido*—Alessandro Striggio rendered the inferno with the dark shades of double basses and trombones; orchestration already had a significant position. However, orchestration rarely shows in the sixteenth century: the composer, as a rule his own interpreter, did not expressly indicate what instruments were to be used. Even as late a score as Cavalieri's *Rappresentazione di anima e di corpo* (1600) advised the conductor to change orchestration to suit the different emotions expressed, but itself made no suggestions. Hence the old prejudice that artful orchestration was born only later, indeed, that it stems from Monteverdi's drama *Orfeo* (Mantua, 1607).

True, this score is a masterpiece of significant coloring. One example may suffice to show its dominant role: when Orpheus enters the land of the dead, he hears a *sinfonia* of two cornets, four trombones, and a jarring reed organ, dark, rigid, inexorable; when with his magic voice he has implored the powers of death to give him back his beloved wife, the same symphony is played *pian piano* with strings and a mild flute organ: the resistance is softening. But Monteverdi was not necessarily the first to achieve such meaningful shades just because he was the first to indicate them in his score. Furthermore this exceptional, indeed unique, indication had nothing in common with modern scoring. It was printed, not before the performance as a binding prescription but after it as a mere souvenir for the guests, which reminded them of how Monteverdi, the conductor, changed "his instruments to suit the different emotions expressed," as so many before him had done. Accordingly the instruments were indicated in the past tense: *Questo Balletto fu cantato al suono di cinque Viole da braccio;* or: *Questo Ritornello fu suonato di dentro da vn Clauicembano, duoi Chitarroni, & duoi Violini piccioli alla Francese;* This ballet *was* sung . . . This ritornello *was* played . . .

The invention and hesitating progress of music printing changed the situation. It implied the wide dissemination of compositions and, consequently, the necessity of telling fellow musicians abroad the right way to perform them. Giovanni Gabrieli in Venice, who died in 1612, seems to have been the first actually to prescribe exact orchestration in modern form.

Pathos, as a rule, both in painting and music, has a predilection for the darker colors. Caravaggio and the Fleming Gerard Honthorst, around 1600, and after them Frans Hals and Rembrandt, contribute the most impressive evidences of such trends: Honthorst was in Italy nicknamed *Gerardo delle Notti*, Gerald of the nights. Victorian interiors, so heavily protected from light, are another example.

Ethos times have on the contrary preferred the lighter shades of musical color. Compare the music around 1450 with the almost whitish colors of paintings in that time. In the Trent Codices, chief musical document of the time (a comprehensive collection of religious and secular music), about 32 per cent of all voice parts are sopranos, 22 per cent tenors, 8 per cent baritones, and only some 4 per cent bassos—an eighth of the number of sopranos.

Again, the importance of voice parts varies: ethos likes the melody in the upper voice, where it is most conspicuous, and pathos likes it below. A comparison of Mozart and Beethoven or, for that matter, of the young and the old Beethoven, shows the point. Young Beethoven, like Mozart, has mostly soprano melodies; Beethoven in his maturity is more interested in basal melodies, such as the well-known double-bass passage on the scherzo of the Fifth Symphony and hundreds of other instances. It is neither a matter of course nor accidental that the straight, popular forms of Italian music, *lauda*, *frottola*, *villanesca*, had the melody in the upper voice. Nor is it mere chance that Pastor Lucas Osiander's *Fünfftzig Geistliche Lieder und Psalmen*, Nuremberg, 1586, transferred the melodies of Protestant chorales to the soprano, in contradistinction to the practice in the time after the Reformation. A pathos period like the later fifteenth century, on the other hand, would give its dances a *ténor*, that is, a ground melody on which the two upper voices had to improvise their parts; and the seventeenth century would build its *passacaglias* and *ciaconas*, and also many of its arias, on ever-recurring *bassi ostinati*, grounds. Nor should we forget the typical invention of low-sounding instruments in times of this kind, of the double-bass sizes of viols, trombones, and bassoons in the age of the *passacaglia*, of the giant *octobasse* in Berlioz's days, or of the tubas in the second third of the nineteenth century. We could add the momentous invention of the organ pedals if we knew their exact date in the fourteenth century.

Speaking of color, attention should be called to the curiously contrasting attitude toward musical instruments in Italy and Germany. Italy has been the golden land of stringed instruments. She created and perfected all the bowed instruments of the Later Ages, and particularly the leading families of the *lira*, the viol, and the violin, up to the marvels from Brescia and Cremona. She gave them the dominant role in orchestral and chamber music long before 1600, in times when elsewhere they were despised or left to the dance. And in return, she assigned a minor part to the wind instruments from the sixteenth century on.

Germany behaved quite differently. In the terminology of the sixteenth and seventeenth centuries, instrumentalists were called either *Stadtpfeifer* or *Kunstpfeifer* (unless they belonged to princely orchestras), that is, town pipers or art pipers. Only the lowest class drew their derogatory title from bowed instruments: *Bierfiedler*—beer fiddlers. Accordingly, most wind instruments were given a place that they held nowhere else and in foreign countries were even credited to Germany. The modern flute was everywhere called the German flute, and the French horn was spoken of as the German horn by the French themselves; the bassoon is first mentioned as being made by a master in Nuremberg, the world center of wood and brass wind manufacturing; the double bassoon and the double trombone were invented in Berlin early in the seventeenth century; the clarinet, again, came from Nuremberg at the end of the seventeenth century; the cromorne derived its name from the German *krummhorn* or bent horn; the brass instruments were given their pistons and valves in Prussia early in the nineteenth century. And much could be added to this list.

France achieved leadership in wind instruments in the nineteenth century; the Netherlands, in harpsichords around 1600; and England in keyboard instruments during the eighteenth and early nineteenth centuries. None of these countries played any role in the manufacture of bowed instruments.

4. *TWO AND THREE DIMENSIONS*

THE SPACE and the objects that our eye perceives are three-dimensional: high, wide, deep. But paintings, being projected on plane surfaces, are only two-dimensional: high and wide. Unable actually to reproduce the third dimension, the painter suggests it by using perspective, either in one or in both of its aspects: aerial perspective, which expresses receding space by gradations of color and intensity, and linear perspective, which gradually reduces the sizes of objects and of their parts according to their greater distance from our eye.

A painted figure, human or animal, gives the weakest illusion of three-dimensional bodiliness when it is rendered in strict profile as on medals or stamps (Plate XIV), or in front view, or even, as in ancient Egypt and southwest Asia, in a combination of the two dimensions. A convincingly all-round figure, on the contrary, would turn its head and torso and limbs so that practically no two of them seem to lie in the same plane. And it also would recur to what Italian art calls *contrapposto*, the counterbalancing of any movement to the left or the fore by a compensatory movement to the right or the rear.

A similar contrast has been described in the juxtaposition of the Delphian Charioteer and the Gaul with His Wife in Chapter VII (Illustrations).

Just as these two sculptures were presented as paragons of ethos and of pathos, the whole contrast of two and three dimensions, of plane and of space, of frontal and all-round, aligns with these trends. Perspective and foreshortening are a matter of mere impression: an object at a greater distance is neither smaller nor dimmer; it only seems to be so. And an arm thrusting forward to the onlooker is not really short and shapeless; this is only how it impresses our retina against our knowing better. Consequently, perspective belongs to appearance not to essence and is, as an odious misapprehension of the eye, the more neglected as a style tends toward ethos. Extreme neglect goes with the oriental carpet where figures, animals, houses are strewn like so many flowers over a neutral ground, without the slightest attempt at individual all-round modeling or proper connection in a common space in which they live and act. The other extreme or, better, one of the other two extremes, might be the panorama, which tries to make one forget its canvas in favor of deceptive illusion.

There is indeed one more extreme when perspective, used by virtuosos in order to interest and thrill their spectators, stresses the accident of some unusual sight. When, for example, Mantegna draws Christ's corpse in a position that any amateur photographer would avoid: foremost the oversize feet, and the rest of the body to the rear in the oddest foreshortening. Or when Caravaggio, in *Santa Maria del Popolo* in Rome, hurls St. Paul from his horse into the depth of the painting. Or again when Mantegna, Correggio, Tiepolo cover the ceilings of churches and palaces with illusionistic figures not to be seen from the front but from below, as if they actually, with feet nearest to your eyes, moved above the ceiling against painted architectures, the verticals of which converge as they do on photographs of modern skyscrapers.

Perspective, foreshortening, *contrapposto*, and kindred notions are at first sight so definitely visual that no bridge seems to lead to music and its purely auditive conditions. Linear perspective, in which the dimensions of objects appear proportionally reduced, has no proper place in music, and reduction, either of intervals or of time values, would not convey any illusion of space, whatever space could be in music.

Music, however, knows aerial perspective or space—visual, extramusical space—expressed by gradations of color and intensity: the impression of some object, procession, or military parade, drawing nearer and nearer and again going away and disappearing has here and there been given by a general crescendo and following decrescendo with appropriately increasing and decreasing orchestration. Wagner himself interpreted the prelude to *Lohengrin* as the solemn descent and subsequent departure of the Holy Grail. But this and the many other examples that any musician can supply move on a comparatively unimportant sideline of descriptive music.

The essential aspect under which music must be given a place in this section cannot show unless we drop the misleading word perspective with its purely visual connotations and concentrate rather on the more-than-visual notions: third dimension and bodiliness.

Western notation, from the indefiniteness of medieval neumes to the almost pedantic accuracy of the modern script, seems to suggest that there is no third dimension in music. In projecting audible sound on a visible surface—a two-dimensional surface—it gives the individual note its place on a vertical reference line according to its pitch or height, while its time value and the succession in time of all notes follow a horizontal staff, that is, width. There is apparently no depth.

But then even the most perspective, spatial, and all-round painting devolves no less on a two-dimensional surface. Its depth and bodiliness are illusions not facts; its dots and dashes, seemingly to the fore or the rear, actually sit side by side in the plane of the canvas.

The fact that the third dimension is, in painting too, a mere product of our imagination under the spell of some suggestive treatment, allows us safely to leave ourselves to the daily experience all musicians have, though hardly any of them are prepared to analyze it and to realize its implications. Faced with the unwonted dualism of plane and corporeal on the one hand, and with the familiar contrast of an unaccompanied oriental melody and a harmonized melody of the West on the other hand, they would not hesitate to call the first plane, and the second, corporeal. Again, of two contrapuntal or harmonic settings, one in the earlier medieval style without thirds or sixths and the other with triads, they would readily call the latter by far more corporeal. And of two harmonic settings, one in simple, sober triads and the other in triads mingled with seventh and ninth chords, this second one would doubtless appear to be a good deal more corporeal, fleshy, all-round. Most of those who accept or even apply such characterization will probably hasten to add that they do so only in a metaphorical sense. But then, what else is a metaphor than the acknowledgment of elemental likeness?

Harmony, then, appears to be the depth, the third dimension in music. Harmony is 'functional': its chords are organically, lawfully linked from the first to the last without an arbitrary shift or jump. True, the chords follow the melody. But just for this reason, each individual note of the melody finds itself not only in a linear way tied to those which precede and follow but also to the march of harmony, which complicates its function and gives it stronger intensity.

And this is exactly what perspective does: it relates the parts of a painting not only with its neighbors but also with a space that, enveloping all of them, gives them a new intensity, significance, and unity.

How close the art of harmony is to the art of space illusion appears from the central law of voice leading: neither counterpoint nor harmony are in favor of 'similar' motion, where the voice parts move in the same direction; and they do not tolerate parallel fifths and octaves. Instead, they prescribe 'contrary' motion, where the voice parts move in opposite directions. That movement would otherwise come to a standstill is the wrong explanation; the mere word 'motion' connected with the epithets similar and parallel disowns it. The actual reason for the (often transgressed) interdiction is that *motus contrarius* is nothing but the musical version of *contrapposto* and as such counterbalances any movement by its opposite to secure convincing all-roundness and third dimension.

Again, harmony, like spatial conceptions in painting, stretches between two extremes. Passing from the unaccompanied melody of the Orient and the Gregorian chant through the contrapuntal forms of the Middle Ages, its evolution brought it to a central position around 1600, in which it supported the span of a melody from its start to the end with a logical, natural, learnable sequence of interrelated chords. But already a movement toward the other extreme had set in: harmony out of sheer delight in chords and their emotional, expressionistic qualities at the cost of melody. Such antifunctional harmony appeared in the so-called chromatic madrigals of the sixteenth century up to Gesualdo da Venosa's *intervalli duri & straordinarj* and to the fascinating harmonic shifts of Monteverdi's *Orfeo*. Again, it is one of the moving forces in the music of the second half of the nineteenth century, with its peak in *Tristan* whose peculiar chords, resolutions, and modulations have given birth to portly tomes of analysis. With Debussy, harmony as a function in the older sense came to an end.

These considerations lead to the last point in this discussion: to the parallel development in painting and in music, of the concept of a third dimension, and therewith to a confirmation by history that the phenomena correspond. The essential phases of this historic development are: lack of both perspective and harmony in the Orient; a slowly growing evolution of perspective and preharmonic music in the basically unperspectivic and unharmonic world of the later western Middle Ages, particularly in the fourteenth century; a radical shift to perspective and harmony proper at the beginning of the Renaissance; perspective and harmony in the uncontested lead up to the second half of the nineteenth century; prevalent disintegration both of space and of harmonic function from the time of impressionism on; and, finally, neglect of both conceptions since the early twentieth century.

Thus, the strictly parallel fate of the two appears to prove that, in vision and in audition, they answer a similar urge of expression.

The dance, too, seems to have had a two-dimensional and a three-dimensional phase in chronological coincidence with the two similar phases in the evolution of painting, one belonging in the Middle Ages and one in the Later Ages. The most typical Italian Baroque poem, Giovanni Battista Marino's *Adone* (1623), describes the art of a prodigious Terpsichore, who, "with marvelous *geometria*," rounds out her space to form a sphere

> and turns about much like a peacock's plumage.
> Her feet outline periphery and center;

One foot rotates outside, and one stands inside.

E rota a quella del pavon sembiante.
Tengono i piè la periferia e il centro;
Quel volteggia di fuor, questo sta dentro.

This is, no doubt, all-round and three-dimensional, in both body and space. And when Terpsichore, before the dance, steps forward and back and bends her knee and tests her foot and "studies where to place her feet," this seems to be a practice similar to what the dancing masters around 1460 had called *compartimento di terreno* or *partire del terreno*, organization of the floor. The new conception of a three-dimensional dance is confirmed at the end of the seventeenth century in Le Feuillet's epochal *Chorographie* of 1699, a dance script, almost indifferent to steps and gestures but—unlike the scripts of the fifteenth century—devised to indicate the floor pattern or progress in space, sideways, back, and forward.

This new insight in the two- and three-dimensional character of both the dance and music will prove helpful when Part III of the book turns to marking out the larger phases of history.

5. PRESENTATION

ARCHITECTS OF PATHOS TIMES have often designed their buildings not only as they should *be* but also as they should *appear*. In Gothic times, the lowly houses of the town were allowed to cluster tightly around the church to stress its upward surge. Many churches of the Baroque are set aslant in the street, so the approaching viewer would see them in a 'picturesque' foreshortening rather than in sober symmetry; and, more than the architects themselves, the artists of the stage avoided all frontality in favor of oblique arrangements and sloping vistas, which stimulate imagination more than the definiteness of frontal symmetry can do.

It is a common knowledge among the curators of museums that such conditions exist in sculpture and painting as well. Most Gothic statues, composed for niches or portals, are meaningless in the open; murals and still lives need different conditions; and many canvases, painted in times of soft-shining wax candles, lose in the crude obtrusiveness of skylight or even of modern light fittings.

In music, the dualism of being and appearing is mainly a question of performance. The symphonic poems of Debussy or Strauss are meaningless agglomerations of notes unless given life and sense by a rendition adequate in phrasing, tempos, intensities. They demand imaginative presentation and need personalities as the performers. Music that *is*, as a thing in itself, can scarcely be affected by the means or ways of performance except from the general angle of good or bad. A chorale or an anthem may be sung by a chorus, or played by the organ or brasses or strings. And in any intensity, loud or soft or *mezzoforte*, it always is and means the same thing solemn, vigorous, great. Finer shades of orchestration, intensity, tempo, or sentiment spoil rather than help; our national anthem is hardly bearable when performed by a self-conscious soloist or, God forbid, by an opera star. While the styles of Debussy and Strauss are individual, chorales and anthems are collective; the former are on the pathos, and the others on the ethos side.

In this spirit, ethos has often left open the choice between all kinds of suitable instruments and even between instruments and voices. The famous collection of 1501 known as the *Odhecaton*, A Hundred Melodies, testifies to such ambiguity: it presents ninety-six songs devoid of their texts to serve as music for instruments. Two generations later, Massimo Trojano's account of the ducal wedding in Munich (1568) proves the purely instrumental performance of vocal pieces: a motet of Orlando di Lasso is rendered by five cornets and two trombones, and French chansons, motets, and madrigals are played on strings. Four years later, *Een Dvytsch Mvsyck Boeck* headed (if I am not wrong) a large number of compositions printed there "to be sung and played on all kinds of instruments," *per cantare e sonare*. Such 'amphibious' music *was*, no matter how it was made to *appear*.

Even where truly instrumental forms excluded singing, the instruments in ethos music were rarely specified. Composers at best allowed for an alternative: *per violino ò cornetto*. As late a work as Bach's *Wohltemperiertes Clavier* (whose arbitrary, too specific English title *Well-tempered Clavichord* fatally falsifies the intentional vagueness of the older German word *Clavier*) can be played on any adequate keyboard instrument including the organ, despite some modern attempts to determine from its style whether it was meant for harpsichord or for clavichord. Actually, it was hardly 'meant' for any one instrument because most of its music was abstract and did not depend on a particular kind of 'appearance.' Which, in turn, is not 'meant' to be a charter for those of our contemporaries who do not hesitate to murder the music of Bach with the full impact of some allegedly modern but in reality outworn-romantic 'appearance' hostile to its style and genius, its abstractness and impersonality.

Masters inclined to join the other side—like the English virginalists around 1600 with their broken chord passages or Domenico Scarlatti early in the eighteenth century or later Liszt and Chopin—on the contrary, created out of the spirit and the peculiar technical conditions of their instruments: one is tempted to say their own, individual instruments and nobody could mistake their works for organ music. Between the two groups, Beethoven would shout at his quartet partner Schuppanzigh who was complaining that some passage was too difficult for the violin: "Do you suppose I think of your miserable fiddle when the spirit takes possession of me?"

Musicians of recent times have taken crescendo and decrescendo for granted; without the gradual change from soft to loud, so they think, music would be mechanical, frigid, and dead. As a consequence, all music, regardless of its style, is being performed in a restless process of inflation and deflation; and particularly our choruses sing works of all kinds indiscriminately in tones coming from nowhere, puffing up to *fortissimo*, and again fading into nothingness.

This is a mistake. Changing volume belongs to certain styles and is misplaced in others. Two thousand five hundred years ago, Confucius stated: "A vulgar-minded man's performance is loud and fast, and again fading and dim, a picture of violent death-agony. His heart is not harmonically balanced; mildness and graceful movements are foreign to him."

Two thousand years later, Palestrina's contemporary Hermann Finck asked the singer to proceed evenly like an organ. In his *Practica Musica* of 1556, he said: "It is very ugly to sing now loudly, now softly." Those who must have known deemed varying intensity in the same piece (not to speak of a gradual increase or decrease of volume) to be not only unnecessary, but repulsive and therefore distorting. Pietro della Valle, a military officer and herald of modern music, confirmed (1640) in his pamphlet *Della musica dell'età nostra* that the older style—before 1600—had not known *piano* and *forte* or, for that matter, the *crescendo* and *diminuendo* of individual tones.

Such reluctance, to be sure, did not reduce music to one unalterable level of intensity. Even as impersonal an art as the Gregorian chant had accepted different volumes for different types of melodies. Guido of Arezzo (d. 1050) had already asked for *forte* in Introits but for the greatest possible moderation in Offertories and Communions. In 1474, a precious incunabulum by the theologist Conrad von Zabern, *De modo bene cantandi choralem cantum*, How to Sing the Choral Chant, gives the general rule that the lower range should be sung with full power, the middle one with medium force, and the higher range with delicacy lest it sound like a roaring bull. The German *Meistersinger*, Craftsmen-Singers, used to perform the first strophe or *Stollen* of a song *mezzoforte*, the second *piano*, and the third or *Abgesang* (epode) *forte*. Nicola Vicentino writes in *L'antica musica ridotta alla moderna prattica* (1555), that chamber music should be soft while choral music should be performed "with the full voice." But according to Silvestro Ganassi, *forte* and *piano* were also used in the middle third of the sixteenth century to express the mood of a piece and, again, Hermann Finck, who so violently opposed any change of intensity during a piece, demanded that cheerful works be sung more loudly than sad ones.

Taste changed toward 1600. Giovanni Gabrieli's *Sonata pian e forte* for brasses and violas (1597) is the first evidence of alternating intensities within the same piece. Michael Praetorius (1619) wants the chorus to sing, now *piano* and softly, now *forte* and briskly, but only once in a while, not too often or too much. In 1631, a mass by the Viennese Christoph Strauss already had *piano, più forte, forte, fortissimo;* and in 1636, Father Mersenne, the French theoretician, enumerated no less than eight shades of intensity.

More important than the gradation of intensities was the smooth transition from soft to loud and vice versa. In 1615, Giulio Caccini gave the first detailed account of the inflation and deflation of individual notes (but by no means of whole passages!). The style of that generation was said, though not with too much authority, to have been kept alive in the way—a hundred fifty years later—the Papal Chapel performed Gregorio Allegri's famous *Miserere* for four and five voices, when young Mozart illicitly wrote it down inside his hat while it was being sung. Many notes were intoned with a crescendo; the tempo was irregular; and toward the end, the piece slowed down and gradually faded away.

Faithful to this school but probably falling behind the leading Italians, the German *Kapellmeister* Wolfgang Mylius' *Rudimenta musices* (1686) cautioned the pupil: "You must not drop from *forte* to *piano*, but gradually let the voice *crescendo* and *decrescendo*."

Actually, the Italians did, or were about to, reabandon this achievement. For Christian Daniel Friedrich Schubart—a German poet and critic who lived 1739–91 but whose book was published only after his death—acknowledged an Italian crescendo style as something quite recent, "created only fifty, sixty years back," that is, early in the eighteenth century. "Previously [around 1700] all pieces of music had been executed at the same intensity of tone, or left to the discretion of the player." (This and the following passage from Reichardt are quoted in the translation by Frederick Dorian, *The History of Music in Performance,* New York, 1942, ch. iii.)

Schubart's statement was correct. A new dynamic style developed in Italy at the beginning of the eighteenth century and was first described by Scipione Maffei in 1711 as being used in concerts of Roman orchestras. Two years earlier, the harpsichord maker Bartolommeo Cristófori in Florence had invented our modern grand piano—the *clavicembalo col pian e forte*—which allowed production of all shades of *piano* and *forte* by the mere touch of the finger. Within a few years, English, French, and German inventors followed; and in 1712, the organ builder Abraham Jordan in London devised the earliest swell.

The Italian orchestra crescendo came to Germany about the middle of the eighteenth century and proved so fascinating that when it was first produced in Stuttgart under Niccolò Jomelli's baton, "the audience gradually rose from their seats." Johann Friedrich Reichardt, *Kapellmeister* of the Royal Opera at Berlin, who later heard the new crescendo in performances of the famous court orchestra of the Elector Palatine, could not but observe: "The masterly effects produced in the Mannheim orchestra by the swelling and diminution of a long note, or of several successive notes . . . would be considered too great an innovation by [the older masters] Hasse and Graun."

Thus, during the one hundred fifty years from the end of the sixteenth to the middle of the eighteenth century, two generations were indifferent to dynamic shades and two favorable to changing intensity. The two former coincided with ethos, and the two latter, with pathos styles. We should pay attention to this fact when we render music of those centuries—not for the sake of some doubtful devotion to historical truth but in order not to destroy its inner coherence.

In doing so, we should be aware of one fact: the interested parties in these generational reversals were Italy and Germany. To France, crescendo was even in the middle of the eighteenth century so far out of the way that Rameau, anxious to use it for a special effect in the prologue of his ballet *Zais* (1748), had to describe it minutely: "Here, each instrument sets in, at first softly, and then insensibly swelling to an extreme *forte*."

The trend of the eighteenth and nineteenth centuries toward an ever-changing intensity was by no means definitive: Stravinsky, exponent of a new antiexpressive style, protested vigorously when Koussevitzky shaded his *Symphonies d'instruments à vent* instead of playing them in a uniform *mezzoforte*.

Tempo, too, depends on the basic contrast of styles. In classical China, rapid tempo was considered vulgar-minded (that is, anticlassic); to the Greeks, a rapid tempo was too nervous, and a slow one too passive and effeminate. Thus, the antithesis reads: moderate versus immoderate, in three degrees, and slow versus fast, in only two degrees of tempo.

Almost two thousand years after the Greeks, in the pathos times of the early fourteenth century, an increase in tempo shows unmistakably in the new symbols for time units which are smaller than any previously used. Again three hundred years later, Bach's son Philipp Emanuel recommended speed in opposition to the traditional slowness of the (ethos-minded) French, and his contemporary Johann Joachim Quantz remarked: "Fast pieces of earlier times [that is, of the most recent past] were played almost twice as slowly as today. *Allegro assai*, *presto*, *furioso*, and so on were not much more rapidly played than *allegretto* today. The many fast notes in instrumental pieces of the German composers of the last generation looked much more difficult and dangerous than they actually sounded. Most modern French have kept a moderate speed in lively pieces." And one more generation later, Mozart condemned rapid tempos: "It is much easier to play a passage quickly than slowly. In the swift passages you can miss notes without anyone's noticing it; but [with a true ethos question] is it beautiful?"

However, the immoderate slowness of some conductors of the Wagner school is not classical either. One should not parry this statement with the incredibly slow performance of the ancient Chinese hymn to Confucius: the hymn is doubtless classic but it is a series of detached notes without rhythm and without the melodic tension that could justify the word tempo at all.

Specific indications of tempo—the outer, countable tempo proper as well as the irrational inner tension—appear in part books of the seventeenth century. Matthias Kelz, a German composer of suites printed in 1658, almost outdoes late Romanticism when he labels his introductory movements as *agiliter*, *animose*, *fuso*, *largo*, *lente*, *nervose*, *presto*, *tardo*. Giovanni Battista Bassani added *prestissimo* in 1677.

It had been quite a shock when the Italians around 1600 began to alternate between *presto* and *adagio lento* in order to differentiate the sections of the same piece. Michael Praetorius tells us in the third volume of his *Syntagma musicum* of 1619 that many a German objected to such practice (just as the Chinese did), particularly in church music. He himself deemed that this kind of "variation and alternation" was neither ugly nor wrong if used with moderation and taste, the better to express the 'affects.'

At the same time, the Italians had begun to depart from rigid tempo even within the same section of a composition. Girolamo Frescobaldi, the greatest organist of St. Peter's, expressly emphasized that his toccatas of 1614 should be as little subject to rigid time as modern madrigals of his day—such as Gesualdo's—which were sung, now languidly, now briskly, according to the meaning of the words and the character of the melody.

Neither tempo nor dynamic shades were inventions of the seventeenth century. No less than seven hundred years before, the so-called Romanian notation which we best know from an antiphonal at Einsiedeln, Switzerland, prescribed by their first letters, *celeriter*, quickly, and three kinds of ritardando: *expectare*, *moderari*, *tenere*, and even two intensities: *frangore* and *clange clamitat* (fortissimo). And all these shades existed in three degrees: *mediocriter*, *bene*, much, and *valde*, very much.

This, better than anything else, shows that there has never been a straight one-way development. All through the centuries, achievements of preceding ages were temporarily stowed away when they did not suit the general style, to be called back in due time.

There is another point. The virtuoso, in the widest sense of the word, was expected freely to embellish the written melody, both in vocal and instrumental music. Although this age-old custom came to an end in the eighteenth century, the concerto-playing virtuoso has tenaciously maintained the privilege and duty to break loose at the end at least of the first movement and to offer an allegedly improvised cadenza with a break-neck display of all his technical tricks. Again, the freedom of improvisation seems to lead the work of art away from essence and deeply into the realm of appearance; and once more this would be a mistake. To pathos, the objects of art live in their appearance only and have no reality, no essence beyond it. All improvisation, on the contrary, whether done on the spot or carefully written down—variations on a given melody, embellishments of the *ripresa* in *da capo* arias, or cadenzas in concertos—acknowledge by their very existence that beyond a hundred different realizations or appearances there is an immanent essence in the composer's mind.

And this is also true of the melody patterns of oriental music. Every Indian piece is but an elaboration on one of the permanent *rāgas* or melody patterns just as every piece of the Near East is but an elaboration on one *maqām*. The patterns are like Platonic ideas without bodies or shapes, which can be defined in their musical and emotional qualities, but do not actually exist as audible pieces, and only appear in numberless, different realizations which answer the definition. Such art is deeply conscious of a permanent essence behind the changing shapes of appearance.

The problem of accidentals, or momentary alternations of the scale in the course of a melody, is quite similar. From the thirteenth century on, the principle of *musica ficta* or *falsa* admitted or even required the sharpening or flattening of certain notes, mostly to make them 'leading.' But the composers, relying on the performer's knowledge and discretion, rarely wrote them down. Uncertain and embarrassed at not knowing how to read the critical notes, we take refuge in the many arrangements for lute of vocal scores—at least in the music of the sixteenth century—hoping to get information from these secondary sources. For tablatures, or fingering scripts, had after all to take sides, since the fingering was different and required another symbol according to whether a note was sharpened or not. But alas, even the lute arrangements, perhaps from negligence, do not always agree; often, one version indicates a sharp or a flat where another demands a natural. With such liberty, accidentals can hardly have been more essential than other forms of expression.

A curious example of such unconcernedness is Johannes Ockeghem's *missa cuiusvis toni*, written sometime in the last third of the fifteenth or the beginning of the sixteenth century—a Mass in Whatever Tone you Want, which could be sung in each of the eight Church modes without changing a single note in the score, just by reading the voice parts in the proper clefs and adding the few accidentals—F sharp or B flat—required by the individual modes. (Readers not familiar with the eight clefs used in the fifteenth century may at least realize that in our modern notation for piano a C major melody reads E minor when a bass clef replaces the original violin clef.) Only too willingly, we call such master-key writing an inartistic pastime. We should however understand that, in the spirit of ethos, it actually means a *recherche de l'absolu* behind the changing appearance conveyed by modes with their sharps and flats.

A decisive, though not final, change came with the monodic style of 1600: Lodovico Viadana's epochal *Cento Concerti Ecclesiastici* of 1602 expressly cautions the singers and the organist to refrain from adding sharps and flats; as far as they are necessary, the composer has taken care of them himself.

Such encroachment on the real or assumed rights of performers is a part of the specific problem of stardom and improvisation. At first sight, exhibition of personal skill as an end seems so closely related to individualistic leanings that it suggests connection with pathos. This is partly true; the Hellenistic and Roman virtuosos as well as Paganini, Liszt, and recent conductors have belonged in such times. But the tragicomedy of arrogant *divas* and *castrati* is at variance with all ideals of genuine pathos. The required unity and significance of the work of art is interfered with when the virtuoso's part is overstressed at the cost of the other parts; if the role of the star is carefully staked off against those of his partners, this acts as a disjoining force; acrobatic technique is tolerated or even favored instead of emotion and nature; and character is necessarily sacrificed to pleasureableness.

A glance at the typical form of instrumental virtuosity confirms this judgment. In the undiluted concerto, Vivaldi's or, later, Viotti's, the role of the orchestra is restricted to hasty *ritornelli* and inconsequential accompaniment while the soloist, intervening between the *ritornelli*, displays his fireworks without any connection with the (however nonexistent) mood and meaning of the work as a whole. In Beethoven's concertos, on the contrary, the solo parts and the soloist himself merge with the orchestra in one symphonic organism which imposes duties rather than privileges upon the performer. A few years after Beethoven's death, Paganini, the archvirtuoso, asked Hector Berlioz to write a concerto for his viola but was thoroughly disappointed on finally receiving the symphony *Harold en Italie*, in which a *viola obbligata*, instead of exhibiting neck-breaking bravura feats, expressed the *melancholia obbligata* of the hero. Berlioz himself lived to hear and admire the final fusion of the soloist and the orchestra in Henry-Charles Litolff's five *symphonie-concerts*.

Pathos times, indeed, did not do away with the virtuoso but tried to assign him a meaningful place in meaningful art.

'Appearance' has in music been a question not only of how but also of where pieces are to be performed. During and after the

Renaissance, the structure of music was often adapted to the particular condition of some local architecture. The somewhat spectacular beginning of such practice, the colorful antiphony of two singing or playing choruses in St. Mark's at Venice around 1550, has usually been described as an inspiration of Adriaen Willaert's, because the two organ lofts in that church face each other and seem to suggest a division of the performers into two answering groups. This is a half-truth only; the pair of lofts had existed long before and the merger of music and space was the result of mental developments, of a new irresistible urge rather than of some chance and its clever exploitation.

Many similar attempts were made in the following hundred years, both in Italy and in Germany and probably also in England, until, in the 1630's, Virgilio Mazzocchi, a Roman composer, wrote for St. Peter's an impressive piece with either twelve or sixteen choruses, we do not know which, set up partly on the ground below the dome, partly on the gallery at roof level, and partly in the dizzying height of the lantern that crowns the dome. The contrast, merger, and echo over such tremendous distances must indeed have made, as an ear witness Pietro della Valle called it, a "marvelous *musicone*," which augmentative evidently meant a big rather than a great music.

Richard Wagner reiterated this effect in the nineteenth century, first in 1843, in the *Liebesmahl der Apostel*, a choral work he wrote for the domed Frauenkirche in Dresden with "voices from on high," and in his last drama, *Parsifal*, where the choruses of the concluding scene sing from the ground, "the middle choir," and "the highest choir."

Wagner, adding the basement to the various musical altitudes, kept the Bayreuth orchestra entirely out of sight, both to unify its sound and not to intercept the voices from the stage, and most opera houses have at least halfway followed his example.

Invisibility of the orchestra, however, was not unprecedented. It had been prescribed in Berlioz's *monodrame lyrique* Lélio *ou le retour à la vie, avec orchestre, choeurs et soli invisibles;* it had been customary in the mysteries of the Middle Ages, in Italian plays of the sixteenth century, and in the Italian opera (and oratorio) until the increasing number and complication of 'machines' on the stage left no space for the hidden orchestra. Goethe, in *Wilhelm Meisters Apprenticeship* (1796), had not only demanded the hidden orchestra but had also given his reasons: "In oratorios and concerts, we are always disturbed by the musician himself. True music addresses the ear only. A beautiful voice is the most general thing that we can imagine, and when the limited individual that puts it forth presents itself to the eye, it ruins the pure effect of such generality." (b. VIII ch. 5)

6. INDEPENDENCE AND DEPENDENCE

THE CONTRAST ESSENCE—APPEARANCE has still another issue: the independence or self-sufficiency of ethos art and the frequent dependence and self-insufficiency of most pathos art. The arts of the ethos side, their individual works, and even parts of their works, rest in themselves and can often be severed from their main bodies and taken away to other places without losing their original meaning and charm; they are self-related. Those of the pathos side are in an entirely different position.

The opposite viewpoints of Mozart and Wagner may illustrate what I mean. Wagner always objected to concert performances of and from his dramatic works, lest they give an entirely wrong idea of his intentions and the meaning of his music. Could there be a greater contrast than the attitude of Mozart who, on January 15, 1787, wrote from Prague: "At six o'clock I went with Count Canal to the *Breiten,* a rustic ball, at which the flower of the Prague beauties are in the habit of assembling . . . [and] saw with wholehearted pleasure how these people jumped around with such sincere enjoyment to the music of my *Figaro,* which had been turned into all kinds of *contres* and *Teutsche*. . . ."

Wagner, intolerant and conceited, Mozart, kindhearted and compliant—is this the clue? Hardly. The two great masters acted and reacted differently because their styles were different. Mozart's music, largely absolute and independent from its place and role in the opera and from conditions of performance, could easily be turned into dances without any harm or blasphemy; Wagner's music, relative and tuned to the outer and inner events of the stage and to the co-reception of visual impressions, cannot well be transplanted into the climate of mere audition.

It is the quality of self-dependence that allows impersonal pieces to change their places without losing their own character or endangering the foreign surroundings. Hans Leo Hassler could around 1600 print his fore- and afterdances in separate sections of his publication and let the players pick out one of each and perform them as a pair; Handel re-used in his oratorio *Joshua* the famous chorus *See, the conqu'ring hero comes* that he had written for *Judas Maccabeus* the year before; Rossini's overture to the opera *Elisa* replaces the lost overture to *The Barber of Seville*. Could one imagine the *Tristan* prelude played instead of the *Meistersinger* overture or a symphony arbitrarily pieced together out of movements from Beethoven's works?

Indeed, it seems that ethos art can easily be transplanted into any different environment, while pathos art is harder to adapt. Folk songs and chorales come off rather well everywhere, in Flemish polyphony no less than in Bach's, in the *Meistersinger,* or in Humperdinck's *Hänsel und Gretel.* But not so individualistic music: even within the same master's personal style, the Tristanesque language of the new bacchanal that Wagner wrote for the later Paris version of *Tannhäuser* is slightly bewildering.

Quite the same is true in architecture. There are few cities in the world without Greco-Roman temples, original or imitated; and for the most part nobody minds them, whether the surroundings are ancient, medieval, or modern. But Chartres Cathedral or the Drapers' Hall from Ypres or a Saxon gabled house would cut a strange enough figure in Athens—of today as well as in the Athens of Perikles. The reason is that, as a rule, the art of pathos, stressing distinctive character and even folkloristic traits at the cost of supernational, all-human significance, of necessity narrows down its own district of validity, while the ancient temple, widening its province from Grecian townships to most of the world, finds a site wherever you care to erect it.

At that, the ethos arts are versatile. We have accepted classic temple fronts for our museums, public libraries, and private manors, for Christian churches, U. S. post offices, and savings banks. We have sometimes looked askance, oftener given a tolerant smile, and oftenest paid no heed to such masquerade. How much more deeply would we resent our banks and postal buildings in the disguise of Gothic cathedrals! Not that the cathedral has kept its halo while the religious meaning of the temple is forgotten. It is the other way around: the Grecian temple, being classical, has little connotation beyond its purely aesthetic qualities; the Gothic cathedral in its pathos cannot well be separated from Catholic service, chant, and incense.

CHAPTER TEN

Close and Open Structures

1. CONTOUR

CLOSE AND OPEN as a leading antithesis of structural trends has been used in recent works and articles on various arts: Gerhard Krahmer in 1923 made it his main division for Hellenistic art; the late Laure Morgenstern in Paris introduced it into the discussion of oriental fine art; and, independently from them, I have found it serviceable in the classification of dances and music. These terms had however been anticipated in a contrasting pair of medieval musical words, the *close* and the *overt*, which designated not two opposite styles but, within the same melody, the half-cadence of the first 'phrase' of a 'period' and the full, definitive cadence of the concluding second phrase.

As a general antithesis, the contrast of open and close again comprises a couple of subcontrasts.

The first and most essential is centripetal–centrifugal, that is, tending toward or away from, a center. Centripetal—one can also say gravitational—implies that a work of art in all its parts crystallizes around a fixed center and whatever motion departs from this focus is bound to return at once as if it were attracted by a magnet. 'Centrifugal,' on the contrary, implies that a work seems to flee from its spatial center and dart outward.

The contrast between centripetal and centrifugal leads to a second pair of opposites, in which one distinguishes between a smooth, untroubled contour and a jerky, jagged profile full of projections in the true sense of the word, of shapes thrown forth and reaching out into the open.

It is hardly necessary to give examples of smooth and of jagged profiles. The Germans have delighted in gables, dormers, and oriels, and the French in forests of chimneys, while the South prefers flat roofs and unbroken façades. Again, the cornices protruding from the otherwise close profiles of Italian *palazzi* are taboo in modern architecture. Towers and turrets, the essential projections of medieval churches, castles, city halls, had been unknown in antiquity and were in Italy at least separated from the buildings proper and even placed quasi casually somewhere off the axis to avoid the feeling of connection; and they in turn so vigorously contradicted the ideals of Louis Quatorze classicism that the church within the vast palace of Versailles was denied them. Contrariwise, a later, more dynamic style undertook to open the horizontal closeness of this *château* by erecting statues on the all too even roof of its park façade.

In sculpture, static styles prefer the outline uninterrupted and round; dynamic styles would pierce the lines and release the arms and legs to thrust into the open. One of the best-known examples, from the sixteenth century, is Jean de Bologne's renowned bronze of Mercury, about to throw himself into the sky to which his arm is showing the way. The theme demands such movement, true; but would a master of the 'close' party have chosen so antistatic a subject?

A parallel dualism is obvious in painting and also in the dance. 'Close' and 'open' show both in the pose and movement of the individual dancer and in choreography; this is the dualism styled 'close' and 'expanded' in my *World History of the Dance* (New York, 1937). The expanded dance "is almost a form of battle, a wild rebellion against the law of gravity" in which the limbs jut out in all directions in an "urge to vivacity and exuberance" (pp. 26, 28). In the closed dance, on the contrary, rhythm flows with measured ease and the limbs hesitate to break through the outline. Such dances "are often surprisingly calm and composed. For unruly power they sometimes substitute charm and grace, even daintiness; for dynamic release, the static ideal, the striving for quiet, steadfastness, and harmonious balance" (p. 34).

In choreography—the art of traversing space in the dance—the simplest, and one of the oldest, closed patterns is 'return' motion, where the dancers take a few steps forward or sideward and return to the starting point with just as many steps in "a static swinging which nullifies every movement and every tension" and in which "the harmonious, satisfying, restful norm is sought" (pp. 168, 169). There are, once more, the ethos epithets static, harmonious, rest, and norm.

Centricity in music is not a mere matter of what the musician calls form but also of melodic and harmonic functions or, better, of gravitation. The Greeks had a 'central' note *mesē* which, as the general pitch tone and the unshakable solar center of the musical space, magnetically attracted the other notes, whatever the key and the course of the melody. The Hindus still use the synonymous term *mādhyama;* the Chinese liken the middle note *chiao* to the center of the world; the Arabs of the tenth century gave one of their notes the name *shams* or 'sun'; and thus our tone name *sol,* which is the Latin equivalent of this last, seems to convey the notion of a solar center.

Music has lost this conception; our pitch tone *a′* is no longer the magnetic center to which all keys refer. Instead, each individual key has its own magnetic final or tonic, to which the melody and the harmony revert again and again unless they are atonal.

To see the contrast of smooth and jagged outlines in music, one may compare the following solemn motive from the third act of *Parsifal* (Example 40) with the passage *Doch uns ist gegeben an keiner Stätte zu ruhn* (But mankind is doomed not to rest in any

Example 40. Parsifal *Richard Wagner*

place) in Brahms' *Schicksalslied,* Song of Fate (Example 41). The first melody worms its way chromatically within a very small range;

Example 41. Schicksalslied *Brahms*

the passage from the Song of Fate juts out in violent, desperate dashes zigzag across the range of human voices. But even this theme strictly reverts to the tonic, in the true sense of Brahms' classicism, and therefore does not show all the possibilities of centrifugal movement. To see what these possibilities are, one has to turn to the expressionistic singing style of Alban Berg's opera *Wozzeck* of 1922 (Example 42).

Not always do centrifugal trends in music appear in wide and jagged outlines. Another evidence of the same force is what modern theory calls a sequence, in which a short motive or theme, oblivious of its tonic, repeats itself in ever higher keys with exactly the same center-fleeing *dynamis* that, for example, the Celtic ornament of the spiral has in art.

2. *ADDITION AND UNIFICATION*

Repetition and addition are the two primeval principles of all composition in art. On a higher level, they develop to unification.

Repetition and addition are serial structures, consisting in sequences of units, without subordination under higher units. A typical example of addition is the beginning of the Bible:

> In the beginning God created the heaven and the earth.
> *And* the earth was without form and void.
> *And* darkness was upon the face of the deep.
> *And* the spirit of God moved upon the waters.
> *And* God said, Let there be light.
> *And* God saw the light, that it was good.
> *And* God divided the light from the darkness.
> *And* God called the light Day.
> *And* the darkness he called Night.
> *And* there was evening
> *And* there was morning, one day.

Example 42. Wozzeck *Alban Berg*

This is a pure sequence of dissimilar units, even when modern translations embarrassedly replace some of the periods by semicolons. It is *a* plus *b* plus *c*, without any attempt to integrate the narrative in a whole of principal and subordinate sentences.

Repetition, on the contrary, is the sequence of similar units, whether it appears as a set of uniform parallel lines scratched on a Vedda's bamboo quiver, as the uninterrupted array of similar columns or windows, as the endlessly chained meanders on a Grecian frieze or some all-over pattern, as a series of equivalent verse feet, or as a strophic reiteration of the same short melody.

Repetition and addition as structural principles are neutral. They convey a feeling of movement without actual progression, of station without rest. They go on but do not carry us anywhere; they stay but do not let our eyes repose.

Both repetition and addition concur in the variation form: the members that constitute a variation are spiritually similar but factually dissimilar, and the pleasure a variation conveys is due to this two-sidedness.

The term is chiefly used in music, where it is oftener than elsewhere the leading principle, because performers, even on the lowest level of civilization, are generally unable to repeat a phrase without changes and also because in music more than one exact repetition is hard to bear. A musical variation can be melodic, dissolving or paraphrasing a theme in ever-faster figuration; or coloristic, with the orchestration changing each time the piece is repeated; or polyphonic, with the theme successively appearing in each of the voice parts; or rhythmic, as in certain suites of the sixteenth and seventeenth century, where each movement reproduces exactly the same sequence of notes, but in the particular rhythm of some dance—the four-four of the pavan, or the three-four of the galliard.

Variation, again, is as a principle neither progressive nor stationary. But here separation begins: a polyphonic variation with the theme successively appearing in each of the voice parts is stationary; it is a set of ever-changing versions, but without progression to a final goal. The individual variations, strictly separated from their neighbors, can often be taken out or exchanged without destroying the whole. Frequently, as in Bach's Goldberg Variations, the theme in its original, unvaried form is repeated after the last variation, thus completing the set and stressing the antiprogressive return character of a form which, better than any other, agrees with Eduard Hanslick's famous definition of music—of all music—as *tönend bewegte Form*, a (meaningless) play of sounding forms.

A melodic variation, on the contrary, dissolving or paraphrasing a theme in ever-faster figuration, is modestly progressive. Many pieces in the Fitzwilliam Virginal Book may serve as examples.

In the fine arts, too, variation is either a stationary alternation or a progressive change. Of the former kind are the columns of some early church, repetitive in shape and size, but different in marble and color—white, pink, gray; or the individually carved capitals of a set of otherwise similar columns. Of the progressive kind is story variation: the three stories of some Roman or sixteenth-century building, similar in size and proportions, but successively following the heavy Doric, the balanced Ionic, and the elegant Corinthian order, so that the theme appears in ever-lighter configuration.

Station and progression are indeed the dominant qualities of all composition beyond the rudimentary stage. Station belongs to styles of permanence, limitation, impersonal serenity; progression serves the styles that aim at boundlessness, personal passion, and change. A *sacra conversazione* of the Italian Renaissance—the Virgin in the middle with quietly bystanding, reverent saints symmetrically turned inward at left and at right—is a paragon of stationary composition. And so is any musical piece in which the first part, repeated after the second, impedes development, progress, and growth.

Both examples, however, belong to a higher class of art, in which the primitive types of mere repetition, addition, or variation are organized in a unified whole, every unit being answered and balanced by a similar unit on the opposite side of a median axis. Such organization is called symmetry.

In architecture, which as a typically stationary art clings to symmetry even in the most dynamic times, this gravitation toward a common axis is of three kinds.

(i) Unstressed: the front extends symmetrically right and left of the central axis without accenting the sides or the axis itself. The axis rests entirely unmarked—as in the earlier Renaissance *palazzo* with its two doors—or else is scarcely marked by the vertex of the pediment, as in Greco-Roman temples and Italian Romanesque cathedrals.

(ii) Double-stressed: the two sides jut out or carry flanking towers, as in the earlier Gothic.

(iii) Single-stressed: the sides, subordinate, yield the stress to the center, which may or may not jut out, as in the later Gothic cathedrals and in the Baroque, or recede, as in the *cours d'honneur* of France, and include an overemphasized portal and carry a single tower or dome.

The first two kinds of symmetry belong rather to ethos, and the latter, to pathos styles.

The alternation of these principles often follows short-lived generational reversals: the new pathos in the last third of the fifteenth century is at once answered by a central door instead of the earlier two doors—as, for instance, in the Banco Mediceo at Milan—or, much more strongly, by a heavy oriel on columns in the middle of the façade, as in Giovanni da Verona's Santa Maria dei Miracoli in Brescia (1488). Again, Bramante's works, characteristic of the early sixteenth century, are quite unstressed; and after 1520, some architects combined two lateral turrets as double stresses with a central dome as a single stress, as did Antonio da San Gallo in his model for St. Peter's.

In painting, all symmetry belongs to ethos whether it is unstressed, double-stressed, or single-stressed, including the pyramidal patterns of the Renaissance. In pathos styles, close symmetry is replaced by an open balance of dissimilar masses, lines, or colors.

In music, symmetry in the strictest sense of the word occurs only under one form, which is not structural at all: the crab canon, a composition that reads backward just as it reads forward. And this one form must not be considered, since its note by note regression obeys the law of symmetry in the letter only, not in the spirit; it can be seen on the paper—and even there only in the way of study and by trained musicians—but cannot be perceived with the ear and hence is unable to give aesthetic pleasure.

Perceptible symmetry in music, according to current terminology, means melodic repetition, not inversion. It is generally understood to denote a 'period,' in which a 'phrase,' ending on an open half-cadence, is repeated but this time closed by a full cadence. In a rudimentary form, such symmetrical periods appear as early as the lowest civilization, indeed in the music of the Veddas and the Patagonians, which Chapter I of this book discussed as the lowest (Example 1); and it has persisted with unparalleled tenacity. It was the formal principle of medieval lays and Church sequences and of many dances and has survived in folk tunes, anthems, nursery rhymes.

The ambiguity of the term 'symmetry' in architecture makes it imperative to broaden its meaning in music, too. Of the two main classes of musical forms, repetitive and progressive, symmetry seems *ex definitione* to apply to repetitive forms only. These, again, are either binary or ternary, according to whether they consist of two or of three main sections.

The simplest forms of binary symmetry are the already mentioned 'period' as a small form, the older sonata with its repeat, as a large form, and, above all, antiphony.

Antiphony is the alternate singing, by two half-choruses, either of each individual line of the text or of two consecutive lines, a practice which has been important from the primitive stages of mankind to Wagner's *Parsifal*, with highlights in Biblical times and in the Italian Renaissance and Baroque. Antiphony is the more fascinating as, dependent upon the face-to-face disposition of the two half-choruses, it forms an actual link between musical and architectural symmetry.

The 'period,' as a musical form, extends from its initial level up to the vertex created by the open half-cadence; and it returns, in the following full cadence, to that level in as many measures. In a similar way, the first section (of the first movement) of the older sonata—Corelli's or Purcell's—extends from the initial level of the tonic up to the vertex created by a modulation to the dominant key at the end of the first and the beginning of the second section, and returns to the tonic.

Ternary forms, on the contrary, have the kind of symmetry that we called double-stressed in architecture, and which in poetry and music is given the formula ABA: the composer, contrasting part A with the different character of part B, closes the form by resuming A. Thus he does in a way what the architect does when he separates the two similar towers of a church front by a contrasting lower middle section. One should however be careful not to liken the musical ABA to the pattern of the French Louis Quatorze palace, where the stress lies on the recessed central part B, not on the projecting lateral parts AA. The musical ABA form existed in medieval church songs, in the Italian *da capo* aria around 1700 (which played so dominating a role in the opera, the oratorio, and the cantata), and in the well-known group scherzo–trio–scherzo of later symphonies.

This latter group is related to ABA forms in the dance (though in the dance the B is a fast movement between livelier sections): the *basse danse*, for example, around 1500 was followed by a *saltarello* or a *tourdion* of different rhythm and tempo and then repeated; and in a similar way its successor, the pavan, was followed by a less stately galliard in triple time and then repeated.

Not much later, in the pathos times of the sixteenth century, the set of three was rearranged: the *saltarello*, then called *tourdion*, changed places with the second *basse danse*—repetitive or return motion yielded to progressive motion, ABA to AAB. In the same pathos times, the French performed their courtly round dances in sets of at least three in growing speed, that is, again in progressive sequence: first the sedate *branle double* for the older people, then the brisker *branle simple* for the younger married couples, and finally the rapid *branle gay* for the unmarried.

The single-stressed symmetry of architecture seems not to apply to music: aesthetically, it means drawing the eye at once to the center and only subsequently allowing it to glide away to either side—which is not feasible in music.

While ethos develops from stationary addition to symmetry, pathos art, explosive, centrifugal, shuns symmetrical patterns, in which its dash would break. For symmetry is, in George Santayana's words, "what metaphysicians call a principle of individuation. By the emphasis it lays upon the recurring elements, it cuts up the field into determinate units; all that lies between the beats is one interval, one individual" (*The Sense of Beauty*, N.Y. 1936, p. 71). From its starting principle—progressive addition—pathos achieves a higher organization in ways that we might appropriately call integration. Such integration deprives the individual parts of all their independence and fuses them into a whole. Symmetry is antiphonic, integration is symphonic.

Instead of a *sacra conversazione*, in which the saints symmetrically flank the Virgin, the men of pathos would shift the Virgin to one side and make the saints advance from the other end of the canvas to greet her, thus suggesting a progression that the Holy Conversation avoids.

In architecture, the most remarkable integration is the Baroque way of uniting the interiors of buildings, in which even sculptures, rarely isolated, formed groups with other sculptures or with parts of the house and could hardly be severed from the room for which they were intended. The individual rooms, in their turn, lost their self-sufficiency and independence; one of them, predominant, gathered the smaller rooms around to be its satellites in a lively play of overlapping, penetration, and foreshortening. And often enough, the remaining partitions became so insignificant that a group of rooms would practically merge into one.

Beyond the unified single house, the Baroque as well as the Hellenists and the Romans proceeded to unify whole sets of buildings, indeed, whole towns and cities. The integration of St. Peter's in Rome and its gigantic square with Bernini's rounded colonnades and, more so, the planned, though never realized, integration of the streets down to the Tiber, is the classical instance of town planning—that is, of thinking in higher units than that represented by a single building. Such town planning implies the creation of fascinating vistas and the correct angle at which a building should be seen in order to offer its best, most picturesque view: appearance wins once more over essence. But, particularly in France, the synthesis of Baroque town planning and strong classicism led to unification under the pitiless rule of strictest symmetry, as in the palace and park of Versailles or the gigantic axis from the Louvre to the Arc de triomphe.

3. DISJUNCTION AND CONJUNCTION

THE BASIC CONTRAST between the styles that follow station and those that strive for growth and progression has two further aspects, which partly overlap with the two forms in which they achieve unification. The first is the dualism of disjunction and conjunction. The ethos artist neatly separates, 'disjoins' the individual parts of his work, lest movement pass from part to part and in its flow interfere with station and rest. The other way around, a pathos artist, eager to move and advance, unites, 'conjoins' the parts of his work, lest barriers from part to part interfere with flow and progression. Disjunction gives a clearer view of things as they 'are'; conjunction conveys a stronger feeling of things as they seem to move and to act.

The contrast of the Greek and the late-Gothic columns is a good example from architecture. The classical column in Greece is crowned by a headpiece or capital, which cuts off its upward surge, while above, the horizontal 'tablature' of architrave, frieze, and cornice opposes passive weight to active force. There is perfect equilibrium, a plus and a minus resulting in zero, which is the ideal of static, restful art.

Quite to the contrary, the later Gothic column, robbed of all arresting, disjoining capitals, juts up to form one piece with the vertical rib above and finds no rest before it reaches the boss high up in the vault. There is no balance; the passive weight is radically suppressed, and the surging force springs up with unresisted violence.

In the ground plan, the Gothic builders opposed from the very beginning the sharp separation, in Romanesque churches, of the nave from the transept and the transept from the choir. In an attempt at unification, they shortened the transept so much that all three sections—nave, transept, and choir—fitted in one rounded, unbroken outline.

As to façades, the three stories of Italian palaces in the fifteenth century—Medici or Pitti or Strozzi in Florence—had been so neatly separated by uninterrupted cornices that one fancies a knife could easily cut them apart. A hundred years later, a central portal would with its decorated *supraporta* pierce the separating line and boldly push into the second story. Indeed, after the precedent of the Palazzo Bevilacqua in Verona (1540), massive pilasters or columns, ignoring the horizontal divisions, would bring together two or three stories in vertical sections.

At the same time, the pathos need of conjunction as against disjunction is impressively shown in the insertion of connecting scrolls or volutes between architectural parts otherwise set off at right angles. Italian basilicas of pre-Romanesque and Romanesque days had honestly showed in their façades that the middle nave was higher than the outer naves; the architects would not have understood why they should conceal this evident fact and shun the resulting right angles in the upper contour. The masters of the Baroque thought and acted differently. Following Giulio Romano's example on San Benedetto al Polirone (*c.* 1542), they filled the two right angles with a large descending volute each, so that the eye, ignoring the actual elevation, glided down from the middle roof along the springy S-curve and smoothly landed on the lateral roofs. Deeply shocked by the absence of connecting links, they indeed went the length of gluing such volutes on older churches, wherever they were given an opportunity; Santa Maria Novella in Florence is an excellent, well-known example. A true thicket of connecting volutes is Santa Maria della Salute at the end of the Canale Grande in Venice (1631–56), where Longhena devised eight volutes between the lantern and the dome and sixteen gigantic volutes, radiating all around, between the dome and the eight-sided church proper.

The same spirit that drove architects to wedge connecting, smoothing volutes into the angular outlines of church façades created in music a typical Baroque form of musical embellishment, which softened any large stride by a slurring scale passage in order to avoid the baldness of leaps from level to level (Example 43). Its names,

Italian *tirata*, German *Schleifer*, recur in the terminology of contemporaneous dancing to indicate what German dancing masters, in bad French, also called *die douce manier*, a Baroque reaction against the angular steps, kicks, and leaps of the Renaissance. And from here, the reader's mind might revert to an earlier quotation from Wolfgang Mylius' contemporary *Rudimenta musices* (1686): "You must not drop from *forte* to *piano*, but gradually let the voice *crescendo* and *decrescendo*."

It means another way of conjunction when certain Gregorian melodies change their endings in order to adapt themselves to the melody immediately following and make the two one piece. It also means conjunction when in the sonata in its earlier form, shortly before 1700, the movements, although contrasted in rhythm and tempo, run into one another and must be played straight through.

The sonata of the following ethos generation is built on the opposite principle: the four movements are separated, and each ends in a full and definitive cadence. Again, the subsequent generations admitted, or even favored, the *attacca* of the last movement without a rest after the preceding one. (Mozart enthusiasts will with delight remember the ingenious, unexpected entry of the *Fandango* after the wedding chorus in *Figaro*). At the end of the evolution of the sonata, about the middle of the nineteenth century, Liszt fused the sections of his famous Sonata in B Minor for the piano (1853) into one single movement and, in exactly the same way, recast the four movements of the symphony (which has faithfully followed the form of the sonata) into the new type of the symphonic poem in one movement.

The contrasting attitudes toward the dis- or conjunction of individual movements is mirrored in another juxtaposition: the eighteenth century tolerated the performance of just one movement from a sonata, symphony, or concerto, a fact that, incidentally, accounts for the seemingly unbearable length of concert programs at that time. Such slicing has not been done in recent years; nor is it deemed in good taste to applaud between the movements, because it gives them a sham independence.

Disjunction and conjunction, though, have nowhere been more important than in the to-and-fro of operatic evolution. On the one hand, there is the typical opera, neatly made up of single 'numbers' —recitatives, arias, cavatines, duets, marches, choruses, finales. Its adversaries, two hundred years ago, called this kind of opera "a bunch of arias." Indeed, every aria, following the *da capo* form ABA, was in itself parceled out in three separate sections and, thus being autonomous, endangered the coherence of the whole. In all real pathos times such weakening disjunction was replaced by deliberate conjunction. Their musical dramas, as opposed to the 'opera,' have in the interest of uninterrupted progression favored 'endless' melody and also effaced the strict caesuras between vocal and instrumental pieces and from solos to ensembles. Even the overture, in the 'opera' an independent potpourri designed to allow belated spectators to enter before the curtain rose, was in the musical drama converted into a shorter prelude which led smoothly into the first scene, if there was a prelude at all. What is more, there has been a tendency to skip the intermission between the acts (which was occasionally done with Wagner's Flying Dutchman) or to condense the drama into one uninterrupted action: Wagner had led the way in *Rheingold;* the Italian *verismo* followed with *Cavalleria Rusticana* and *Pagliacci;* and so did Richard Strauss in *Feuersnot*, *Salome*, and *Electra.*

The second of those aspects which partly overlap with the different integrations of stationary and progressive styles is the dualism of contrast and uniformity. Ethos art, in need of disjunction, resorts to striking contrasts; pathos art, on the contrary, rather tries to deaden contrast, which too easily destroys the intensity, unity, and one-way progression, both in form and content. Thus, the ballet master Jean-Georges Noverre, as a pioneer of pathos, wrote in 1760: "It is a capital mistake to mingle opposite *genres*, the serious and the comic, the noble and the trivial, the *galant* with the burlesque."

The two viewpoints—mingling and parting—are clearest in the master-and-servant motive of the opera. Both Tristan and Isolde have important servants. But Kurwenal and Brangäne, on a level with their masters and serving them as devoted friends, are strictly kept apart from one another and even hostile, in order to intensify the concentrated drama between the two heroes without contrasting it with a play of their own. In the *Meistersinger*, one step away from radical pathos principles, Hans Sachs' apprentice David and Eva Pogner's nurse Magdalena have their understanding with gifts of cakes and sausage and at long last get engaged to be married. They duplicate Eva's and Walter's courtship on a lower level without becoming vulgar. The *Magic Flute*, on the contrary, lives on the forced and somewhat nauseating contrast between the couples Tamino–Pamina and Papageno–Papagena, which is the eternal contrast between the uplifted spirit of the noble and the hackneyed mind of the vulgar. Papageno, though in his far-fetched connection with

Tamino not properly his servant, is indeed, like Don Giovanni's Leporello, the *servo ridiculo* whom the Italian opera had created in 1634 (Stefano Landi's *Alessio*) in the very moment in which it had given up the pathos ideals of its beginnings.

In nonscenic music, this contrast is fundamental in the classic sonata form: the very first movement exposes a first, leading theme, energetic, masculine, and in the main tonality, and contrasts it with a subsequent second theme, more lyrical, feminine, and in the 'dominant' key, a fifth higher. It was a revolutionary act when Robert Schumann gave his piano concerto Op. 54 one subject only.

Orchestration, too, has known two poles. The ideal of contrast is reached when the sixteenth century alternates from piece to piece between bodies of different timbre; when the seventeenth century opposes groups of strings, wood winds, brasses, and voices, answering each other in choral antiphony; and when Wagner, in his least dynamic work, *Parsifal* (1882), repeats his themes in descending order from delicate flutes and oboes to the warmer horns, from horns to the mellower strings, and from strings to the solemn trombones. The other pole, integration, is achieved either by the free and ever-changing penetration of all the instruments, as in *Tristan* or anywhere in Strauss and Debussy, or by reducing the gamut if not the *glissando* of colors to an almost complete monochrome of strings, as often in the seventeenth century.

We need not leave the seventeenth century to find the analogy in painting: Rembrandt delighted in the free penetration of all colors and shades in the Night Watch of Amsterdam (1642), and in the practical monochrome of the darkest hues in his Syndics (1662), both in the Rijksmuseum. New Yorkers have an outstanding example of monochrome in the marvelous symphony in red of Velasquez's Cardinal Velasco in the Metropolitan Museum.

Ethos times hardly knew penetration or monochrome. To realize this difference, it suffices to glance at some *sacra conversazione* of the Raphael generation with its full, unbroken colors: the Madonna in red and blue, and the saints, one in white, one in red, the third in yellow, and the last in green. But more so, the Egyptians and the classical Greeks used to paint the various parts of the temple and even its reliefs in glaring, contrasting colors the better to detach them from each other—red, yellow, blue, and green. In the same order of thought, Pheidias' Athene of gold and ivory was typically disjunct on the strength of a variety in materials that kept the flesh apart from the hair and the garment. Almost two thousand five hundred years later, Max Klinger resumed this ethos motif in his statues of Salome (1893), with amber eyes and painted hair, Cassandra (1895), and the well-known Beethoven (1902), all in the museum of Leipzig.

It only means one step beyond the conjunction of parts—which is an opening of inner barriers—when in pathos times the work of art opens its frame. This should not be understood too literally: to avoid a frame is difficult and not even desirable: most people have experienced its power when some aesthetically insignificant bit of scenery, caught and cut off in a driver's mirror or an archway, of a sudden attracts and delights.

But even these two chance frames constitute two opposite cases: the arch does actually insulate the piece of scenery that it frames and makes it complete in itself, without inviting the onlooker's imagination to visualize its continuation left and right. The driver's mirror, on the contrary, provides no flanking; the piece of scenery that it catches is incomplete and 'open.' The ethos man would find it lacking in form, but to the pathos man it would appeal as stimulating and 'natural.'

The strictest ethos masters, discontented with the wooden frames outside, have indeed a liking for painted, compositional boundaries inside. Their figures have no life beyond the frame, and their sceneries must rest confined between a stagelike wing of rock or tree on either side.

Artists from the other camp—early examples are the Flemish miniaturists around 1400—would cut right through the composition with the frame, as if it were the border of the driver's mirror. They indeed would cut through bodies so that the nearest appear as half-figures or busts. There is no feeling of stagelike limitation and pose but, on the contrary, the suggestion of an unlimited expanse beyond our field of vision. In a similar way, an artist of the pathos camp would paint the ocean or a grassy plain right to the frame, without any flanking wings, to suggest that they are only artificially cut off, and that imagination should see them in their boundlessness. It was not his fault when around 1900 some fools began to carve and color frames which then, instead of insulating the picture, continued it with trees and clouds in bas-relief.

Painting has been opened, not sideways only but also forward, by addressing the onlooker and effacing the spiritual distance between him and itself. This happens in portraits, the eyes of which pursue the visitor whether he stands at the left or the right. It also happens where some minor figure in a group turns his face away from the scene described and looks at the public, to create a contact; indeed, such a figure, looking out of the picture, sometimes points with his index finger at the hero, to guide the spectator's attention and make him a witness.

To help the illusion that the observer is a party to the play, the north Italians often painted their pictures as seen from below, that is, from the level on which the public actually stands.

The proscenium, so frequent in north Italian paintings of the Renaissance, is a similar, though spatial, way to connect the two worlds in and outside the canvas. A few steps lead to the 'stage' of action; some accessory figures, uninteresting and uninterested, loiter about; a fruit, not called for by the theme of the picture, is dropped somewhere in the foreground and reaches forward beyond the edge of the stage. So there are two realities, the scene proper and an ante-scene, which, switched between the stage and the public, lessens the distance between the two.

The sculptor's frames are the socle and the niche: the socle separates the statue from the ground; the niche separates it from its environment. Strictness respects them; freedom trespasses. Both forms of violation—of the niche and of the socle—have been frequent in most pathos generations. The two together occur in Verrocchio's tabernacle on Or San Michele in Florence (1483): Christ stands on a socle in the niche, while Saint Thomas, touching his master's wound, is half outside the niche without a socle of his own. Encroachment for lack of socles is complete in the twenty-four stone animals that flank the Road to the Thirteen Tombs at Chang Ping Chou in China (fifteenth century). The highwater mark was reached, in the eighteenth century with the strange processional figures that the Spaniard Zarcillo carved for Murcia (today in the Ermita de Jesús), particularly the Last Supper: thirteen disconnected, wooden statues, which, life-size and realistically painted, sit around a real table on real chairs, while the public is allowed to walk around them. This is full-illusionistic 'waxworks,' made almost to deceive the faithful; but they are so well made and so honest and strong that they silence any criticism on general aesthetic grounds.

Insulation has gone almost entirely when monuments in our streets show not only the great man's bust but also some nondescript allegorical figure who hails the hero in a disconcertingly theatrical gesture or, worse, points his finger at him like a showman and looks invitingly at the public. It is also almost absent when a statue is sitting on a grave as if she were a living mourner: the grave is a complete and insulated organism, and the woman something intermediary between the work of art and the visitor. This has even happened in a decidedly classic atmosphere: Canova's tomb for the Duchess Maria Christina in Vienna (1798–1805) is a funeral pyramid in relief against the wall of the church with mourners in the round, who approach the open door (a motive taken up a hundred years later, 1899, in Paul-Albert Bartholomé's *Monument aux Morts* in the cemetery of Père-Lachaise in Paris). Classicism, however, is entirely absent from René de Saint-Marceaux's monument to the International Postal Union in Bern (1909), with real water, natural rocks, and the five continents floating round the earth. There is a borderline where pathos ends and bad taste has the field.

In architecture, the contrast: insulation–encroachment shows in the degree to which a building reaches out into its neighborhood. Examples are a good many North Italian villas of the seventeenth century with their adjoining arcades thrown far out into the parks like feelers, and Lorenzo Bernini's concave colonnades in front of St. Peter's in Rome, which like open arms receive and embrace the square.

That this applies to music, too, appears from a comparison of the preludes to the *Meistersinger* and to *Tristan,* both created by the same master in the same decade. The former, following the pattern of the traditional overture, is very finite in the irrevocability of its firm and full beginning on the tonal triad and its unmistakable ending—despite the *attacca* of the chorale in the wings, which starts on the last beat of the prelude. The *Tristan* prelude, on the contrary, sets in indistinctly with a groping, harmonically problematic stride in the dark; indeed, one famous conductor used to give the first upbeat with so vague a gesture that the twelve 'celli could not but start individually and thus add to the infinite character of the beginning.

4. TECTONICS AND ATECTONICS

Tectonics and atectonics indicate whether a style does, or does not, stress the structural articulation of buildings and bodies, the balance of weight and support in architecture, and the physiological workability of man as an object of sculpture and painting. A triumph of tectonics was the Greek temple in its marvelous equilibrium of vertical forces and horizontal weights—but also the Gothic cathedral, which quite openly displays its supporting framework of buttresses, piers, and ribs; and no less tectonic are the skeletons of modern steel architecture, like the Eiffel Tower in Paris or George Washington Bridge in New York.

Atectonic buildings of the East, including Byzantine churches, show picturesque masses in obscured relation and with decorative surfaces rather than a clean contrast of horizontal and vertical functions. Atectonic builders of the West often play with surprise and deception. A Baroque church, seen from the front, would appear to be taller than it actually is: you enter and are disappointed to see that the naves are lower than you expected; you return outside and realize that the front wall is higher than the building itself. The same is true of secular edifices in the Baroque; as Martin Shaw Briggs nicely puts it, "it was a point of honor among these architects that, so far as possible, a stranger entering one of their palaces should imagine its dimensions to be greater than was actually the case."

Dotti, who in 1723 erected the Santuario di San Luca high above Bologna, gave the church an oval exterior and a Greek cross interior; how a purist would shrink from such a heresy! A quite different specimen of atectonic architecture is Asam's St. Nepomuk Chapel in Munich (*c.* 1720), whose ceiling does not rest on the (visible) walls, but extends above and beyond them (to invisible walls) to suggest the infinite sky. This is sham architecture but at least ingenious. Any short trip through a nineteenth-century town would provide an astonishing collection of make-believe architecture of a much lower order: stucco pilasters glued on façades and pretending to carry what is actually supported by iron posts inside; gables that suggest imaginary roofs or attics; turrets that nobody ever would or could ascend.

The contrast of tectonics and atectonics goes down to the last architectural detail. The Doric capital, a simple cushion of stone, forms an organic, seemingly resilient pad between the carrying column and the weighing tablature; the Corinthian capital, a delicate cluster of leaves, is decorative and full of life but unable to reconcile push and pressure. Greek columns, straight and slightly bulging like the muscles of carrying arms, are tectonic. The screwed or rifled columns of the later Middle Ages and those of the Baroque, first evidenced 1580–85 in Veronese's Triumph of Venice on the ceiling of the main reception room in the Palazzo Ducale, suggest a violent movement upward and, exaggerating their function, give the lie to the rigid material they are made of; a Romanesque knotted column with two or more entwined shafts is decorative and fantastic but entirely dematerialized and unable to convey the idea of firm support. In a similar way, the Romanesque pulpits whose supporting columns rest on couchant lions—as in the baptistry of Pisa (1260) and the cathedral of Ravello (1272)—embarrass tectonic-minded eyes, which would anticipate that the heavy weight of stone must eventually break the spines of the beasts.

One thinks of Vitruvius who, living in the ethos time of Emperor Augustus, exclaimed: "How can you admit that reeds are able to support a roof, or that the candelabra could bear the dome of a temple with all its decorations, or that a tender and trembling stem could carry the weight of a seated figurine?" (Quoted from Lionello Venturi's *History of Art Criticism*, N.Y. 1936, p. 56).

Tectonic, more than atectonic, sculptors and painters are anxious to suggest the play of bones and muscles under the surface of skin and attire. In this urge, they meet the fashion designers, who, as a rule, bare the joints of the body—ankles, wrists, and neck—in ethos times, but much less so in times of pathos. No ethos generation could have invented ruffs or high boots or farthingales.

Decoration and ornament, so intimately connected with costume, reflect the contrast tectonics—atectonics better than anything else. Ornament in itself does not belong to any definite group of style; it can be close or open, limpid or involved, seriated or integrated, symmetrical or asymmetrical, calm or feverish, abstract or near to forms of nature. The question is not how ornaments are, but how they are used. They may be suppressed altogether, as they widely are today, or at least applied sparingly; or else they may be introduced so lavishly as to choke the structure they are called upon to adorn. They may respect the structural lines and strictly limit themselves to filling nonstructural parts, as panels, friezes, pediments, or profusely and ruthlessly overgrow the structural carriers. Many façades of the French Romanesque and of the later fifteenth century, the marvels of the luxuriant, delicate plateresque or 'silversmith' style in the

Spanish Renaissance and, strongest of all, the styles of the ending Baroque and the Rococo, give a good idea of atectonic decoration.

The form-dissolving quality of atectonic decoration nowhere shows better than in the ornamental treatment of the column. While, as the main support of everything above, it is kept untouched and clean in all tectonic, and even in moderately atectonic styles, in late Romanesque art it is unhesitatingly shaped or adorned in fanciful ways. The columns in the northern door of St. Peter's in Moissac and those from St. Guilhem-le-Désert (before A.D. 1206) in the Cloisters in New York are hatched, scaled, or even serpentine; and many others are covered with luxuriant ornaments from foot to capital. And this is also true of the Baroque: those in Churriguera's sections of Salamanca Cathedral (1732) belong in the same family.

In music, all the graces, diminutions, or coloraturas, which we comprise under the common names of musical ornaments or musical decorations, are very different in form and scope. They connect intervals, enliven individual notes and supply longer passages with rounded flourishes; they are either unwritten and left to the skill of the trained performer, or written out in ordinary notes, or symbolized in conventional signs. But however they appear, they are the casual 'appearances' of melodies that exist or at least can be reconstrued in their ground form, that is, in their 'essence.' It tallies with this pathos quality, when the Hindus say, a melody without graces "is bald" and "cannot smile," since graces "are the very pulse and breath of melody and give the individual note its weight, shade, and meaning."

Within this general nature, ornament extends all the way from pathos to radical ethos. It often sacrifices character to superficial beauty and technical bravura, which excludes it almost entirely from Gluck and from the romantics, but granted it an all-important role in the formal music of France in the age of the Couperins. On the other hand, it would, in the right form and at the right place, convey a tension that cannot be easily reached by other means.

Nothing equals the excitement of a long, preparatory trill; and the emphatic 'turn' of four or five notes rapidly circling around the principal note, so frequent in Wagner's works from *Die Feen* to *Parsifal*, is with him not a subsequently glued-on grace but a lifting gesture of the strongest emotional power. Still, as typical a pathos composer as Wagner does not use embellishing grace notes, except in caricaturing Mime's falsehood, or the tailors' parade in the last act of *Die Meistersinger;* and the mere idea of mordents in a song of *Tristan* or *Parsifal* would be ludicrous.

On the other hand, we saw that as emotional a style as the Indian cannot exist without graces. The discrepancy must probably be explained by the vital difference between the two styles: the irrealistic character of Hindu music and the strong realism of the later Romantic style. To Wagner, graces (except the 'turn') meant glued-on, 'embellishing' ornaments. But embellishment is incompatible with character or nature: man's speech varies in height and intensity; it goes up and down and is now loud, now soft; but it has no trills or appoggiaturas. Thus Wagner's adequate idiom was melody with a continuous change from *fortissimo* and *forte* to *mezzoforte*, *piano*, and *pianissimo*. India, on the contrary, does not imitate speech and instead strives for an utterance as far from everyday conversation as possible. Therefore she does not seek expression through a restless crescendo and decrescendo but rather through graces which bend, enliven, and deflect the rigid lines of melody.

Accordingly, graces and varying intensity seem to a certain degree to exclude one another. Where graces are meant to be the means of expression, there is no room for varying intensity; where, on the contrary, graces appear in a style using varying intensities, they lose their emotional power and become mere embellishments. Performers of older music should take this fact to heart. They should, for example, realize that the overdecoration of harpsichord music early in the eighteenth century is conditioned by the rigidity of the instrument and becomes meaningless—to say the least—on a piano played in the dynamic style of the nineteenth century.

Musical overdecoration is synchronized with overdecoration in the fine arts. For Romanesque times there is no direct proof that secular music was overdecorated but its evidences, the notations of troubadour songs, are possibly mere skeletons since some of these songs, still alive on the coasts and isles of the west Mediterranean, are sung in a florid style as remote from the pedantic notes of these texts as a human being in flesh and skin is from his bones.

We are better informed about the musical practice in Churriguera's time: we know how Couperin's and Rameau's works almost choke under the impact of piled-up grace notes in all their voice parts; and we have some difficulty in accepting the ornamental saturation of Bach's chorale-preludes, which does not fit our preconceived idea of solemn grandeur. Even where the composer did not care to write the ornaments out, the performers, if soloists, were expected freely to adorn his sober text. For, in Ludovico Zacconi's words (1592), "the composer only bestowed pains upon arranging the notes according to the rules of harmony." Hermann Finck had in 1556 already said ornamentation depended on "the skill, gift, and personality of the performer; everyone does it in his own way. Many think the basso, and others, the soprano, should be colored. In my opinion, all voice parts must be adorned, not throughout, though, but only in the proper places, and not in all voice parts at once." The composers themselves, or their friends and pupils, have left us priceless documents of this practice: Girolamo dalla Casa (1584) and Giovanni Bassano (1591) 'diminished' works of Palestrina and Lasso, and Francesco Geminiani played the sonatas of his master Corelli—as published in a version of his own in Hawkins' *General History of the Science and Practice of Music* (1776)—in which all solid lines are dissolved into flourishes and coloraturas, and the slow movements are past recognition.

While music responds to overdecoration in architecture with an overdecoration of its own, it also meets—in fact and in time—deception and surprise in its own way: the theory of music speaks of a 'deceptive' cadence—*cadenza d'inganno*, in Italian, and *Trug-*

schluss, in German—when modulation, avoiding logic and normalcy, leads to an unexpected chord. Both arts enjoy the same delight in taking the public unawares.

The other aspect of tectonics and atectonics in music is the contrast between a regular progress and an irregular nonprogress of the voice parts. In the fugue and other contrapuntal forms, a certain number of voice parts, two, three, four, or more, move from the beginning to the end of the piece without changing in number; they may individually pause for a few measures but they never disappear; nor can an additional part join in. Atectonic pieces, conceived in terms of melody, harmony, rhythm, or color instead of counterpoint, ignore this law; when there are episodes of a polyphonal character, the composer does not fix any compulsory number of voice parts; he does not hesitate to drop or add a part for reasons of fingering or expression; and he feels free to interrupt their progress and proceed in passages, chords, or other designs opposed to part setting. It is the case of Chopin versus Bach. Johann Sebastian himself, according to Forkel's biography, is said to have called the atectonic way *manschen,* a German dialect word, which the old English translation of Forkel's *Life of Bach* (London 1820, p. 68 f) embarrassedly skipped, and which may least inadequately be translated as 'botching.'

This survey of the manifold aspects of style shows, still more than the preceding outline of comparative art history has done, that art depends on a dualism of antagonistic forces which shape its spirit and its form. It now remains to see how such dualism determines, not only the nature, but also the fate of style.

PART THREE

The Fate of Style

CHAPTER ELEVEN

Art and the Crises of History

1. OUTER EVENTS

STYLES, THOUGH OFTEN OVERLAPPING, follow each other in time: the manuals present Old Christian, Romanesque, then Gothic and later the Renaissance, subsequently the Baroque, Rococo, Classicism . . . Why has there been such sequence? Have the artists jumped about like the capricious creators of fashions and fads to stun an ever-restive public? Does style denote a personal language, shaped by some genius and aped by minor prophets, until we forget it when another genius charms the world with novel words? Or are styles the stations in a one-way development from humble beginnings in the dawn of time to growing wealth and beauty? Is it perhaps true that Gothic art was so much riper than its Romanesque precursor? And was not the Renaissance still better than the Gothic style—just as mankind has from the sinner Adam's days improved more and more until he is now well-nigh angelic?

Serious historians, ridding themselves of ideas so poor and inadequate, have often tried to connect the evolution of art with our numberless crises—economic, social, religious, political. Indeed, the arts, created by man as the faithful expression of his will and urge, and reflecting the ways of ages and nations, must also mirror the nonartistic features of the common cultural ground in which they have their roots. Not even lonely masters are exempt. Rightfully, Lewis Mumford says in *The Condition of Man* that all our questions as to the condition of man "remain bottomless until one places man in the frame of a particular historic moment: for his nature reveals itself only in the acting out of his particular drama; and it cannot be understood by a static external analysis, since time and purpose and development are of its essence."

But Mumford does not say that the artists, like seismographs, record all economic, social, political quakes. Discussing Greek decadence, he states instead: "The disintegration of Hellenic civilization came with such heart-breaking swiftness that even the wisest of the Greeks did not know what had happened to them. The collapse was all the more shocking because it occurred during a period of intense cultural vitality. Corruption from within and violence from without shattered the organic structure of life; but . . . a good part of the art we now behold in museums, was a product of the period of retreat."

Any art historian has found similar examples of radical discrepancy. Otto Kümmel, speaking of the period after the T'ang Dynasty (A.D. 618–907), says: "In all the misery of political history in that time, Chinese art seems to have put forth its noblest bloom" (*Die Kunst Chinas, Japans und Koreas*). "Very frequently, a bloom of the arts disguised brutal, merciless habits," says Alfred Leroy in his *Histoire de la Peinture Française;* and in another passage of the same book, he confesses that "in the face of the marvels of illumination in the thirteenth century . . . we have some difficulty to understand the dualism of these serene visions and the barbaric conduct."

In 1356, in one of the worst episodes of the Hundred Years War, King John I of France was taken prisoner after the disastrous battle at Maupertuis and was four years later forced to cede all Aquitaine to Edward III of England. Moreover the country, already weakened by endless warring, suffered from almost continuous revolutions, the bloodiest of which was *la Jacquerie*, the uprising of the peasants in 1358. And yet, the nation was not only able to produce the greatest composer of the century, Guillaume de Machaut but also to prepare for the marvels of the Flamboyant style.

Or, to switch to Spain: Philip II, who ruled during the second half of the sixteenth century, plunged his country into misery and moral disintegration; whole quarters were deserted, crafts died out, and the treasurer's collecting box rattled from house to house, from street to street. And this was the Spain of Cervantes and Lope de Vega, of Greco and Victoria.

If art is able to ignore the trends of outer life, we must revise our first impression that art is a mirror of mankind's actions and sufferings. In doing so, we should from the very first realize that events and developments, though long prepared, hit man with lightning speed while works of art and, more so, styles need a long, long time to take shape. I am not thinking of the technical side, not of manual work or finish. I mean rather the slow process, from the personal experience and reaction of the artist as a man to the mature expression of the same artist as the creator of a lasting, superpersonal work. Gustav Mahler wrote his *Kinder-Totenlieder* out of the long stored experience of a suffering, pitiful heart, before death answered the call and actually took one of the composer's own children. He would hardly have been willing or able to set them after the blow had struck.

The more personal a work of art is, the longer it takes to evolve. Beethoven never went out without a notebook to jot down some first melodic inspiration. Only later—and often much later—he worked and reworked these sketches until everything abrupt, rhapsodic, improvised had gone. The earliest sketches of the Ninth Symphony appear in the notebooks of 1815; the work was finished in 1823, eight years later. In this long process of maturing, the symphony tells a good deal about the inner development of Beethoven's personality but nothing of the events or developments outside, of Napoleon's fall or Metternich's reactionary politics and the debacle of democratic freedom.

The word freedom evokes the case of the Third Symphony, written in 1804 and called the *Sinfonia Eroica.* Is not its original dedication to the Consul Bonaparte one of the weightiest documents to prove that the outer world forces the doors of the studio and inspires, leads, and shapes the work of art? Once more, no. For, when somebody had told Beethoven that his hero of liberty was about to make himself emperor and to re-establish tyranny, he tore out the frontispiece with the dedication, crumpled it up, and trod on it. The dedication, not the score. He then merely replaced the dedication to Napoleon by a more general one "To the Memory of a Hero" without changing one note. In other words, the symphony had not been inspired by Napoleon; the work of art was the original thing, and Bonaparte could be exchanged for any other hero.

How little the heroic character of this E flat major symphony depended on Napoleon and how much on the inner balance of Beethoven's creative personality follow from the meaningful sequence of Beethoven's nine symphonies: they alternate in character so that the odd-numbered symphonies are more or less 'great' or even heroic, while the even-numbered ones are lighter if not playful.

A year later, Napoleon won a crushing victory over the Austrians at Austerlitz, not too far from the gates of Vienna, where the master was busy with *Fidelio* and the three Leonores, with the gay Fourth Symphony, the Concerto for Violin, the G major Concerto for Piano, the quartets op. 59 . . . Was this his anguish, dejection, defeat?

Such detachment is indeed typical; every artist has something of Archimedes, who after the fall of his native city of Syracuse was so absorbed in a geometrical design he was drawing in the sand of his garden that when the enemy soldiers entered to slay him he only warned them not to disturb his circles.

When the Thirty Years War haunted Germany, when the courts and communities that had supported art broke down, the country boasted of her three great S's: Scheidt, Schein, Schütz. True, Schütz wrote, besides a lost opera, religious music only, which could easily be interpreted as a cry of distress or an attempt at solace. But then, Scheidt and Schein, and numberless smaller masters, composed secular music, dances and songs, which could not possibly have any spiritual connection with the great war.

Germany knew another long and devastating war from 1756 to

1763. With the treasure chests empty, the orchestras were reduced and the opera houses closed. When peace came and they were re-opened, the public did not rush into the repainted loges and parterres, to hear Italian operas, in a language that it did not understand, with conventional actions and characters that could not but bore, with a music that had become academic and empty. King Frederick the Great of Prussia resorted to force: every night, a company of grenadiers was ordered to the opera house to cover the desertion. The deserting public, meantime, adored a new type, the comic or beggar's opera, with its vernacular language, simple actions from everyday life, and popular music. Was this a consequence of the war? It was not. The movement had begun in Italy with Pergolesi's *Serva Padrona* (1733) and in France with Jean-Jacques Rousseau's *Devin du Village* (1752) long before the Seven Years War, and it was actually a part of the great movement that transformed all European arts about the middle of the eighteenth century.

In the French Revolution, Gossec became the official composer of the Republic. He wrote the *Chant du 14 Juillet* and addressed hymns to the supreme being, to nature, liberty, humanity, equality; but no unheard-of style was the outcome. Grétry composed the Feast of Reason; but was it revolutionary? Lesueur, in his turn, retired to the country when the Revolution began in Paris and returned only in 1793 with two scores, *Télémaque* and—of all things— *Paul et Virginie*, the innocent idyl of two children in the bosom of nature.

The short episode of the horror opera has been mentioned. There is the *Marseillaise*, however, the darting, ravishing song of freedom, which has no equal in the world. But alas, the original melody, written by Rouget de l'Isle, a dilettante and officer, was notably inferior and had to be changed piecemeal during a hundred years, until a special committee gave it final shape in the peaceful year 1887.

No music that is directly connected with outer events or currents can be seriously considered as a work of art, even without discussing banalities like *Giovinezza* or the unspeakable *Horst Wessel Lied.*

Nobody would earnestly compare Beethoven's Battle of Victoria with his symphonies or, for that matter, Wagner's *Festmarsch* for the Centennial Exhibition in Philadelphia (1876) with the *Götterdämmerung* which he finished in the same year.

2. *INNER TRENDS*

It is more promising to shift to the inner developments of which the outer events are mostly the symptoms. Parallels in this field have often been drawn, and it has almost become a truism today to connect the political currents in later Greece with her subjective art; medieval universalism and clericality with Gothic art; the new society in the cities of the Renaissance with their vocal chamber music; the enlightenment of the eighteenth century with its *style bourgeois*.

Such connections are perfectly legitimate, and even indispensable, as long as they are not supposed to imply a priority of politics: we should not rashly derive aesthetic from political trends, or even from social or religious facts. Rather, they all have a common root beneath the visible surface of history.

Almost unanimously, historians have credited Christendom with shaping the arts of the Middle Ages. In view of the dominant and almost exclusive role of church building in medieval architecture and the tyrannic sway Biblical themes held over sculpture and painting, such credit is doubtless suggestive, if not convincing. But style as such is little concerned with aims or conditions, and Christian art found its expression in idioms as different as Abyssinian panels, Byzantine icons, and Gothic reliefs. It is man, man the divine, who shapes his art and shapes his religion in the image of his soul and longing.

It is easy to motivate the form of Lutheran chorales or Calvin's psalms with the need that religion had of permanence, essence, and subordination of the individual with his personal emotions, and also of the simplicity that allowed everybody to join in congregational songs. But secular music, too, was in those times interested in square, symmetrical melodies of popular character. Again, this type of melody was in keeping with the trends of all the arts in the first and the third generations of the sixteenth century.

The counterreformation, again, has been made responsible for the art of the Baroque, and particularly for its architecture: to win over the hostile or indifferent masses, the Jesuits needed an art impressive, overawing, sweeping, and hence, theatrical and loud. But why, then, had the Baroque its blossom in Italy, which, being Catholic throughout, was least in need of such a style, and why the great reserve with which it was received—if at all—in those Catholic countries which had an urgent Protestant problem, like France and South Germany? And would not the favor given to Palestrina's style in the name of counterreformation justify exactly the opposite opinion that the counterreformation led art to austere simplicity and transparence?

These considerations should indeed caution against a unilaterally religious explanation or, better, against deriving styles of art from nonartistic movements. This does not mean that there is no relationship between the arts and life. It only means that we should look for common impulses given to art and to life by hitherto unknown processes rather than at random trace them to one another.

The French Revolution favored mass choruses to sing the hymns to liberty, equality, fraternity and other new songs of the new time. Again, the obvious explanation is undoubtedly correct: the revolution needed mass choruses to express mass feeling. And again this explanation is not sufficient. For as early as 1784, years before the revolution and outside France, the English had commemorated George Frederick Handel in five monster concerts with five hundred twenty-five performers, and similar commemorations were held at Westminster Abbey in the following years with apparently increased numbers of singers and players. And likewise before the peak of the Revolution and outside France, Karl Friedrich Fasch in Berlin, predecessor of Zelter, founded in 1790 the Sing-Akademie as the first new-type public chorus of burghers—of moderate size in the first year, indeed, but of rapidly increasing proportions—

and neither old Fasch nor Zelter or their good singers had revolutionary or proletarian leanings.

In both cases, and in numberless others, some very general trend in the evolution of mankind controls all forms of human expression and all ways in which they act, be they politics, economy, thought, or art.

There is one more point of importance. The facts of outer life are spontaneous and often erratic; the evolution of art is much more regular. For art is reflection, not action. Man's acts may be rash; his art is deliberate and carefully prepared. The breath of history reminds one of the air in the bellows of a harmonium: the player operates the upper feeder bellows in irregular pushes; but the wind passes the reservoir bellows to be equalized before it becomes artistic tone.

It is the vision of this regular breath in the history of art that the following chapters will try to convey.

CHAPTER TWELVE

Phases

1 . *THREE EXAMPLES: FROM 1460 TO 1560*

No generation is homogeneous: no style can be of a piece. Stragglers cling to past ideals, and pioneers anticipate the future; beginners cope with seasoned masters, rash temperaments with wary natures, independent minds with conventionalists. The picture of the many overlapping and contradictory tendencies is never quite unequivocal and often so dim that to pick out one of these as *the* style of an epoch seems hopeless or at best arbitrary.

In most generations, however, the situation is unmistakable enough to allow for a dependable diagnosis. Such are the three generations that flourished in the one hundred years between 1460 and 1560, in the then leading countries, Italy, France, and the Netherlands.

The earliest of the three generations, betraying trends in the loud, capricious eccentricity of fashions, drove naturalism in the arts to the extremities of violence, brutality, and ugliness. Even where naturalism appeared in milder forms, it meant excitement with racing, gesticulating, shrieking figures and with overcrowded scenes in which no empty spot was tolerated. Virtuosity in perspective stressed the incidents of appearance at the cost of essence; symmetry and balance were shunned. The given themes from Grecian myth and Bible legend left but little space for other topics except, of course, the portrait. And yet, a casual escape into life, and even into the tragedy of life, shows what the artist's eye perceives. Sculptors stress illusion, or round and soften the outlines of reliefs; the architects open their façades and, avoiding the baldness of all too sober fronts in a *horror vacui* similar to that of the painters, lapse into decoration, if not overdecoration.

Music, turning away from the neatly balanced and almost harmonic style of the generation before, created, or rather re-created, a boundless melody in fantastic, expressive, and passionate lines. Expressiveness was, with the invention of the *tremulant*, even forced upon the rigid aloofness of the organ; and the predilection for showy sizes, so seldom absent in styles of this kind, appears in canons for thirty-six voice parts and huge, unheard-of double-bass viols.

No doubt, the last third of the fifteenth century belonged to pathos.

Things were different in the first third of the sixteenth century. In the province of form, the two outstanding paintings analyzed in Chapters V and VII, Raphael's *Sposalizio* and Leonardo's Last Supper, are not only simple and limpid but so strictly centered and symmetric that we fancy we can see the auxiliary charcoal lines with which their geometric patterns were constructed. In the same spirit of centrality, canvases are often cut to the circular *tondo* form, and architects try their hand at round and polygonal structures. In music, the plain, symmetrical forms and strict tonality of popular music come to the fore: *laude*, *strambotti*, and *frottole* dominate music printing; and even the Netherlanders dam the flowing polyphony of their masses and motets.

To the softly gliding 'conjunction' of parts, the static ideals of the time oppose a clean-cut 'disjunction.' Leonardo's and Raphael's paintings keep the well-balanced groups of figures strictly apart; works of music are unmistakably divided into periods and phrases with separating cadences; and fashion taboos the uninterrupted tights that men had worn in previous decades. In color, smooth transition from shade to shade would not be in keeping with such disjunction. The painters indulge instead in the outspoken contrast of strong, unbroken colors; and the musicians answer with the antiphonic alternation between the two higher and the two lower voices.

Contours are 'close' and rounded in costume as well as in the fine arts, music, and the dance.

Reason is set above imagination. Musicians delight in symbolic themes, which are neither perceived by the ear nor created by a shaping genius but synthetically put together in a cold process of substituting the names of notes for the similar vowels of either the text or the title. The architects believe in Vitruvius' orders and 'correct' proportions rather than in inspiration, just as the sculptors and painters look for eternal canons of human beauty. In doing so, their eyes review the visible and the readable relics of classic antiquity, which seem to grant the final answers to their questions. Poetry revives the spirit and language of Rome, and even music, unable to copy the melodies of two thousand years ago, at least bows to the ancients by conforming to the long and the short syllables of Latin meters.

No passion shows, no clamorous glee or mourning. Emotion is restrained, in fine art as in music, and often yields to serenity, if not to coolness.

The following generation gives an equally excellent instance of pathos.

Delight in life is paramount, particularly in France—delight in vitality and plain truth, in the uncouth and the juicy. One sings unpolished street and soldiers' songs, one likes the taste of spicy chansons and heartily enjoys the ribaldries of Rabelais. Even the court appropriates the untamed dances of the people, prefers the faster to the slow, joins with relish in suites of increasingly rapid branles, and is especially fond of *voltas*, in which the cavaliers fling up and show off their ladies. Tragedy appeals to the public's lust for horror: Giraldi Cintio's famous *Orbecche* (1541) stages no less than four murders, one suicide, plus incest, and the audience happily cries, sobs, and faints.

Sculpture, in Italy as in France, responds in its own way. Far from statuesque restfulness, it strives for agitated movement, athletic vigor, and passionate tension, although it also finds the way to decorativeness and elegance.

Painting tackles gigantic tasks. Paolo Veronese's huge canvas of the Feast at Cana and Michelangelo's Last Judgment would have been impossible a generation before; and Tintoretto's Paradise in the Ducal Palace at Venice is the largest mural ever conceived. Composers do not stand back; they increase the usual number of voice parts up to forty and organize them in choruses that blend or contrast.

And yet, this generation is also fond of intimate art in small and smallest size and appreciates the delicately chased saltcellar of Cellini's hand, just as it appreciates the subtleties of madrigals and short chansons.

The forms are seldom close or regular; symmetry is dodged, and disjunction hardly ever used, in music as in painting or sculpture. Accordingly, emotion is dominant in all shades from the violent passion of Michelangelo's Last Judgment down to the petty and not altogether heartfelt sentimentalism of Italian madrigals and French chansons.

And fashion, on the dot, reverts to loud and showy extravagance.

2. *INNER DIVERGENCES*

Even pictures so striking as the three generations just analyzed are not without flaws. The great pagan Michelangelo, who made of Christ an athletic Apollo unwilling to carry the cross (Plate XIX; the disgusting loin-cloth and the aureole should not be blamed on him), and Goudimel, who wrote the austere psalter of the Huguenot church; the ribald Rabelais, who so heartily laughed, and the dainty masters of the madrigal, who hardly dared to smile; Tintoretto's gigantic mural and the intimate art of the short chanson; the vulgarity of street songs and the elegance of Cellini's chased delicacies; the stormy passion of the great sculptors and the weakly *ohimè's* of the madrigalists—do they not contradict each other and in this contradiction menace the veracity of the style of 1530 as I have pictured it?

We need not dwell upon this single example. Not one pathos style —and for that matter, no ethos style either—has been without such seeming incongruence. Monteverdi's mythical heroes coincide in time with Caravaggio's cheats, the neat and smallish canvases of the Dutch with Rubens' big tableaux, the refined elegance of the Rococo with the brutish vulgarity of the later Hamburg opera, Gluck's grandiose passion with Greuze's dairy girl who mourns for her broken milk pot.

Our fathers read Zola after tea and sympathetically interested themselves in destinies that liquor stores and slums had modeled. And at night, they were willingly caught in the dream worlds of Lohengrin's swan and the church of the Grail. In art exhibitions, Courbet's sweating toilers rubbed shoulders with the Blessed in Boecklin's Elysium. And all this was modern, more or less disreputable and taboo for well-bred youngsters, but fully up-to-date. Affirmation and negation stood closely alongside—the pitiless world as it was and romantic escape into fairyland. Charles Darwin and Felix Mendelssohn were born in the same year, 1809, indeed, in the same month, February. This is almost a symbol. Materialistic science and romantic music, socialism and Germanic gods, technique and psychology crowded into the same congested room. Ernest Renan, who witnessed these paradoxical attitudes, was probably right in saying that "the more a man develops intellectually, the more he dreams of the contrary pole, that is to say of the irrational, of repose in complete ignorance" (translated by Irving Babbitt).

Far from giving the lie to the inner coherence of the styles just touched upon, the seeming paradoxes rather prove the amazing vastness of their scope. Nor is there any inconformity in their diversity. Cohesion should not be looked for in the homogeneity of their elements but in the common opposition against the preceding style. And of contrasts there are always two or more. To put it in the language of logics: black has not only the 'contradictory' contrast white, but also the 'contrary' contrast of anything not black, including gray and red and blue. The difference between two successive styles is oftener contrariness than contradiction.

As a consequence, no collective reaction to a certain style can be expected to be one and unequivocal, even were the reacting generation uniform and single-minded. If ethos is moderate in its useful sizes, the immoderation of pathos could exaggerate in both directions, to titanic and to midget sizes; impassible serenity can be antagonized by the whole range of emotion between violent passion and cheap sentimentalism; noble dignity, by either affected elegance or vulgar clumsiness; idealistic beauty, by either character or homely ugliness.

'The' style of an age is often a purely defensive alliance of different, indeed, of opposite styles against the trends of the age before.

The wide expanse that opens in either direction of style helps to explain why no two phases have been alike; why the pathos generation of 1530 spoke a language different from the idiom of the pathos generation of 1470; why Romanticism was not Baroque, nor the Baroque a flamboyant Gothic. The many ways provided by the two basic conceptions allow for divergent results, and the ever-changing complexity of conditions takes care that despite all similarity in attitude and action no constellation is exactly repeated.

One of the dissimilating factors—of which Chapter XIV (The Dominance of the Individual Arts) will disclose another—is what we might call cumulative experience. Even so striking a parallel as Greece–Renaissance would suffer from the elementary difference that the Renaissance had Grecian vases, statues, temples, verses, all within easy sight and reach, while the ancient Hellenes of necessity knew nothing of the wonders that the Renaissance was to achieve after two thousands of years.

Still, one should not dwell too much on cumulative experience. A generation may have access to the piled-up knowledge and creativeness of all bygone generations (as ours has)—it will unshakably stand on its own individual ground if an own ground it has. The very same impulse that enforces a certain trend of style will steer the artist through that infinite storehouse of the past, blind him where he should not be concerned, but direct his attention to those of the treasures which might help him to find his personal way. The very word Renaissance, 'renascence,' proves that a later time with different leanings had to open people's eyes to the relics of antiquity, which, though visible and readable, had had but little meaning in the Middle Ages.

CHAPTER THIRTEEN

The Alternation of Phases

1. TIDAL CHARACTER

THE WORD 'PHASE,' used to indicate a generational style of either ethos or pathos character, implies more than just a mere alternation between the two. For, to use Lewis Mumford's words, "all life-maintaining changes are in the direction of equilibrium" (*The Condition of Man*, New York 1944, p. 6). The word 'phase' actually implies a recurring cycle of changes, such as the sections across comparative art history in Part I show with impressive clarity: everywhere and at all times, style proceeds between serenity, strictness, and moderation, on the one hand, and freedom, passion, and exaggeration, on the other hand, thus balancing the trends that seek discharge.

However, these phases do not simply reciprocate like green and red in traffic lights, as an alternation of two quiescent stages. Rather, they are currents which flow forward and back under the impact of some mysterious magnetic force and would be better compared to the restless to-and-fro of the tides. Ethos and pathos are not states; they are two opposite directions in which the styles of art recede and flood.

As a consequence, most styles belong to one of the two categories not by nature but only by the direction from which they are reached: the same quality in a style would be an expression of pathos when it follows an ethos phase, and vice versa. To use a simile: in an impressive test of relativity, you fill three bowls with hot, tepid, and cold water; you dip your hands, first, one into the hot and the other into the cold water, and after a short while, both into the tepid water—this latter will seem to be cool to the hand from the hot bowl and warm to the hand from the cold bowl.

The tidal motion of art asks for a revision of several current misconceptions. There are in the main three of these, two that are incompatible with the ceaseless movement of style, and one, with the tidal form of this movement.

A first misconception is the idea of some steady one-way evolution, every step of which seems to be the product, indeed, the fulfillment of the foregoing, and at once the seed of the following phase. The three thousand years of Egyptian art, then, were just the basement on which the art of Greece could stand; Romanesque prepared the Gothic style, and the Gothic style was the necessary step toward the Renaissance; Bach was the forerunner of Haydn, and Haydn, the sire of Beethoven; and it was only logical that Alexander Ulibishev, in his amateurish Mozart obsession, claimed that God had created the world in order to make the *Magic Flute* possible. By implication, this better-and-better conception means 'progress' in the sense of the eighteenth century and suggests that modern art, the fruit of so many thousands of years of cumulated and ever outdone skill, must be superior to anything created before, even if our masters do not always reach the individual genius of earlier men. It is in this spirit that, in the idiom of French art historians, the older masters, particularly those of the later Middle Ages, are still called *les primitifs*, as if they were paleolithic cave dwellers.

Such steady development forward and upward is not even true of mere technique, where at the worst it could be possible; and it is quite certainly not true of spirit and temperament, which are not and cannot be subject to progress, because they belong neither to the intellect nor to manual skill.

Besides, this naïve conception has innumerable times been discredited in the history of fine arts. Practically all centuries, far from overestimating their own achievements in this field, have imposed the 'ancients' as the unattainable paragons of art on their contemporaries; and the last two centuries, so particularly fond of progress and evolution, not only admired and worshipped but foolishly copied Greco-Roman temples, Gothic cathedrals, and Baroque palaces.

The false conception of progress has done some real harm in music: in the clash which necessarily results when a living, modern performer tries to rouse an old composition asleep on its paper, the performer is only too easily convinced that the style in which he himself has been trained is, in an absolute sense, superior to what the older masters could do on their technically inferior instruments and in their lesser maturity. The best service to render to old music, then, would be a performance in the style of our own, so glorious time, with all its 'expression,' its unruly *crescendi* and *decrescendi*, *fortissimi* and *pianissimi*, *accelerandi* and *rallentandi*. While any painter has the sense to realize that Raphael's composition requires Raphael's colors and would be reduced *ad absurdum* by applying Cézanne's, musicians again and again exclaim: "If Bach had known the marvels of our modern pianos, organ skyscrapers, and mass orchestras!" However nonsensical all if-exclamations are, there is a simple answer to this antihistorical and antilogical question: Bach would either have rejected the modern marvels because they were due to a romantic attitude foreign and even hostile to him (just as the English harpsichordists of the seventeenth century ignored the timbre- and intensity-changing pedals that someone had invented against the trends of his time), or else he would have written in a quite different style, which again would have implied a quite different mind. In one sentence: he might have achieved great mastership, but would not have been Bach.

Here, too, one should take to heart the warning of Mumford that every man must be placed in the frame of a particular culture and a particular historical moment. And one could add what Ruth Bunzel said in *General Anthropology* (p. 576): that art is "continually in a state of tension, an exciting condition of unstable equilibrium between the exuberance of individual imagination and the weight of tradition as expressed in formal patterns."

A second misconception is responsible for the mischievous 'transitional' styles of our handbooks. Since style never stops flowing, hither or thither, there is no such thing as a lasting style. "Style is but a momentary state of equilibrium" (Elie Faure). And since there are no lasting, regular styles, there cannot be transitional, irregular styles: all style implies transition. Therefore, the numberless allegedly transitional styles should at long last be dropped from the vocabulary of serious historians.

The third misconception has led to the intolerance in which our books abound and to the mutual dislike among classicists, modernists, progressists, radicals, futurists, and whatever other slogans the fencers and crusaders may invent. Like any intolerance, this, too, is based on ignorance and the incapability of getting away from the narrow limitations of one's self.

The tacit assumption behind such arrogance is that the two sides are stationary phenomena, and its noble aim is to eliminate the hostile phenomenon and to keep the good side for all eternity. Alas, they just are not stationary. They are movements, which either go on in the same direction or else turn, and in going on too far would leave the realm of art: the ebb that we call ethos would inevitably lead to the dearth of soulless academicism; and the tide of pathos, to a springtide of destruction and anarchy.

Fortunately, there is no such alternative. For, in Erich Kahler's words, "every principle that is carried out to its fullest implications is bound to reverse itself" (*Man the Measure*, New York, 1943, p. 464). Which amounts to Matthew Arnold's more concrete statement that in an epoch of convention and dry rationality there finally arises the need of "storms, passion, effusion, and relief" (and vice versa).

It seems, however, that actual reversals are possible only in the tense atmosphere of high civilizations. Where no such tension calls for continual balance through action and reaction, the situation is different. Chapter I of this book mentioned the 'pathogenic' style in primitive singing, which "derives from savage shouts and convulsive panting" but is "eventually dammed up"; and the youthful rhapsodic style of Balinese orchestras has in the less spontaneous civilization of Javanese courts yielded to an impassionate, even, and almost static movement without rhapsodic traits. The visible arts contribute ornaments—particularly in works of penmanship—which in their flourishes, arcs, and jagged dashes are born from instantaneous motor impulses and only later set in regular, unemotional patterns. The motor impulses that act on the throat and the limbs, once sprung from emotional urges, are brought under control and move away from pathos while from responses to stimuli they slowly pass to well-planned art works. Instead of regular reversals, we find a steady cooling off.

The tidal movement of style answers the frequent, wondering questions why certain turns or achievements in the evolution of art received no proper response in the decades to follow and were adopted only at a much later time instead of changing, at once and for good, the style of their own time and of the times to come; why Michelangelo could be so unmistakably Baroque long before the style that carries this name set in; why Palestrina, by so much his junior, could be so entirely un-Baroque; why Diderot about 1750 and the anticlassic Storm and Stress of the later eighteenth century seem so strangely out of place in their separation from Romanticism proper. Alfred Leroy has, in his *Histoire de la Peinture française*, unwittingly coined an excellent word to characterize such (seeming) misplacement: the illuminations in the Bible of Moutier-Grandval, in the ninth century, were, as he says, an attempt at naturalism "*sans lendemain.*" Actually most art has no tomorrow. But it certainly has the day after.

A good example of such an atavistic jump from today to the day after tomorrow is the English invention of the earliest organ swell in 1712, so well timed with the invention of the expressive piano in

Italy, England, France, and Germany and yet unable to reach continental organ building before the pathos year of 1764 when it was given to the organ of St. Michael's in Hamburg. The answer, within our simile, is: when the tide for any reason fails to wash some piece of driftwood ashore, there is little chance that this will happen in the following ebb; but the next flood tide will easily carry it along.

The tidal movement also answers another question: why are so many ethos phases apparently more dynamic than certain pathos phases, and vice versa? Again, because the phases are not stationary centers but directions in which the styles devolve. The same spot on a shore may lie in the reach, now of the flood, now of the ebb.

2. GENERATION AND PERSONALITY

THE QUESTION, WHAT POWER could cause a turn of the tide, must in different times necessarily be answered in different ways. Pathos periods, individualistic, liking personality, and delighting in biography, will be only too prone to concede the place of honor to the greatest individuals of every generation rather than to the vague, anonymous forces of the masses or the times. But this would hardly be a satisfactory interpretation of what actually has occurred; nor should the answer be given out of philosophic and, still less, out of political convictions at all. Nothing but sober analysis can help.

To this end, the following short paragraphs relate a few facts from history.

Giotto (*c.* 1266–1337) painted the Franciscan frescoes in the Upper Church at Assisi when he was about thirty years old. He made them eloquent, dramatic, passionate, in strongest contrast to his later works in Santa Croce at Florence which, apparently created in the 1320's, were reserved and monumental. Monographers have called this contrast the normal evolution from an emotional young age to sedate maturity. But such is by no means the obligatory growth, normal as it may seem; the following example works the other way around.

Andrea Orcagna, born not before 1308, was a mature painter and sculptor when the naturalism of the 1350's broke in—mature in his severe, hieratic solemnity, which did not allow of drama, emotion, or even three-dimensional conception. Not only did he swerve from this line when he painted a Triumph of Death and comply with the violent naturalism that the subject imposed; his later works, the Birth and the Death of the Virgin (the latter dated 1359) in Or San Michele at Florence and particularly the sublime altar of St. Matthew in the Uffizi (1367–68) are more dramatic and three-dimensional than his earliest certified work, the altar of the Strozzi in Santa Maria Novella.

Around 1415, the two great Italian sculptors, Nanni di Banco and Jacopo della Quercia, were almost suddenly converted, in unison with their contemporaries, from a solemn classical style to an agitated dynamism.

The striking contrast between the first and the second bronze door of the baptistry in Florence, both from Ghiberti's hand, are a parallel example of this shift.

Donatello (1386–1466), the *terribile*, greatest sculptor of the fifteenth century, was a decided naturalist all his life. Still, in a middle period, between 1433 and 1453, and particularly in the bronze reliefs at Sant'Antonio in Padua (1445–48) and the equestrian statue of Gattamelata (1453), he tried to express himself with more restraint, only to relapse into a truly Baroque style for the remaining twelve years of his life.

The Flemish painter Roger van der Weyden (1400–64) has been discussed in detail in Part I. Fifty years old, this master of an agitated, overemotional style experienced a thorough turn to ethos in 1450 and broke for good with the strong pathos of his earlier works.

For Mantegna (1431–1506), 1456 was the critical year. Severe, grandiose, statuesque in his first period, he advanced far toward pathos in the three periods into which historians have divided his later works, from the overdecorated altar of San Zeno in Verona (1456–59) to the audacious perspective of the Lamented Christ in the Brera at Milan.

Leonardo da Vinci was an ethos master in the almost pedantic strictness of his symmetrical paintings and the enthusiasm for mathematics, rules, and theory; in the quiet noblesse of his madonnas and apostles; and in the serenity of Mona Lisa. Yet he dissolved all hard contours in the golden atmosphere of his chiaroscuro and was so fond of nature as it *appeared* in all its whim and ugliness that he would follow cripples and idiots who came in his way until he had impressed their traits and gestures on his mind. However, was it mere chance that of his dated works the naturalistic study of the hanged Bandini and the equally naturalistic St. Jerome in the Vatican were done respectively in 1479 and around 1481, the caricatures between 1485 and 1493, and the anatomical studies between 1485 and 1490, that is, in a naturalistic epoch, while the Last Supper and Mona Lisa were painted, the former from 1495 to 1497 and the latter in 1503, when the new classicism set in?

The work of the Flemish painter Gerard David (1460–1523) has been divided into three distinct phases: the first, 1484–98, with the Skinning of the Bribed Judge Sisamnes, naturalistic; the second, 1498–1511, climaxing in the Madonna with Saints in Rouen, very strict, symmetric, and quiet; the third, 1511–23, cool, academic, and from chiaroscuro relapsing into unbroken colors. Again, the decisive crisis is shortly before 1498, in accordance with the generational reversal.

To resume: early in the fifteenth century, Nanni di Banco and Quercia, both coming from a strictly classicistic style, turn to pathos at the same time, around 1415. The new pathos period comes to an end with Donatello in 1445, with Roger van der Weyden in 1450. Ethos again ends with Donatello in 1453, with Mantegna in 1456, and is after an interruption of forty years restored by Leonardo in 1495, by David in 1498, and, as the following paragraph shows, by Michelangelo in 1497.

Michelangelo's early works around 1500 betray indeed the full impact of the momentous turn that art took on the threshold between the two centuries. While his David (1501–3) was still a child of the late *quattrocento* with some of Donatello's traits, the *Pietà* in St. Peter's (1497–1500), the Madonna in Bruges (1500–2), and the *tondo* of the Holy Family in the Uffizi were as close to the new 'classical' style as Michelangelo's explosive personality permitted. True, he always despised color, light, and shadow and exalted the supremacy of hard-drawn lines; he disdained protruding limbs and theatrical gesture, and never was interested in individual models or portraits. All this would have given him a good standing in the Italy between 1500 and 1525. But he had nothing of her restful sereneness, and even where his figures seem to be absorbed in peaceful contemplation, they are about to jump up and take action.

Michelangelo's volcanic nature erupted very shortly after his initial tribute to static ideals. The vast ceiling of the Sistine Chapel, which he covered with frescoes from 1508 to 1510, already abounded in the grandiose, energetic, and eloquent torsion of the bodies that twenty years later became the common property of a pathos generation.

Twenty years later, when the time was ripe, not when Michelangelo showed the way. Even he, who has been emulated and imitated as no other sculptor ever was, did not revolutionize his generation; the change that his genius anticipated came in due time—the inner law of his epoch was stronger than his personal example.

To jump to France: a quarter of a thousand years later, in the 1790's, Jean-Antoine Houdon, the sculptor, renounced his naturalism and, in not quite convincing forms, sacrificed his work to the spirit of classicism. And to end with an American master of our days: Charles Lewis Fox, the once conventional painter from Maine, resumed his painting after a rest of fifteen years and did so as a modern artist. "There is an almost prophetic expression of what has become the trend of the art of our day, and this though he lived during this time in a hermitlike retreat from the world of his fellow artists and workers."

Lafuente is right when he says in the Phaidon book on Velásquez: "There is in style a 'cultural imperative' which holds sway over individuals and collectivities, from which these cannot free themselves: which is a something given, a foundation for every personal reaction."

A genius can soar to dizzying heights and delve to depths inaccessible to his contemporaries. But he cannot step out of the time into which he is born.

The many experiences that the history of art provides give at least a provisional answer to the initial question as to what power could cause a turn of the tide. Not the individual genius as such inaugurates a style, and even the greatest master is at best in a position to impose his manner or style upon epigones. The generation as a whole goes its own collective ways, without depending too much on the great or their blindfold followers. Indeed, its reversals drag the individual masters along, the great and the little, and redye them without spoiling their native, personal patterns. Not the masses, either, form a style; nor have the social, economic, religious factors more than contributory power. The momentous impulse comes from impalpable forces which, while shaping both the outstanding individuals and the slower masses, cannot in their dimness be grasped.

Such an explanation—if an explanation it is—will doubtless hurt those who believe in 'realistic views.' But realists are often like children who grab at the moon, without comprehending that the big white ball is out of reach of their hands. Spirit would not be spirit if it could, like tangible facts, be fully explained by sober, simple data. You may easily prove that a certain style was introduced in a certain country after some man had in such-and-such a year traveled abroad and seen the advanced expression that foreign masters had found; and still you have failed to prove why the style he carried home was accepted, though there had been no readiness to accept it in a hundred similar cases a few years before.

Generally speaking, the 'influences,' on which so many art historians live, only seldom mark artificial interferences with otherwise continuous developments. They always prerequire a natural receptivity, owed to inner developments, for this very kind of influence. They are stimuli rather than meddlers and have much less importance than they are generally given.

CHAPTER FOURTEEN

Cycles

1. GIANT CYCLES

THE WORD 'PHASE,' used in the preceding chapter to indicate a prevalent generational style of either ethos or pathos direction, implies the existence of a *cycle*, that is, a regular recurrence in the same sequence of the two phases. In this recurrence, it means much more than just an alternation of the two directions; for, to quote Lewis Mumford again, "all life-maintaining changes are in the direction of equilibrium." Style, as our section across the history of art has shown, finds equilibrium in a regular alternation between serenity and passion, between strictness and freedom, between beauty and character, much as man keeps his balance walking by regularly throwing his weight from the left to the right foot, and back from the right to the left. It does not matter, in doing this, whether he counts the complete double step as left–right or as right–left; or, for that matter, whether he counts the tides as ebb and flood or as flood and ebb; these microcycles of two phases do not interest us beyond the fact of their existence.

It is more important to know that generational reversals are not independent or exclusive. Just as the regular alternation of daytime warmth and nighttime cold is embedded in the wider span of seasons warm and cold, so the generational changes are embedded in wider cycles, revolving in orbits high above the hasty swarm of small reversals. They are known under the current names of Gothic, Renaissance, or Baroque, and even under the wider conceptions of Antiquity or Middle Ages.

GIANT CYCLES

The vaster cycles of hundreds of years, or a thousand, are nowhere more striking than in the history of architecture. Martin Shaw Briggs is right: architecture "is too structural, too permanent, too eternal, one might almost say, to be blown from its course by every trifling aesthetic movement."

The temple of the Greeks scarcely changed in a thousand years; it remained the same rectangular, simple pattern with columns up to the tablature and with a shallow pediment on top. There were three 'orders' or patterns, to be sure: Doric, Ionic, Corinthian; but they lived greatly side by side and did not differ except in proportions and minor details.

In medieval architecture, the history of art distinguishes two successive styles, the Romanesque and the Gothic. The Romanesque style lasted about seven hundred years, from the sixth to the thirteenth century (or, according to a different interpretation, at least a quarter of a thousand years, from about A.D. 1000 to the thirteenth century), and the Gothic style, three or four hundred years, from the twelfth to the fifteenth or sixteenth century. But in the slow development from the comparatively static Roman basilica to the final dynamic cathedral with its north-south transept, its ambulatory around the apse, its turrets and towers, its growing perfection of vaults and ribs, and its ever-increasing tendency toward dematerialization and verticality, they form one uninterrupted cycle, spanning a good thousand years, in which the alleged, disreputable "style of transition" is a mere fiction.

To cover the architectural development since the Middle Ages, the term Renaissance has—though not in this book—been extended from the beginnings of the Renaissance proper to World War I, or over five hundred years, because it was impossible to find essential differences between the so-called Renaissance proper and its varieties, which have been very unsatisfactorily designated as Baroque, Rococo, Classicism, Empire, or otherwise.

It is hardly necessary to emphasize how much both music and painting changed in each of these enormous epochs. During the

Romanesque and Gothic centuries, polyphonic music evolved from the primitive *órganum* in parallel fourths or fifths to the marvels of Dutch and Flemish masses; and while architecture stuck to the basic principles of the Renaissance, painting veered from van Eyck to Titian, from Rembrandt to Watteau, from Ingres to Manet. In music and painting, the generational changes were much stronger than in architecture.

There have been several reasons for so different a fate. One of these is the momentous distance between the creator and his creation. Musicians and painters express themselves directly; they jot down their fleeting visions—gestures, chords of color, melodies—and often let them stand without elaboration. The architect, on the contrary, has an exasperatingly long way from inspiration through practical considerations and physical necessities to the final realization of his dream—if he ever sees realization. None of the gigantic cathedrals was finished by the master who had made the original plan, and his successors, decades or even centuries later, though little scrupulous about following the initial design, had to respect the parts already built and to adapt their new ideas to the former style. Even the overdelicate northern spire of Chartres Cathedral, added three hundred years later (1507–13), in all its heterogeneity does not offend. In a similar spirit private buildings were expected to serve a good many generations of descendants and could not yield too much to generational or personal whims.

All this resulted in a continuity of style which in other arts, and particularly in music, was neither necessary nor desirable. Before printing became habitual, music was often performed one single time and forgotten—as late as the eighteenth century, Bach composed five annual courses of cantatas, one for each Sunday, and he little thought of reverting to any of them. Music was not always even written down; the master, improvising on the spur of the moment, allowed his vision to materialize in a flash, die away, and leave no trace.

The arts of painting and sculpture had neither the fugacity of music nor the longevity of architecture; even larger commissions were generally finished within a few years. They reckoned with months and years, where music reckoned with hours and days, and architecture, with centuries.

Yet painting and sculpture, too, have evolved in giant phases and cycles. Only, such phases and cycles are here less easily detected because the two arts have been so strongly subjected to generational reversals. Even as striking a trait as, say, the golden background against which medieval painters set off their holy figures was not consistently in use for longer ages and cannot conveniently serve to denote a phase or a cycle. But then, the conventional golden ground was in itself just one of the factors concerned in the all-important problem that has actually ruled the ways of the arts for hundreds and thousands of years: the problem of space.

Three-dimensional space was not altogether unknown or unwanted in the Middle Ages. However, it had but little theoretical backing or guidance and forcibly played an insignificant role in the comparative irrealism of medieval art which, on the whole, was more interested in merely suggesting than in actually representing the visible world. As a consequence, the figures that the artists shaped were allowed to live in almost complete insulation, detached from space, from air, and from light.

A radical turn came only in the middle of the fifteenth century with Italy's geometric research for perspective—with more and more correct foreshortening, with the disengagement of the once frontal arrays of acting figures, with the opening of distant bluish vistas, with cast shadows, and with the consistent three-dimensional *contrapposto* of the parts of human bodies, in both painting and sculpture. No generational reversal before our own days could ever affect these spatial achievements: two-dimensionalism and three-dimensionalism, coincident with the Middle and the Later Ages, are the main characteristics of the two giant phases.

To the dance, the fifteenth century seems to have given—outside the age-old wooing pantomime—the couple pattern proper, which it has retained ever since. It had existed in the Middle Ages, to be sure, but so exceptionally and evidently so late that the German minnesinger Neidhart von Reuental at the beginning of the thirteenth century almost wonderingly speaks of dancers who "moved about as if they were husband and wife"—*geuden giengen sie gelîch Hîwer an einem Tanze* (H. 63, 28).

The three-dimensional character of the dance in the Later Ages has been discussed in Chapter IX (Two and Three Dimensions).

Music, too, had its fateful turning point in the fifteenth century while Italian architects, sculptors, and painters were creating the Renaissance. As long as the fine arts had persisted in their two-dimensional attitude, music had been 'linear,' proceeding either in one single, unaccompanied line, as in the Gregorian chant, or else combining these originally single lines with other simultaneous lines in the way of a counterpoint essentially different from the harmonically based polyphony of the Later Ages. To be sure, the old counterpoint, as in the *órganum*, the conduct, or the motet, excluded dissonant friction on accented beats, but only between adjacent voice parts, and it was so little concerned with anything resembling harmonic progression or unified 'space' that composers invented the simultaneous voice parts one by one and successively, first the *ténor*, then the *duplum*, and finally the *triplum*. Indeed, they often composed alternative voice parts to be sung at pleasure.

When Johannes Tinctoris, Flemish author of the earliest dictionary of music (*c.* 1475), somewhat boastfully said that his compatriot Dufay had written the first music worth listening to, he testified in his own exaggerated way that a radical break beyond the range of generational reversals had taken place in Europe. Guillaume Dufay and his generation in Italy and Burgundy had indeed initiated another giant phase, in which, after the recognition of thirds and sixths as consonances, music was conceived of as a functional progress of chords with melody, rhythm, and polyphony only as dependent factors.

This giant phase of harmony coincided with the phases of Renaissance and post-Renaissance architecture and of three-dimensional vision in sculpture and painting, just as the giant phase of linear music had coincided with the phases of medieval architecture and of two-dimensional vision. Such coincidence confirms what a previous chapter has pointed out: that harmony and three-dimensionalism are interrelated.

However, Debussy's parallels, Scriabin's fourth chords, Schönberg's atonality have dissolved and defunctionalized the harmonic system of the last four or five hundred years. At the same time, the independence of voice parts in the latest polyphony, and particularly in jazz, draws closer to medieval counterpoint. The fine arts, too, have done away with all the principles familiar to the five hundred years of the Later Ages: 'modern' architecture is strictly opposed to the aims of our immediate past; and special museums for modern painting and sculpture indicate by their very existence the radical break from tradition.

A new giant circle seems to have set in.

It seems, however, that all these qualities ultimately depend upon one general contrast in attitude, which might be called sectional perception as opposed to total perception.

Medieval painters created additively. Any scene they depicted would be a sum of figures and objects, a woman plus a child plus a hut plus a tree, not an indivisible whole, of which the woman, the child, the hut, and the tree, linked by and for one optical impression, were the constituent, inseparable parts. Perspective, as the unifying medium of spatial vision, had no place in an art that aimed at insulation rather than unification. Again, the medieval painter and his public did not mind the simultaneous appearance of consecutive scenes on the same painting as if they had happened at strictly the same moment, say, in the story of St. John the Baptist, the banquet of Herod, king of Judea, the decapitation of the saint, the presentation of his head at table, and Salome's dance; or all the phases of Christ's passion scattered about one common landscape, with the

Last Supper, the trial, the crucifixion. The painting was to be read section by section, not seen at one glance as a whole.

The medieval theater was conceived in a similar spirit: the successive *mansions,* Herod's throne, the manger of Bethlehem, Mary Magdalene's perfume shop, the tabernacle of the Last Supper, Christ's Sepulcher, and so on were aligned in the back of the stage as *décorations simultanées,* and the scene (and therewith the attention of the audience) shifted from one to another as the drama progressed.

The same happened in medieval music, as in the case of counterpoint versus harmony. The two, three, four voice parts of an early motet had their own, individual life and significance; they were coexistent in a spatial and a spiritual, but not in a perceptual, sense. Even the (perceptual) condition that they must form consonances on the main beats was imposed on neighboring voice parts only, not on all of them. It is, again, sectional as against total perception.

Architecture, too, was additive. While, for instance, the Baroque conceived of all parts and rooms of a building (or even a town) as the organic, inseparable elements of a whole that hardly allowed of later changes, the Middle Ages paid little attention not only to the proper organization of rooms (not to speak of town planning), but did not even keep to any definitive, binding first plan. Hence the obvious delight of medieval builders in continuing unfinished churches in their own way and in leaving them unfinished to future generations to carry on as they deemed best. Hence also the charming, picturesque disorder of medieval castles with their purely additive growth from a donjon and living wings to the chapel and a hall of assembly, without stylistic harmony, or symmetry, or even balance.

The Middle Ages had gone when Leonardo da Vinci asked the painter to complete the various parts of a figure only after having sketched the whole.

This book, however, does not undertake neatly to partition the whole history of art into a number of ready-made cycles with their subdivisions. So rigid a system would hardly be feasible or even desirable. Too much depends on the critic's viewpoint. A problem like this—should antiquity be opposed to the Middle and the Later Ages as to two giant cycles of equal rank, or to one Cycle of the Nearer Past with the Middle and the Later Ages as its phases—would be differently answered by the man whose mind is focused on the contrast of the pagan and the Christian spirit, and by him who sees in Gothic art a sharper contrast with both Antiquity and the Later Ages than between Antiquity and all the Nearer Past together. Considering our ignorance of the musical styles and of the dance during almost the whole first thousand years A.D., this alternative would anyway not be in the sphere of this book, which draws its conclusions from the unanimous testimonies of all the arts.

The following pages, therefore, only try to convey a general idea of the subsumption of generational reversals under cycles, which in their turn are the phases of still larger cycles.

2. *THE CYCLE OF ANTIQUITY*

THE GREEK PHASE of the giant Cycle of Antiquity evolved from heavy, monumental pre-Doric and Doric temples to the 'classic' style of the Golden Age in Perikles' time, in which Doric weight was counterbalanced by Ionic mellowness; and again from the well-balanced classical style to the slender elegance of late Corinthian temples and the oversize of Pergamon. Greek sculpture developed from a frontal, static archaism to the serene equilibrium of Pheidias, and thence to Baroque exhibition of overfed muscles, voluptuous gods, and sensational subjects. Greek painting changed from the two-dimensional Geometric style of early vases to the "noble simplicity and quiet grandeur" of the classical age, and thence to illusion, chiaroscuro, and—as Part I said—"the malodorant reality of craftsmen, beggars, topers with rags and wrinkles."

Of music, we know at least that it paralleled the dynamism of the seventh and sixth centuries; that at the end of the Golden Age of fine arts, composers swerved from the austerity of "the old stuff," as Timotheos said, to what Plato scorned as "musical illegality"; and that the archaistic Delphian hymns of the second century coincided with an archaism in the fine arts. All evidences confirm, no evidence contradicts, the strict parallelism of the arts.

In the dance, we can with sufficient clearness distinguish an earlier 'emmelic' phase, with the emphasis on harmonious groups, and a later phase, of professional solo dancers, who displayed personal skill and veered to the side of emotion, character, and caricature.

The full account of the evolution in all the arts has been given in Chapter II.

Despite generational reversals, the curve of development obviously moved toward an ever-increasing pathos. It would be rash, however, to assign ethos preponderantly to the archaism of preclassical times.

The Roman phase was greatly dependent on Grecian art. But statues of Hellenic appearance and Hellenic columns or capitals on Roman buildings should not mislead our judgment: architecture and sculpture were radically different. Greek builders had been concerned with two-dimensional fronts; the *cellae* or inner rooms for the god and his priests had merely been accessories behind those fronts. The Romans, on the contrary, conceived in three dimensions; primarily they created spaces, bounded by walls and opening upward in audacious vaults and domes. After the Etruscan manner, they rested the masonry on arches made of wedge-shaped pieces, while they restrained the columns, chief structural parts of Greek architecture, to a more and more decorative role. They also built their houses in several stories; and they did not hesitate to overcrowd façades with statues and reliefs as decorative fillers.

Sculpture, in its turn, went to a degree of picturesqueness that Greece had never achieved. Reliefs, with elaborate landscapes or architectures as backgrounds, were plastic paintings rather than sculptures projected on planes; and the statues and busts were designed for vivid effects of shadow and light. Music gave the instruments a greater share than Greece had given them; the dance was descriptive and pantomimic; and all the arts, including music, strove for sizes that the Greeks had hardly ever considered.

On the whole, the Roman style was the pathos phase of the giant Cycle of Antiquity, whose ethos phase had been provided by a thousand years of Grecian art. Any subdivision between the phase as a whole and the to-and-fro of its generational reversals is not yet feasible.

3. THE CYCLE OF THE MIDDLE AGES

ROMANESQUE ART can hardly be outlined in a few words. Its national, and even regional, characteristics are too manifold and different and, except in early ivory carving, its sculpture needed so long a time to master technical difficulties that it only counts in the last one hundred years before the Gothic style sets in. Two statements, though, are safe enough to be pronounced. At first, the style as a whole, extending far into the Mediterranean countries and greatly under the sway of meridional taste, kept essentially more to the ethos side then the 'barbarian' Gothic could or would ever achieve.

Its architecture was additive, insulating, disjunct; but in the later part of the high Romanesque period, from 1115 to 1150, and still more in the (German) late Romanesque, during the one hundred years between 1150 and 1250, it disavowed these qualities in favor of a certain integration and conjunction. And it also proceeded from compact, inexorable blocks to a livelier play of light and shadow effects by a higher relief of its projecting parts and here and there —as in Pisa—by the lacework of thoroughly decorative, blind arcades. In its last period, it indulged in truly Baroque details, such as scalloped arches and screwed or twisted columns. Sculpture, too, with its climax in the violent ecstasy and passion of the tympans in Moissac, Vézelay, Autun developed to pathos.

Of music, we do not know enough to indicate so general a trend but we know at least that the beginnings, in Charlemagne's time, were rather static, and that the following centuries dynamized the original forms. Still less can the dance be taken as a parallel; we hardly know what the knights and ladies danced and are completely ignorant as to how they did it.

The Gothic cycle, coincident with the ruin of imperialism and feudalism and the rise of cities, bourgeoisie, and capitalism, was basically realistic. Writers began to express themselves in prose, and artists dared to look at nature, to observe, and to do away with the ready-made patterns of workshops, though still in a timid way. In his curious sketchbook, one of the most precious relics of the middle of the thirteenth century, the architect Villard de Honnecourt proudly—though not very convincingly—comments on his drawing of a lion: "*Bien sacies q cis lions fu contrefais al vif.*" Mark that this lion was drawn from life. It was reserved to Cennino Cennini, around 1400, to recommend the study of nature. And again, as an unmistakable trait of the nearing end of a cycle—he postulated that light and shade should run into one another instead of forming unbroken contrasts.

Sculpture, in the words of Elie Faure, French art historian—"strongly recalls the progression of the schools of antiquity from archaism to academism, with their passage through a point of equilibrium wherein science and sentiment, rising to their loftiest certitude, shine from the same focus. Romanesque [no: early Gothic art of the twelfth century] has the smiling strength and the rhythmical stiffness of the sixth century of Greece; the art of the thirteenth century is calm and mature like that in which Pheidias and his precursors affirmed their complete self-possession. Afterwards, in France as in Greece, virtuosity—descriptive, naturalistic, and picturesque—gains the upper hand little by little."

It is tempting to add another quotation: Mary G. Houston, writing on *Medieval Costume in England and France*, is struck by "the noble simplicity of construction and natural silhouette of the thirteenth century, compared with the slender elegance of the fourteenth, and the riot of variety and exaggeration in the fifteenth century."

Gothic music shared with Gothic architecture the delight in open work: coincident with the delicate lace of Gothic tracery, in the thirteenth and fourteenth centuries, musicians used the strange, indeed unique, technique of the *hoquetus*, in which either individual notes, or smaller groups of notes, were alternately performed in one of the two voice parts, while the other part had a rest. And like the other arts, music reached in Machaut's generation a flickering, flamboyant climax, before the fifteenth century proceeded to sedate clearness and sober simplicity. Nor should we forget that at that time the music for the dance, sung of old by the dancers themselves as ballads or *rondeaux*, was taken over by instruments: vocal music lost its exclusiveness and instrumental music conquered its earliest stronghold.

The general direction of Gothic art from ethos to pathos is obvious. Compared with the Romanesque, it kept on the whole to the pathos side.

Jan Huizinga and other historians have often insisted on the fact that late-medieval man, in his nervous tension, hopelessly staggered from extreme to extreme without balance or rest, from fanatical love to fanatical hatred, from the angelic to the satanic, from exuberant joy to despair. In such a mental pattern there is little room for the serene equilibrium and wise moderation for which all ethos times have striven. Gothic minds, concerned with heaven rather than earth, had no longing for the perfect proportions and canons of beauty that the ages before and after kept alive. Nor were they able or willing to build their music on harmony, which is the art of leading back from dissonant tension to consonant rest. Life, nature, and the body, paramount in the art and science of later centuries, were nothing but peripheral accessories in the spiritual universe of the Middle Ages; and the sober senses, evoked in the Renaissance, had little part in the creative process of medieval art. Inspiration drew its shapes from dream and memory, and less from observation.

The almost classic episode in Gothic art around 1225 or, for that matter, the vagaries of the Baroque, do not invalidate this argument: they are divergent phases within two larger ethos cycles.

The whole cycle of the Middle Ages, comprising the Romanesque and Gothic phases, extends from the end of the Roman empire to the fifteenth and, in the North, even to the sixteenth century. The focus of architectural activity was the church; only in the later part, the city hall became almost equally important. And about the same time, the proportions of the church changed in the direction of unified space. Sculpture, nearly exclusively in the service of church decoration, hardly left the wall as its natural background and was on the whole, except toward the end of the period, frontal rather than all-round. The history of medieval painting leads from rigid pseudo-Byzantine murals to the lively, nature-inspired easel pictures of fifteenth century Flanders, and from conventional illuminations of gospels and psalters to the delightful Hours of French and Netherlands masters. And painting, too, was preponderantly two-dimensional though in its last one hundred years, say, from Ambrogio Lorenzetti's City Life mural in the Hall of the Nine at Siena (1340's) with its amazing tangle of edifices, streets, and squares, it was earnestly interested in the problem of spatial depth.

The music of the Middle Ages evolved from the heavy, static note-against-note *órganum* of Charlemagne's time to the daring naturalism and spirit of the fourteenth century and to Machaut's and Landino's intricacies. And further on, music developed into the novel art of the English and the Burgundians; and without entirely abandoning its basically linear, horizontal style, it turned under Italian and English leadership to an almost harmonic conception. This development implied the growing importance of *musica ficta,* that is, of 'leading' semitones to soften the rigid church modes (C-sharp-D instead of C-D, F-sharp-G instead of F-G) and hence the passage from the Dorian mode to minor and from the Mixolydian mode to major.

The general trend of the Middle Ages thus went from ethos to pathos.

4. THE CYCLE OF THE LATER AGES

The later ages, extending from the end of the Middle Ages to World War I, are sharply set off against the preceding style as a whole but by no means against the immediately preceding last phase of the Gothic. For in all their difference, indeed, in their contrast, their natural constellation forces upon them a partial similarity that here and there makes clear distinctions difficult. As a whole, the Middle Ages in their irrealism and two-dimensionality had been on the ethos side, with all their meandering through generational reversals and through larger cycles; and the Later Ages, in their realism and three-dimensionalism kept mainly to the pathos side. But as we saw, the Middle Ages, following the normal course of all the cycles, ended in a phase of relative pathos, with serious attempts at space and realism; and the Later Ages, obeying the same immanent law of evolution, set in with definite ethos. The late Gothic and the early Renaissance, one adding pathos to ethos, and the other ethos to pathos, could not but run into one another in more than one place, in the rendition of space, for instance, or in the harmonic conception of music.

The prevalent trait of the Later Ages is realism. Architects focus on the palace not on the church; sculpture is all-round; painting, and also the dance, are quite definitely three-dimensional; and music rests on the functional progression of chords, even where the style is seemingly polyphonic or else dependent on melody only.

The cycle began in austere simplicity with Brunelleschi's churches and with those motets and masses of Dufay that a decade spent in Italy had helped to shape. It ended in the radical naturalism, pseudo-elegant *Jugendstil*, and screaming expressionism of the early twentieth century. Generational reversals of unusual violence carried the arts now to the classic, now to the anticlassic or dynamic side; and yet, in all this to-and-fro, a general trend toward increasing sensuousness, illusion, and magniloquence can hardly be mistaken.

Nevertheless, the earlier eighteenth century accomplished a thorough reaction, thus ending the Baroque and its Rococo aftergrowth —a complete break in conditions, aims, expression, and techniques. From this a second ascent from ethos to pathos developed in a way similar to the first but with a weight of classicism less than that which the earlier ascent had had to carry along. The two phases have no official names. So we will temporarily, tentatively, and somewhat reluctantly call them the Greater Renaissance and the Greater Romanticism.

The Cycle of the Greater Renaissance, extending to approximately 1730, has the Renaissance proper and the Baroque as its phases. The Renaissance laid stress on limitation, perfection, and essence, notwithstanding the substrate of pathos that it had in common with the Baroque. The Baroque, on the contrary, relied on boundlessness, change, and appearance. It overtaxed the possibilities of the stage, of stone, of music, of instruments. It mingled the arts, mixed painting and sculpture with architecture, and music with speech and space, and united all of them in the *Gesamtkunstwerk* of the opera. It fused the divine and the secular, the holy and the erotic, and even lifted the barrier that separates the work of art from life and nature. It strove for impressive sizes—of buildings, paintings, music pieces and performances, instruments, scorebooks—and, being picturesque, in art and costume gave color, light and shadow a never-heard-of significance at the cost of line and drawing. It created the nineteenth-century way of giving emotional expression to music by unruly changing of force and tempo. And it unified the structural plans in all the arts, replacing additive co-ordination of the parts by the most radical subordination under one coherent concept.

Most ethos qualities prevail in the Renaissance proper, most pathos qualities, in the Baroque. The Renaissance is the ethos, Baroque the pathos phase of the Greater Renaissance Cycle.

Many observers will be inclined to place the caesura at, or shortly after, 1600. In doing so, they are under the spell of the word 'baroque,' which even today, after a long period of widening significance, still cannot, and possibly never will, get rid of its original connotations: oblique, irregular, bombastic, theatrical. But the opposite is true: the period doomed to carry this unfortunate name exalted the ideals of classic regularity and simplicity, and the French erected a dozen academies to enforce them; men of the Baroque age created England's inexorable classicism; and even Italy, homeland of the style, never forgot her national heritage.

Seen from this angle, the so-called Baroque need not begin on a 'baroque' phase in the usual sense of the word; and once this has been admitted, the way is open for an unprejudiced search for the strongest caesura in the Greater Renaissance Cycle.

Architectural facts point to the 1560's. The two patriarchs revered as the highest authorities during the Baroque, Vignola and Palladio, set the standard with their books of 1563 and 1570. But the answer is particularly impressive in music. Here, too, the year 1600, with the appearance of two or three new operas, the *stile recitativo*, and the thoroughbass, has been a favorite of those who are partial to nice round numbers. Actually, at least one real opera had been performed three years before, and forerunners can be traced all through the last third of the century; recitatives existed at least in the 1570's; and the thoroughbass had slowly become indispensable. The striking events of 1600 were already a summit reached by the pioneers after decades of climbing.

But a cycle begins at the foot of a mountain. It begins where a trickling, poor, infantile beginning first appears at the side of the rich and ripened style of the past. In the music of the sixteenth century, it begins where we are at a loss to reconcile the rigid, clumsy recitatives of the *Ballet de la Royne* or the sober, threadbare division-variations for instruments with the wonders of Palestrina's masses or Lasso's motets. It begins where musicians from different camps, dissatisfied with the 'moderns,' turn their backs on polyphony and search for another style, expressive, natural, limpid. How this happened has been described in Part I in Cross Section 1567.

With the line between the Renaissance proper and the Baroque drawn in the 1560's, both phases, despite their opposite character, show a general trend from ethos to pathos. The former phase started with the quiet simplicity of 1430 and ended in Michelangelo's violence; it stretched from the hard-drawn paintings of Pisanello to the mellow chiaroscuro of Titian and Tintoretto, from the sober chordal *lauda* to Gombert's unbridled polyphony. The latter phase started with the purism of the 1560's and ended in the orgies of the late Baroque and the flamboyant elegance of the Rococo. And it spanned the period of the figured bass from its timid beginnings to the powerful and almost superhuman ending with Handel and Bach.

The Greater Renaissance Cycle as a whole, comprising the Renaissance proper and the Baroque as its two phases and extending roughly from 1430 to 1730, was itself the first phase in the larger Cycle of the Later Ages. As such, the Greater Renaissance was the ethos phase of a giant pathos cycle. Both in France and in Italy, Leone Battista Alberti's classicistic principles and Vitruvian orders in architecture, academic rule in sculpture, *gran maniera* in painting restrained the styles of art, however far Donatello's naturalism, Michelangelo's high tension, and the extravagances of the Baroque would throw them out of gear. Indeed, the arch-Baroque Bernini considered himself a classicist just as Michelangelo had done; and all the leading architects were ardent classicists: Brunelleschi and Bramante, Vignola and Palladio, Wren and Mansard.

Music clung to strict and static forms despite the escapades of the *stile recitativo* and the freedom of the dying madrigal; the most exuberant, passionate melodies were forced into the iron clasps of *ostinato* basses or grounds, and the imitative forms of polyphony, averse to symmetry, culminated in the inextricable weaving of the fugue. The dances, too, were strict in form; the *basse danse* in 1500, the *courante* in 1600, the *minuet* in 1700 were very formal dances which did not allow for emotion or ecstasy.

Not even Spain or Germany, countries where the most baroque Baroque existed, could entirely ignore this strong component of ethos common to all stages of the Greater Renaissance including the Baroque. No wonder, then, that in basically moderate countries like France and England (and hence in America) the popularly Baroque qualities of this phase were rather a thin, transparent veneer above an often academic classicism.

Greater Romanticism as the title of the phase from 1730 to about 1910 cannot be introduced without apology. In presenting it, the author risks the objection of critical readers to listing the rationalism, the enlightenment, and the classicism of the eighteenth century under romantic styles, and his less sophisticated readers claiming, on the authority of this book, that Lessing, Gluck and David were romantics.

Still, the reasons in favor of this title are stronger than the reasons against it. In a negative way first: it is the common fate of all names of styles to be narrower, much narrower, than the scope of art in the ages they are called upon to cover: the 'Renaissance' spans more than just the renascence of antiquity; the 'Baroque' is preponderantly un-'Baroque'; and even 'Romanticism' proper denotes a time in which architecture, sculpture, and Goethe's poetry indulged in classic revivals. In a positive way: Romanticism is the only leading attitude that openly or secretly steered the arts through two hundred years of contradictory currents. If in a sketchy way we describe Romanticism as the delight in self-expression, in an ever-unsatisfied longing, in sensitive shades, in vagueness, dream, and death, we will find it raising its head when the tearful eighteenth century adores aeolian harps and glass harmonicas, when Bach's son Karl Philipp Emanuel parts with his beloved clavichord in an astonishing rondo, when Diderot relishes ruins, when Rousseau writes confessions, when the Storm and Stress assails bourgeois and classic art.

To architecture, the Greater Romanticism meant the suspension of creative power. Only France was able to keep a noble tradition from the Louis XV style to the Second Empire. In the rest of the world, during those two hundred years we find ourselves confronted with Greek and Roman, Romanesque and Gothic, Renaissance and Baroque revivals—a motley menu of poorly warmed-up dishes. But then, Romanticism, in its stress on emotion and dream, was basically unarchitectural and seldom sculptural. It forcibly left its chief expression to the arts of color and sound, to painting and music.

The Greater Romanticism was the period of painters who in spite of David and Cornelius shied from academic recipes and the *gran maniera*. These men were fascinated by life as they saw it in all its aspects—high and low, tragic and comic—and they discovered the charms of nature under the impact of open air and changing light. It was the period of deeply emotional, personal, indeed, egocentric music under the guidance of German masters. And the very fact that, ever since the middle of the eighteenth century, most musicians have unfortunately considered digestible music to have begun with Haydn proves at least how momentous that reversal was. And lastly Greater Romanticism was the period of the waltz which, informal and passionate, had forced out the minuet and, in general, the age-old courtly dance by open, individually performing, stately couples.

Again, a division into two phases is rather obvious although there are no distinctive titles in readiness. The older phase kept to the ethos side. Architecture, in its nature little compatible with a romantic attitude, was incapable of independent ideas and escaped into Roman and Greek revivals. Classicists were also dominating in sculpture, since plastic style and romantic spirit could not well be reconciled. Even painting stood under the leading influence of the arch-classicist David. Music clung to formal strictness decades after Beethoven's death; Weber, Schubert, Mendelssohn rarely left the realm of classical structure; and even the opera, romantic in spirit and subjects, followed the classical plan of separate 'numbers' until Richard Wagner recast it into a music drama.

The reversal came about the middle of the century. Wagner outlined the break with tradition in 1850 with his pamphlet The Work of Art of the Future, written while he was developing from the style of *Lohengrin* to the radical styles of the *Ring* and of *Tristan*. The painters, Millet, Manet, Whistler, Courbet, and the leading authors, Dickens, Balzac, Flaubert, indulged in a new naturalism. And the classic revivals in architecture yielded to the more dynamic Gothic revival.

Many traits in this second phase recall Baroque ideals: town planning on a large scale particularly in the France of Napoleon III, gigantic orchestras and enormous organs, magniloquence, and theatrical gesture. Thus, the reader might call this phase the Baroque phase of Greater Romanticism. He would also be within his rights—and even more strongly, perhaps—to call it the naturalistic phase, as opposed to the classicistic phase. This book, however, refrains from coining handy names for the two ages. Suffice it to state that the Greater Romanticism developed in an ethos and a pathos phase, and that as a cycle it went in the same direction almost steadily, from Gluck's *Orfeo* to Strauss's *Electra*, from Greuze's melodramatic scenes to van Gogh's expressionism, from sober classicistic building to the banal overdecoration of what the English call Edwardian, the Germans Wilhelminian, and the French *le style Emile Loubet.* So steadily did it go that it allowed no coincident ethos opposition—from Puvis de Chavannes or Fauré in France, from Burne-Jones in England, or from Feuerbach and Brahms in Germany—to interfere with its force as a generational reversal.

5. *THE TRENDS OF THE CYCLES*

TWO MAIN RULES of evolution follow from the discussions of this chapter.

Every cycle starts on an ethos *phase and ends on a* pathos *phase.*

Every phase develops from ethos *to* pathos.

These rules apply whether the cycle in question is a giant or a smaller cycle.

The consequence is that a certain style might belong to the ethos phase of a pathos cycle or vice versa, and that again the giant cycle of which this cycle is a part does or does not agree with the trend of the phase. This seems to be the most important key to the fact that nearly all the styles have elements of either direction. The Baroque, at once so disconcertingly classicistic and anticlassicistic, tends to pathos as a part of the Later Ages; to ethos, as a part of the Greater Renaissance, which is the ethos phase of the Later Ages; and again to pathos, as the concluding phase of the Greater Renaissance. And Romanticism is so desperately contradictory in its anticlassical soul and classic form because it tends to pathos as a part of the Later Ages; and again to pathos, as a part of the Greater Romanticism, which is the pathos phase of the Later Ages; but Romanticism also tends toward ethos, as the incipient phase of the Greater Romanticism. Graphically:

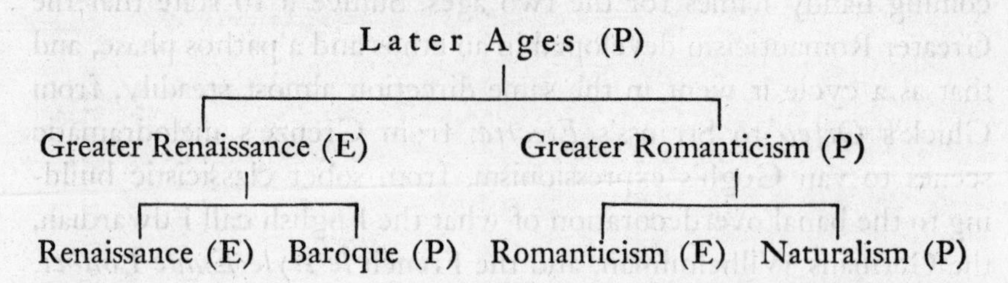

Readers fond of figures and diagrams could easily make a qualitative analysis of any one of the styles.

It is important to notice that the same trend guides the evolution of the individual musical forms which—quite differently from the situation in the fine arts—crystallize in well-defined types under consistent names to last for one or several centuries and, notwithstanding stragglers, reach their end with the cycle in which they belong. It will suffice to outline the destinies of two such types: the fugue and the sonata.

In the widest sense of a musical composition in which each voice part successively enters with the same initial theme but then continues in its own, individual way, the fugue fills the whole cycle of the Greater Renaissance. Timid beginnings of such a free imitation are found in Dufay's generation. The following age of Ockeghem, in the last third of the fifteenth century, raises the thorough imitation of the entries to the leading principle of all nonpopular vocal music; and the masters around Isaac and Hofheimer model instrumental pieces after the same pattern. From the 1540's on, this instrumental form appears under its definitive name *ricercar*. Though alive until Johann Sebastian Bach wrote practically the last one in his Musical Offering of 1747, the *ricercar* had its bloom before it yielded to the fugue late in the sixteenth century. It treated several themes imitatively but in succession, so that it consisted of disjoined, more or less independent sections.

When, about 1600, the cycle turned to the pathos side, the seriated *ricercar* developed into a unified form, the fugue. Here, a melodic 'subject,' imperfect, meaningless without the things to follow, starts unaccompanied but is after a few measures answered at the distance of a fifth or a fourth by a second voice, which takes the lead, while the first proceeds in an accompanying counterpoint. In a similar way, the other voices answer the subject, until all of them—two, three, four, or five—have joined. After this first 'exposition,' the voice parts modulate away from the original key and throw the subject to each other like a ball, or shrink, enlarge, or even invert it. The tension grows, the texture tightens, and at last, closely on one another's heels in a breathless *stretto*, the voices repeat the subject without waiting for their fellow parts to finish with it. Motion never stops; no cadence brings a break; indeed, as Vaughan Williams nicely puts it, "a sonata movement may be said to be sewn together, a fugue to be woven." One central idea runs through the fugue from its first note to the ultimate climax; and even a double, triple, or quadruple fugue, with two, three, or four subjects instead of one, means only complication, not abrogation, of this principle.

While the fugue shared its end with the Greater Renaissance (all later fugues were conscious archaisms), the *sonata* extended all over the Later Ages. After a long period of conflicting, ever-changing phases, the first quarter of the eighteenth century, a time of ethos, gave the sonata a strict, distinct, and logical form. It usually kept four movements only, two slow and two fast, and the fast ones were subdivided into two sections with repeats—one starting on the tonic and ending on the dominant, and the other, starting on the dominant and ending on the tonic. In this perfect symmetry and closeness, the sonata around 1720 was essentially more 'classic' than the so-called classic sonata of Haydn-Mozart times.

This latter form took shape in the second quarter of the eighteenth century, first in Italy, and then in Germany. Its initial movement generally opens with the main theme and passes to a contrasting second theme in some related key. The exposition of these two themes is repeated and then followed by the development, in which the composer is free to play off one theme against the other and to use all the potentialities the thematic material provides. The coda brings the first theme back, triumphant and uncontested.

The slow movement frequently has the form of variations on a strictly built theme; the brisk movement, a minuet or scherzo, is symmetrical and often interrupted by a contrasting trio. And the last movement has the alternating form of a rondo or the symmetrical form of a fast dance.

The movements after the first are definitely 'close' and 'classic,' and so is the first movement, the sonata proper, in the contrast of its two themes, in the repeat of the exposition, and in the coda, which in a way leads back to the starting point. But its development is not close; it means action and dramatic progress.

It is to this dynamic element that the sonata owes its existence far beyond the so-called classic period, indeed, to the end of Romanticism. Such survival was made possible by the growth of the development not only in size but also in importance; and, characteristically, conductors often hesitate to obey the repeat signs in Beethoven's expositions lest, being in themselves developments, they might become meaningless. Abandoning the original pattern, the composer would even drop the contrasting second theme, as Robert Schumann did in his Concerto for Piano and Orchestra, Op. 54. The last movement, originally just a Sir Roger and happy ending, is in a similar way conceded a development of its own—as early as Mozart's G minor Symphony—and becomes an important final act, which transforms the sonata (and its derivatives) from a playful alternation of quick and slow movements into a musical drama in four acts. A further condensation into one act was ultimately reached in Liszt's symphonic poems and his one Piano Sonata in B minor.

Thus, all ethos traits became attenuated, and the pathos traits increased.

The individual dances do not seem to share in the typical evolution from ethos to pathos and cannot without due allowance serve to understand the march of styles. A few examples will easily show that the dance has obeyed a different law of growth.

The *galliard*, first spoken of at the end of the fifteenth century as a folk dance in Lombardy, appears as the successor of the 'leaping' *saltarello* shortly before 1530 and is characterized as bold and wanton. In 1536, Antonius de Arena, author of a curious poem on the dance, feels reminded of a cockfight and, in 1549, an Italian, Simeone Zuccolo, describes how the spectators egg on the girls with shouts and cries until they do their utmost. Moreover, it is pantomimic. But canon Thoinot Arbeau's *Orchésographie* of 1588 records these features only as reminiscences from his early years: the pantomime has been dropped, and the galliard is not much more than a rhythm with several step patterns.

The *saraband* was first mentioned in 1583 as a dance of unparalleled sexual suggestiveness "with absurd twists of the body, hands, and feet." Forty years later, Giambattista Marin, the bombastic poet, protested against its savagery: "The girls with castanets, the men with tambourines exhibit indecency in a thousand positions and gestures. They let the hips sway and the breasts knock together. They close their eyes and dance the kiss and the last fulfillment of love." And yet, the saraband must have greatly changed. For even before Marini's oratory, it had been danced within the frame of a comedy at the Spanish court, the strictest of all, and in 1625, it appeared in a French court ballet. Never again, up to the last known date of its existence, 1697, was there any mention of lust, barbarism, or even temperament; Mersenne, the most important source of the century, said in 1636 just that it was performed in gliding steps. From an orgiastic dance it had developed to a frigid pattern of steps in stately rhythm.

The *minuet*, too, had a concentrated existence of three or four generations and would be a good example of a larger cycle. But there is hardly a trace of any evolution in the extant sources, except for the stylistically quite irrelevant changes in its floor pattern —figures 8 and 2 and letters S and Z—in the early years of its life.

The *waltz* conquered Germany in the 1760's and in not so many years was leading in the balls of Europe. It had the qualities of pathos: expression, spirit, character, passion. "The girls looked half mad and ready to swoon"; the Viennese waltz surpassed everything "in wild fury"; and in 1782, a doctor's pamphlet warned against the new exertion. Alas, expression, fury, passion, character went; the waltz became sedate and 'classical.'

As matters stand, all dances may reflect the cycles in which they belong but do not share in their development. While the galliard mirrors the wanton spirit of the 1530's, and the waltz the naturalism of 1760, they—and probably all dances—had the same disastrous fate: to start in a dynamic, passionate phase and to end as static, dispassionate step patterns. Such development is normal; in their need for rejuvenated dances, the courts and the citizenry had again and again reached for those of peasants and foreign peoples in which dynamic power and motor impulse were still unbroken. Such were the Lombardian galliard, the Americo-Spanish saraband, the Alpine waltz. But away from its homeland and social conditions, a folk dance cannot but lose its freedom and force. It declines to poor, unvaried designs and at last survives as a merely musical model.

Dancing, nevertheless, was probably not altogether exempt from generational changes. A dancer might scrupulously preserve the choreography and step patterns of some dance all through its lifetime despite the growing pathos of style and yet comply with all specific trends of the age, by changing what the sources hardly ever mention: tempo and mood, pose and motor type, the width of the steps, and the scope of gesture.

It would be unwise, then, to base the synchronization of the dance merely on those characteristics which under the protection of some distinctive name recommend themselves as units and to neglect the often more important features which do not show in the special patterns or descriptions of 'the' courante or 'the' galliard, but in all the dances of a certain time or nation. A courante of the sixteenth century is in essential qualities of step and carriage doubtless closer to galliards of the same period than to courantes a hundred years later. And it is much less the minuet as such that forms a cycle than its gliding, bending steps with the feet no more than one foot apart.

Still less than social dancing can the ballet be used as an illustration. Technical and wholly unemotional in the main, it has greatly lived its own life without sharing in the reversals due to changes in emotional attitude, just as the technical skills of the circus and the bullfight have lived their own lives unconcerned with the ever-new developments of art proper. The tenacity of the ballet is in retrospect outlined in the revolutionary *Lettres sur la Danse et les Ballets* that the dancing master Noverre published in 1760 against the old ballet. The traditional ballet master, he says, would, in a mythological ballet, place the nymphs and fauns in parallel lines, all the nymphs in uniform poses and all the fauns with arms raised to the same height. He would never place five nymphs on the right, and seven on the left side. But, he asks, was not the result cold exercise instead of spirited action?

The full significance of Noverre's description is that, in an age with spirit, warmth, and free asymmetry as its ideals, the ballet still held to the frigid style of Louis Quatorze. Such timeless traditionalism, however, has not precluded occasional reconditionings under the hands of creative artists like Noverre or Vestri or Diaghilev.

It is evident that neither the countermovement of social dancing nor the inertia of the ballet apply to the sensitive art of modern stage dances.

6. THE DOMINANCE OF INDIVIDUAL ARTS

THE ARTS HAVE NOT, and could not have, contributed in the same measure to all the phases and portions of phases: they are too different in nature, weight, and tempo. Architecture, as an organization of motionless space, is static, tectonic, and mostly symmetrical; and it is also basically permanent, impersonal, and emotional. Thus dominated by ethos qualities, it necessarily plays its most significant role in ethos times but grows weak in its creative powers in pathos generations.

Music, on the contrary, as an organization of time and therefore of motion, is basically transitory, dynamic, and, owing to the affective character of sound, emotional and personal. Thus dominated by pathos qualities, it necessarily plays its most significant role in pathos times but weakens in generations of ethos.

Sculpture and painting have their positions mostly between the two polar arts—sculpture, as a rule, closer to architecture and painting nearer to music; indeed, they almost coincide. The fourteenth century, with Giotto and the Sienese masters, with Machaut and Landino; the seventeenth, with Rembrandt, Rubens, and Velásquez, with the opera, the new orchestra, and the new chamber music; the nineteenth, with Whistler and Manet, with Wagner and Brahms, are striking examples of the pictorial and musical leadership in concluding phases.

It would be rash, however, to associate all ethos phases with a predominance of architecture, and all pathos phases with a predominance of music, while sculpture and painting were proportionally distributed. It is rather this way: as the cycles, whether small or large, develop from ethos to pathos, they evolve from the ethos to the pathos arts.

All cycles give predominance, in their incipient stages, to the visual arts and often to architecture and, in their final stages, to music.

It is not difficult to give historic evidence.

The dominance of architecture is particularly impressive in the earlier Romanesque where sculpture, painting, and music cannot seriously challenge the perfection of the cathedrals of Pisa, Toulouse, or Bamberg, however important they are. Music, on the other hand, grows in importance from the *órganum* in Charlemagne's time to that of Leoninus.

In the Gothic Cycle, architecture and sculpture fill the beginnings and even the center almost to capacity, while painting and music begin their conquest in the thirteenth century and are predominant from about 1300 on, both in France and in Italy.

The Renaissance sets in with architecture, with Brunelleschi's pilgrimage to the relics of antiquity in Rome, with the type of church and palace that he and Michelozzo created and with Alberti's architectural theory. Music, on the contrary, was so little dominant that from 1430 to about Michelangelo's death in 1564, Italians lived chiefly on Netherlandish music, the late Gothic character of which they changed but little in their own direction. At the end of the Renaissance proper, about 1560, the Flemings still held most key positions in Italian music but had created typical Italian forms, like the madrigal. The greatest Italian, Palestrina, by far outshone the contemporary 'mannerists' in the fine arts.

Two leading names, however, appeared in architecture, Palladio and Vignola. But, both as builders and as theorists, they were the patriarchs of the coming Baroque, to whom two centuries of designers paid their homage—including those who glued the interrupted 'Palladian' pediments on the windows of our white wooden Georgian houses. They marked, in the 1560's, a new start not an ending, while Palestrina, the finisher, was leading polyphonic music to a glorious climax. At the same time, a new generation of musicians was timidly beginning to express itself in ways quite opposite to those of Palestrina's generation. Renouncing the rich, sophisticated polyphony of the 'moderns,' they created the recitative, the emotional monody, the simple *balletto*, which, listened to alongside masses, motets, madrigals of the older masters, displayed the wooden meagerness characteristic of incipient musical styles.

The following seventeenth century, the age of Rubens, Velásquez, and Rembrandt, belongs mainly to the painters. At the end of the Baroque, from about 1700 on, architecture, without producing new ideas, lived to a flamboyant end in the elegant, decorative orgies of the Rococo. Sculpture and painting declined. But music, steadily growing from Monteverdi and Gabrieli on, became predominant in the age of Bach and Handel, the Neapolitan opera, and Jean-Philippe Rameau. The fine arts hardly had names of equal weight to match.

Looking over the Greater Renaissance as a whole, it is fairly safe to say that the contribution to architecture was greater around 1430 than around 1550, and also that, on the contrary, the musical achievement at the end of the second phase was more important than that at the end of the first phase. This implies a development from fine art, especially architecture, to music not only in the two smaller cycles, but also in the larger cycle.

Things were scarcely different in the cycle of Greater Romanticism. While the Handel-Bach generation marked a spectacular sunset, musical style reverted from riches and complication to simplicity, indeed, to wooden meagerness and often to not more than two skeletal voice parts, but subsequently music grew in importance, scope, and means, until around 1900 it was the dominant art. It assumed authority in every respect not only for edification or mere entertainment but as a spiritual power, which permeated the misty skies of *Weltanschauung* and even meddled in politics. Indeed, in an age of materialism and sober sciences, music created waves of intoxication unheard-of in previous centuries and conquered poetry itself: "Music above all," said Paul Verlaine; and of Stéphane Mallarmé *Le Petit Larousse* nicely states that "*sa muse est plus soucieuse de musique que d'intelligibilité*"—his muse is more concerned with music than with intelligibility. It was only normal that architecture, the natural antipode of music, proved in the heyday of music quite unable to shape any style of its own and helplessly staggered from revival to revival, since reverent, yearning retrospection to ideals and patterns of some distant past is the only trend in Romanticism that can affect so impersonal an art.

Comparing the whole Greater Romanticism with the Greater Renaissance, we cannot overlook that the preponderance of music over painting, sculpture, and architecture appears to be much stronger than it was at the end of the Greater Renaissance, in the times of Handel and Bach. This gives the giant cycle of the Later Ages a growth toward the musical pole similar to that which the evolution of the Middle Ages has shown.

In the new cycle of which we are witnessing the onset, architecture again has the lead and is so far the only art in modern form that has been able to take root in actual life. This can hardly be said of present-day sculpture or painting—not to speak of the almost desperate struggle of contemporary music for recognition, affection, and importance. Do not blame it on the composers nor, for that matter, on the audiences; the cause of the present situation is not lack of mastery or want of willingness but, beyond control of man, the inexorable law of the evolution of art.

7. *DOMINANCE OF INDIVIDUAL NATIONS*

THE SHIFT FROM ART to art often implies a shift from nation to nation. For "it is given to every nation to embody and display to the world some side of the great formative tendencies which have lead to the development of humanity. Each people can assimilate some of these better than other peoples" (Percy Gardner, *The Principles of Greek Art*).

Such a shift is particularly obvious whenever a nation, too deeply absorbed in one of the arts, has no energy left to spend on the others. Nowhere are one-sidedness and, as a consequence, variation from nation to nation more striking than in the Greater Renaissance between the fifteenth and seventeenth centuries. While the creative power of Italy was concentrated upon the visual arts, the country had not one outstanding musical figure to match the unprecedented host of prominent architects, sculptors, goldsmiths, and painters. So sensible was the musical vacuum that the courts, while fostering native masters in the visual arts, recurred to musicians from the Lowlands and Burgundy. The Curia engaged Dufay, Brasart, and Josquin des Prés; the Este in Ferrara, Obrecht; the Medici in Florence, Isaac; the Gonzaga in Mantua, Cypriano de Rore, Orlando di Lasso, and Jacob van Werth; the republic of Venice, Adriaen Willaert. Indeed, men from the North created the national madrigal of Italy and the polychoral style of Venice. Not that the country was unmusical. Everybody delighted in music, sang, and played, and particularly the visual artists themselves. Paolo Veronese has left a unique document in his gigantic Wedding at Cana in the Louvre, where he portrayed himself and his fellow painters Titian, Tintoretto, Bassano as viol players entertaining the guests (Plate XXI). But little gift and energy was left for creation in music.

This situation lasted all the one hundred and twenty or thirty years of Italy's overwhelming activity and influence in the fine arts. It came to an almost sudden end when after 1564, the year of Michelangelo's death, the unique quality and importance of Italian art declined. The reversal became complete within a few decades: Rubens, Hals, Rembrandt left far behind what their Italian fellow painters had to offer. But Netherlandish music, insignificant after Orlando di Lasso, yielded its supremacy to Italy, which in turn kept the musical leadership from the days of Gabrieli's international studio in Venice and the exportation of Italian madrigals to England in 1588 to the age of Mozart.

Again, about 1760, in the time of Padre Martini and Piccini, the Germans, rarely in the focus of the scene, came to the fore at least in music, and particularly in instrumental music, to hold this front position for a century and a half up to World War I.

The nations mainly involved in shaping post-Roman art of the West have been, in alphabetical order: England, France, Germany, Italy, the Lowlands, and Spain. The following pages try to convey an idea of their artistic mentalities.

England's attitude toward the arts has been determined by her salient national qualities: devotion to life and nature, good humor, common sense and rationalism, sobriety and reserve. As a necessary consequence, inherent moderation has tempered all expression of pathos. A Romanesque massiveness, stressed in central towers above the intersection of nave and transept, and a powerful horizontal trend distinguishes English from continental Gothic with its immoderate verticalism—just as the massiveness of third and sixth consonances distinguishes the music of medieval England from the less corporeal fourths of continental music. The English Baroque keeps carefully away from the loudness of many Italian, German, Spanish works of that style; and its musicians ignored almost completely the essential features of Italian Baroque music. They cared little for the recitative and were utterly uninterested in the opera before the times of Purcell. They left the tragedy to Shakespeare, just as the French left it to the spoken verses of Corneille, and they clung in music to the milder dramatic form of the masque, as the French preferred the ballet to the opera proper. England also was opposed to orchestral ensembles and stuck by preference to their chamber concerts with only one instrument to each voice part.

Moderate styles, on the other hand, reached England more easily than other countries. The Elizabethan time accepted Italian madrigals and sonnets when Germany, France, and Spain had closed their borders, and its greatest church music by William Byrd or, later, Orlando Gibbons was very close to the polyphonic styles of Rome and Venice. English architecture of the seventeenth century lived on the classical spirit of Palladio and Vignola; the Classic Revival of the later eighteenth century was perhaps more heartily welcomed than in any other land; and in the nineteenth century, the pre-Raphaelites had an influence that similar movements on the continent had not.

It would be a grave mistake, however, to interpret English reserve as sereneness and to call the British an ethos nation. If this they were, they would not have perpetrated the Gothic style, as nowhere else; Shakespeare could not be their greatest master; nor would they have produced Charles Dickens, Byron, or Shelley, or, for that matter, Hogarth, Constable, Turner.

The Netherlands and Spain, on the contrary, have been preponderantly on the anticlassical side. The ideals of Greece and even of Rome, canonic proportions, mythology, great subjects did not agree with those of Holland or of (what is now) Belgium, for they found delight in nature, intimacy, and everyday life. In turns, they have led the arts of Europe, now in painting, now in music: in painting, at the end of Gothic times and in the seventeenth century; in music, during the Renaissance proper, from Dufay to Lasso. Their architecture, from Gothic centuries on, has always been on a highly respectable level, though it was not influential (except for the latest style). Sculpture, as generally in lowlands, has rarely been important. The same is true of the dance—the Burgundian and Brabantian *basse danse* of the fifteenth century belongs to France rather than to the Netherlands.

Spain's anticlassic attitude was of a different kind. In an unparalleled fusion of mysticism and brutal naturalism, she knew no joy of life or harmony, and sereneness was foreign to her fanatic, passionate soul. Ethos hardly reached her; but all the pathos styles of Europe lived in Spain to extremes unknown elsewhere. Cathedrals—in Seville, in Zaragoza—were given five or seven naves instead of the continental three; the strict reserve of Italian buildings broke down to excessive decoration; flamboyant Gothic and the later Baroque outdid their continental paragons in glittering superabundance and vehemence. Aiming at convincing illusion, the sculptors and painters often led their faithful public to the fringes of waxworks and theatrical gesture. As Santayana says in *The Middle Span:* "Baroque and Rococo cannot be foreign to a Spaniard. They are profoundly congenial and Quixotic, suspended as it were between two contrary insights: that in the service of love and imagination nothing can be too lavish, too sublime, or too festive; yet that all this passion is a caprice, a farce, a contortion, a comedy of illusions."

Spain is profoundly musical. But her music, though highly developed, has always been too national, too folkloristic to pass the frontiers often. Her dances, on the contrary, were able to expand into Europe early in the Baroque when the ballrooms, after having exhausted native resources, were badly in need of rejuvenation.

Germany has begot a host of excellent masters in all fields of art; but none of them—except her musicians after the later eighteenth century—was able to play a supranational, normative role. She abounds in buildings that imitate Italian Baroque or French classicism; none of the national styles of Germany ever found its way to France or Italy—neither the brick façades of the North nor the high-gabled *Rathäuser* of Saxony nor the onion towers of Bavaria. There is, or was, a statue of Raphael in front of the Academy of Art in Dresden but there never was a statue of Dürer before the Roman or the Florentine Academy. Hans Holbein's great success in England and his appointment as a painter to the court of Henry VIII is the one exception that confirms the rule: he was more classical minded than any other German painter and better able to weld the intenseness of the northern peoples with the balance of the South.

The same is true of music and, still more clearly, of the dance. Germany remained "undisturbed by all the changes and fashions of the international world launched now in Italy, now in Spain, and now in France" (Curt Sachs). Caroso's important book *Il Ballarino* (1581) emphatically confined itself to the dances *sì all'vso d'Italia, come à quello di Francia, & Spagna*. Germany did not count.

Even foreign styles so close to national needs that they later were claimed to be genuine German entered with considerable delay. Gothic architecture and the poetry and music of the knights reached the German border only a hundred years after the French had begun to develop them.

The deepest reason for such stunning isolation is the lack of balance in the national character of Germany and, therewith, the dominant pathos of her art. Pathos, as the end of Chapter IX and again the end of this Chapter XIV make evident, is mostly prone to cling to folk tradition against the supranational trends of ethos and humanism. The best of German art is actually high-bred folk art; the picturesque *Rathäuser* with their giant gables are peasant houses; and the sculpture of the South German Baroque derives from native wood carving. Dancing in Germany meant rustic turning in couples cheek by cheek, in the *Ländler* of hobnailed mountaineers as well as in the patrician dances that the French philosopher Michel de Montaigne, traveling through Augsburg in 1580, wonderingly watched in the house of the Fuggers.

Mountaineers and patricians in closest connection—this illustrates the vital point: that in Germany the lack of a central court and an art-loving aristocracy spared the upper class the fate of being lifted into the realm of a uniform, colorless clique and granted them a steady nearness to the common man and to their native places, but also that German art kept to a great extent the limitations of a bourgeois character, indeed, of provincialism.

Folk, provincial, and burgher art is conservative and toughly resists interference and development. And it also resists exportation, like domestic wine which must be drunk in its habitat.

The only folk art apt to be exported is the dance. For, in the words of the author's *World History of the Dance*, "when the dance in a too highly refined society becomes anemic, . . . fresh blood must be taken from the dance of foreign peoples, who are more primitive in their way of life and superior in physical mobility and expressiveness." Actually, the medieval languages of France and Italy have several South German words for dances—*danse*, *espringale* and *danza*, *ridda*, *tresca*, *trotto*—which points to the exportation of the dances themselves.

It is for this same reason that many hundreds of years later, at the end of the eighteenth century, the world, bored to death with the overrefined minuet, availed itself of an unbroken dance of German mountaineers—the waltz.

The art historian Max Hauttmann once said that German art appears to be at its best and strongest in the final stages of a period. This observation is confirmed and explained by the concurrence of three statements in this book: that "every cycle starts on an ethos phase and ends on a pathos phase"; that "every phase develops from ethos to pathos"; and that all German art is essentially oriented to the pathos side. No wonder, then, that German art is better at home in the final than in the initial stages of cycles and phases. But this, of course, is true of all the national pathos styles.

Though pathos often gives preference to color at the cost of drawing, the Germans, essentially virile, sober, austere, have frequently sneered at the delicate intricacies of the palette. True, there has been a continuous current of excellent colorists from Matthias Grünewald through Caspar David Friedrich to Böcklin and Max Liebermann. But it seems that Germany has always given her best in black and white, in Dürer's prints, in Rethel's drawings, Menzel's woodcuts, Klinger's etchings.

Still, with all her pathos, indeed, because of her pathos, Germany has had an eternal longing for the ethos of Greece and of Italy, for balance and harmony; and it was a German who gave voice to this desire in pointing at the "noble simplicity and quiet grandeur" of the Greeks. It shows in the Renaissance movements of Charlemagne, Otto II, and Frederick II, between 800 and 1250; in the *mâze*, the spirit of moderation that the knights of the Hohenstaufen proclaimed in the twelfth century; in the humanism of 1500; in the pilgrimages to Italy of Dürer, Goethe, Cornelius; in the Helena problem of *Faust* and its second, 'classic' Walpurga night, responding to the Nordic Walpurga night in the first part of the drama.

While the longing for form of those who crossed the Brenner aimed at harmony, balance, serenity, the Germans at home had a no less imperious, though different, sense of form, inevitable in a country so fond of neatness, order, and organization. Bach's fugue, still orthodox in a time when French and Italian masters were dissolving its strictness, would be a striking symbol of organization and method. And since such sense of form has been particularly strong in the Protestant North and center, much more than in the Catholic South, the terms sobriety and prosiness might adequately be added to neatness and order. Music again provides the outstanding examples, not with Bach to be sure, but with the so-called Berlin school of the lied and the North German school of the symphony around 1760, as opposed to the South German schools of Vienna and Mannheim. But it is only fair to add that, just as in England, the spirit of sober prosiness also caused a healthy dislike of rhetoric, pose, and theatrical gesture, which reacted against the flamboyant excesses of the Gothic and the Baroque, fostered the honest matter-of-factness of Chodowiecki and Menzel, and armed Johannes Brahms against the Wagnerian camp.

Why, then, were the Germans after 1760 able to export their music, indeed, to become as dominant in music as they were in the dance? Or, more precisely, why did they become the uncontested masters of the Western concert halls and even of Western musical homes? The problem boils down to finding the reason why, in the greater Romanticism, France and, more so, Italy were unwilling and unable to contribute essentially to the stock of symphonic and chamber music. France, to be sure, had always been averse to instrumental music of some length—"*sonate, que me veux-tu?*". Italy, on the contrary, had given birth to the basic forms of symphonic and chamber music: the *canzone*, the *sonata da camera*, the *sonata da chiesa*, the *ricercar*, and the *toccata*. She had even played a decisive role in shaping the later form of the sonata and, hence, of all instrumental music. Why did she withdraw in the middle of the eighteenth century? The reason seems to spring from the different character of the new music.

This specifically romantic instrumental music is lyric in its smaller forms, in Mendelssohn's *Lieder ohne Worte* or Schumann's *Träumerei;* it is dramatic in its larger forms, sonatas and symphonies. But it always means something beyond a merely sensuous perception and beyond reason, something vague, which never can be fully grasped with the ear alone and never can be expressed in clear, unequivocal words. In this capacity, music was, in the poet Wackenroder's enthusiastic words, "the art of the arts" and, as Robert Schumann said, "romantic in itself." Music of this kind was seldom heard in the provinces of French or Italian art: going beyond the perception of the senses was against the fundamental attitude of Italy; going past the borderline of reason was not given to France; and vagueness was foreign to both. Thus, romantic music rested chiefly with German masters. Not before the second half of the nineteenth century did the French make some serious efforts in the direction of instrumental music with Saint-Saëns, César Franck, and Vincent d'Indy. The Italians remained passive even then.

One of the two regulating powers in Europe has been Italy where, as in no other country, the reversals of generations have followed as neatly and as radically as happens only in nations that cover the widest range of style and keep it meticulously in balance. Both the moderate, classic Renaissance and a wild, orgiastic Baroque were created in Italy. And yet the Renaissance hardly ever froze to pale and lifeless academicism. And even at the climax of the Baroque, the Latin spirit of moderation, perfect form, and sensuous beauty seldom and for a short while only allowed the artists to break loose: *nil nimis*, not too much.

The second counterbalance has been the regulating power of France. She was the founder of Gothic art; her impact helped the 'awakening' Italy in the fourteenth century; and she was leading in the dynamic styles of the nineteenth century. And yet her static forces have always been stronger, indeed, decisive. She withstood all attempts at introducing the Italian Baroque and successfully kept from exaggeration even where styles invited to freedom and whim. (Compare the reserved Rococo of the Château de Versailles with the orgies of the *Zwinger* in Dresden.) The very word *goût*, repeated to capacity in French art criticism, means restraint, harmonious balance, limpidity.

This unique equilibrium of her culture is however not the quiescent result of some Platonic law of the mean but on the contrary it is the continual rebalancing of active, opposite forces. Expanding from the Channel to the Mediterranean, from the Lowlands and

Germany to Spain and Italy, embracing Celtic, Latin, Germanic, Catalan, Basque and Greek populations, France has welded the elements of central, western, southern climates and styles. She is the golden land of tradition, schools, and academies but also of revolution and daring heretics; she opposes inexorable reason to dreams and vagaries but never lacks the temperament to outwit logic where it threatens creative imagination; and while in the worst of extravagance she insists on *goût*, on form and measure, there is a grain of Romanticism in her coolest classicalism.

Owing to this balance, France has been the chief center of western thought. The whole cycle of medieval art with the Romanesque and Gothic phases, with the polyphony of Tours, Limoges, and Paris and the songs of troubadours and trouvères, was controlled by the French, and most of the musical figures were French—Hucbald, Odo, Leoninus, Perotinus, Garlandia, Croix or Cruce, Vitry, Machaut. Only the two hundred years from about 1430 to 1640 stood under Italian hegemony: the renascence in the fine arts, the madrigal, the monodic style and the opera were Italian. But the French, about the middle of that span, had already wrested the leadership in social culture, the dance, and costume from the Italians. And the following quarter of a millennium, up to our time, again was mainly French in attitude. The monarchies all over Europe followed the pattern set at the court of Versailles; the battle of the *tiers état* against them was fought in Paris; and the most advanced ideas in politics, economy, science, and art found their earliest wording in France. Architecture, in Europe as in the new world, availed itself of models from France, just as the world of fashion obeyed the *haute couture* of the Rue de la Paix. Painters from all corners of the world crowded in studios on Montmartre to learn from David and Ingres, Corot and Courbet, Manet and Monet. In poetry and novel, any enumeration would be ridiculous—no literature has had an equally universal validity beyond the bounds of Europe; none has been so 'modern' through the ages, so daringly pioneering, so perfect in style.

The German art historian Arthur Weese expresses the same idea on the second page of his *Skulptur und Malerei in Frankreich im*

XV. und XVI. Jahrhundert (1927): "*Seitdem der französische Künstler als nationale Einzelfigur im europäischen Kunstleben auftritt, wendet er sich zu jeder künstlerischen Aufgabe, die ihm die Zeit, das Kunstwollen seiner Epoche und der eigene Genius stellen, immer wie zu einer Angelegenheit des menschlichen Glückes überhaupt, als wäre sie ihm aus dem Schoße des ewigen Schicksals erwachsen. Er weiht sich ihr und widmet ihr seine Kräfte um der Menschheit willen.*" Which, shorn of luxuriant redundancy, means: From the time when the French artist appears in European art, he turns to every task as if it were a matter of human bliss and eternal destiny, to give it all his force for the sake of mankind.

Have those countries which travel their own byways outside the supranational highway shared in the reversals, phases, and cycles of the main development? It seems that the answer would in general be affirmative with the one restriction that the innate and ineffaceable pathos character of such nations, as an immutable substrate, necessarily affects all ethos phases and therewith dims, weakens, and often shortens them. This is quite certainly true of the Netherlands and of Spain: how evenly, for example, the two hundred years of the Baroque pass in these countries compared with the clean-cut alternation in France and Italy! Things are much less even and plain in England or Germany.

English art has always been a mean between the two extremes—she moderates all pathos trends but is, despite her academy, reluctant to accept pure form for the sake of form. Hence such words as Renaissance, Baroque, Rococo, Romanticism or Empire are nearly meaningless in English art.

The cycles as such agree: the Anglo-Norman style coincided with the Romanesque, the Early English style with the high Gothic, the Decorated style with the later Gothic, the Perpendicular style with the Flamboyant. The Renaissance at first showed around 1515; later, the architectural classicism of Inigo Jones and Christopher Wren matched with the classicism in French architecture while

Purcell and, after him, Handel wrote in the contemporaneous Italian style. John Pepusch and the *Beggar's Opera* met the continental era of the common man; Walter Scott and Lord Byron joined the inter-European Romanticism; and the Gothic Revival seconded the anticlassical currents of the 1850's in the rest of Europe. The only difference is that the English as a whole used to linger when the tide pointed to ethos; for instance, despite some bolder pioneers of the Renaissance, they persisted in Gothic traditions even more and longer than Germany.

The Netherlands cycles paralleled the cycles of France, at least from Gothic centuries on. The Gothic phases coincided and also those of the Renaissance; but, as in France, the latter overlapped with the Flamboyant style so much that the picturesque City Hall of Oudenarde dates from as late as 1525–35. In the Baroque, the arts of the Netherlands not only coincided with the styles in the other countries; in painting, they even had the lead. Later on, they faithfully seconded the classicists of 1800 under the sculptor Guillaume Godecharle, the impressionists under the painter Jozef Israels, the naturalists under the sculptor Constantin Meunier; today, they are in the van of modern architecture.

Germany, too, has shared in the common European phases and cycles but has lingered whenever the tide would turn toward ethos, and more so than England: she stuck to the Romanesque a hundred years longer than France before she accepted the (ethos beginnings of the) Gothic style, and in a similar way hesitated for a century to take over the art of the troubadours and trouvères as the model for her minnesongs.

But she swiftly drew abreast once such styles had left their initial stages. The classical Gothic in Germany, around 1230, of which the cathedrals in Wechselburg and Freiberg (Saxony) were the outstanding monuments, coincided exactly with the classical Gothic of France. Later, the Renaissance was hardly able to uproot the Gothic traditions of Germany and often rested satisfied with horizontalizing Gothic patterns; but it unmistakably set in at exactly the time when Italy entered her high Renaissance—in the days of Raphael, Leonardo, and Titian. Germany's Rococo was simultaneous with the Rococo of the French. And from 1760 on, the German development almost strictly paralleled the evolution of the arts in France or, at least in music, even took the lead: the two classicistic sculptors Canova and Dannecker were born in the consecutive years 1757 and 1758; the ethos masters Rauch, Ingres, Schinkel, Cornelius, Klenze, Schadow were all born within the twelve years from 1777 to 1789; the two outstanding muralists, Puvis and Feuerbach, in 1824 and 1829; and both Lehmbruck and Picasso, in 1881.

The pathos nations of Europe were not to be the leading stars on the world stage of art. But they were called from the wings whenever the tide turned to pathos—Germans in some phases of Romanesque art and, as musicians, in the Greater Romanticism; musicians from the Flanders at the end of the Flamboyant style, and her painters, together with those from Spain, in the Baroque. At last, in the second half of the nineteenth century, the Scandinavians, Slavs, Hungarians, and other nations who had lived on what before had been the periphery shifted nearer to the center, particularly in the fields of poetry, music, and the dance; and they did so, not only because the climax of all pathos cycles implied the readiness to accept folklore and exoticism but more so because in their native pathos they were able to contribute to the main trend of the age.

So general a characterization of national trends and developments seems, however, to wrong the much more complicated fate of style. A front position on the stage of world-wide art, though often conceded and owed to one individual nation, requires a more-than-national character.

This is a ticklish subject to discuss; for the slogans national and international are perhaps the cheapest among the many cheap, misleading, dangerous trade-marks of our time and need re-examination more than any of them. What, after all, is national, what international, what more than national?

Nation, to use a simile, is the native soil in which a tree has taken roots—the soil that gives it sap and support. No tree can live without its soil, not the charming slender birch in your garden nor the majestic cedar. But the two are given to grow to different destinies: the birch, intimate, kindly, is confined to your garden; the cedar, tall and expanding its branches far beyond the hedges of your plot, becomes a landmark visible from miles away. To end our simile: international is the tree from some foreign country artificially kept in a pot in your hothouse.

Folk art and rural architecture are—like the birch in the garden—national or, better, nothing but national. A white New England town, a warm-brown, balconied *dorf* in Switzerland, a red Norwegian village, all charming in their own way and inextricably tied to landscape, climate, and human habits, can seldom be transplanted without becoming soulless curios. The same is true of English pewter, Swedish weavings, Andalusian *azulejos*. And folksong is no exception.

But even individual art is often nothing but national and can for this reason attain a charm, an aroma denied to greater art. It is as a rule confined to its own realm, be it national, tribal, or local—as, for instance, dialect poetry—and attracts outsiders only in the way in which the life of foreign lands attracts the tourist. How definitely Russian! How typically Spanish! How truly American!

And yet, the very individual character of such art, as opposed to collective folk art, is stamped with a sharper seal by time than by nationality. It is easy to tell modern architecture from Gothic buildings but not so easy to distinguish between the works of even lesser Dutch and American masters within the modern style. Any tyro in the history of music readily ascribes a motet written in Palestrina's style to the later sixteenth century but it needs a highly trained specialist to attribute this motet to Spain, or Italy, or Flanders.

This eclipse of the national is almost complete in the realm of the great. Shakespeare's works, translated, are read in German schools side by side with Goethe's and Schiller's; Palestrina's masses are sung in St. Patrick's in New York and in the cathedral of Cologne as they are in St. Peter's in Rome; Michelangelo's *Pietà* is fully at home in Brugge in Flanders, and Rodin's Thinker could easily stand on a Florentine piazza, on the Red Square in Moscow, or in front of the White House. Nobody would exclaim: How English is Shakespeare! How French is Rodin! How Italian is Michelangelo! Just as nobody would emphasize how German Mozart was, or as no Protestant or Catholic who sings a psalm of David would think of its Jewish creator. The inner size of these men has outgrown the limits of nationhood; they have entered the lofty realm of supranational humanity; they are landmarks.

The supranational character that the preceding paragraphs have claimed for any front position conceded to a nation will now be easily understood. Not only individual masters but styles as a whole must reach the supranational stage before they attain a world-wide importance. The song of the troubadours, expanding all over France and over Italy, Spain, and England, and after a hundred years begetting the art of the German minnesingers, was more than French; and more than French was the spirit that had shaped it—the spirit of an inter-Christian knighthood thoroughly averse to nationalism. And so was the Gothic style, created by Frenchmen in France, but in a universal conception far beyond the limitations of nationhood. Otherwise it would not have conquered the world from England to Sicily and from Spain to the Holy Land; nor could the Germans so long have misclaimed that this was their own, their truly national style. In a similar way, the Baroque was more than Italian and the waltz more than German.

Where and whenever this supranational element is deficient, a style has little chance beyond its native soil. A striking example is the music of Spain, so brilliant in its dances, *villancicos*, *romances*, and motets: it has been admired, enjoyed, and loved abroad, but nowhere accepted as a part and expression of non-Spanish peoples.

Still, even in the lofty sphere of the great, in which the national element seems so much rarefied, the attitude toward nationalism is by no means unquestioned. As a rule, the pathos times, *ex definitione* interested in character, distinctive features, and distinctive environment, love to stress the fascinating diversity of men and settings, both abroad and at home. The love of diversity abroad has led to exoticism; love of diversity at home, to folklore. And from overdone folklore, there are only a few steps on the slippery way to nationalism, chauvinism, and hundred-percentism. Pathos ages look at the past, at myth and history, and revert to styles of times gone by, which they claim with, and oftener without, justification, to have been created by their national forebears. They revive and foster native idioms, and accent all racial, national, tribal affiliations to the point of intolerance, hatred, and arrogance. Wagner boasted in Bayreuth of having built a "German art," and Debussy answered by adding *Musicien français* to his name.

Ethos, on the contrary, striving for archetypes, perfection, and permanence, looks through all the distinctive appearances at the common essence of nations and races and emphasizes the basic unity of mankind. Its followers do not rest satisfied with being citizens of their countries but are at once cosmopolitan *Weltbürger* or citizens of the world, as Goethe called himself. They are humanists and in older days would have conversed in Latin or, later, in French, or even would replace the native styles in art by classic revivals. It was in this spirit that Gluck in 1773 claimed to aim at a style of music that could affect every nation and efface the "ridiculous" differences of national styles. And twelve years later, the Frenchman Paul Gui de Chabanon, glorifying Gluck's life work, spoke, for the first time, of music as "the universal language of our continent," which all too narrow limitation was duly outdone when a few years later the German poet Wilhelm Heinse celebrated music, in his Musical Dialogues, as "a general language, which the Iroquois understands as well as the Italian."

In the same decades in which these men exalted the world-wide span of music, a classicistic art had sprung up, nobody knows where —in France, in England, in Germany?—an art that defies anyone who tries to find Italian spirit in Canova, German in Schadow, Danish in Thorwaldsen. For once, the power of ethos had conquered nation and race.

Thus a last aspect of the eternal dualism in art has opened: nation versus humanity. But this last antithesis, too, is more than an alternative of good and bad. Any stubborn persistence in the direction of nothing-but-national art inevitably leads to barren horizons and ultimate poverty; any stubborn persistence in the direction of supranational art inevitably leads to shallow, colorless uniformity. Rather, the two directions complement one another and need an alternate stress to secure the balanced march of style, just as we human beings shift our weight from foot to foot lest we lose our poise and steadfast motion.

Epilogue

THE SEQUENCE OF STYLES, bewildering and often discouraging, in the light of facts cannot appear as a straight evolution, as a continual ripening, progress, improvement. Nor has it been a haphazard result of the senseless, ever-changing caprices of taste or the fruit of personal leadership. Infinitely more logical, lawful, inevitable, the grandiose orbit of art meanders in generational turns, which in their to-and-fro safeguard eternal motion and balance. The generational phases, again, form in cycles evolving from ethos to pathos. And the cycles themselves are embedded in ever larger cycles of similar trends, up to the giant cycles that envelop all of them—their complicated course reminding us of the orbit of the moon, which in a triple revolution rotates around the earth, and with the earth around the sun, and with the sun around the center of the galaxy.

All the arts share in this orbit. Now one would have the lead, and now another; and the stages of their journey overlap and differ. And yet their march is co-ordinated like the march of the voice parts in a fugue which, accelerated or delayed, following at a normal distance or in a breathtaking *stretto*, proceeding in larger strides or hasty tripping, achieves the greatest unity of a master's plan that music has ever created. Architecture, too, and with it sculpture, painting, music, and the dance are the voice parts in a gigantic fugue: none of them, in all their freedom, can swerve from the course the master has set. For they are man's creation and possess no life, no breath, no motor power but that which comes from him. In however different ways they mirror the trends of ages and nations, they cannot get away from man or from each other. Springing from one urge, they are united in the one indelible commonwealth of art.

Epilogue

The sequence of styles, bewildering and often discouraging in the light of facts cannot appear as a straight evolution, as a continual ripening, progress, improvement. Nor has it been a haphazard result of the senseless, ever-changing caprices of taste or the freak of personal leadership. Intimately more logical, lawful, inevitable, the grandiose rhythm of art measures in generational moves, which in their to and fro safeguard eternal motion and balance. The generational phases, again, form in cycles evolving from ethos to pathos. And the cycles themselves are embedded in ever larger circles of similar trends, up to the giant cycles that envelop all of them—their complicated course reminding us of the orbit of the moon, which in a triple revolution races around the earth, and with the earth around the sun, and with the sun around the center of the galaxy.

All the arts share in this orbit. Now one would have the lead and now another, and the [illegible] of their [illegible] overlap and differ. And yet their motion is co-ordinated like the motion of the voices in a fugue which, accelerated or delayed, following at a moment's distance or in a breathtaking stretto, proceeding in larger strides or lazy stepping, achieves the greatest unity. [illegible] that mankind has ever created. [illegible], too, and with it sculpture, painting, music and the [illegible] parts in a gigantic fugue; none of them in all their freedom, can swerve from the course the master has set. For they are man's creation and possess no life, no breath, no motor power but that which comes from him. In however different ways they mirror the trends of ages and nations, they cannot get away from man or from each other. Springing from one stage, they are united in the one indelible consciousness of Art.

Index

INDEX

INDEX

INDEX

The
Commonwealth of Art